Witness
The future Catholic Church in Australia

Philippa Martyr

Connor Court Publishing Pty Ltd

Published in 2025 by Connor Court Publishing Pty Ltd.

Copyright © Philippa Martyr

ALL RIGHTS RESERVED. This book contains material protected under International and Federal Copyright Laws and Treaties. Any unauthorised reprint or use of this material is prohibited. No part of this book may be reproduced or transmitted in any form or by any means, electronic or mechanical, including photocopying, recording, or by any information storage and retrieval system without express written permission from the publisher.

Connor Court Publishing Pty Ltd.
PO Box 7257
Redland Bay QLD 4165
sales@connorcourt.com
www.connorcourt.com

ISBN: 9781923224582

Cover Design by Maria Giordano

Cover photo by Giovanni Portelli Photography/Catholic Archdiocese of Sydney.

Printed in Australia.

Jesus showed himself to the Eleven and said to them:
'Go out to the whole world; proclaim the Good News to all creation. He who believes and is baptised will be saved; he who does not believe will be condemned.'

- Mark 16: 15-18

Through the Cross, and only through the Cross, the gates of the kingdom will be opened. Only through the Cross will the sharp swords in the hearts of men be beaten into ploughshares, and the wickedly designed spears of their plans and ambitions be made into pruning hooks in the service of a fruitful harvest.

- Hans Urs von Balthasar, 'Palm Sunday', in *You Crown the Year With Your Goodness* (1982).

I felt like a lone passenger on a sinking ship, who had played 'Nearer My God to Thee' three or four times, SOS'd till the batteries had run out, shot off his last rocket, and was now preparing to dance the Charleston on the top of the wheelhouse.

– Lennie Lower, *Here's Luck* (1930).

Contents

Figures and Tables   viii

Acknowledgements   x

Introduction   1
- How did we get here?   1
- 'Consultative' processes   7
- A bit about me   11
- Oh, those Boomers!   14
- What you can expect   15

Chapter 1 – Where *is* Everybody?   23
- Bob Dixon, data king   23
- Why aren't Catholics coming to Mass?   25
- Nature takes its course   29
- Where's the data?   30
- Why ARE Catholics coming to Mass?   31
- What about converts?   33
- Why focus on Mass-going Catholics?   35
- Dioceses, eparchies, and ordinariates   37
- The upside: there's no priest shortage   45
- The downside: there's a laity shortage   47
- Conclusion   50

Chapter 2 – Family Life in Catholic Australia   56
- What's the recipe for a Mass-going adult?   56
- The 'vocation' that nobody wants   62
- Till death us do part …   67
- … but not always   70
- The incredible shrinking Catholic family   76

Older Catholics	80
The other older Catholics: the faithful departed	82
Conclusion	84

Chapter 3 – Parish Life in Catholic Australia — 90

What are our parishes like?	91
A young people problem	104
Lex orandi, lex credendi – and vice versa	111
The sacrament of Reconciliation in the parish	113
What is a parish meant to be?	114
Parishes that are already changing	118
Conclusion	122

Chapter 4 – The Catholic Clergy in Australia — 128

Australia's bishops	130
Diocesan priests in Australia today	134
Permanent deacons	151
Making things better	153
Conclusion	155

Chapter 5 – Religious Life and New Apostolates in Australia — 162

The numbers	166
Everything old is new again	174
Other ways of witnessing	178
Risks and blessings	184
Conclusion	185

Chapter 6 – The Business Arm: Catholic-Origin Organisations in Australia — 190

Corporate soteriology	191
Diocesan bureaucracies	195
Catholic-origin schools in Australia today	201
Catholic-origin universities and chaplaincies in Australia	207

Catholic-origin hospitals and health care in Australia today	220
Catholic charities	223
Whatever happened to the Australian Catholic media?	226
Conclusion	229
Chapter 7 – Making It All Work	**239**
Our part in our downfall	241
Changing our families	244
Changing our parishes	249
Changing our dioceses	259
Changing our clergy	269
Changing our business arm	273
Conclusion – the season of the furrow	279
Appendix 1 – Possible Research Projects	**287**
Appendix 2 – Data Sets on the Catholic Church in Australia	**289**
Bibliography	**307**
Index	**337**

Figures and Tables

Figure 1. Numbers of Mass attenders ('00) and diocesan clergy in Australia, 1990-2021.   46

Figure 2. Number of people undertaking different parish roles in the Catholics in Australia Survey 2022 (CIA2022).   95

Figure 3. Gender balance of people undertaking different parish roles in the Catholics in Australia Survey 2022 (CIA2022).   96

Figure 4. Priestly ordinations in Australia, 1970-2021, Annuarium Statisticum Ecclesiae.   141

Figure 5. Percentage of non-Catholic students enrolled in Australian Catholic-origin primary and secondary schools.   208

* * * * *

Table 1. Western-rite dioceses in Australia by state or territory, 2021.   37

Table 2. Eparchies and Ordinariates in Australia, 2021.   40

Table 3. Estimated projected numbers of Sunday Mass-goers by diocese in Australia, 2051.   48

Table 4. Marriages involving at least one Catholic, selected years.   68

Table 5. Marriages conducted by a Catholic minister of religion in Australia, selected years.   68

Table 6. Australian Catholic marriages by country of birth of spouses, 2008-2020.   69

Table 7. Diocesan seminaries in Australia.   141

Table 8. Australian religious personnel, 1901-2016.   167

Table 9. Use of admissions checks by religious communities in Australia, 2014.   169

Table 10. MPJPs operating in Australia and their original communities.   172

Table 11. Irving Janis's eight characteristics of groupthink.   201

Table 12. Proportions of government and other funding in the income of Catholic-origin schools in Australia, 2022-24 – examples. 205

Table 13. NSW Catholic charities, government revenue and donation revenue, December 2023. 224

Table 14. Baptisms in Australia, *Annuarium Statisticum Ecclesiae*, 1970-2021. 289

Table 15. Catholic marriages in Australia, *Annuarium Statisticum Ecclesiae*, 1970-2021. 291

Table 16. Annual variations in diocesan clergy numbers, Australia, *Annuarium Statisticum Ecclesiae*, 1970-2021. 293

Table 17. Western-rite Catholic seminarians in formation in Australia by state, *Official Directory of the Catholic Church in Australia*, 1990-2021. 295

Table 18. Western-rite permanent deacons in Australia by state, *Official Directory of the Catholic Church in Australia*, 1981-2021. 296

Table 19. Eastern-rite and Ordinariate permanent deacons in Australia, *Official Directory of the Catholic Church in Australia*, 1992-2021. 297

Table 20. Australian Catholic dioceses – estimated financial position (equity), 2023. 298

Table 21. Catholic-origin schools and enrolments in Australia, 1981-2021. 300

Table 22. Catholic students enrolled in Catholic-origin schools as a percentage of all enrolments by state and diocese, 2016 and 2021. 301

Table 23. Selected Australian Catholic-origin school authorities – estimated financial position (equity), 2022-2023. 302

Acknowledgements

Many of the arguments you will find in this book were first aired in my regular column in the Archdiocese of Sydney's *The Catholic Weekly* newspaper, so if you recognise some of my more pungent turns of phrase, that's why. Thanks to Peter Rosengren and Adam Wesselinoff, past editors of *The Catholic Weekly*, for encouraging me to air these pungent turns of phrase in the first place.

I've been talking with and listening to concerned Mass-going Catholics in Australia for around 35 years now. In my time as a columnist at *The Catholic Weekly* since 2019, I've also received emails (and sometimes written letters sent to my work address) from over 70 people. I always answer my emails and letters, and your thoughts, prayers, and feedback have helped to shape me as a writer and as a Catholic. I'm grateful to you all, even if I sent you a rather stern response (you know who you are). Your emails and letters have also helped to inform the contents of this book.

I know that when you ask a Catholic a question about the Church, you get very different answers, depending on how often that person goes to Mass. That's why I cast a wide net for people to help me with this project – but I only asked the people who I knew were regular Mass-goers, and on the younger side. They are the best-informed Catholics around: they're right where the action is, especially when we're talking about the future of the Church in Australia.

For this book, I've consulted men, women, priests, religious, and the married, single, divorced, employed or otherwise; parents of families, members of the eastern Churches, those born overseas, converts, same sex attracted people, and those who work in the Church on a paid or volunteer basis. They live in different dioceses in New South Wales, Queensland, Victoria, Tasmania, and Western Australia (I'm sorry about South Australia, but I don't know anyone who lives there). Almost all of them were aged under

60. It's not a representative sample, and I haven't tried to make it one, but I think it's a pretty good range. I've also used some of the anonymous written comments left by participants in the Catholics in Australia 2022 survey (CIA2022).

I'm hugely grateful to everyone who took part and gave me their own words to use. Some of them have asked to be anonymous or pseudonymous. Those who used their own names are Ben, John, Josh, Fr Joshua, Lauren, Miriam, and Paul. Those who didn't are Alan, Annie, Anonymous, Belinda, Charlotte, Colin, Daisy, Diane, the Dominican Sisters of St Cecilia, Ethan, Eloise, Gerard, Fr Geoffrey, Fr Harrison, Isla, Fr Jason, Katrina, Lawrence, Leah, Fr Michael, Oliver, Petra, Fr Robert, Rachel, Fr Stephen, Steve and Helen, Sr Teresa, Tori, Fr Vincent, William, and Sr Yvette.

But I also needed Catholic statistical data, and so I went to the most reliable sources that I could find – the *Official Directory of the Catholic Church in Australia*, and the *Annuarium Statisticum Ecclesiae* ('Statistical Yearbook of the Church', published annually by the Vatican). To access reasonably complete runs of these, I used the Archdiocese of Perth's Archives and Information Governance Office, the Veech Library at the Catholic Institute of Sydney, and the Mannix Library at the Catholic Theological College in Melbourne. The staff in the university libraries at the University of Western Australia and the University of Notre Dame Australia also helped with hard-to-find sources. Thanks to everyone who expedited my work in these places.

A special thank you to a *very* special group of people: every Church bureaucrat, professional Catholic, dodgy theologian, affronted chairperson, disgruntled ex-cleric, episcopal non-letter/email-answerer, crank 'reformer', parish bossy-boots, and ecclesiastical handball-passer with whom I have had the pleasure of dealing in the last 35 years. You have made me the Catholic woman I am today, and without you, this book would never have been written.

There are some odd little thank-yous that I don't want to leave out.

- Deacon Bruce Talbot, who used the Balthasar quote that appears at the beginning of this book in his Palm Sunday homily in 2024. This put me on to the collection of Balthasar's essays *You Crown the Year with Your Goodness*, in which I also found a marvellous essay on being an authentic Christian witness which helped to inform this book.
- Dr Larry Chapp, American theological writer whose sharp insights, dry wit and verbal panache sustained me through many dry spells. I also thrashed out some of the ideas in this book in earlier form on his blog *Gaudium et Spes 22*.
- Professor Tracey Rowland, whose book *Unconformed to the Age: Essays in Catholic Ecclesiology* appeared while I was writing this book. Tracey's book provides the theological backstory for what I'm trying to say with the data, and I'd highly recommend it.
- The data wonks: Robert (Bob) Dixon, whose data analyses and commentaries I have referred to in this book; Ben Clements and Stephen Bullivant, whose Catholics in Britain 2019 survey formed the basis of the Catholics in Australia 2022 survey; and the team at the National Centre for Pastoral Research (NCPR), whose thorough and patient work has also informed this book.

The rest of you know who you are and are terrified of being identified in these acknowledgements. Breathe easy – your secret is safe with me. God bless you all.

Philippa Martyr.

Introduction

How did we get here?

What is the Catholic Church in Australia? It's a mighty spiritual force that flows like a river, transforming lives and saving souls as it goes. It's also incredibly small, shrinking rapidly, and burdened by a lumbering, asset-rich, people-poor, sclerotic carapace running on increasingly large sums of government money, unwilling to adapt to rapidly changing conditions, with a reverse Midas touch for evangelisation and a reputation for covering things up. An Australian priest who I'll call Fr Robert said to me, 'It is as if two different churches exist side by side, the one co-mingled with the other, each considering the other to be the darnel and themselves to be the wheat.'[1]

The Church in Australia is in real crisis, but no one seems very concerned about this. The Catholic schools are full, the hospitals are financially solvent, and we're getting good returns from the diocesan real estate portfolios. But we're also showing a massive decline in the area that really matters – actual human beings going to Mass, which is the most robust external measure of our relationship with God as a pilgrim people. Our last national count of Sunday Mass attendance in 2021 turned up a figure of just 417,000 people – less than the population of the Australian Capital Territory.[2]

Imagine if the Church in Australia were a football club. The hundreds of thousands of people who used to belong to the Catholic Football Club (CFC) have gradually lost interest in football over the last fifty years. We still hold the fixtures every winter, but it's now down to a handful of elderly players who toss the ball around gently to each other, unwilling to risk injury. A slightly larger handful of mostly elderly spectators watch them from the almost-empty stands.

But down the road there's a gigantic, heavily government-subsidised Catholic Football Club hotel, spa, and casino complex which is open to the public. It's making money hand over fist, and you can go there whether you're a CFC supporter or club member or not. Everyone's enjoying bar snacks, spending money in the casino and spa, and watching pretty much anything but football on the big screens.

Every now and then, someone suggests that the government shouldn't be subsidising the CFC hotel and spa complex like this. After all, it's taxpayers' money, and not everyone is a football fan or club member. But they're always drowned out by howls of outrage. CFC members are taxpayers too! Just look at the benefits to the community! Isn't it important to keep up the old traditions? And just look at the sheer numbers of people it employs! Then everyone goes right back to whatever they were doing before they were so rudely interrupted.

The Plenary Council which the Catholic Church held in Australia with considerable fanfare from 2018 to 2022 was an opportunity to tackle this and many other troubling issues. It nicely exemplified the war between a fringe group of ageing Catholic liberals and the ordinary people who just wanted their Catholic patrimony back. I watched with interest as it lurched from side to side – now looking like it might address the real problems, then dragged into the weeds of time-wasting over marginal issues, and then hauled back on track again.

Then we all saw the gloves come off on 6 July 2022 at the Second Assembly of the Plenary Council, with enraged delegates determined to force the Council to produce the kind of Church they'd been demanding for decades.[3] It would have been great if they'd had some genuinely new ideas. But all they had was the same formula that they've been wheeling out since the 1980s: married priests, women deacons as a back door to women priests, Holy Communion for everyone, lay-led parishes, women preaching, women doing everything else except cleaning the church, many more salaried church professionals, and unlimited amounts of consequence-free sex for everyone who wants it.

This is the same formula that's emptied Protestant churches the world over and has the Anglican communion flailing about in its death throes. It's an agenda tailored to suit the whims of a very small, very privileged group of older and mostly white Catholics who are dying to get up on the sanctuary and show us what they've got – preferably on a salary. This agenda also doesn't represent the *sensus fidei* – the 'sense of faith' or 'spiritual instinct' that can be found in Catholics when they're properly formed in their faith – no matter how often its proponents say it does.[4]

This time, the carefully curated working groups didn't quite manage to wash out the authentic Catholic faith and practice that still exist in Australia at the grassroots. Ordinary Mass-going Catholics pushed back hard and stopped them. None of this was secret; it was all very public, and quite cathartic. These people had already said out loud that this was their 'last chance' to get the kind of Church they wanted,[5] but thankfully they failed.

And at what cost? No one has ever produced any kind of financials for the Plenary Council, but it would be wonderfully illuminating to know how it was all paid for, and by whom, and in what amounts. Sadly, the calls for increased corporate governance and transparency in the Catholic Church don't extend to us seeing this kind of information.[6] We are not off to a flying start for the new transparent Church in Australia if the Plenary Council couldn't even be transparent about itself.

It's not just the self-styled 'reformers' that are the problem. There's a widespread lassitude in the Church in Australia today that was identified as long ago as 1999 by Archbishop (later Cardinal) George Pell. When asked 'What is the biggest threat, in your opinion, to the Catholic Church today?', he replied, 'Oh, that we'll just merge into the background. We're a minority church, fewer than 30 per cent of the people, and we'll just take on the colours of our society, and that we'll become the bland leading the bland.'[7] This is what US bishop Robert Barron and theologian Dr Larry Chapp have since called 'beige Catholicism': a phenomenon that's numbing and extinguishing the fire at the heart of the Church.[8] We've spent so long trying to blend in with the rest of Australian society that our authentic Catholic identity as brothers and sisters of a crucified God-Man has almost completely disappeared.

The root cause is that we've largely lost – or deliberately washed out – our sense of the supernatural. Catholicism exists because we believe God became a human man and everything that goes along with that, most of which is a matter of historical record. But today in the Church in Australia, you will find embarrassment about the supernatural at every turn. Much better to focus on our charitable work and how many people the Church employs: it plays better to our secular audience. Also, it removes the awkwardness of having to acknowledge that you are a created being who will one day die, but not cease to exist. And then what?

Fr Geoffrey, a priest living in Australia and with many years of pastoral experience, said to me that '[the] laity spend more time in the secular *mores* than they do in the Catholic spiritual one,' so naturally, they don't want 'to be different from others in the secular culture'.[9] Beige, comfortable middle-class Catholicism – that terrible seamless integration into the modern pagan world – has almost strangled Vatican II's urgent call to personal holiness. Tori, a young mother, really feels this.

> Raising three small children makes you very conscious about how they are instructed and formed in a far more intentional way than perhaps you have ever been about your own spiritual life. As such, you suddenly become very aware of bad, feminised liturgy and the absence of actual meaningful actions by those in positions of Church leadership at both a local and broader cultural level. Who are the current Australian faith warriors I should point out to my kids as examples of courage and selflessness?[10]

Paul, a divorced father of three in his forties, agrees.

> Christ's message in the New Testament centres around forgiveness, compassion, meekness and love. But by the same token, he doesn't pull his punches when calling out what he will and won't accept. He came to divide; he says so very clearly. ... He took this message all the way to the Cross, standing for us when we cannot. That's the engagement I refer to when speaking about the lack of the same. I believe the Church actively loses the younger generations when it refuses to stand firm and draw them into her holy presence but rather tries to lull them in by placating and appeasing.[11]

But in spite of this – or perhaps because of it – most Catholics in Australia have found more enjoyable things to do on a Sunday. Who wants to sit for an hour in a beige church, listening to beige music, and watching a ritual you know nothing about and don't believe in?[12]

You can see the influence of this comfortable mentality in the slowness of Catholic-origin schools to respond to their plummeting numbers of Catholic enrolments and the incredibly low rate of Mass attendance among the students' families. It's in the slowness of Catholic-origin universities to grasp their incredible opportunity to evangelise barely catechised young Catholics and bring them (often for the first time) to a knowledge and love of Jesus Christ. It's in the diocesan tendency to talk about what a great employer the Church is through its schools and health care, while ignoring the fact that this is mostly done on taxpayers' money while practically no one goes to Sunday Mass anymore.

Let's return to what Fr Robert said: 'It is as if two different churches exist side by side, the one co-mingled with the other.' I would like to start drawing a line between these two entities. One of them is the Church proper – what I call the **parochial-diocesan Church**. This is the most ancient and most important structure in the Catholic Church; it's literally *what it is* in its visible form, and it's the structure that's most closely oriented towards serving the Church's mission. It's made up of parishes and dioceses where Catholics live, worship, and are governed by Church authorities.

The other structure is what I have called the 'carapace' (and on one memorable occasion, the Borg), and what Australian theologian Tracey Rowland calls 'Catholics Inc'.[13] It's everything else that's grown on the parochial-diocesan Church over time like barnacles and has fused so closely to it now that some people can no longer tell the difference between this and the real thing. In fact, some of them have come to prefer it to the real thing, and to see it as Catholic core business in Australia. And, as I have discovered while writing this book, quite a lot of it is running on taxpayers' money.

Is it wrong for the Church to take money from the State? Not according to the Code of Canon Law (canon 797) which tells us that 'civil society' should support parents' freedom of choice to educate their children as they see fit, and even subsidise this. But this is quite a specific instance relating to children's education; it's not a free-for-all. And once you start taking government money, where does it stop? The Church in Australia is, I believe, teetering on the verge of finding out, and not in a good way.

I am aware that a lot of Catholics, even Mass-going ones, don't have too much of a problem with the Church taking government money. But historically, when the Church has formed an alliance like this with the State, it has never ended well for the Church. In Australia and elsewhere, taking the money has led to bigger everything, which means employing more people, fewer of whom are likely to be Mass-going Catholics, or even on the same side as the Church. Fr Jason, a younger priest who works in an urban diocese, explains:

> ... many in the Church are working against the teachings of Christ, knowingly or unknowingly. As a result, often a common understanding of what the Church is and believes cannot be assumed. There is a challenge to reclaim a common language. So often there is the facade that we,

together as a Church, are united, but in reality, we are so divided with very different worldviews. As well as seeing this in parishes, this is most pronounced in institutions such as Catholic schools, hospitals etc.[14]

It also means that many Mass-going Catholics – the people most likely to have supernatural beliefs, and who try to conform their lives to these – increasingly feel like unwanted strangers in their own Church. Alan, a married father of six in an urban diocese, has felt this.

> We live in a secular society – we experience this at the workplace and other areas of life, so we expect to be treated like freaks when we speak our true beliefs in that atmosphere. It's when the Church also treat us like weirdos for wanting to focus on Catholic education for our children, living by standard Catholic teaching, and doing charity to those really in need.[15]

I am here to tell you that everything is not okay in the Catholic Church in Australia. But I am not going to repeat the usual litany of problems. I and my extended network of advisors are also going to provide you with some solutions if you want them. You could have employed an expensive consultancy company to come up with solutions for you – and chances are that your diocese has already done this. But instead, here are solutions from people with skin in the game, and for a modest price. It's about saving the salt and light that remains in the Church here, opening the way to restoring some of our losses, and continuing our God-given mission to preach the gospel in and out of season.

'Consultative' processes

I'm partly writing this book because I know that many ordinary Catholics in Australia today don't trust or respect their bishops, chanceries, and diocesan bureaucracies. This mistrust is rooted in the decades of bad experiences they suffered simply because they were concerned about the Church and tried to do something about it. William, who works for the Church, said that 'often it doesn't take much to have a label put on you – conservative, reactionary or whatever – for expressing mainstream Catholic views in terms of faith.'[16]

Over the last few decades, ordinary Mass-going Catholics have been made fun of, dismissed, ignored, and treated with contempt by many comfortably employed professional Catholics, including some bishops. As married-father-of-four Colin put it, one of the biggest problems in the Church in Australia today is:

> an episcopate that is largely estranged from the rank-and-file practising Catholics who are faithful to Church teaching. The overwhelming impression is that practising Catholics who are faithful to the perennial teachings of the Church are on the lowest rung of the ladder; the bishops are more worried about offending just about every other grouping of people in Australia today.[17]

Largely cosmetic consultation processes have also stifled genuine discussion and debate about the real problems in the Church in Australia and how to fix them. This loss of trust has done harm to the Church in Australia that's as great as the clergy sexual abuse crisis, and it will take a long time for our bishops to win that trust back.

Let me give you an example of why ordinary Catholics like me have so little faith in 'consultation' now. In March 2024, the following notice appeared in my Sunday parish bulletin. I have changed all the names below.

> **Synodality Response by Parishioners**
>
> The parishes of St Alpha, St Beta, St Gamma, St Delta, and St Epsilon have prepared a draft response to the Synthesis Report [for the Synod on Synodality].
>
> We are seeking comments from parishioners on the draft before it is submitted.
>
> A copy of the response and the Vatican report can be obtained by emailing [email address] with a heading COPY

OF REPORT PLEASE.

Please respond by return email – [Wednesday of that week].

I usually go to Mass at St Delta's and was surprised to learn that 'we' were preparing a draft response. 'We' must have been at it since October 2023, and it was now March 2024. But for some reason, 'we' now had barely three working days to respond to a prepared submission that none of us had seen.

I can never resist a challenge, so I emailed the man I'll call Bernie (who inserted the notice and provided his email address) and got a copy of the draft submission and provided feedback on it. The submission contained factual errors and plenty of Boomer-style liberal Catholic boilerplate. But even though I asked him a couple of times how the document came to be written, and who had been invited to contribute to it and why, Bernie refused to tell me. He sent me a list of dates of purported meetings that had been held – but there were apparently no minutes taken at any of them.[18]

Eventually Bernie told me that I should make my own submission to the relevant diocesan office, which I did. I understood that in doing so, I may as well have been pointing a radio telescope at a random part of the night sky and hoping to pick up a friendly wave from an alien civilisation. Today, I am still waiting for that office to acknowledge that they've even received what I sent them. (That's not true – I'm not waiting at all, because I know it will never happen).

This is one of many instances where a Church consultative document has been prepared through an opaque and controlled process. The non-elect ordinary Catholics are lucky if they're given a tiny window (in this case, barely three working days) in which to make 'comments' – not to contribute to the actual drafting of the document. There's no communication, no feedback, and no nothing.

Many parishes and dioceses have useful people like Bernie who enjoy this sort of work. The Plenary Council was full of them, to the point where one journalist described it as a gathering of the Church's HR department.[19] The Synod on Synodality in Rome was full of them. Your local Diocesan Pastoral Council – which is heading your way if it hasn't already arrived – is full of them.

Fr Michael, with many years of first-hand experience of these people, thinks that they're not quite done yet. 'Thirty years ago we used to say that those non-believing Catholics (unconverted, private interpreting, relativistic, worldly, new age, skeptical-of-the-supernatural Catholics) would be gone in ten years, but there are still enough around to cause great trouble in the Church.'[20] These useful people are often employed by the Church, frequently with backgrounds in Catholic education, or are retired ex-professionals, well off and well educated. They love enabling processes like this to produce the outcomes they think are best for the Church.

What they think is best for the Church usually follows the same predictable pattern of increased liberalisation of Church teachings on sex and marriage, laicisation of the clergy, and clericalisation of the laity. They write confidently about the needs and desires of Catholic youth when it's doubtful that any of them has spoken to anyone aged under 40 at Mass for years. They're also full of the Church's need to embrace 'diversity' when their experience of this is limited to their wife's gay nephew who thinks all religion is stupid.

Fr Harrison, a younger priest who works in Victoria, has seen the same tin ear in action.

> My biggest frustration is that the bishops-as-a-class, and many 'establishment Catholics' – that is, senior clergy; senior religious; and senior lay professionals in paid work for the Church – devote so much time and energy to post-conciliar debates about married clergy and female ordination and a sexual revolution in Catholic moral theology. I have no interest in these reforms, and among under-50s I think this is typical. They are still hot-button

issues to older Catholics, and to younger people *outside* the Church (hence the coverage these issues attract in mainstream media), but I think under-50s *in* the Church consider them hackneyed and irrelevant.[21]

So has Fr Jason: 'It seems to me that there are no priests under 60, or even 50, who are okay with the wackiness we have seen throughout our Church over the last decades. That's not to say that they are all faithful priests, but there is clearly a shift to me.'[22]

The Catholic Boomer agenda has already landed like a lead balloon and is well on its way to the bottom of the ecclesiastical ocean. Its proven failures are all around us, and if you can't see them, have a look at the churches which rolled out the same policies years ago – if you can still see them. Fr Geoffrey was a convert from one of them: 'the devastation in these churches is such that they are unlikely to re-emerge as a continuation of the Church of the Apostles.'[23]

A bit about me

Someone else should have written this book a long time ago, but they didn't. It's probably because they were afraid of being ostracised or losing their job. Thankfully I am not a church employee, and I also have the hide of a rhinoceros, so I can say things in public about the Church that a lot of people wouldn't dare. In fact, I've been doing this pretty much all my adult life.[24]

Long story short: in the late 1970s, my family fled a parish that fell to bits in the first wave of liturgical grooviness, and we became liturgical nomads. If you're not familiar with the term, these are Catholics who go from parish to parish to try to find a spiritual home where they can go to Mass in peace. During the great unrest of the 1970s and 1980s, there were a lot of us, and there still are – but more on that in my chapter on parish life.

My Catholic-origin school was academically excellent but riddled with doctrinal nonsense driven by radicalised Boomer nuns. My mother protested to the school regularly about the doctrinal nonsense, only to be told repeatedly to take me out of the school. I remained in the school, which was a useful apprenticeship in how to be a thorn in an institution's side by simply existing.

When things got very bad in the Church in Australia in the late 1980s – which was probably when the Boomers were approaching full strength – ordinary Catholics began to organise. We had no internet, but we had newsletters and mailing lists, and we started to read more and more overseas periodicals like *Crisis* magazine that helped us to understand what was going on in our parishes and schools. In Melbourne, the courageous Brian and Maureen Schaefer created and invested in a small co-operative, the John XXIII Fellowship, which supplied excellent books from the newly founded Ignatius Press and other small printing houses which were trying to salvage something from the ruins.

The Schaefers also published *Fidelity* magazine, which was a lifeline for many disaffected and confused Catholics at this time, and I wrote for it a lot in the mid-1990s. I also wrote a bit for the National Civic Council's *AD2000* magazine – but only a bit, because I can get quite salty in print, and they were trying to avoid bringing the heavy hand of the episcopate down on their heads.[25]

Elsewhere, I've documented the times where I think the pushback from ordinary but organised Catholics helped to turn the tide in Australia, one of which was the magnificent *Statement of Conclusions* drama after the Australian bishops' embarrassing *ad limina* visit to Rome in 1998.[26] The papacy of Pope John Paul II did wonders for ordinary Catholics in Australia, who felt that even if there was a thick layer of bureaucratic awfulness between us and him, at least he was on our side. I think the pushback against the Plenary Council was another watershed moment in the history of the Church here, where ordinary Catholics spoke up vigorously and made a huge difference.

The other thing I've noticed over time is how skilled those ordinary Catholics – the ones who are quietly pursuing holiness in their many walks of life – are at making alternate arrangements. Buckminster Fuller, the American architect and futurist, is purported to have said, 'In order to change an existing paradigm, you do not struggle to try and change the problematic model. You create a new model and make the old one obsolete.'[27]

This is what I'd also like to learn more about and talk more about – how ordinary Catholics are slowly and quietly rebuilding their part of the Church locally and pursuing holiness and the love of God through it. I know that many older Catholics refuse to believe this because they think all younger Mass-going Catholics are starchy traditionalists with no sense of social justice. They are wrong. Instead, the efforts of younger Catholics are making the hard shell of money, lawyers, bureaucrats, and other stuff that isn't integral to our mission, obsolete in the best possible way.[28]

This means that sometimes in this book I'm going to write about God in exuberant and advice-giving ways. That's because I do believe that it's only through each one of us living out Vatican II's call to personal holiness that the Church will have a future at all in Australia. This might sit a bit oddly alongside the hard-headed data with which I intend to stun you into submission, and the many personal observations that I've also included here. But the Church is complex: it's spirit and life – and full of deeply flawed human beings just like me.

We can't fix the problems in the Church primarily through governance and committees and roundtables and policies, although they have their place. We fix them primarily through living holier lives: being better people with closer relationships to God and with each other, conformed to the commandments and immersed in the sacraments. This is an unstoppable force which allows the real Church to simply bypass obstacles and re-form somewhere else. This is how it's survived for so long: it's the grace of God in action. No human institution could have managed this over two millennia – not with the idiots we've had in charge.

Oh, those Boomers!

If you're a younger Mass-going Catholic, it's easy to get mad at the Catholic Boomers. You may well see them as the main architects and enablers of the current problems in the Church.[29] This is part of a bigger conversation we're having in Australia where Boomers are blamed for the current housing shortages, unsustainably large pension commitments, and for having taken advantage of the good times to enrich themselves.[30]

The reason we're having this inter-generational spat is that at least some of this is true. The Boomer generation – especially the ones who still describe themselves as the 'children of Vatican II' – were the architects of much of the mess we see in the Church today. They had lots of fun in the 1970s and 1980s changing the liturgy to suit themselves and settling into comfortable diocesan jobs as professional Catholics. These are the people whose felt banners, anodyne hymns, and clay altar-ware have made younger Catholics cringe for years.

And they've been persistent. The people at the recent Plenary Council sessions were overwhelmingly Boomers, many now well into retirement but with active minds and a strong desire to continue the work of a lifetime to re-make the Church in their own image.[31] They're probably still dominating your diocese and your local parishes: enmeshed in the music ministries, parish councils, Church agencies, local Catholic charities, and on the boards of Catholic health care providers and schools.

There are two things we can say about this. One is to remind younger Catholics of what is unkindly called the 'biological solution': the Boomers will have largely gone to their eternal reward by 2050. Part of the reason I am writing this book is to show you what's likely to be left for you to inherit, and where you can do your best work and target your remaining resources so that the (probably) much smaller future Church can thrive.

The other is to remind the same group of young Catholics that many of the Boomers they see in church today are the good guys. They've stuck around through the felt banners and awful hymns because they really believe. They've often felt isolated, helpless, and alone as their fellow Boomers forced their pet changes on everyone else. They've run newsletters, magazines, prayer groups, and all sorts of other networks to support like-minded faithful Catholics during the very dark years when there was no internet to help them.

These people have borne the brunt of years of being treated as nuisances and troublemakers by their local bishops, dioceses, and schools. They are often badly shell-shocked from decades of fighting in an undeclared guerilla war in their own Church. They want to see you reclaim the future Church and thrive in it. So don't tar them all with the same brush.

What you can expect

I promise you that this book will be at least readable and at best entertaining and informative. It needs to be read by ordinary Australian Catholics as well as people in charge who need to make better-informed decisions about the future. It will look in each chapter at both our weeds and wheat in key areas: Catholic family life, our clergy, our parishes, our religious life, and our business arm.

I will be using published data sets, but also the data from the Catholics in Australia 2022 survey (CIA2022), a national survey of over 2,300 Catholics Australia-wide which produced some very interesting data. This survey largely replicated the Catholics in Britain 2019 survey led by Dr Ben Clements at the University of Leicester and Professor Stephen Bullivant at St Mary's University Twickenham.[32] Stephen and I recruited differently for CIA2022, but we found similarities as well as interesting differences in these two Catholic populations. You will find references throughout this book to CIA2022's eleven summary reports.

I'll finish with my take on where we might be by the year 2050 or thereabouts, and what we can do about it. Fr Harrison provides a sketch of what he thinks the future Church in Australia might look like.

> I share Pope Benedict's hopes and expectations of a smaller, more spiritual Church. Not a 'smaller and purer Church,' which is a common misattribution. The Church will always be full of sinners, which means there's room for me. But it will be 'more spiritual' in the sense that it will be less influential, own less property, run fewer services, have less money. That's no problem to me, because the Church has been in decline for as long as I remember. Less power means less worldliness. Less influence, but more credibility.[33]

Ethan, a father of four who works for the Church, said similarly that:

> Ratzinger spoke of a smaller Church, not as something to be hoped for but as a reality. But he said that this would be the cause of a greater sense of evangelical and apostolic creativity, and I think that this is correct. I think the Church in the future will be smaller, and I hope that dioceses are smaller, such that bishops will be able to know their priests well, and many of their lay faithful, too.[34]

I believe that there are real signs of growth, life, and positive change in the Church here, but they are not what the Boomers think they should be (payrolled married clergy and female deacons; sexually diverse young people flocking into our safe-space churches). Nor are they happening among the increasingly sclerotic diocesan agencies, or the corporations that make up the affluent business arm of the Church in Australia. Yes, young Catholic Australians are going to Mass, and yes, they're involved in authentic growth – but they're avoiding all this other stuff like the plague.

I can tell you a bit more about this younger Catholic demographic, because we captured some interesting data about them from CIA2022. Catholics in Australia used to be a reliable

Australian Labor Party (ALP) voting bloc. But we found that now, only the older Catholics – the Boomers, and especially those who no longer go to Mass regularly – still vote for the ALP in large numbers.

Instead, in the 2022 federal election, the CIA2022 sample of younger Mass-going Catholics voted far more for the Liberal-National coalition (29%), for populist parties like One Nation (17%), and for confessional parties like the Australian Christians (10%). If you were a TAFE or vocationally trained Mass-goer, the percentage who voted for One Nation (17%), United Australia Party (20%), and the Australian Christians (25%) was even higher. There was a gender difference as well. Young male Mass-goers were more likely to vote for One Nation (19%) and the United Australia Party (11%), while young female Mass-goers showed a stronger preference for the Australian Christians (14%).

This puts this younger demographic completely at odds with other young Australian voters, who are much more likely to vote ALP, Greens, or Teal Independents.[35] It may also put them at odds with the generally centre-left political vibe of most of Catholic officialdom. Instead, they more closely resemble the increasingly conservative voting blocs seen in the US and Europe. The very worst thing Catholic officialdom could do now is to dismiss these young voters as rubes and neckbeards who need to be bullied into voting in a more socially acceptable way. The best thing would be to engage with them and listen to them about why they're choosing to vote the way they do.

Over the years I've been lucky enough to meet and talk with invested Mass-going Catholics from all walks of life – priests, religious, and lay people who have thought long and hard about the same issues and are often involved with the solutions in progress. This book aims to represent people who are often voiceless in the Church in Australia today – they generally aren't invited to contribute to panels or roundtables or even diocesan pastoral councils. And if they are invited, they can't attend, because they have demanding jobs in the real world during the week, and young families to raise outside of that time.

Many of my participants have asked to be pseudonymous, and for me to be discreet about revealing their locations. Their chief fear is that if 'they' find out there's a flourishing parish or ministry or group somewhere, 'they' will find a way of ruining it. 'They' can be the local bishop, or the local chancery office, or just some diocesan busybody who will find a way of sterilising the seeds sown by the Holy Spirit in that corner of the Church in Australia.

This level of mistrust is understandable – but it's also risky. Some new movements and groups should be on the local bishop's radar, because Mass-going Catholics (like everyone else) are prone to sin. Cult-like groups can form quickly and do people real harm. You need only think of the so-called 'Little Pebble' William Kamm in NSW,[36] or the Bethel Community in Western Australia,[37] to see how badly this can end. It's important to rebuild our trust in church leadership in Australia, and I think we can. However, it will take bishops who behave in a trustworthy manner, stop treating their flocks like idiots, and stop outsourcing their pastoral responsibilities.

The future of the Catholic Church in Australia will depend on its ability to witness – hence the title. The Greek word *martyros*, from which my surname also originates, means 'witness' – someone who stands up in court, but also someone who might pay for their testimony with suffering and even death. For us as Australian Catholics, surviving as a Church is going to mean increasingly looking different and acting differently from the culture around us. It is probably going to mean turning off the tap of government money. It may also mean enduring an increasing rate of soft and perhaps hard persecution from the State.

But witnessing is actually our daily job as Catholics. German theologian Hans Urs von Balthasar understood this.

Only people who have totally forgotten and lost themselves, to be found by God, have any effect on others as witnesses of Christ. ... If the lives of Christians do not witness to the truth of Christianity, that is, that Christ is God and man, who has died for our sins and risen again, what use are sermons and catechisms and all the libraries of theology? Christianity is intended to be true not *in itself* but *in us*: we ourselves, in our lives, in our believing, hoping, and loving, in our suffering and victory, are meant to be the Lord's witnesses.[38]

Don't lose heart – we've been here before. I always recommend that troubled Catholics should read the Book of Nehemiah. Like Nehemiah, we're looking at a broken wall, an exposed city, and a demoralised population. Nehemiah organised everyone and asked them *to repair the part of the wall that was in front of their house*. This is subsidiarity in action – it doesn't get more local than that, and local is beautiful, and small is also beautiful. (Yes, they had to repair the wall fully armed because they were being attacked on and off while they did it – but they still got it done.)

I have said elsewhere that in the Church right now, 'we are in the season of the furrow, rather than that of the harvest.'[39] So how can we best get ourselves ready for that great task? Without further ado, let's get stuck in.

---

[1] Fr Robert, personal communication, 11 June 2024.

[2] National Centre for Pastoral Research (NCPR). (2024). *Australian Catholic Mass attendance report 2021*, https://ncpr.catholic.org.au/wp-content/uploads/2024/05/Mass-attendance-in-Australia-2021-FINAL.pdf

[3] Coppen, L. (2022, July 7). A day of drama at Australia's Plenary Council. *The Pillar*, https://www.pillarcatholic.com/p/a-day-of-drama-at-australias-plenary

[4] Rowland, T. (2024). *Unconformed to the age: essays in Catholic ecclesiology*. Emmaus, 18-19; International Theological Commission. (2014). *Sensus fidei in the life of the Church*, https://www.vatican.va/roman_curia/congregations/cfaith/cti_documents/rc_cti_20140610_sensus-fidei_en.html

[5] Fewtrell, T. (2022, July 5). Canberra Catholics say Church's Plenary Council could be a last chance for reform. *The Riot Act*, https://the-riotact.com/

canberra-catholics-say-churchs-plenary-council-could-be-a-last-chance-for-reform/572400; MacKinley, S. (2020, February 18). 'Listen to what the Spirit is saying': Monsignor Peter Jeffrey Oration, https://sandhurst.catholic.org.au/news-events/1309-listen-to-what-the-spirit-is-saying-shepparton-feb-2020/file; Martyr, P. (2020, June 7). Precisely which Church? A response to the Plenary Discernment Papers. *The Catholic Weekly*, https://www.catholicweekly.com.au/precisely-which-church-a-response-to-the-plenary-discernment-papers/. More recently longtime 'reformer' John Warhurst has signalled defeat, Warhurst, J. (2024, May 19). Painful times for church reformers. *Eureka Street*, https://www.eurekastreet.com.au/article/painful-times-for-church-reformers

[6] It's worth reading the report *The light from the Southern Cross: promoting co-responsible governance in the Catholic Church in Australia*, which got a lot wrong, but it did get this bit right. You can find it at https://www.catholic.au/s/article/Church-Governance

[7] Cited in Cook, M. (2021). 'Naked to mine enemies': Cardinal George Pell and the media. *Church, Communication, and Culture*, 6(1), 80-98. https://doi.org/10.1080/23753234.2021.1882317

[8] Hadro, M. (2016, June 26). How not to be a 'beige Catholic', according to Bishop Barron. *Catholic News Agency*, https://www.catholicnewsagency.com/news/34095/how-to-not-be-a-beige-catholic-according-to-bishop-barron; Chapp, L. (2020, December 11). The choice: bourgeois well-being or conversion to Christ: beige Catholicism and the challenges of the young priest. *Gaudium et Spes 22*, https://gaudiumetspes22.com/blog/the-choice-bourgeois-well-being-or-conversion-to-christ-beige-catholicism-and-the-challenges-of-the-young-priest

[9] Fr Geoffrey, personal communication, 11 June 2024.

[10] Tori, personal communication, 31 August 2024.

[11] Paul, personal communication, 29 May 2024.

[12] Martyr, P. (2021, September 28). Beige Catholicism emptied our churches. *The Catholic Weekly*, https://catholicweekly.com.au/dr-philippa-martyr-beige-catholicism-emptied-our-churches

[13] Martyr, P. (2021, March 5). Stranded under the Southern Cross: news from a shrinking Church. *Gaudium et Spes 22*, https://gaudiumetspes22.com/blog/stranded-under-the-southern-cross-news-from-a-shrinking-church; Martyr, P. (2021, October 6). Plenary voices: Philippa Martyr. *The Catholic Weekly*, https://catholicweekly.com.au/plenary-voices-philippa-martyr/; Rowland, *Unconformed to the age*, 102.

[14] Fr Jason, personal communication, 13 June 2024.

[15] Alan, personal communication, 29 April 2024.

[16] William, personal communication, 17 October 2024.

[17] Colin, personal communication, 20 May 2024.

18 Martyr, P. (2024, July 18). How to be ignored during the synodal process. *The Catholic Weekly*, https://www.catholicweekly.com.au/instrumentum-laboris-synod-2024/

19 Cited in Rowland, *Unconformed to the age*, 86.

20 Fr Michael, personal communication, 9 August 2024.

21 Fr Harrison, personal communication, 30 May 2024.

22 Fr Jason, personal communication, 13 June 2024.

23 Fr Geoffrey, personal communication, 11 June 2024.

24 Martyr, P. (2012, December 1). Reaping the whirlwind. *Quadrant*, https://quadrant.org.au/magazine/2012/12/reaping-the-whirlwind/; Martyr, P. (2021, August 26). Liturgical fallout of the seventies. *The Catholic Weekly*, https://www.catholicweekly.com.au/dr-philippa-martyr-liturgical-fallout-of-the-70s/

25 One of the best contemporaneous summaries of the problems in the Catholic Church in Australia in the 1980s is Gilchrist, M. (1986). New class, new church. *Quadrant*, 30(9), 44-47. Gilchrist identified the new nomenklatura of Catholic bureaucracy and the contradictions of having a lavish business arm alongside falling Mass attendance rates.

26 Martyr, Reaping the whirlwind; Baker, M. (2011, May 24). *Paul Brazier*, https://www.superflumina.org/brazier_tribute.html. You can read the Statement here: https://www.catholicculture.org/culture/library/view.cfm?recnum=1046. For the other side, I'd recommend Lockwood, G. (2011, February 21). *The Catholic right in SA Labor*. Australasian Society for the Study of Labor History, https://labourhistorycanberra.org/2015/04/the-catholic-right-in-sa-labor/

27 The textual origin of this quote remains elusive, even for diehard Fuller fans online. If you find it, drop me a line at philippa.martyr@gmail.com. But I liked the idea so much that I used it in a paper in 2017 at the Dawson Colloquium in Tasmania, Martyr, P. (2018). Let's call the whole thing off? God, truth, and Buckminster Fuller. In D. Daintree (Ed.), *Creative subversion: The liberal arts and human educational fulfilment*. Connor Court. Audio at: https://cradio.org.au/cradiotalks/talk-lecture-series/dawson-centre/lets-call-whole-thing-off/

28 Martyr, Stranded under the Southern Cross.

29 Lucas, A. (2023, March 13). Boomers or bust? On Vatican II and generational arguments. *Catholic World Report*, https://www.catholicworldreport.com/2023/03/13/boomers-or-bust-on-vatican-ii-and-generational-arguments/

30 Sato, K. (2023, December 7). Baby boomers are scapegoats for ills of the world, Charles Sturt University researcher says. *ABC News*, https://www.abc.net.au/news/2023-12-07/baby-boomers-scapegoats-clive-hamilton-history-csu/103179636

31 Warhurst, Painful times for Church reformers.

32 Clements, B., & Bullivant, S. (2022). *Catholics in contemporary Britain: faith, society, politics*. Oxford.

33 Fr Harrison, personal communication, 30 May 2024.

34 Ethan, personal communication, 30 May 2024.

35 Chowdhury, I. (2022, June 6). Young Australian voters helped swing the election – and could do it again next time. *The Conversation*, https://

theconversation.com/young-australian-voters-helped-swing-the-election-and-could-do-it-again-next-time-184159

[36] Drewitt-Smith, A. (2023, June 22). Paedophile cult leader 'Little Pebble' William Kamm granted bail after alleged breach of court orders. *ABC News*, https://www.abc.net.au/news/2023-06-22/paedophile-cult-leader-faces-court-alleged-breach-of-bail/102509370;

[37] Prichard, J. (2008, July 10). Catholic community shuts after Archbishop's apology. *WA Today*, https://www.watoday.com.au/national/western-australia/catholic-community-shuts-after-archbishops-apology-20080710-3crr.html; Coyne, B. (2008, June 28). What lessons can we learn from the Bethel Covenant Community? *Bishop Accountability*, https://www.bishop-accountability.org/news2008/05_06/2008_06_28_Coyne_WhatLessons.htm

[38] Balthasar, H. (1982). What is required in witnesses. *You crown the year with your goodness: radio sermons*, trans G. Harrison. Ignatius.

[39] Martyr, P. (2019, November 21). Why get over it isn't enough for victims of clerical sexual abuse. *Church Life Journal*, https://churchlifejournal.nd.edu/articles/why-get-over-it-isnt-enough-for-victims-of-clerical-sexual-abuse/

Chapter 1

Where is everybody?

I've begun this book with a big assumption: that in Australia, we are a rapidly shrinking Church. According to the 2021 Census, around 20% of Australians still call themselves Catholics (that's around 5 million people). But we don't see most of them at Mass on Sunday. We see around 8% of them, which in 2021 was estimated at around 417,300 people across the country.[1]

But am I right about this? Surely if the entire Mass-going Catholic population in Australia had shrunk to less than the size of the population of Tasmania, we'd have seen panic-stricken people working frantically around the clock to do something about it?

I haven't noticed a great sense of urgency. Browse any diocesan website or open any Catholic newspaper or magazine, and everyone's smiling. They're cutting birthday cakes with 100-year-old nuns and standing around with small groups of well-groomed children in Catholic school uniforms. There is no hint that anyone thinks we're beginning a demographic winter that will seriously reshape the Church in Australia by the year 2050.

Bob Dixon, data king

If you've never heard of Robert (Bob) Dixon, a research officer for the Australian Catholic Bishops Conference (ACBC), I am about to remedy that. Bob Dixon was one of the first people to measure and comment on the decline in Mass attendance in Australia. Back in 1996, he said that 'attendances have been falling for at least twenty years'[2] (from as far back as 1976) and he found a 1989 national survey showing that only 29% of Catholic adults attended Sunday Mass. Dixon estimated the 1996 national Mass attendance rate to be around 18-19%, with some dioceses as high as 25% and some as low as 15%.³ He also described the decline in Mass attendance at diocesan level as 'obvious and inescapable.'⁴

It's very hard to count Mass-going Catholics, and estimates of church attendance are generally too generous.⁵ Every five years in Australia since 1996, parishes have been asked to do a count of their Mass attenders for four successive Sundays in May. All that data gets pooled at diocesan level and forwarded to the National Centre for Pastoral Research (NCPR; run by the ACBC), and they clean it up, analyse it, and release a report.

The last report on what's now called the 'National Count of Attendance' was released in 2024 and described data collected in 2021 after most churches in Australia had re-opened after COVID19.⁶ The national rate of Sunday Mass attendance was around 8%, and 23 of Australia's 28 Western (Latin) Catholic dioceses had total attendances of under 10,000 people. Catholics in non-Latin communities – Chaldean, Maronite, Melkite, Syro-Malabar, and Ukrainian – have astonishing attendance rates by comparison, but these are tiny groups of people, and these Mass attendances rates may not last another generation.⁷ We will look at a breakdown of all these figures later in this chapter.

My research into rates of Mass attendance during and immediately after COVID19 found that perhaps around 70% of very regular Mass-goers were trying to go back to churches once they'd reopened – but the less regular attenders were less diligent about coming back.⁸ But even if 70% of the 2016 total came back to Sunday Mass, that would still reduce our national total down to 420,000. And that's pretty much what happened.

I wonder sometimes if the reason no one seems to be worried is that historically, Australia has always had quite small numbers of Mass-going Catholics. Dixon thought that even in the 1950s, our alleged golden era, the attendance rate nationally was around 65%, rather than the 75% sometimes quoted.⁹ If it was just 65%, that's only around 1.3 million Mass-attending Catholics nationally¹⁰ –

which is still about three times as many as we have now. But was it even this high? One tantalising estimate from South Australia in 1956 puts the number of Mass-goers at just 12% of the Catholic population.[11] And that's meant to be the good old days.

The takeaway message here is that since 1989, researchers have been telling us that there are problems with falling Sunday Mass attendance. That was 35 years ago. I haven't seen many signs of action from church leadership on this issue, but perhaps they're still trying to make up their minds whether this is a real problem or not.

Why aren't Catholics coming to Mass?

A huge amount of ink has been spilt on this question. Everything has been blamed, from *Humanae Vitae* to the clergy sexual abuse crisis to bad homilies to the patriarchy. But we already know some answers, because the ACBC has commissioned two projects which explored it – the Catholic Church Life Survey in 1996, and a more specialised report eleven years later in 2007 (led by Bob Dixon).[12]

The 1996 study found that the chief reason Australian Catholics gave for not going to Sunday Mass any more was because they 'No longer feel that being a committed Catholic requires going to Mass every week'. A substantial 32% of respondents chose this as the most important reason, followed by 'Disagreement with the Church's teaching on, or attitude to, personal sexual issues' and 'No longer accept many Catholic beliefs', at 9% each. The 2007 report basically confirmed this, and came to the following conclusion:

> These results show that once people stop going to Mass, the degree to which they accept Catholic beliefs and moral teachings is likely to decline. The notion of 'believing without belonging', that people who no longer attend church maintain religious beliefs and moral attitudes similar to those held by church attenders, is not supported by the evidence presented here. There may well be exceptions but, for most Catholics, levels of belief will

eventually decline if they do not participate in the life of the Catholic faith community.[13]

Professor Stephen Bullivant and I also surveyed a group of just over 2,000 Australian Catholics in 2022 (CIA2022), and asked them why they did or didn't go to Mass. Those who didn't (374 people) told us that the most important reasons for them were, 'I don't see it as sinful to miss Mass', and 'I disagree with the Catholic Church's stance on certain issues.'[14]

It doesn't get more obvious than this. Australian Catholics don't go to Mass on Sundays because they don't believe they *have* to go, and because they don't believe core Catholic teachings or disagree with them. I'm certain that things like clergy sexual abuse have put some people off, but for the most part, the data is very consistent. People don't go to Mass because they don't believe what the Church teaches to be true. It's unreasonable to expect them to behave otherwise.

But knowing why people *don't go* to Mass, and knowing why they *slowed down* or *stopped going* to Mass, are two different questions. Mass attendance is a complex thing, and it's unlikely that just one adverse event would stop a fervent Catholic in their tracks and make them simply give up. It's more likely that there's a range of different factors working together to slowly erode their Mass-going over time.

There's another problem with asking people why they don't go to Mass anymore. Human memory is notoriously unreliable, especially over time (sometimes called 'recall bias'). For example, I have met priests who left the active ministry decades ago to get married. There's nothing wrong with that – I'm glad they left to get married instead of having a string of unhappy secret lady friends.

But after the clergy abuse crisis became public, I noticed that more priests who had left the active ministry were saying that they had seen child abuse happening when they were in the active ministry, and that was the real reason why they left. And perhaps it was – in which case, I wish they'd made a bit more noise about it back then, especially after they left the active ministry and had nothing left to lose.

There are many sides to this. Some of it is about not remembering, or only remembering what you want to. Some of it is also what is called 'social desirability bias' – we tell people what we think they want to hear. If I stopped going to Mass and I had to give people a reason why, I'd immediately pick the clergy abuse crisis, because that's the one thing everyone understands. But because of this, the people who really did give up Mass-going because of experiences of clergy sexual abuse – and they absolutely exist[15] – can get lost in the mix.

It also looks like many Australian Catholics since 1970 were 'pre-programmed' to stop going to Mass as adults because of one simple demographic change since 1966: the Catholic Church relaxed its marriage restrictions on 'mixed' marriages. These are marriages between a Catholic and a non-Catholic. It suddenly became much more likely that a Catholic in Australia would be born in a family where one of their parents wasn't a Catholic, and/or didn't go to church themselves.[16] I'll say more about this in the chapter on family life.

If you think that changing the Church's teachings on sexuality would bring everyone rushing back to Sunday Mass, I should remind you that Australian bishops and priests almost universally turned a blind eye to *Humanae Vitae* from 1968 onwards. That's why some Catholics at Mass every Sunday use artificial birth control, and possibly do all sorts of other things that the Church doesn't recognise as the right use of their sexuality, and don't think twice about it. In fact, some of them are quite proud of it – like the elderly gentleman and pillar of a local parish who told me, 'I put my wife on the Pill as soon as it became available'.

Disagreeing with the Church's teaching on important things doesn't seem to be a barrier to these people attending Mass every

Sunday. Perhaps they are simply less honest than the people who stay away in droves because they don't want to worship a God they don't believe in. Or perhaps they are less well-instructed than the other Catholics around them. Or perhaps they don't really care. Perhaps they like the social aspects of Mass and Church life. Perhaps their children are at the local Catholic school, and they feel like they must come to Mass there, for a while at least.

There's probably a good research project here waiting to happen, and in June 2024, the NCPR announced a two-year project to inquire more deeply into the reasons why people don't attend Mass any longer.[17] The last time they did this was 2007, when they produced the above-mentioned small-scale but very thorough study that was meant to inform the ACBC about the problem and stimulate them to try to turn the tide around. That was in 2007. How's that been working out in your diocese?

There's a well-known and well-worn solution to the problem that gets trotted out every time we have this conversation. If we just changed the Church's teaching on (whatever is annoying the more liberal Catholics this week), we'd get our numbers back. They usually point to various Protestant churches and communities who have appointed gay men and women to ministry and senior leadership positions, have vigorous music ministries, and generally bear no resemblance to the Catholic Church at all.

But I'd suggest that's not going to work, based on some interesting data that recently appeared in the US. These same Protestant communities and churches are dying on their feet. It's estimated that in another 30 years, less than 12% of all Americans will belong to any one of their long-established Protestant communities. Younger people especially have been abandoning them in droves.[18] The Anglican Church in Australia has also lost a huge number of its younger adherents in the same period, despite introducing women clergy and bishops and eagerly pursuing whatever causes are currently fashionable. The high death rate among elderly members is also catching up with them.[19]

Nature takes its course

Speaking of the death rate, that's another important factor that the blame-assigners have missed. The awkward thing about being over 60 years of age is that you're statistically more likely to die sooner. Of our approximately 600,000 Mass-going Catholics in Australia back in 2016, around two-thirds of them were over 60 years of age.

This – and the high rate of funerals in my own parish – got me wondering about the declining rate of Mass attendance we were seeing happen every five years from 1996. Was there something else going on? We didn't really know, because I was the only person morbid enough to go and look at Australian death rates for the over-60s and do some maths.

I used the Australian Bureau of Statistics (ABS) data on how many Australians die each year over the age of 60 and worked out how many of them were likely to identify as Catholic, based on the Census data for that period. Then I used the over-60 estimated Mass attendance rates to estimate how many of those over-60s were probably Mass-going Catholics.[20]

Between 1996 and 2001, the Church in Australia shed around 99,000 Mass-going Catholics.[21] According to my estimates, just under half of those were very likely to be our over-60s dying (around 42,000 deaths). Over the next five years to 2006, we shed around 56,000 Mass-going Catholics, of whom around 44,000 may simply have died.

There was one other interesting development in the twenty years between 1996 and 2016. The rate of women Mass-goers showed a sharp decline, from 21.4% of the female Catholic population in 1996 to just 13.9% in 2016.[22] Is this a case of women being driven out of an uncaring Church by the patriarchy? Possibly – but it's more likely to be elderly women Mass-goers dying. The number of women aged over 60 who die each year in Australia is generally slightly larger than the number of men, because women tend to live a bit longer than men.

Some people may still be voluntarily leaving, but I believe that the Church in Australia's biggest losses right now are those caused by the inevitable death of our biggest group of Mass-going Catholics: the parents of the Boomers. This generation – born before 1946 – was a very faithful group in terms of attending Mass. In 2024, the last of their children – those born in 1964, who grew up in the post-conciliar Church – will turn 60. But by 2050, the Boomer Catholics will be almost all gone. That's just twenty-five years – less than one generation away.

Before you panic too much, I haven't allowed for a corresponding number of babies being born during this time who might be at least nominal Catholics, and around 8% of those babies will have parents who both go to Mass, so they might stick around in the future. If there were plenty of Mass-going Catholic families having more than three children, numbers in the pews could remain stable and even rise steadily and organically, as a percentage of these children would continue to come to Mass in adulthood.

But Catholic families in Australia are now much smaller overall. We have a top-heavy population pyramid of Mass-goers aged 70 years and over, supported on a much narrower stem of Mass-goers under 70.[23] I think that nothing short of a miraculous fertility explosion – or a great sign in the heavens that converts all our non-Mass-going brothers and sisters – can reverse this trend. Mass immigration of church-going Catholics only solves the problem for around one generation. The next generation inevitably begins to lapse under the influences of high living and poor catechesis.[24]

Where's the data?

The laborious way in which I worked all this out should also prompt questions about what sort of data the Church collects on its own people, and where you can find it. It's quite hard to find reliable data at a national level for things like numbers of baptisms and adult receptions (converts) into the Church every year, and numbers of Catholic marriage ceremonies. A lot of the data goes straight from diocesan level to the Central Office of Church Statistics, which is part of the Vatican's Secretariat of State, and which publishes an annual yearbook of this data called the *Annuarium Statisticum Ecclesiae*.[25]

So I had to find a library (or two) in Australia with a complete or nearly complete run of this. Because I did, I have been able to collect data on baptisms, marriages, ordinations, first Holy Communions, and Confirmations in Australia for most years over that time. Much of this is now in the appendices to this book, and there is an online version available as well (see Appendix 2). The *Annuarium* also contains some complex and fascinating data on the number of annulments in Australia each year. I haven't had time to sift through and unpack it, but if someone wants an Honours or Masters project, this annulments data would be a good one.

I have heard some amusing and probably true stories of how inaccurate some of this Australian data is. Certainly, the marriage data in the *Annuarium* doesn't match up with the marriage data by Catholic ministers of religion collected by the ABS. The moral of the story is that good data is hard to find, and it's worth making a real effort to collect it in as consistent a way as possible – even if it means the diocese has to employ someone scary to go round and check all the parish registers manually and cross-examine the parish priests. I will say more on this in the final chapter.

Why ARE Catholics coming to Mass?

There are Catholics in Australia who are still going to Mass every Sunday and during the week, so the Church's teachings clearly aren't putting everyone off. Knowing what keeps people engaged and connected to the Church is valuable information, and the best people to give it to us are the ones who turn up pretty much every Sunday (or more often).

The CIA2022 study was open to anyone in Australia who identified as Catholic, but to my surprise, around 75% of those who responded were at least Sunday Mass-going Catholics. I was even more surprised by the number of younger Catholics (those aged under 40) who responded.[26] This has given me a fantastic opportunity to find out about the 'survivors' – the people who are still going to Mass, and especially those who are younger Catholics.

Dividing the survey participants into 'Weeklies', 'Irregulars', and 'Nevers' in terms of Mass attendance showed some very interesting differences.[27] It turns out that regular Mass-going Australian Catholics are literally a different type of Catholic from those who go to Mass irregularly or never. They're much more faithful to the Church's teachings, for starters.[28] Around a third of all Weeklies were also aged under 40, which is an even more important group of Catholics – if they stick around, they will form the backbone of the future Church in Australia.

These people can tell you why they go to Mass so often. Around 90% of them said that two reasons were very important to them: 'It helps me to feel closer to God' and 'It helps me grow in my relationship with Jesus in the sacraments'. Just over 80% also chose a third reason: 'I feel a need to receive the sacrament of Holy Communion'. They also knew what *wasn't* important to them as a reason for going to Mass: around 85% said that pleasing or satisfying spouses or parents wasn't important as a motivator. The next most popular choice of not-important reasons (50%) was 'The Church asks me to attend'.[29]

This isn't a crisis of practice or habit – it's a crisis of faith. It's clear that nominal Australian Catholics aren't coming to Mass because they don't think they have to, and they don't agree with the Church's teachings. It's also clear that Mass-going Australian Catholics are coming to Mass because they really want to, and don't have a problem with all or most of the Church's teachings. There's a very clear division between these two outlooks on life, and no amount of moving the Church's external furniture around is going to make a difference.

What about converts?

I'm so glad you asked. We don't seem to have any official data on converts – adults who were baptised as Catholics, or adults who were already baptised and have now been received into full communion with the Church. There's some data available on baptisms of people aged more than seven years, and the number has gently increased. In 1970, we baptised around 3,600 people aged over seven, but in 2017 it was over 4,700.[30]

Fr Harrison, working in Victoria, has been keeping track of his converts.

> After a decade, they number nearly a hundred, and I've discerned a pattern. Church scandals and hypocrisy don't figure much in their thoughts. They are attracted by the intellectual arguments of online apologists, like Bishop Robert Barron, Taylor Marshall, and even Jordan Peterson (who is not, himself, a believer). Or they are attracted by the mysticism of the saints and wish to deepen their spiritual lives.
>
> The feedback from [Rite of Christian Initiation of Adults] classes is consistent: they love learning more about the sacraments and prayer, they want more moral and social doctrine; they want to volunteer in social outreach; and they cherish their new home in a welcoming community. They have little interest in the inner workings of the Church, and even less interest in the battery of proposed reforms.[31]

Fr Robert, working in a different urban Australian diocese, said of the people he's assisted into the Church that:

> the many converts and reverts ... usually attribute their conversion or reversion to traditional worship, orthodox teaching (including that regarding sexual morality), strong Catholic identity (including priestly identity), and a strong sense of the vacuousness of the ideologies (especially that of the far left). This seems to me to be the one real area of growth among indicators of strong decline in the Church's life at other levels.[32]

I'd love to know more about the converts in the Church in Australia today. The CIA2022 study was able to find a few things out:

- Around 13% of our total sample (or nearly 300 people) were converts.
- Just over one-third of them were former 'Nones' – people with no identifiable religion before they became Catholics.
- Another one-third were converts from a range of Christian denominations, and a quarter were converts from Anglicanism.
- Very few were converts from other non-Christian religions.
- Around two-thirds had become Catholics between the ages of 20 and 39 years.[33]

Around half were aged under 40 years, and the other half aged over 40. Around half lived exactly where you'd expect to find Mass-going Catholics: the archdioceses of Sydney, Melbourne, Brisbane, and Perth. Around three-quarters of them were also Weeklies, and the younger converts were more likely to be Weeklies than the older ones. Around half were married (mostly to other Catholics) and had children, and interestingly around 20% of all these converts identified themselves as Latin Mass attenders.[34] They polled across all questions in the survey as strongly believing Catholics.[35]

Is this group typical of all converts in Australia? We don't know because we don't have any other data. But it's a start. There were some excitingly large groups of catechumens and others received into the Church at Easter 2024 in Sydney,[36] Brisbane,[37] and Melbourne.[38] Fr Joshua has also seen things turn around in his parish recently.

> We've got 11 [Rite of Christian Initiation of Adults] entrances this Easter [2024] with another 6 lined up for next year. Having no one received in the church last Easter. We had no altar servers; now we have about 8-9. Mass attendance is up by about 150 people … we have just strived

to do the basics well – good community, good teaching/ preaching and good music ... We also did a letter drop at Christmas[39] and have reached out to migrant groups as well.[40]

So I hope someone's writing all this down – tracking converts would be another terrific research project.[41]

Why focus on Mass-going Catholics?

This is an area where some church consultative processes (like the Plenary Council) and I part company. They have invited participation from Catholics who don't go to Mass, and from non-Catholics. On the contrary, I think that we as a Church should consult much more with the Catholics who are deeply invested in the Church's future in Australia, and who demonstrate this by regular Sunday Mass attendance. They are much more likely to represent the *sensus fidei* than an assortment of people sporting a Catholic 'identity' that could mean anything to anyone.

As I said before, Weeklies are a different group of Catholics from Irregulars and Nevers. Irregulars and Nevers are strongly in favour of changing the Church's teaching in core areas.[42] Of course they are – they're not the ones who will have to live with any consequences. They can say whatever they like about Church teaching, and usually do.

In fact, the CIA2022 study showed that if you're going to ask any big group of Australian Catholics questions about the Church, you need to know some important things about them before you analyse the answers. You need to know their age, their Mass attendance rate, where they were born (in or outside of Australia), if they're a convert or not, and how much Catholic schooling they've had.

These factors really seem to affect how a person answers questions about Catholic belief and practice in Australia today.[43] The one that seems to matter the most is Mass attendance rate. If we don't take these factors into account when we analyse their answers, we will get very peculiar survey results with misleading 'average' responses.

This might help explain why it's common to read opinion polls about 'Catholics' and their 'beliefs' that don't seem to bear any resemblance to the lived reality of Mass-goers' beliefs. That's because most respondents are Irregulars and Nevers, who make up the majority of 'Catholics' in Australia, and who are cheerfully sharing their own widely divergent views of what the Church should teach.

There's another reason why I think the Mass attendance rate is an important number. How do you measure how well the Church is doing its job? The single best indicator of how well the Church is delivering its core business is the Sunday Mass attendance rate. We're probably at the point where the only people still going to Mass are doing so because they really believe in the Church's teachings, and they really want to maintain their relationship with God and the Church. Everyone else has already gone.

This is what Ben Clements and Stephen Bullivant called the 'minority effect' of Catholics in the UK. Clements and Bullivant think this group of 'survivors' might be deliberately doubling down on their religion and living in a consciously counter-cultural way.[44] Less flatteringly, I've called it our 'Catholic weird', and suggested we embrace it. I would like to work out the algorithm for Martyr's Law: the smaller a local Church gets, the weirder it gets, because only the weird people stay attached to it when there's no earthly reason to do so.[45]

Some people don' t like the term 'practising Catholic'. They tell me that we're all practising Catholics, whether we go to Mass or not. Hans Urs von Balthasar also reminds us that Church statistics are just statistics, and that we can't use them to judge people's moral worth or their spiritual merits.[46] I'm happy to accommodate everyone by using the term 'Mass-going Catholic' instead.

I think it's important to have clear terminology for the group of

Catholics who are involved very regularly with the Church where it really matters: the parochial-diocesan Church through regular Sunday Mass attendance. This is growing more important because we are now a religious minority in Australia. I also think that with our shrinking numbers, a priority for future clergy distribution should be to ensure that Mass-going Catholics can continue to have access to the sacraments. For that, we need to know where they are – so let's find out.

Dioceses, eparchies, and ordinariates

Australia is a big country, even if it only has a tiny Church. So where are the weeds and the wheat in terms of numbers? Are things equally bad all over?

There are 28 Western or Latin-rite dioceses in Australia (Table 1) – 'Roman Catholics' with bishops and archbishops – plus several eparchies and ordinariates. An **eparchy** is what Eastern Catholics call their main organisational unit, and it's equivalent to a diocese in the Western Church. The five eparchies currently active in Australia are, in alphabetical order, the Chaldean, Maronite, Melkite, Syro-Malabar, and Ukrainian eparchies.[47]

Table 1. Western-rite dioceses in Australia by state or territory, 2021[48]

States, provinces, and dioceses	Mass-going Catholics, 2021	Mass attendance rate of Catholics in diocese, 2021	% of all Western-rite Mass-going Catholics in Australia, 2021
NSW and ACT			
Armidale	2,950	7.8%	0.8%
Bathurst	3,523	5.7%	0.9%
Broken Bay	14,138	6.9%	3.7%
Canberra-Goulburn	10,725	7.1%	2.8%
Lismore	5,391	5.5%	1.4%

Maitland-Newcastle	5,443	3.7%	1.4%
Parramatta	27,871	8.6%	7.2%
Sydney	61,247	10.4%	15.9%
Wagga Wagga	5,439	9.3%	1.4%
Wilcannia-Forbes	1,447	5.7%	0.4%
Wollongong	12,064	6.1%	3.1%
Victoria			
Ballarat	7,117	8%	1.8%
Melbourne	83,925	8.1%	21.8%
Sale	7,733	6.2%	2.0%
Sandhurst	5,619	6.6%	1.5%
Tasmania			
Hobart	4,062	5.7%	1.1%
Queensland			
Brisbane	39,735	5.8%	10.3%
Cairns	3,070	5.6%	0.8%
Rockhampton	4,745	5.1%	1.2%
Toowoomba	3,420	5.8%	0.9%
Townsville	3,787	5.5%	1.0%
South Australia			
Adelaide	19,848	7.8%	5.2%
Port Pirie	2,036	9.2%	0.5%
Northern Territory			
Darwin	4,061	10.4	1.1%
Western Australia			
Broome	592	7.9%	0.2%
Bunbury	3,757	6.6%	1.0%
Geraldton	1,254	5.9%	0.3%
Perth	40,333	9.8%	10.5%
Total	385,332	7.0%	100 %

Let's start with the Western Catholic dioceses. In Australia, they're organised into five **provinces** that roughly match our state borders: Sydney, Brisbane, Melbourne, Adelaide, and Perth. 'Sydney' takes care of NSW and the ACT, while 'Adelaide' takes care of South Australia and the Northern Territory. 'Melbourne' also takes care of Tasmania's lone archdiocese of Hobart. 'Brisbane' handles Queensland, and 'Perth' handles Western Australia.

It's good to know about the provinces, because with the dire state of Mass-going in Australia, they may be a future way of administering the Catholic Church in Australia. At the very least, we might see more of the *in persona episcopi* solution. This is when Rome keeps two dioceses running as separate entities but appoints a single bishop to manage both.[49]

For example, at the time of writing (June 2024) there were four dioceses in Western Australia, but only two bishops in charge of them. The Archbishop of Perth, Timothy Costelloe (aged just over 70), was overseeing Perth and was also the apostolic administrator for Bunbury diocese. The Bishop of Geraldton, Michael Morrissey, was overseeing Geraldton and the diocese of Broome in the same way. He's also in his early 70s, and he has a total of less than 2,000 Mass-going Catholics to worry about.

Bishops usually retire at the age of 75. If the Vatican was concerned about the tiny numbers of people involved, they'd unite the dioceses of Perth and Bunbury, and Broome and Geraldton, *in persona episcopi*. Archbishop Costelloe's successor would run Perth and Bunbury, and Bishop Morrissey's successor would run Geraldton and Broome.

But as of late 2024, Broome acquired a new bishop, Tim Norton SVD, who at the age of just 66 might find himself managing Geraldton as well as Broome in the future.[50] Norton was followed in January 2025 by Fr George Kolodziej SDS, who was appointed the new bishop of Bunbury. A spokesperson for the Archdiocese of Perth apparently said that both appointments would help meet the needs of more than 60,000 parishioners across both dioceses.[51] Perhaps that's the number of Catholics there, but the combined Mass-goers total around 4,300. It's hard to see why dioceses with such tiny numbers of Mass attenders have been given new bishops, but perhaps their job will be to turn this situation around.

What about the eparchies, ordinariates, and the personal prelature – the 'non-geographical dioceses'? Who are they, what do they have to offer the Church in Australia today, and how are they tracking? I'd like to spend a bit of time describing these communities, because most Western Catholics in Australia don't have a clue about them. I'll start with the oldest presence in Australia (the Melkites) and work forward to the newest (the Syro-Malabars).

Table 2. Eparchies and Ordinariates in Australia, 2021

	Mass-going Catholics, 2021	Mass going Catholics as % of 2021 Census population	% of all Eastern and Ordinariate Mass-going Catholics in Australia, 2021
Chaldean	6,657	47.2%	20.5%
Melkite	1,785	57.8%	5.5%
Maronite	13,661	29.0%	42.0%
Syro-Malabar	8,352	81.1%	25.7%
Ukrainian	1,664	57.7%	5.1%
Military Ordinariate	65	–	0.2%
Personal Ordinariate of Our Lady of the Southern Cross	333	–	1.0%
Total	32,517		100.0%

The **Melkite** Catholic Eparchy of Australia, New Zealand and All Oceania is made up of members of an ancient group of

Christians derived from the Church of Antioch. The Melkites use the Byzantine Rite, and their form of the Mass – 'the Divine Liturgy' – is celebrated primarily in English or Arabic, or a mix of both, together with some Greek. Melkite Catholics will ordain men who have been married for at least 5 years before ordination, but married men do not become bishops.

The first Melkite mission was set up in Australia in 1891, and the Melkite Diocese of Sydney was finally erected as an eparchy in 1987. Known as the Eparchy of St Michael Archangel of Sydney for Melkite Greek Catholics of Australia, it was first led by the Most Rev George Riashi. By 2021-22 they had thirteen parishes and twenty priests.[52] The 2006 Census estimated their numbers at 1,982 nationally,[53] but by 2021 this had risen to 3,086.[54] The eparchy currently has five churches in NSW, three in Victoria, one each in Queensland, South Australia, and Western Australia, and a planned mission to the ACT.[55]

The **Maronites** are the largest of the eparchies in Australia in terms of population, mostly based in the Sydney area, and mostly originating from Lebanon. The Maronite Eparchy of Australia, New Zealand and Oceania also has its own liturgical calendar, rites of Mass and sacraments, liturgical language (Syro-Aramaic), religious orders, and saints (like St Maroun, who the community is named after). Maronite priests may be married before ordination, but their bishops are expected to be celibate.

The first Maronite mission was established in Sydney in 1898 and was eventually erected as a diocese in 1973 (the Diocese of St Maroun of Sydney), first led by the Most Rev Abdo Khalife. In 2021-22 they reported a community of some fifteen parishes and over 50 priests.[56] The 2006 Census identified 29,053 Maronites in Australia, and by 2021 this had risen to 47,014.[57] You can see how large this community is, but also how it's mostly based in NSW, by the number and distribution of their churches. They have a cathedral, co-cathedral, and 11 churches in NSW – but just two in

Victoria and one each in South Australia, Queensland, and Western Australia.[58]

The **Ukrainian** Catholic Church can trace its origins to the original Christian conversion of the Russia and Ukraine region. The largest of the Eastern rites globally, it's also one of the smallest in Australia. Parish priests can marry before ordination, but bishops are unmarried men, and they also have their own religious orders of men and women. Ukrainian Catholics traditionally celebrated the Divine Liturgy in Old Slavonic, but mostly today it is celebrated in modern Ukrainian or English.

The Ukrainian Catholics were first established in Australia in 1958 as an **apostolic exarchate** – a small group of Eastern Rite Catholics who found themselves in Latin Rite territory. It was originally called 'the Apostolic Exarchate for Ukrainians of Byzantine Rite in Australia' and was first headed up by the Most Rev Ivan Prasko. In 2006 the Census estimated that there were around 3,600 Ukrainian Catholics in Australia,[59] but by 2021 the Census figure had fallen to 2,882.[60]

In 1982 the community was elevated to become the Eparchy of Saints Peter and Paul of Melbourne for the Ukrainians.[61] By 2021-22, the Ukrainian community had 22 priests, mostly diocesan. According to their website, in 2024 there are four parishes in Victoria, two in the ACT, three in NSW, one in Queensland (plus missions), two in South Australia, one in Tasmania, and two in Western Australia.[62] And in late 2024 in a move that absolutely no-one predicted, Pope Francis nominated Australia's Ukrainian eparch, Bishop Mykola Bychok CssR, as Australia's newest and currently only cardinal.[63]

The **Chaldean** Catholic Eparchy of Saint Thomas the Apostle of Sydney are Catholics who worship according to the rites of the Chaldean Church, a 'Church of the East' which is of ancient origin. Today, most Chaldean Catholics live in either Iraq or the United States, but some live in Australia, mostly on the east coast.

The eparchy was first established in 2006 in Australia, and its first eparch was Most Rev Jibrail Kassab. They have their own form of Mass, liturgical calendar, liturgical language (Syriac/Aramaic) and customs. Their priests can marry before ordination, but bishops must be celibate. The local eparchy has two churches in Victoria and a future planned mission there,[64] and one church in Fairfield, NSW.[65] In 2021, there were 14,103 Chaldean Catholics in Australia.[66]

The **Syro-Malabar** Eparchy of St Thomas the Apostle is made up of Catholics mostly from the Kerala region of India. It's another Eastern church of ancient origin, with a long and famously well-inculturated history in India. The Mass or 'Holy Qurbana' (East Syrian liturgy) and sacraments are generally celebrated in Malayam, the language of Kerala, or in English in Australia. It was established in Australia in around 2014, and the first eparch was Most Rev Bosco Puthur. With around 4.2 million members worldwide, it's a very large group outside Australia, and a rapidly growing one inside it: in 2021, there were 10,301 Syro-Malabar Catholics in Australia.[67]

Syro-Malabar priests are celibate, and in 2022 there were around 30 diocesan and nine religious priests in Australia, serving 43 parishes.[68] Many of the Syro-Malabar priests in Australia also have **bi-ritual** faculties – this means they can say not just the Holy Qurbana, but the Western rite of Mass as well (the 'Novus Ordo'). This isn't just something a priest can decide to do by himself. He needs the permission of his bishop, and the bishop of the other rite. He also needs to be properly trained in the other rite of Mass.

Because Syro-Malabar priests are celibate like Western Catholic priests, this also makes them very portable. That's why, with the addition of bi-ritual faculties, you will now find them serving as parish priests in Western-rite parishes. They have clergy and churches widely distributed across Australia: eight churches and a mission in Victoria, 12 and a mission in NSW, 12 in Queensland, one in Tasmania, three in the Northern Territory, two in Western Australia and three in South Australia.[69]

An **ordinariate** is a canonical structure that's also equivalent to a diocese, but it often has national boundaries instead of local ones because it's set up to manage a small number of people spread over a large area. The Military Ordinariate manages all Catholics in the armed forces, who are a highly mobile and dispersed group of people.[70] The Personal Ordinariate of Our Lady of the Southern Cross is one of the ordinariates created by Pope Benedict XVI to provide a home in the Catholic Church for former Anglican clergy and laity who wanted to worship in their traditional liturgy, but as Catholics.[71] It was established in Australia on 15 June 2012, and its first Ordinary was Monsignor Harry Entwistle. In 2021, the Ordinariate had 14 parishes across Australia, Japan, and Guam, with 23 parish priests, one permanent deacon, and three seminarians in formation.

There's also the Personal Prelature of the Holy Cross and Opus Dei, which is an international apostolate. This was founded in Australia on 28 November 1982, although the movement had been active in Sydney since 1963. You can read the names of every priest incardinated in the prelature in the *Official Directory of the Catholic Church in Australia*. Opus Dei also has a very public website, so if it's meant to be some kind of Catholic secret society, it's clearly not delivering on that.[72]

I should probably state that I am not now, nor have I ever been, involved with Opus Dei. Over the last thirty years or so, people who disagreed with me about the Church have accused me (and 'accused' is the right word) of being a shill for them. However, the truth is that their spirituality has never really appealed to me, and my experiences with 'The Work' have been – like my experiences with every other apostolate, parish, ministry, and office in the Church in Australia – mixed. I have some further thoughts about apostolates and movements in Australia which I'll unpack further in the chapter on religious life.

These tables give us a clear picture of where the living,

breathing, Mass-going Church in Australia is holding on, and where it's really struggling and in danger of extinction in the next ten to fifteen years. The struggling end can be seen in rural and regional dioceses like Broome, Geraldton, Wilcannia-Forbes, Port Pirie, Armidale, Cairns, Toowoomba, Bathurst, Bunbury, Townsville, Darwin, Hobart, and Rockhampton, all of which now report fewer than 5,000 Mass-going Catholics in total, often spread out over vast distances from priests and from each other. The Eastern rites have high rates of Mass attendance, but very small numbers of people. They may have a lot of new migrants, but they struggle with the same issues as all migrant Catholics – they find it increasingly hard to keep their children and grandchildren going to Mass on Sundays.

At the healthier end of the Church, population-wise, are the archdioceses and major population centres: Melbourne, Sydney, Brisbane, and Perth, all of which have around 40,000 or more Mass-going Catholics. Around half of all Mass-going Catholics in Australia currently live in these four archdioceses, so we are a heavily urban/suburban Church. But the dangers of being otherwise are already beginning to show – for example, the Archdiocese of Perth is much bigger in land size than Sydney or Melbourne but has about half as many Mass-going Catholics.

The upside: there's no priest shortage

The good news about the shrinking numbers of laity in the Catholic Church in Australia is that it means there's no priest shortage. I know this might surprise you, because this has been one of the most persistent myths about the modern Catholic Church in Australia. That's because all the calculations were being made based on the nominal Catholic population (5 million), not the actual Mass-going population (417,000). I can show you what this looks like (Figure 1). This shows the number of Mass-going Catholics dropping abruptly while the number of diocesan priests in Australia declines very gently over the same period.[73] I've had to shrink the Mass-goers down, but I've done it proportionally so you can see both sets of data on the one chart.

Figure 1. Numbers of Mass attenders ('00) and diocesan clergy in Australia, 1990-2021

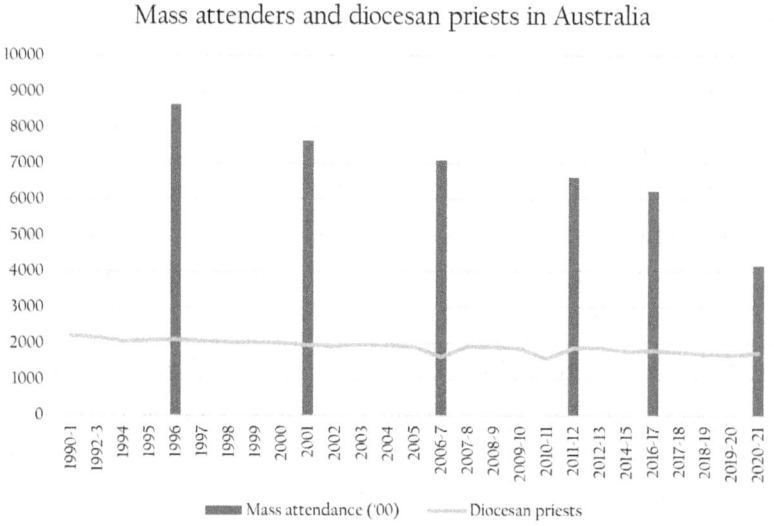

I've only counted **diocesan** priests here (priests who work for the local bishop), because **religious** priests (those in religious orders) can be transferred in and out of dioceses, so their numbers tend to fluctuate more. For the most part the number of diocesan priests has remained steady. To be fair, this includes all diocesan priests, even the ones who are retired. But when you realise that most priests really only work with and for the people who come to Mass and the sacraments, the burden becomes lighter.

I used several sources for my priest numbers: the *Annuarium Statisticum Ecclesiae*, the *Official Directory of the Catholic Church in Australia*, and the website Catholic-Hierarchy.org (at the time of writing it had data from around 2020-2022). I then compared these numbers to the number of Mass-going Catholics in each Western-rite diocese.[74] There were just over 2,700 priests in total – that's diocesan and religious priests combined – and 385,332 Western (Latin-rite) Mass-going Catholics.

This means that the ratio of priests to Mass-going Catholics in Australia in 2021 was about 1 to 143. That's a modest Sunday congregation. If around a third of all the priests were too elderly or infirm to do this work, that takes us down to 1,800 priests – 1 for every 214 Mass-going Catholics. This again would not pose a huge problem for the average priest. If we just used diocesan priests, there were about 1,700 of them in 2021-22 – so that's around 227 Mass-going Catholics for each diocesan priest.

Of course this is just maths, and real life is different, because lots of our priests aren't in the right places. If you live in the archdiocese of Sydney, where there's a diocesan priest for every 300 or so Mass-going Catholics, it's easy to find another Sunday Mass if your parish priest is unwell that week. But if you lived in the diocese of Lismore in northern NSW, where there's one diocesan priest for every 130 or so Mass-going Catholics, the nearest Catholic church with Mass available might be a long drive away. A typical parish priest in Sydney might have 800 people at Sunday Masses, with youth ministry, a mothers' group, a men's group, a busy RCIA ministry, a large choir, and the annual fundraising fete. Meanwhile, his brother priest in the diocese of Wilcannia-Forbes has to drive for hours to say Mass twice a month for a tiny Catholic community close to the state border.

In my chapter on the clergy, we'll look at things like ordination numbers. But for now, rest assured that the Church in Australia is in more danger of running out of laity than priests.

The downside: there's a laity shortage

So, if we're down to around 417,000 Mass-going Catholics now, what might we look like by 2051? The first thing I have to stress is that this is just **data modelling**. Data modelling isn't the same as fact or reality; if you change even one tiny bit of the 'recipe', you get a different outcome.

There are some people in the Church who think this kind of thing is a bad idea. This includes a woman religious in a senior diocesan role (not my diocese) who emailed me early in 2024 to say that it was outside our scope to guess the future size of the Church in Australia because this is in God's hands.[75] I agree with Sister that it's in God's hands, but he also gave us the gift of reason and asked us to use it.

What I've done is work out what each diocese lost in 2011-2016, and then in 2016-2021, as a percentage of its total Mass-goers. I've averaged this out for each diocese to create an 'average loss' for the ten years between 2011 and 2021. All I've done then is take that same average loss forward in ten-year intervals.

For example, the archdiocese of Adelaide had an estimated 19,848 Mass-goers in 2021. Their average loss from 2011-2021 was 20.7% of all their Mass-goers. Every 10 years forward, I subtracted 20.7% of the Mass-going population. This means that by 2051, the archdiocese of Adelaide may have just 9,893 Mass-goers.

This table shows what the total number of Western (Latin rite) Mass-goers might be in Australia by 2051 (Table 3). I think we're looking at just under 200,000 people, because I don't think we can make up our losses from an increased birth rate alone now. If I allow for 10% loss of diocesan priests over the same period, we end up with almost 1,300 of them, which means it's around 1 priest for every 150 or so Mass-goers. I think the national Mass attendance rate will be around 5%. I'm allowing for fewer people identifying as Catholics in the national Census as well, because I suspect we'll be down to around 10% willing to identify as Catholics nationally, or 3.7 million nominal Catholics in a projected Australian population of 37 million.[76]

Table 3. Estimated projected numbers of Sunday Mass-goers by diocese in Australia, 2051

Diocese	Estimated Mass-goers 2051
Melbourne	38,128
Sydney	31,680
Perth	25,244
Brisbane	18,950

Parramatta	12,293
Adelaide	9,893
Broken Bay	6,097
Wollongong	6,052
Canberra-Goulburn	5,448
Sale	4,643
Darwin	4,493
Ballarat	3,332
Wagga Wagga	3,215
Sandhurst	2,710
Bunbury	2,465
Lismore	2,186
Hobart	2,161
Townsville	2,023
Rockhampton	2,011
Cairns	2,009
Maitland Newcastle	1,639
Armidale	1,638
Port Pirie	1,278
Bathurst	1,256
Toowoomba	1,167
Wilcannia Forbes	569
Geraldton	541
Broome	440

Obviously, this is grim. It's also not certain. It could be less or more, because there's a lot we can't control, like papal elections, episcopal appointments, government persecution, Catholic migration numbers, religious worker visa conditions and numbers, international events, and even eschatological events.

What will this (hopefully) brave new Church look like? We might have to take the Eastern Rite churches more seriously. If they can maintain their current numbers to 2051, they will give us an additional 32,452 Mass-going Catholics. The Traditional Latin

Mass community in Australia has also grown measurably since it was included in the National Count of Attendance as a Mass said in a language other than English (from 763 attenders in 2006 to 3,379 in 2021).[77] If they kept increasing their numbers, even by just 50% over every five years, they would account for around one-fifth of Australian Mass-goers in 2051.

Migration might also be on our side. I looked at the Australian net migration figures for 2022-23, what countries of origin were represented, and then at the Catholic populations and likely estimated Mass attendance rates in those countries. I made it at around 35,000 likely new Mass attenders migrating to Australia in that year. If the federal government continues to take the same number of migrants from Catholic-dominated countries with relatively high Mass attendance rates, right through to 2051, and if the estimated Mass attendance figures are correct, it could make a real difference. But Fr Vincent, a priest in Victoria, put it like this:

> Now, as a migrant myself, I am all too happy to see more people come to Australia and fulfill their God-given purpose in the Church here in Australia. Skilled migration can help the Church grow, just as it helps to grow the economy. However, it cannot be the sole source of Church growth, as it will risk the grassroots Australians becoming 'a Church on the margins,' and we will lose them to other groups.[78]

Of course, all these migrants would have to stay in Australia, still be alive in 2051, and keep going to Mass every Sunday. If they did all this, we'd have almost a million new Mass-goers by 2051. Catholics born overseas would then make up around 70% of the entire Mass-going population in Australia, and our parishes would look (and sound) excitingly different.

Conclusion

There's some good news and some bad news. The bad news is that we're rapidly running out of laity in the Church. We've known about this for some time, but there's been a certain lack of urgency about changing direction so far. By 2051, we're likely to be looking at a very small group of Mass-going Catholics in Australia – maybe less than 200,000 people.

Some dioceses in Australia, demographically, are already at death's door. There are skeleton crews of clergy basically keeping the lights on for a smaller and smaller number of Mass-goers, and it's hard to see a future beyond the next five years, let alone 25 years. Perhaps we can learn from the Eastern Catholics in Australia and set up mission posts in these territories for our increasingly tiny congregations.

The good news is that we can see where we're likely to end up. Hopefully at some point we will galvanise ourselves into doing something about it. There are some parts of the Church that are geographically and demographically alive and well – large numbers of Mass-going Catholics and plenty of clergy within driving distance. These will be called on to do more of the heavy lifting in the future.

Good news again: we're not running out of priests. We also don't seem to be losing adults hand-over-fist because of the essential awfulness of the Catholic Church. Instead, our numbers of laity are now dropping mostly because we have an upside-down pyramid in the Church based on age, and all those older church-going Catholics are dying in higher numbers than the young ones.

It's likely that the huge increase in marriages between Catholics and non-Catholics in Australia since 1970 has produced the effect always predicted with 'mixed' marriages – the faith of the Catholic spouse will weaken, and the children won't come to Mass. There's not much we can do about people dying or deciding to marry non-Catholics: changing the Church's teachings won't bring them back.

More good news: today, there's pretty much no material or social advantage to being a Mass-going Catholic in Australia. In fact, it's quite the opposite. This means that the people you see around you on Sundays at Mass are likely to be the people who really believe in it all, and really mean it.

In our next chapter, we'll look at the core building block of the Catholic Church in Australia – the Catholic family. We'll look at the weeds and wheat and identify some trends that might show us a way forward to a smaller but healthier and more committed future Church in Australia.

---

1 Rossi, M., & Scappini, E. (2014). Church attendance, problems of measurement, and interpreting indicators: a study of religious practice in the United States, 1975–2010. *Journal for the Scientific Study of Religion*, 53(2), 249-267; National Centre for Pastoral Research (NCPR), *Australian Catholic Mass Attendance Report 2021*, https://ncpr.catholic.org.au/wp-content/uploads/2024/05/Mass-attendance-in-Australia-2021-FINAL.pdf; Burge, R. (2023, October 12). The Catholic Church is in trouble in places where it used to dominate. *Graphs About Religion*, https://www.graphsaboutreligion.com/p/the-catholic-church-is-in-trouble

2 Dixon, R. (1996). *The Catholics in Australia*. Bureau of Immigration, Multicultural and Population Research, 92.

3 Dixon, *Catholics in Australia*, 92.

4 Dixon, *Catholics in Australia*, 92; Dixon, R. (2024). Mass attenders' attitude to the sexual abuse crisis in the Catholic Church in Australia: Part 2: Detailed results from the most recent survey. *Pointers Bulletin of the Christian Research Association*, 34(2), 1–5.

5 Rossi & Scappini, Church attendance; Clements, R. & Bullivant, S. (2022). *Catholics in contemporary Britain*. Oxford University Press, 10-15. The foreword to each National Count of Attendance in Australia explains how the counts are made and when. Obviously, age must only be guessed in each count, as most parishes do not register Mass attenders and don't ask them for their age or date of birth, so the figures on the age groups attending Mass are at best rubbery.

6 NCPR, *Australian Catholic Mass attendance report 2021*.

7 It is difficult to find data on Sunday worship attendance rates for Eastern Rites churches outside Australia – almost as hard as it is to find accurate counts of their numbers worldwide. But I did find one figure for Ukrainian Catholics and their Mass attendance rates. Pew Research Center. (2017, May 10). *Religious Belief and National Belonging in Central and Eastern Europe*, http://assets.pewresearch.org/wp-content/uploads/sites/11/2017/05/15120244/CEUP-FULL-REPORT.pdf

8 Martyr, P. (2022). Factors affecting Australian Catholics' return to Mass after COVID19 church closures. *Journal of Religion and Health*, 61(5), 4245-4259. https://link.springer.com/article/10.1007/s10943-022-01618-1

9 Dixon, *Catholics in Australia*, 93-94.

10 Philips, W. (1987). Religion. In W. Vamplew (Ed.), *Australian historical statistics*, Academy of the Social Sciences in Australia, https://socialsciences.org.au/wp-content/uploads/2019/10/29-Historical-Statisitics-Chapter-25-final.pdf provides a state-by-state breakdown of the Catholic population in 1954, from which I compiled my total of 2,056,707 Catholics nationally.

11 Philips, Religion, gives a total of 125,770 Catholics in 1954, but an estimate of 'church members' of just 14,500.

[12] Dixon, R., Bond, S., Engebretson, K., Rymarz, R., Cussen, B., & Wright, K. (2007). *Research project on Catholics who have stopped attending Mass: final report February 2007*. ACBC Pastoral Projects Office, https://ncpr.catholic.org.au/pdf/DCReport.pdf

[13] Dixon et al., *Research project*, 66.

[14] Martyr, P., & Bullivant, S. (2023). *The Catholics in Australia Survey 1 – Mass attendance*, https://papers.ssrn.com/sol3/papers.cfm?abstract_id=4646161

[15] Martyr, P., & Bullivant, S. (2024). *The Catholics in Australia Survey 8 – Irregulars and Nevers*, https://papers.ssrn.com/sol3/papers.cfm?abstract_id=4912660, 25.

[16] Martyr, P., & Bullivant, S. (2024). *The Catholics in Australia Survey 6 – Family life*, https://papers.ssrn.com/sol3/papers.cfm?abstract_id=4855996

[17] Ang, D. (2024, June 7). National study to investigate reasons for decline in Mass attendance. *The Catholic Weekly*, https://www.catholicweekly.com.au/national-study-to-investigate-decline-in-mass-attendance/

[18] Hodge, B. (2024, April 4.) The faith of the next generation. *The Pillar*, https://www.pillarcatholic.com/p/the-faith-of-the-next-generation; Sandeman, J. (2024, April 28). Mythbusting: conservative denominations grow, progressive ones shrink. *The Other Cheek*, https://theothercheek.com.au/mythbusting-conservative-denominations-grow-progressive-ones-shrink/

[19] Shearer, C. (2017, June 28). Number of Australian Anglicans falls by 580,000 in five years: Census 2016. *Melbourne Anglican*, https://tma.melbourneanglican.org.au/2017/06/number-of-australian-anglicans-falls-by-580000-in-five-years-census-2016/

[20] These can be found in each of the NCPR's 5 yearly reports on Mass attendance at https://ncpr.catholic.org.au/national-count-of-attendance/

[21] Dixon, R., Kunciunas, A., & Reid, S. (2008). *Mass attendance in Australia*. ACBC Pastoral Projects Office, https://www.ncpr.catholic.org.au/pdf/SummaryReport_MassAttendanceInAustralia.pdf

[22] NCPR, *Australian Catholic Mass attendance report 2016*, 6.

[23] NCPR, *Australian Catholic Mass attendance report 2021*, 9.

[24] See for example Crockett, A., & Voas, D. (2006). Generations of decline: religious change in 20th-century Britain. *Journal for the Scientific Study of Religion*, 45(4), 567–584. https://doi.org/10.1111/j.1468-5906.2006.00328.x, and the classic study, Mol, J. (1965). The decline in religious participation of migrants. *International Migration*, 3(3), 137–145. https://doi.org/10.1111/j.1468-2435.1965.tb00878.x

[25] Catholic Church. *Annuarium Statisticum Ecclesiae*. Vatican: Central Office of Church Statistics.

[26] Martyr & Bullivant, *Mass attendance*.

[27] Clements & Bullivant, *Catholics in Contemporary Britain*, developed this three-level categorisation and found similar variations in their results from the Catholics in Britain 2019 survey.

[28] Martyr, P., & Bullivant, S. (2024). *The Catholics in Australia Survey 3 – Believing*, https://papers.ssrn.com/sol3/papers.cfm?abstract_id=4723637

[29] Martyr & Bullivant, *Mass attendance*, 30.

[30] Data taken from the *Annuarium Statisticum Ecclesiae* for most years between 1970 and 2017.

[31] Fr Harrison, personal communication, 30 May 2024.

[32] Fr Robert, personal communication, 11 June 2024.

33 Martyr & Bullivant, *Mass attendance*, 9.

34 Data taken from the CIA2022 raw data set.

35 Martyr, P. & Bullivant, S. (2024). *The Catholics in Australia Survey 3 – Believing*, https://papers.ssrn.com/sol3/papers.cfm?abstract_id=4723637

36 Cramsie, D. (2023, April 28). On God's beat: police officer among 200 new Catholics welcomed into the church. *The Catholic Weekly*, https://www.catholicweekly.com.au/on-gods-beat-police-officer-among-200-new-catholics-welcomed-into-the-church/; Ally, D. (2024, April 24). Sydney's baptism boom has us beaming with pride. *The Catholic Weekly*, https://www.catholicweekly.com.au/sydneys-baptism-boom-has-us-beaming-with-pride/

37 Higgins, J. (2024, February 19). Hundreds take the next step on path to baptism and confirmation in Brisbane. Catholic Leader, https://catholicleader.com.au/news/qld/hundreds-take-the-next-step-on-path-to-baptism-and-confirmation-in-brisbane/

38 Melbourne Catholic. (2023, February 28). The journey to Easter: catechumens and candidates celebrate the Rite of Election. *Melbourne Catholic*, https://melbournecatholic.org/news/the-journey-to-easter-catechumens-and-candidates-celebrate-the-rite-of-election

39 Cox, V. (2023, December 19). 10,000 Christmas Mass invites go out to Queanbeyan residents. *Catholic Voice*, https://www.catholicvoice.org.au/10000-christmas-mass-invites-go-out-to-queanbeyan-residents/

40 Fr Joshua, personal communication, 24 March 2024.

41 See Cronin, C. (2013). Interpreting research results of parish mystagogy. *Australasian Catholic Record*, 90(1), 71–80, https://search.informit.org/doi/epdf/10.3316/informit.246311803077022 for an example of how a project like this can be run.

42 Martyr & Bullivant, *Believing*, 17.

43 Martyr & Bullivant, *Believing*.

44 Clements & Bullivant, *Catholics in contemporary Britain*.

45 Martyr, P. (2021, March 5). Stranded under the Southern Cross: news from a shrinking Church. *Gaudium et Spes 22*, https://gaudiumetspes22.com/blog/stranded-under-the-southern-cross-news-from-a-shrinking-church

46 von Balthasar, H. (1982). What is required in witnesses. In von Balthasar, H. *You crown the year with your goodness: radio sermons*, trans G. Harrison. Ignatius.

47 For a good explainer, see Waters, I., & McGuckin, R. (2016). Eastern Catholic churches in Australia: canonical issues for Catholic clergy and pastoral workers. *Australasian Catholic Record*, 93(1), 81–89.

48 NCPR, *Australian Catholic Mass Attendance Report 2021*.

49 Coppen, L. (2024, May 23). Is Italy's *in persona episcopi* experiment for diocesan mergers ending? *The Pillar*, https://open.substack.com/pub/thepillar/p/is-italys-in-persona-episcopi-experiment

50 Higgins, J. (2024, October 14). Pope Francis appoints Bishop Tim Norton as the Bishop of Broome. *Catholic Leader*, https://catholicleader.com.au/news/australia/pope-francis-appoints-bishop-tim-norton-as-the-bishop-of-broome/

51 Williams, A. (2025, January 15). Faith Workers Alliance says new WA Catholic Bishops a chance to rebuild trust. *ABC News*, https://www.abc.net.au/news/2025-01-15/new-catholic-bishops-for-broome-bunbury/104796430

52 *Official directory of the Catholic Church in Australia*, various years.

53 Ibid.

54 Australian Bureau of Statistics (ABS). *2021 Census, Religious affiliation in Australia* (Excel spreadsheet), Table 4, https://www.abs.gov.au/statistics/people/people-and-communities/cultural-diversity-census/2021/Census%20article%20-%20Religious%20affiliation%20in%20Australia.xlsx

55 *Melkite Catholic Eparchy of Australia, New Zealand & All Oceania*, https://www.melkite.org.au/community. Thanks to Fr Collin Nunis of the Melkite community for reviewing and improving this paragraph for accuracy.

56 *Official directory of the Catholic Church in Australia*, various years.

57 ABS, *2021 Census, Religious affiliation in Australia*, Table 4.

58 *Maronite Eparchy in Australia, New Zealand and Oceania*, https://maronite.org.au/

59 *Official directory of the Catholic Church in Australia*, various years.

60 ABS, *2021 Census, Religious affiliation in Australia*, Table 4.

61 *Official directory of the Catholic Church in Australia*, various years.

62 *Ukrainian Catholic Church – Australia, New Zealand and Oceania*, https://catholicukes.au/

63 Osborne, P. (2024, November 7). Bishops hear from Cardinal-designate Mykola Bychok. *ACBC Media Blog*, https://mediablog.catholic.org.au/bishops-hear-from-cardinal-designate-mykola-bychok/

64 *Our Lady Guardian of Plants Chaldean Catholic Church in Melbourne*, https://chaldeanchurch.org.au/

65 *St Mary's Assumption Chaldean Church*, https://www.stmarysassumption.org.au/

66 ABS, *2021 Census, Religious affiliation in Australia*, Table 4.

67 Ibid.

68 *Syro-Malabar Eparchy of St Thomas the Apostle, Melbourne*, https://syromalabar.org.au/priests/; see also https://www.catholic-hierarchy.org/diocese/dmesm.html for 2022 clergy numbers.

69 *Syro-Malabar Eparchy of St Thomas the Apostle, Melbourne*, https://syromalabar.org.au/

70 *Catholic Diocese of the Australian Military Services*, https://military.catholic.org.au/

71 *Personal Ordinariate of Our Lady of the Southern Cross*, https://www.ordinariate.org.au/

72 *Opus Dei*, https://opusdei.org/en-au/page/opus-dei-in-australia/

73 I compiled this data from the various National Counts of Attendance plus the annual data reported to the *Annuarium Statisticum Ecclesiae* on diocesan priest numbers in Australia, as this number was generally slightly lower than that in the *Official directory of the Catholic Church in Australia*.

74 *The Hierarchy of the Catholic Church*, https://www.catholic-hierarchy.org/

75 Sr Teresa, personal communication, 17 July 2024.

76 ABS. (n.d.) *Population projections Australia (2022-2071)*, https://www.abs.gov.au/statistics/people/population/population-projections-australia/latest-release

77 Martyr, P., & Bullivant, S. (2024). *The Catholics in Australia Survey 9 – Traditional Latin Mass (TLM) attenders*, https://papers.ssrn.com/sol3/papers.cfm?abstract_id=4942220

78 Fr Vincent, personal communication, 31 August 2024.

Chapter 2

Family life in Catholic Australia

The health of the Church in Australia depends on the spiritual health of the people in it. The bedrock of this is family life, where most Catholics live from birth to natural death. In the Catechism (1665-1668), we call the family the 'domestic church', and that's what it should be.[1] It's generally the place where future adult Catholics receive their formation in faith and practice.

In this chapter, we'll look at some important dimensions of Catholic family life in Australia. We'll begin with single people, then look at marriage, and then at children. Finally, we'll finish with older adults and how they fit into Catholic families today, and where we might be going with this.

What's the recipe for a Mass-going adult?

How do you turn a newly baptised Catholic baby into a Mass-going adult? Is there a recipe that works every time? There's a lot of current and available research into families and religion, and it's found some important factors that help a child believer to grow into an adult believer of any religion.

Simply having your child baptised as a Catholic doesn't work. From 1970 to 2021, we baptised over three million children in Australia under the age of seven, and almost 200,000 people who were older than seven years.[2] Numbers are shrinking: in 1970 we baptised around 75,000 children under seven, but by 2021 this had fallen to around 38,000. Almost none of these children have grown up to be Mass-going Catholics, mostly because their parents aren't Mass-going Catholics either.

The Australian Catholic Bishops' Conference (ACBC) currently says:

For an infant/child to be baptised into the Catholic Church there are two requirements:

1. At least one parent of the infant/child consents to the child being baptised into the Catholic Church.
2. There needs to be a well-founded hope that the infant/child will be raised in the Catholic religion.[3]

I can imagine most parish priests exercise a lot of latitude with Point 2 and willingly baptise a child of non-Mass-going parents in the hope that 'something will stick'. The reality is that most parish priests know that the parents have no intention of coming to Mass regularly, and don't want any adult catechesis. To avoid unpleasant scenes, the baptism goes ahead without too many awkward questions.

Multiply this by around 50,000 baptisms a year, and it's easy to see why we have so few Mass-going young Catholics. This clearly isn't working, so we need to re-think our approach. There must be a middle ground between what we're doing now, and simply refusing to baptise babies presented by non-Mass-going parents and families. I'm just not sure where that middle ground is.

What *does* help a Catholic baby to grow into an actively Catholic adult? Having an actively religious father in the home is an important factor. So is having a family that's happy to talk about religion during the week (not just on Sundays). If parents can explain the weirder bits of belief and practice to their child in a way that makes sense, rather than just telling them 'It's just what we do', this helps.[4] A warm, affectionate family with routines of prayer, fun, and service to others helps as well.[5]

We also found that overall, our participants' fathers were less likely to be Catholics and less likely to go to church than their mothers. This feature of Australian Catholic life – the religious mother and the less churchy father – is an interesting one. Certainly, the Church has struggled for decades (some would say millennia) to get men to be more involved in church.[6] Petra, now in her mid-sixties, was in this situation.

> ... I was married to a lapsed Catholic (lapsed due to the physical abuse he apparently suffered from the Christian Brothers at his Sydney school) whom I always hoped would return to the faith. ... I naively thought that my example and teaching alone would be sufficient to keep my children Catholic, and didn't fully comprehend that my husband's resistance to returning to the faith (until he finally did return in the last few weeks of his life) would potentially be more influential on them than my example (two out of three children still practise).[7]

It really helps if your parents are both Catholics, and both regular Mass-goers. In the Catholics in Australia Survey (CIA2022), the people we called 'Weeklies' were very likely to have two Catholic parents, and mostly those parents were weekly or more frequent Mass-goers.[8] The 'Irregulars' and 'Nevers' were more likely to have a non-Catholic parent, and either or both of their parents were not regular Sunday church goers.

How likely is it that an adult Catholic in Australia today would have a non-Catholic parent? There's pretty much a 50-50 chance. In 1966, the Church relaxed its former restrictions on what used to be called 'mixed' marriages– marriages between a Catholic and a non-Catholic. Before that time, the rate of 'mixed' marriages in Australia was around 21%.[9] From 1970 it skyrocketed to around 50% of all marriages involving a Catholic. It stayed at this level for decades – in fact, the number of 'mixed' marriages every year usually outstripped the Catholic-only marriages. But around the year 2000, the balance began to tip back towards more Catholic-only marriages, and it's been rising ever since.[10]

The children of those 'mixed' marriages that took place in Australia between 1970 and 2000 – and there were around 450,000 such marriages – are now aged between 25 and 55. With just one Catholic parent, your chances of being taken to Mass regularly as a child are lower. It's not surprising that we see so few of this age group in our parish churches on Sundays. We almost pre-programmed it that way by relaxing the restrictions on who Catholics should marry.

But overall, there's no one factor that makes Catholic children grow into adult Mass-goers – and conversely, no one factor that drives them away. It seems to take a village to produce a committed adult Mass-goer, but it starts with a Mass-going family that forms their children well. It also takes grace, but that's harder to quantify.

I know it would be easier if we could just blame our adult children's lapsing on poor Catholic schools, or cringe-making youth Masses, or them getting in with the wrong crowd at university. But as it turns out, the quality of that initial family faith formation at home is hugely important, no matter where your child goes to school. Miriam, a Catholic homeschooling mother of two young adults and one teenager in Western Australia, agrees: 'As far as faith formation goes, that can still fail whether you homeschool or not. ... But I feel confident that diligent parents can achieve that regardless of schooling choices. [My children's] friends are testament to that, and none of them homeschooled.'[11]

Families do the heavy lifting in forming their children in the habits of being a Catholic – Sunday Mass, regular Confession, regular personal prayer. Regular Confession is a habit that's learned in the family, but its practice has almost died out in many parishes in Australia. This was probably accelerated by the COVID19 restrictions imposed in some dioceses, which made it virtually impossible for many priests to hear any Confessions at all.[12]

Are people staying away because they're scared of 'the box'? If we re-introduced the Third Rite of Reconciliation, would this help?[13] I think it's unlikely, mainly because there's one group of Catholics who have shown that they're not afraid of 'the box' and not at all inhibited about going to Confession. According to CIA2022's data, the Weeklies are going to Confession quite regularly – around two-thirds go at least several times a year.

In fact, the 18–29-year-old cohort are standouts who go to

Confession very regularly – we spoke to 352 of them altogether from all over Australia, and two-thirds of them go to Confession at least monthly. If this group of young people clearly isn't afraid of individual Confession of their sins to a priest, it's hard to explain why mature adults are staying away in such numbers.

CIA2022 also found that most Catholics who rarely go to Mass almost never go to Confession. Of course they don't. They don't believe in it, or they don't think it's necessary. These are the reasons why they don't go to Mass on Sundays, so it's likely that this extends to their beliefs about Confession as well. There's a good research project lurking in here: asking people who identify as Catholics how often they go to Confession, and why they go, or don't go.

Forming your children to go to Mass and Confession regularly is one thing. Families also need to make those all-important connections between Catholic theory and Catholic practice outside of church. If children see the virtues being modelled and consistently taught by their parents – apologies, forgiveness, sharing, kindness, affection, tolerance, patience, joy – they begin joining those dots earlier. A firmly on-side family environment can also give the children protection against the ill effects of lukewarm Catholic schools and cringe-making youth Masses.

Having two Catholic parents usually means that children get sent to a Catholic school, and our CIA2022 participants were no different. But here, we found a big difference in the under-40s and the over 40s. The over-40s were mostly sent to exclusively Catholic schools for both primary and secondary education, but the under-40s weren't. Many of them had never been to a Catholic school at all.

There's anecdotal evidence to suggest that younger Mass-going Catholic parents in Australia have been opting out of the Catholic school system for some time now. Some are choosing home schooling or sending their children to local government schools, or a mix of both.[14] Unfortunately, there's not a lot of research available on this.[15] I am happy to get the ball rolling, so I asked a few of my Sunday Mass-going Catholic friends about it – all spread out across Australia, with different ages, ethnicities, family sizes, incomes, and priorities.

Most of them got straight back to me, and you'll see just how diverse and often fluid these decisions are, and the reasons behind them.

> We homeschooled our four boys. It was mostly about not wanting to be beholden to school meetings and parts of their curricula, having an idea who our boys were hanging out with, and giving them opportunities to pursue knowledge of things they love further than they could with class time constraints. (Gerard, 4 children, NSW)[16]
>
> Homeschool, and Protestant high school for one child for senior [high school]. Why – because we initially moved around a bit and also because my Catholic education sucked! I don't think homeschooling is the answer, though, because although I was bullied throughout two Catholic primary schools and one Catholic high school – that was another reason – and yet my kids have been bullied in Catholic homeschooling too. (Charlotte, 6 children, an Australian diocese)[17]
>
> Five of my children go to ... a non-Catholic private school. Why: because of its Christian family values and ethics and high academic focus. I couldn't send my children to Catholic schools ... (as much as I like the idea of single sex schools) because the [local] Catholics schools are run by anti-Catholic Marxist homosexual lunatics. (Alan, 6 children, an Eastern States city)[18]
>
> We went for Catholic schools – carefully chosen for the best available/affordable. I know they are not perfect, but better than the alternatives (I get to hear a lot of horror stories). I don't homeschool because I know I would be lousy at it, and at least two of my kids love the social aspect of school. (Daisy, 3 children, WA)[19]

> The older two were homeschooled. But when the 4 [year old] was born the older two were sent to school for a year and then another. However, during COVID we pulled them out and homeschooled them. ... I have made changes to my work life balance to be closer to my family because they are always home and working less means I am with them in their learning and playing – essentially being part of their lives which makes mine more fulfilling too. (Lawrence, 4 children, WA)[20]

> In the end we decided on a state school mostly because we had friends who either had kids there or were willing to send their kids there. ... One mum had older kids who had all gone to [state school] and her kids seemed to be nice and have retained their faith. ... Ultimately, we followed someone we trusted and who had the same view of education. (Annie, 4 children, WA)[21]

> My husband and I decided on our daughter's current school, a Uniting all-girls private K-12 school ... I felt our current option provided the best holistic education, with a focus on pastoral and wellbeing, no political agendas, and education excellence for girls without the bitchy reputation. Our daughter still learns about God at weekly chapel lessons (the Uniting way), and I try to fill the Catholic gaps. ... I could not homeschool to save my life! (Belinda, 1 child, Queensland)[22]

I'm certain there's more where that came from – and I am really hoping that someone out there is doing a research project on this, because if they're not, they should be. I'll say more about Catholic-origin schools in the chapter on our business arm.

The 'vocation' that nobody wants

Let's say you're lucky enough to have grown up as a Mass-going Catholic adult in Australia today. You're likely to have at least three Catholic friends in your closest circle – Catholic social networking and Mass attendance usually go together.[23] You're also likely to say that you feel very closely affiliated to the Catholic Church, especially if you're aged under 40.[24]

But now you'd like to raise some future Catholics of your own, but you can't seem to get a date. Or you get a date or even a few dates, but it just goes nowhere. This is a burgeoning problem among Mass-going Catholics in many Western countries – the lack of other like-minded Catholics of the opposite sex who want to get married. There's been a flurry of articles about it in different Catholic periodicals for many years now.[25]

There's a marriage drought in most Western countries today.[26] There's lots of reasons for this: a real fear of divorce, fear of commitment, a private sexual smorgasbord available through casual sex and porn use, and the high costs of living, higher education, and buying a home. Women have more opportunities than ever to work and explore careers that they enjoy, and this means that they might put off marriage and childbearing or opt out completely.[27] Faithful young Catholic women don't want to use artificial forms of birth control, so the best way to save for a house deposit and remain child-free at the same time is for them to delay marriage.

The Church in Australia has been actively promoting married life for decades now. This has been great for struggling married couples, but it's made many single Catholics feel like failures and freaks. Some are struggling because they believe that their future spouse is pre-ordained by God: that there is 'The One' out there somewhere, and that perhaps they either missed them or lost them or rejected them. (These ideas are not Catholic; they come from some strains of evangelical Protestantism that can influence well-meaning Catholics looking online for robust guidance on living a Christian life.[28])

Katrina, some of whose adult children are now seeking spouses, points out other challenges.

> A lot of the problems faced by young men and women seeking either life-partners, or just like-minded friends, is trying to combine work and distance to travel for events after a long day. I would hope that as families are forced to move further out of city areas just for affordability, [more

Catholic] groups will start to resurface, but they do need a core of motivated and committed individuals to guide them.[29]

A single woman in her 30s in Sydney said in CIA2022 that:

> We don't have much connection with church leadership... and it is so hard to meet young Catholic working adults. Where is the Church in this? It is one of the most important things to nurture faith is the support we have around us, sometimes I feel alone in my faith and it's hard to find people like me.

I understand why the Church at the diocesan level has swung so hard behind marriage in the last thirty or forty years: the impact of easier divorce on most Western societies has been grim. But if we make entering the married state the principal goal of a Christian life, then we won't prepare young people properly for the real goal, which is getting to heaven.

And if we don't really understand marriage, then we don't really understand consecrated celibacy and the priesthood. They simply look like second-best options for people who were too ugly or too weird to get married.[30] Rachel, single and over 40, knows what I mean:

> The toughest challenge is the total irrelevance to Catholic culture of single women over the age of 40, except as a source of free labour, and, if we are very lucky, a form of diversity-hire window-dressing. Genuine incorporation into the Catholic community is very difficult.[31]

I've read Catholic singles literature for years and found it unsatisfying, partly because I have a low tolerance for what I call the Cupcake School of Lady Catholic Journalism. Quite a bit was written by married people, or by single women creating an extended (and successful) personals ad.[32] The overwhelming message was that achieving a Catholic marriage was the goal of a woman's existence, and that her energies were best directed towards this before it was too late.

But this left out so many people: men (remember them?), same sex attracted Catholics, and those with careers, disabilities, or family responsibilities that made marriage unlikely or impossible. Thankfully some Catholic heavyweights chose to differ, like the late Fr Benedict Groeschel, Mary Beth Bonacci, Jessica Keating, and Luanne Zurlo. These writers respected the complexities of the human heart and resisted any urge to tidy single people up.[33]

US writer and researcher Michael Altenburger says that we spend too much time trying to make the Church 'produce' something – priests, religious, married people. This leaves single people as sort of unwanted industrial by-product.[34] And yet Altenburger says that ultimately, we're all single. We're single before we go into religious life or priesthood or marriage. Some of us remain that way or revert to it later in widowhood or divorce. This makes the single life the foundation of all other states of life and vocations in the Church: 'Single people are not outliers or attached patches awkwardly stitched on to the neat quilt of the Church – they are the fabric itself.'[35]

A person never leaves their 'single life' – they bring it with them. The single person you were is the married person, priest, or religious you will become. If we can't help single Catholics to live faithfully, then how can we expect these same single people to become good spouses, religious, or priests? Marriage, religious life, and priesthood aren't crime prevention programs or fix-it workshops for people with deep-seated problems.

Being a single Catholic is also not just about holidays and unbroken sleep (although the unbroken sleep is a plus). Singleness can become a powerful source for good in the Church. But before this can happen, many single Catholics need to work on their self-pity, anger, and chastity, usually through good spiritual direction. Single Catholics need a mix of good friends – and they must learn how to *be* good friends in return. The theology of healthy, sincere adult friendship needs a lot more exposure and development, especially in youth ministry.

Katrina, a married mother of eleven, has valued the single Catholics in her life and can tell you what this looks like in practice.

> Side by side with families are single adults, who can sometimes do for children what parents cannot. ... We don't see religious in our parishes very often, but a single adult living a full life is a valuable witness to children (and the rest of us). Not all are called to marriage, marriages break down, some recognise that marriage isn't for them, some are very dedicated to their work and Church. What wonderful mentors these individuals could be! The clever woman who taught me to play the organ (and was phenomenally patient with the teenage me) was a Doctor of Microbiology and an expert in her field. She was modest and humble, caring for her ageing mother, and I had no idea of this until she'd taught me for about six months![36]

There's a subgroup in the single Catholic population who are same sex attracted, some of them deeply. They've decided to try to live chastely, with inevitable humiliating bumps in the road. They're in our parishes, coming to Mass every Sunday. You might know some of them, but not realise it. I know some of them, and their witness is awesome.

The reason you don't know them is because these people have spent their entire adult lives trying not to be boxed into a 'gay identity' that doesn't really represent who they are. They're also trying to avoid being told by well-meaning but badly informed Catholics that 'God made you this way', 'You should just get a partner', and 'You can get married now'.

Not everyone wants to be part of a minorities box-ticking exercise. This is an unhappy effect of a corporatised Church: we are presented with a shopping list of minorities who must be 'included'. This shows an unfortunate blindness to the minorities already quietly thriving in the Church, worshipping away happily because their identity as a son or daughter of God is more important to them than anything else.[37]

These courageous individuals don't always believe that God 'made' them same sex attracted, and they appreciate time and space to seek healing for their emotional wounds, whatever they may be. Living out their Catholic faith has brought them far greater interior freedom and exterior happiness. They probably won't out themselves to you because they don't want to be fawned over as the token same sex attracted person. They just want to be left alone to have good friendships with healthy and safe people, strive towards personal holiness, and keep on developing a loving relationship with God.

Maybe we need to think about these people before we next start talking glibly about 'inclusion'. In fact, I'm writing about them here with trepidation. My greatest worry is that if the Church finds out about these people, there will suddenly be a new diocesan office for them led by someone on a full-time salary, and they'll be pestered out of the Church altogether.

Till death us do part ...

The single Catholics are on to something: Catholics in Australia just aren't getting married like they used to.[38] In 1970, there were around 31,000 marriages involving Catholics, but only half of those were to other Catholics. By 2021, there were only around 5,460 Catholic marriages in Australia – but 60% of those marriages were between two Catholics (Table 4).

Government data also shows that religious marriage ceremony numbers have been dropping since the early 1970s, and since 2000, more Australians marry in a civil ceremony than in a religious one (81% versus 19%) (Table 5).[39] After 2020 the ABS aggregated all the marriage celebrant data, so we can't pull out the Catholic marriage data from that anymore – so the Church in Australia really needs to collect and publish this data.

Table 4. Marriages involving at least one Catholic, selected years[40]

Year	Both Catholic	'Mixed'	Total	% Catholic	% mixed
1970	15,540	15,259	30,799	50.5%	49.5%
1977	11,347	12,765	24,112	47.1%	52.9%
1987	11,824	11,776	23,600	50.1%	49.9%
1997	9,505	9,742	19,247	49.4%	50.6%
2007	7,135	7,123	14,258	50.0%	50.0%
2017	4,458	3,437	7,895	56.5%	43.5%

Table 5. Marriages conducted by a Catholic minister of religion in Australia, selected years[41]

Year	Number of Catholic marriage ceremonies	As % of all Australian registered marriages
1996	19,155	18%
2001	16,365	16%
2008	13,901	12%
2011	11,978	10%
2016	8,603	7%
2019	6,306	6%
2020	3,522	4%

Who you marry, matters. Do you want your children to marry other Catholics? Understandably, the CIA2022 Weeklies thought it was very important, compared to a very low level of interest among Irregulars and Nevers. Weeklies were around 30% more likely to have a Catholic spouse than Irregulars, who were in turn around 30% more likely to have a Catholic spouse than Nevers.[42] Younger Catholics (those aged under 40) were also more likely to be married to another Catholic, as were people born outside Australia, and converts.[43] This confirms the marriage data we have already from the Church and the State.

There were other factors that seemed to affect the answers. For example, the bigger the family, the more emphatic the parents were about wanting their children to marry other Catholics. Being born outside Australia also seemed to relate to people wanting their children to marry other Catholics.[44] The youngest age group (18–29-year-olds) were most likely of all age groups to rate this as 'very important', as were those with no Catholic schooling.

There's something else happening: Australian Catholics are increasingly marrying people born in a country different from their own. We only have data from the ABS for 2008-2020 for this (and then for just 13 years), but it's very interesting (Table 6).

Table 6. Australian Catholic marriages by country of birth of spouses, 2008-2020

Year	Marriages performed by a Catholic minister	Both spouses born in Australia	Both spouses born in same o/s country	Spouses born in different countries
2008	13,901	72%	4%	23%
2009	13,047	72%	4%	24%
2010	12,386	71%	5%	24%
2011	11,978	69%	5%	25%
2012	11,015	71%	5%	24%
2013	10,532	70%	5%	25%
2014	9,975	70%	5%	25%
2015	9,975	70%	5%	25%
2016	8,603	68%	6%	26%
2017	7,316	67%	6%	27%
2018	6,926	66%	7%	27%
2019	6,306	67%	7%	26%
2020	3,522	64%	8%	28%

This could be, say, an Australian-born child of migrants marrying someone from the same culture who's arrived in Australia more recently. But it can also be Australian-born Anglo-Celtic Catholics marrying across cultural and ethnic boundaries. Anecdotally I could have told you this, because I've seen my Catholic friends' children making these marriages quite happily. I think it's a great way to break down some of the social and cultural barriers at parish level that may exist between Catholics born in Australia and those born overseas.

If we want a future Catholic Church in Australia made up largely of people who believe and live like Catholics – going to Sunday Mass, receiving the sacraments, and forming sustaining parish communities – then the best place to start is with young married Catholics who are on the same page about religion. They are more likely to raise their children to go to Mass and Confession, and to believe and live like Catholics. Marrying other like-minded Catholics helped to hold the Church together before 1966, and it's now voluntarily re-emerging as a factor in building the future Church.

... but not always

Marriages don't always work out, and that includes Catholic marriages. For people aged over 15 who identified as Catholic in the 2021 Census, the rate of divorced or separated people has gone up from 8.9% in 1996 to 11.7% in 2021. The national rate is 10.6%.[45] So nominal Catholics, at least, are more likely to be separated or divorced than the general population in Australia – but this might be because they're also slightly older than the general population.

What about Mass-going Catholics? The CIA2022 study found that 5.4% of our participants were separated or divorced.[46] I went back and looked at the raw data, and the divorce rate among the youngest Catholics was less than 1%, but it rose gradually until the age group of 60-69 years where it peaked at 11.6%. But as we know, averages can be a bit tricky when you're measuring Catholics – other factors come into play, such as their Mass attendance rate.

So I compared Weeklies, Irregulars, and Nevers. The highest divorce rate in the Weeklies group was 9.9% (which fell in the

60–69-year age group). Irregulars and Nevers were far more likely to be divorced than Weeklies. Overall, most of the divorced people who are still going to Mass on Sundays are likely to be retirement age or beyond.

Divorce has damaged the Australian Catholic community in different ways. The Dominican Sisters of St Cecilia here in Australia shared this insight:

> Due to the breakdown of family life in our society as well as the modern secular culture in which we are immersed, religious formation must look different than it did even just 25 years ago. Women need more time for healing, time to detach from the world, time to foster interior silence to truly hear the voice of God.[47]

Paul, a 42-year-old man who divorced several years ago, said:

> The first thing I'd say here is that divorce is awful. Truly awful. It's a pain that can't be articulated … Anyone seeking to give advice/comfort/assistance to someone in the midst of that is wise to be aware that you are dealing with a person who is (in an almost terrifyingly literal sense) falling apart. Through the grace of God, I managed to move past this, but I suspect there are people who never get past this first place. Profound gentleness and compassion [are] required for these people.[48]

Oliver, a divorced father in his forties, had to suffer both personal heartbreak and public scandal.

> In my case my wife established [a] relationship with [a] colleague working in [a] senior role for [a diocese] which she gave as part of the reason for ending the marriage. Zero reaching out to me from [the organisation]. I am not aware of any evidence by them to encourage her to rethink or to reconcile. As far as I am aware, zero consequences for the male colleague (ex-principal) involved.[49]

Divorced Mass-going Catholics often find themselves in no man's land when they first get divorced. On the one hand, there are the married Catholics who will look askance. They know (or at least believe) that divorce is socially contagious, so they tend to edge away.[50] Diane, a Mass-going Catholic who left an abusive marriage in her late fifties, knows what that feels like.

> Loneliness after the divorce has been a continuing challenge for me. I have gone to secular social groups and have made several good friends that are not Catholic. So I'm not saying the Church has to fix everyone's loneliness, but a more open and matter-of-fact (and charitable) attitude about the reality of divorce and the burdens it places on the divorced person, especially if they have partial or full care of one or more minor children, could be very helpful and a bit of balm to a hurting soul already struggling and abandoned by someone who promised to love and honour them for life.[51]

A subset of Mass-going Catholics believes divorce is always gravely sinful and damages the Church to a terrible degree. Sometimes they are kind enough to say this out loud to a divorced person's face. Some even suggest penances that the divorced person can perform for the rest of their life to atone for what they've done. Diane has had to grapple with this.

> The anxiety and sense of failure for a divorcing person is deep enough without the added burden of blame that stems from that attitude. The conditioning to take all responsibility for all the problems in the marriage and subsequent divorce is very hard to shift, even though I know it is absolutely wrong. I have only really come to grips more closely with what the Church actually teaches about divorce and nullity since beginning the divorce process.[52]

Paul suffered similarly, and personally did not feel able to receive Holy Communion until his marriage had been formally annulled.

> I didn't receive Communion for many years after my divorce …. What I came to understand was that by doing

this, I was effectively telling the Lord that there was something he was unable to forgive. I was placing my guilt in a higher position than him. A priest who became a close friend helped me to that realisation, to which I am eternally grateful.

I remember vividly the first time I received Holy Communion after my divorce [and annulment]. All in all, it took me about 5 years to do the necessary work to get to that place. I've never had a clearer understanding of the phrase 'God is God, you are not God' than I did in that moment.[33]

This burden of shame is galling for the Catholic man whose wife left him for another man (or woman), or the Catholic woman who is divorced because her husband tried to force her to use artificial birth control. It's especially hard for the spouse who has fled a chronically violent, abusive, or unfaithful marriage and has taken their children with them to protect them.[54]

At the other end of the scale are the helpful people who assume that you'd like to start dating and get re-married now. The fact that you have no annulment and are still sacramentally married is no obstacle to these people. Sometimes local dioceses don't help: one divorced Catholic told me ruefully that she believed her local Church's 'pastoral' approach to divorced Catholics was to give them all annulments so that they could all get remarried as quickly as possible.

When Catholic marriages are in trouble, we all need to pitch in and help as much as we can – if we can. But some marriages can be damaged beyond repair, especially if there is violence or persistent abuse. In those cases, the Church recognises that those two people and their children should no longer live under the same roof, sometimes permanently. The *Catechism* (2383, 2386) and the Code of Canon Law (1151, 1153.1) both allow for legal separation in grave circumstances. In a country like Australia, legal separation should always include a legal divorce, so that both spouses have a chance at financial stability, especially the spouse who is carrying most of the child-raising load. It's also essential to legally divorce before you start the annulment process.

It's true that you will meet the occasional divorced Catholic who clearly has a personality disorder, or whose abusive behaviour caused their own misfortune. I don't think they're representative of most. If you don't know what to say to a divorced Catholic when you meet them for the first time, try these: 'I'm so sorry that happened to you.' 'That must have been really hard for you and your kids.' 'How are you doing now?' 'What can I do to help?'

Couples are presumed to be sacramentally married until there's an annulment. While not every divorced Catholic has an invalid marriage, we seem to have a very high rate of successful annulments. I also know people personally who've gone through the humiliation of defending the sacramentality of their marriage to a tribunal, but they've been given an annulment anyway. Diane said:

> I think a stronger differentiation – or even a complete separation – between the civil and sacramental elements of marriage might well prevent a greater number of ill-founded sacramental marriages taking place. I think bishops need to become more outspoken and solid and assist their priests to be a lot more strong in refusing to preside at sacramental marriages except where both parties are known practising Catholics with a strong commitment to their faith. Careful examination about sexual health and orientation could also save some young people from later grief.[55]

This is a difficult area, because on the one hand, the high rate of annulments can look like everyone gets one free pass for a 'starter marriage' from the Church. This is probably not the message a Catholic diocesan marriage tribunal should be sending.

On the other hand, Pope Francis, Pope Benedict XVI, and others have suggested that a sizeable portion of Catholic marriages today are invalid because the couples aren't entering into them with proper formation and the right intentions.[56] Fr Vincent, who works in Victoria, said, 'The numbers seeking to marry in the Church are dwindling. When they do, they have their own ideas of what marriage is, and often, it doesn't quite stack up to what the Church thinks about marriage'.[57]

One solution is much more intensive and realistic marriage preparation, and – unpopularly – more barriers to having a Catholic marriage ceremony until you've gone through a lot more hoops. The quality and type of marriage preparation varies immensely from diocese to diocese, and from priest to priest. Over the years, I've heard many horror stories of facile, sentimental and largely meaningless Catholic marriage preparation, both from the couples involved and those priests and lay people who had to deliver it. This does no one any favours.

If the Church were ever unlucky enough to have me working full-time in Catholic marriage preparation, I would make it my goal to have around 40% of all my couples break off their engagements. This is the estimated percentages of marriages in Australia for the period 2003-2022 that ended in divorce.[58] Hopefully more broken engagements would lead to fewer messy divorces and fewer children involved. The FOCCUS program[59] comes highly recommended as a tool for finding the weak spots in a relationship and helping a couple to slow down and do more realistic preparation for a lifetime together – or end their engagement.

Priests and other marriage preparers also need a lot of upskilling on the signs of abuse and coercive control, or even just plain incompatibility, in the engaged couples they counsel. Diane said:

> I wish the Church was more openly supportive of what it requires to safely leave an abusive marriage ... Some difficulties can be sorted out with counselling and therapy and love and prayer. Abuse is not one of those difficulties. Leaving is the only way to manage it and leaving is fraught with difficulty and danger.[60]

These problems are often visible before marriage, but might be missed by an inexperienced pastor, or swamped by all those other important discussions (bridesmaids, music, flowers).[61] Above all, it's important to keep reminding a couple that engagement is not the same as marriage, and booking a church and a reception venue doesn't mean you have to go through with it – even if you have paid a deposit. Losing a deposit is probably cheaper than the average cost of a divorce in Australia with at least one lawyer involved.[62]

I now believe that good Catholic marriage preparation should always take place with one eye on the emergency exit. This is in stark contrast to the more common model of marriage preparation that poo-poos every concern as cold feet and propels a couple inexorably towards the ceremony. Sensitive marriage preparation means keeping an ear open for the uncertainties and addressing them honestly (and usually individually with the person concerned, away from the partner). You may save a life.

Meanwhile, we have a real problem with divorced Catholics in our churches because we still don't quite know what to do with them. I suspect it's our idol worship of the intact marriage at all costs that may have led us to treat them – perhaps unconsciously – as second-class citizens. Perhaps if we had shown more love and support to divorced Catholics, most of whom can be admitted to Holy Communion, then we wouldn't be grappling today with the issue of divorced-and-remarried Catholics, many of whom can't be admitted to Holy Communion.

The incredible shrinking Catholic family

Most people don't know that Australian Catholic families have been shrinking in size since before the 1950s. A long-forgotten paper based on the 1954 Australian Census found that the birth rate of Australian Catholic women born around 1879 or earlier was nearly 5 children, but for Australian Catholic women born in the twentieth century, their birth rate almost halved to 2.5 children. The author came to an inescapable conclusion:

Whatever the reasons for doing so, and whatever the means they use (whether the 'rhythm' method sanctioned by their church, or some other), Catholic Australians are, as a group, practicing some form of birth control. And they are doing so effectively enough to have produced quite rapidly a substantial reduction in their fertility.[63]

Having 2.5 children in 1954 was sufficiently above replacement rate then, but the Catholic birth rate has since fallen further. Given that 90% of the Catholic population is largely indistinguishable from non-Catholic Australians, it's fair to assume that the nominal Catholic birth rate in Australia is close to the national average of 1.63 births per woman.[64] In the CIA2022 study, the most common family size was between 1-3 children (41% of the sample). Just 18% of our survey participants had a family of 4-6 children, and only 4% had 7 or more children.[65] Most of the bigger families, unsurprisingly, were also Weeklies.[66]

Smaller families wouldn't be a pressing problem if all the children practised their faith, and then raised their own children to do so as well. But in Australia, this hasn't happened. The Church in Australia has found various ways of not looking at this problem which exactly parallel the secular Australian government's response to our falling birthrate.[67] We've eagerly welcomed Catholic migrants who go to Mass more than the locals do, and we've imported more of our labour force (priests) from overseas. In 2004 Australian treasurer Peter Costello offered Australians a baby bonus to have 'one for mum, one for dad, and one for the country'. Perhaps the Church in Australia should have done the same?[68]

For many years now, people have told me that almost everyone of reproductive age who goes to Mass is using artificial birth control, in defiance of the Church's teaching. Some of these people are ardent supporters of the traditional Latin Mass (TLM) and are keen to point out the differences in family size between a TLM parish and a typical non-TLM parish in Australia.[69] Others are equally ardent supporters of a change in the Church's teaching on the use of artificial birth control

They both have a point. The CIA2022 study identified a group of 291 people who attended TLM parishes regularly, and more of them had larger families (4 or more children) – 26%, compared to 22% of the other Catholics we surveyed. When I looked just at Weeklies, there was still a gap – 28% of TLM Weeklies had larger families, compared to 24% of the other Weeklies. So it's true that TLM attenders tend to have larger families than non-TLM Mass-goers, but not by much.

We've been fighting about artificial birth control since the late 1960s and the promulgation of the papal encyclical *Humanae Vitae* by Pope St Paul VI in 1968.[70] This encyclical explained why the use of artificial birth control was not consistent with Catholic moral teaching and wasn't an option for faithful Catholics. And yet the impression is that everyone ignored this and went ahead with it anyway.

Is this true? And how can we find out? When you look at various polls about this topic, the data is quite messy. The polls don't always tell us who they're asking: Mass-going Catholics, or nominal Catholics. They sometimes just ask about a person's beliefs about birth control, rather than what they're doing about it. Sometimes they ask about lifetime use of birth control, which will give you a different result again.[71] There's no recent published data available describing Australian Catholic use of family planning methods, so we asked people to tell us about it in the CIA2022 study.

It turned out that a huge number of our participants weren't using any form of birth control at all. These were mostly young and single, or old and past the need for birth control. We put them to one side and looked instead at the married, cohabiting, or otherwise apparently sexually active participants, who made up about a quarter of our total group.[72]

We found that our married Catholics were much more likely

to use natural family planning or natural fertility awareness (NFP/NFA). We also found that our single sexually active Catholics and cohabiting Catholics were much more likely to use artificial birth control. Most of the married Catholics who were using any kind of family planning already had children, but the singles didn't. I think this shows two different mentalities: one is about spacing births or limiting family size, and the other is about avoiding having children outside of marriage.[73]

So then we divided up the birth control users into those who used family planning methods approved by the Church (NFP/NFA and safe period/abstinence) and those using unapproved methods (withdrawal, barrier methods like condoms, hormonal methods like the Pill and intrauterine devices (IUDs), or permanent surgery for sterilisation). Two-thirds of all the birth control users had used unapproved methods in the last 12 months, and the remaining third had used only approved methods. Only 9% reported using a mix of both.

The approved methods users were – no surprises – overwhelmingly Weeklies. They were more likely to be married, to be women, and to be aged under 40. They were also more likely to have a slightly larger family. This confirms a lot of other findings from the same survey: there is a group of younger and more conservative Catholics in Australia who are faithful to core Catholic teachings and practices across the board, including regular Mass attendance. It turns out that they are also mostly faithful in their use of Church-approved forms of family planning.

There was another group who were even more interesting: those who we might call the 'NFP-adjacent'. The most popular unapproved methods of birth control in the sample were inexpensive *ad hoc* methods like condoms and withdrawal, both of which are compatible with secular natural family planning approaches, but not approved by the Church. Some of these people might be just doing this occasionally as part of a 'mostly NFP' approach.[74] I'd love to know more about how NFP is working out there for Catholics in Australia, especially this possible 'NFP-adjacent' group, and I think this would also make a fantastic research project.[75]

I decided to map all this out as if it were a Sunday parish congregation. In this virtual parish of around a thousand Catholics, look around you. Most of the married Mass-goers you see are not using any kind of birth control, because they don't need it (they're too old). Of those who are currently having families, we can divide them into two groups. The slightly bigger group are using Church-approved methods of family planning, and the slightly smaller group are using unapproved methods. The single Catholics you see at Sunday Mass are largely not any using birth control at all.

There's also strong agreement between what the CIA2022 participants said they believed about the Church's teaching on birth control, and what they're doing in their own lives. Approved method users supported traditional Church teaching on birth control far more than unapproved method users. Those who were using unapproved methods were also those most likely to support a change in Church teaching on birth control.[76] Of course they are – but it's nice to see it confirmed in the data.[77]

What this means is that if you're going to do a survey of Catholics and ask them about whether they think the Church's teaching on birth control should change, you should also ask them about what types of birth control they've used in the last 12 months. You'll find a strong relationship between using an unapproved method and wanting the Church's teaching to change. It joins the list of important things to ask in any Catholic survey, like Mass attendance rate, before you start producing any figures purporting to represent 'Catholics' as a whole.

Older Catholics

You wouldn't be a Catholic today if it wasn't for older Catholics. They taught you, either directly or indirectly, about your faith and helped you to foster it. You owe them a lot. Catholicism is a religion of tradition – we openly acknowledge every Sunday that we are part of a long unbroken heritage of faith. We in turn have a responsibility to hand on that sacred knowledge to the next generation. I sometimes remind people that we're like the Aboriginal peoples of Australia in that we're only the custodians of sacred knowledge – it's not ours to tamper with or 'update', because it's our duty to pass it on intact.

The single biggest group of Mass-going Catholics are those aged over 70. It's lonely being under that age in church, but it's also lonely watching your friends dying off. The lady who ran the cake stall at my local parish told me one day that things hadn't been the same since three of her best bakers died. You may laugh, but this is the reality at parish level: far more dispatches than hatches and matches. In fact, it was attending Mass at a parish with a high rate of funerals that first alerted me to the fact that natural deaths might be driving our plummeting Mass attendance rates.

How we treat our remaining vulnerable and frail elderly as they leave us, one by one, will help to define the future Church in Australia. This includes the Boomers in our parishes, even those who have annoyed us terribly. Aged care in Australia is in crisis, including Catholic aged care. The Royal Commission into Aged Care Quality and Safety (2018-2021) exposed the horrifying conditions of most aged care homes in Australia, and the neglect, malnutrition, sexual assaults, and lack of dignity experienced by those who live in them.[78] Given the chronic staff shortages since COVID19 and 'quiet quitting' in Australia, those conditions are unlikely to have improved much since then.

Can a Catholic person – a faithful, believing, Mass-going Catholic – ever put an elderly relative into institutional care, knowing how awful the conditions are, and how life-shortening it's likely to be? In some cases, they may feel they have no choice because the relative has dementia, or they have been vigorously requesting admission. And yet it's increasingly possible for more older people to remain safely in their own homes (even with dementia), and to plan to die there with proper care and management. It takes motivated relatives, access to an aged care package of funding, and the willingness to collaborate with the elderly relative and allow them as much freedom and autonomy as possible. It's hard work, but it's also very worthwhile. As Catholics, we can and should be doing better with the care of our elderly.

I'm also really encouraged by the examples of multigenerational living that are starting to be trialled by some Catholic families.[79] This is where several generations of one family live together and are mutually interdependent – grandparents babysit and are cared for in their very old age, parents work and raise children, and children learn to share in the common household tasks, including aged care. It's something our Maronite brothers and sisters can teach us about, because it's stronger in their culture than in most of the Church in Australia.[80] Hopefully this will protect at least some elderly Catholics from having voluntary – or not so voluntary – assisted dying imposed on them in an increasingly overcrowded public health system.

The other older Catholics: the faithful departed

There's a final group of people who make up the biggest part of any Catholic family, and that's the faithful departed. I'm mentioning this here for a reason: Australian Catholics' belief in the existence of purgatory seems to have really tapered off.

We asked CIA2022 participants whether they believed in various core doctrines. Just 63% of the total sample believed in the existence of purgatory. Even among the Weeklies, only 76% believed in purgatory, compared to the 94% who believed in heaven. The older our participants were, the less likely they were to believe in purgatory. This last one is a puzzle, because surely with death approaching, enlightened self-interest should kick in and make the doctrine of purgatory much more appealing.

We don't have a lot of research literature on this (which makes it another excellent project for someone). Stephen Bullivant and Ben Clements found in 2019 that only 46% of their UK-based Catholic sample believed in purgatory – but that was a mix of all sorts of Catholics.[81] A recent EWTN poll of likely Catholic voters in the US found that 65% believed in purgatory.[82] Given that belief in the existence of purgatory has been a defining belief of Catholicism for centuries, it's really curious as to why belief in its existence seems to have declined like this, even among Mass-going Catholics. For me, it's a good measure of that broader loss of supernatural belief that I identified in the introduction.

The Holy Souls are an important part of any family – or at least, they should be. Prayer for family members who have died, attendance at funerals, and cemetery visits for All Souls and at other times during the year are all important parts of children's Catholic faith formation. This may have been lacking in recent years, which may also be why belief in purgatory has declined so much.

Australian mainstream culture is not good at dealing with death. Most funeral companies advertise with images of sympathetic looks and solitary flowers. You rarely see a coffin, even in the background. People no longer die at home; we mostly die in hospitals. Children are kept away from funerals because it's 'scary'. Increasingly, we aren't even buried from a church. Fr Harrison, a priest working in Victoria, told me:

> In the past decade, I have performed fewer and fewer weddings. ... The funerals I do perform are predominantly for the very old – people in their 80s and 90s: my grandparents' generation. The funerals of younger people – my parents' generation and my own – are predominantly conducted in funeral parlours, officiated by funeral directors.[83]

For those lucky enough to be buried from a church, a typical Catholic funeral in Australia today canonises the departed and makes it clear that God should be thanking his lucky stars that this person is now with him in heaven. We say fewer and fewer

Requiem Masses and more and more 'celebrations of life'. It's considered almost insulting to suggest that we might need to pray and have Masses said for them.

Some families have let these customs lapse because they don't want to have to explain to their children that Grandma might not be in heaven yet. To be blunt: if you don't teach your children to pray for their deceased grandparents and others, they're much less likely to pray for your soul when you die. It's time to revive a solid catechesis and practice of prayers for the faithful departed at family level. Normalising and reviving prayers, Masses, and devotions for your own deceased relatives will also help to drive broader changes at parish level.[84]

Conclusion

Catholic families are important. We all need to work hard at getting them healthy and happy, and keeping them that way. Catholics who marry other Mass-going Catholics are more likely to keep going to Mass themselves, and raise children who will also go to Mass. The same goes for the other sacraments.

It's encouraging to see that younger Catholics in Australia are now taking steps to try to shore up marriage and family for themselves, and to learn from the mistakes of the post-conciliar generation. They are marrying other Catholics again in greater numbers, and those who are probably at the same level of Mass-going as themselves. They're also marrying more across ethnic and cultural boundaries, where the priority is that the other person is a regular Mass-goer first and foremost. They are more obedient to the Church's teaching on the transmission of life and are more generous in welcoming children than many of their parents' generation.

But a Catholic family can still be a hot mess. Everyone knows – or is part of – a Catholic family like this. I am the youngest of seven children, most of whom still go to Mass at least sometimes. I have 23 nieces and nephews, one of whom has gone to God already (I hope), and only two of the others go to Mass on a regular basis. I pray for them all every day, because that's literally all I can do.

Families are our domestic churches. But they're also the building blocks of our parishes. Young Catholic families have the capacity to do real good in their local parishes – but it's going to be uphill work. Let's see what's out there in parish-land.

---

[1] Catholic Church. (1994). *Catechism of the Catholic Church*. Vatican.

[2] Data taken from the *Annuarium Statisticum Ecclesiae* for most years between 1970 and 2017.

[3] Australian Catholic Bishops' Conference (ACBC). (2021, November 8). *Who can be baptised?* https://www.catholic.au/s/article/Who-can-be-baptised

[4] Smith, C., & Adamcyzk, A. (2020). *Handing down the faith: How parents pass their religion on to the next generation*. Oxford University Press.

[5] Gray, M., & Popčak, G. (2023). *Future Faithful Families Project: successfully raising Catholic children to be active Catholics as adults.* Center for Applied Research in the Apostolate (CARA), https://275132.fs1.hubspotusercontent-na1.net/hubfs/275132/_peytoninstitute/Research/HCFM-CARA%20Summary%20FFF%20Report.pdf

[6] Pew Research Center. (2016, March 22). The gender gap in religion around the world. *Pew Research Center*, https://www.pewresearch.org/religion/2016/03/22/the-gender-gap-in-religion-around-the-world/

[7] Petra, personal communication, 25 August 2024.

[8] Martyr, P., & Bullivant, S. (2024). *The Catholics in Australia Survey 8 – Irregulars and Nevers*, https://papers.ssrn.com/sol3/papers.cfm?abstract_id=4912660

[9] Mol, H. (1970). Mixed marriages in Australia. *Journal of Marriage and Family*, 32(2), 293–300. https://doi.org/10.2307/350137

[10] The *Annuarium Statisticum Ecclesiae* for 2021 has the rate at 60.7% Catholic-only to 39.3% mixed marriages.

[11] Miriam, personal communication, 14 May 2024.

[12] Martyr, P. (2023). Australian Catholics' lived experiences of COVID19 church closures. *Journal of Religion and Health*, 62, 2881-2898. https://doi.org/10.1007/s10943-023-01823-6

[13] The Third Rite of Reconciliation involves communal absolution without individual Confession. It's meant to be used in cases of grave emergency, eg. a plane is about to crash and a priest on board gives general absolution to everyone present. The only other use is when there are far too many people present for priests to hear everyone's Confession individually. In some dioceses in Australia, notably in Queensland, there were experiments with its wider use at parish level as a way of circumventing the need for individual confession of sins. This – which was in effect a liturgical abuse – was stopped after the Australian bishops' *ad limina* visit to Rome in 1998.

[14] COVID19 and its fallout may have led to an increase in homeschooling in general

in Australia, if Western Australia is anything to go by. Thompson, H. (2024, August 12). More WA families are opting to home-school their kids. Here's why. *WA Today*, https://www.watoday.com.au/national/western-australia/more-wa-families-are-opting-to-home-school-their-kids-here-s-why-20240725-p5jwkd.html

[15] English, R. (2015). Use your freedom of choice: reasons for choosing homeschool in Australia. *Journal of Unschooling and Alternative Learning*, 9(17), 1-18; Slater, E., Burton, K., & McKillop, D. (2022). Reasons for home educating in Australia: who and why? *Educational Review (Birmingham)*, 74(2), 263–280. https://doi.org/10.1080/00131911.2020.1728232; McLean, F. (2018, May 3). Why we sent our children to local state schools. *The Gospel Coalition* (Australian edition), https://au.thegospelcoalition.org/article/sent-children-local-state-schools/; Williby, B. (2019, July 29). Public schooling Catholic kids. *Blessed Is She* [blog], https://blessedisshe.net/en-au/blogs/blog/public-schooling-catholic-kids

[16] Gerard, personal communication, 9 May 2024.

[17] Charlotte, personal communication, 9 May 2024.

[18] Alan, personal communication, 9 May 2024.

[19] Daisy, personal communication, 9 May 2024.

[20] Lawrence, personal communication, 26 May 2024.

[21] Annie, personal communication, 21 May 2024.

[22] Belinda, personal communication, 9 May 2024.

[23] Martyr, P., & Bullivant, S. (2024). *The Catholics in Australia Survey 4 – Belonging*, https://papers.ssrn.com/sol3/papers.cfm?abstract_id=4767155; Clements & Bullivant, *Catholics in contemporary Britain*, 62-3.

[24] Martyr & Bullivant, *Belonging*.

[25] Bonacci, M. (1999, February 1). Love and the single Catholic. *Crisis Magazine*, https://crisismagazine.com/vault/love-and-the-single-catholic; Keating, J. (2016, September 13). Single by default. *Church Life Journal*, https://churchlifejournal.nd.edu/articles/single-by-default-by-jessica-keating/; Hitchings, A. (2019, May 2). For want of a lot of good men. *The Catholic Weekly*, https://www.catholicweekly.com.au/for-want-of-a-lot-of-good-men/.

[26] O'Sullivan, F. (2015, October 15). Where Europeans are most likely to be single vs married. *Bloomberg*, https://www.bloomberg.com/news/articles/2015-10-14/maps-of-where-europeans-are-more-likely-to-be-single-instead-of-married; Brown, A. (2020, August 20). A profile of single Americans. *Pew Research Center*, https://www.pewresearch.org/social-trends/2020/08/20/a-profile-of-single-americans/

[27] Willis, O. (2018, June 17). 'I don't yearn for someone to complete me': Why more women are staying single. *ABC News*, https://www.abc.net.au/news/health/2018-06-17/why-women-are-staying-single/9873956; Bennett, J. (2017). *Singleness and the Church: a new theology of the single life*. Oxford University Press.

[28] Thomas, G. (2013). *The sacred search*, David C. Cook, is a Protestant book on marriage preparation that deals with this myth. I also strongly recommend it to Catholics discerning marriage.

[29] Katrina, personal communication, 20 June 2024.

[30] I first worked out these ideas in a talk to the Dawson Colloquium in Hobart, Tasmania in 2018. This was later published as Martyr, P. (2020). Clothed with the

sun: Christianity and the liberation of women. In D. Daintree (Ed.), *Heart to heart: thriving in a post-Christian world*. Dawson Colloquium.

[31] Rachel, personal communication, 25 August 2024.

[32] I liked Stimpson, E. (2012). *The Catholic girl's survival guide for the single years*, Emmaus Road. Emily Stimpson married in 2014, but her book is the only one I've read that isn't Cupcake School.

[33] One of the best and most practical books on the theology of lay singleness I've ever read is Zurlo, L. (2019). *Single for a greater purpose: a hidden joy in the Catholic Church*. Sophia Institute.

[34] Altenburger, M. (2017, November 29). Single life is more fundamental for Christianity than both married and religious life. *Church Life Journal*, https://churchlifejournal.nd.edu/articles/single-life-is-more-fundamental-for-christianity-than-both-married-and-religious-life/

[35] Altenburger, Single life.

[36] Katrina, personal communication, 20 June 2024.

[37] For more information see Eden Invitation, https://www.edeninvitation.com/

[38] Mol, Mixed marriages in Australia.

[39] Australian Bureau of Statistics (ABS). (2022, November 10). *Marriages and divorces Australia*. https://www.abs.gov.au/statistics/people/people-and-communities/marriages-and-divorces-australia/2021/marriages

[40] *Annuarium Statisticum Ecclesiae*, various years.

[41] All data is taken from the ABS series *Marriages and divorces Australia* for the relevant years. These can be found at https://www.abs.gov.au/statistics/people/people-and-communities/marriages-and-divorces-australia

[42] Martyr & Bullivant, *Family life*.

[43] Ibid.

[44] Ibid.

[45] National Centre for Pastoral Research (NCPR). (2023). *Social profile of the Catholic community in Australia, based on the 2021 Australian Census*, 7. https://ncpr.catholic.org.au/wp-content/uploads/2023/04/2021-Social-Profile-of-the-Catholic-Community-in-Australia-R.pdf

[46] Martyr, P., & Bullivant, S. (2023). *The Catholics in Australia Survey 1 – Mass attendance*, https://papers.ssrn.com/sol3/papers.cfm?abstract_id=4646161, 7.

[47] Dominican Sisters of St Cecilia, personal communication, 15 August 2024.

[48] Paul, personal communication, 29 May 2024.

[49] Oliver, personal communication, 17 August 2024.

[50] McDermott, R., Fowler, J., & Christakis, N. (2013). Breaking up is hard to do, unless everyone else is doing it too: social network effects on divorce in a longitudinal sample. *Social Forces*, 92(2), 491–519. https://doi.org/10.1093/sf/sot096

[51] Diane, personal communication, 20 May 2024.

[52] Ibid.

[53] Paul, personal communication, 29 May 2024.

[54] Martyr, P. (2023, December 7). When getting out is the only way to go on. *The

Catholic Weekly, https://catholicweekly.com.au/when-getting-out-is-the-only-way-to-go-on/

55 Diane, personal communication, 20 May 2024.

56 Wooden, C. (2016, June 18). Too many couples do not understand marriage is for life, Pope says. *National Catholic Reporter*, https://www.ncronline.org/too-many-couples-do-not-understand-marriage-life-pope-says

57 Fr Vincent, personal communication, 31 August 2024.

58 The ABS calculates a divorce rate per 1000 people, rather than indicating the number of marriages that end in divorce. This figure of 44% was obtained by adding up all the marriages and divorces in this period and working out the divorces as a percentage of all the marriages. https://damiengreer.com.au/family-law/statistics/marriage-divorce-statistics-australia/

59 https://www.foccusinc.com/foccus-inventory.aspx; Williams, L., & Jurich, J. (1995). Predicting marital success after five years: assessing the predictive validity of FOCCUS. *Journal of Marital and Family Therapy*, 21(2), 141–153. https://doi.org/10.1111/j.1752-0606.1995.tb00149.x.

60 Diane, personal communication, 20 May 2024.

61 Many thanks to the Australian Confraternity of Catholic Clergy (ACCC) branch in Perth, who hosted me on 11 April 2024 as a guest speaker on domestic violence in the Church in Australia, where we discussed marriage preparation – the diversity of methods and approaches used was very noticeable, and this was a valuable insight for me.

62 The Separation Guide. (2024). *How much does it cost to get a divorce or separate?* https://theseparationguide.com.au/how-much-does-it-cost-to-get-a-divorce-or-separate/

63 Day, L. (1964). Fertility differentials among Catholics in Australia. *The Milbank Memorial Fund Quarterly*, 42(2), 57–83. https://doi.org/10.2307/3348716

64 ABS. (2022, October 18). *Births, Australia*. https://www.abs.gov.au/statistics/people/population/births-australia/latest-release

65 Martyr & Bullivant, *Mass attendance*, 8.

66 Ibid., 25.

67 Campbell, R. (2023; January 9). One for the country: do we need another baby bonus? *Sydney Morning Herald*, https://www.smh.com.au/national/ageing-population-falling-birth-rate-do-we-need-another-baby-bonus-20230108-p5cblr.html; Murphy, H. (2024, April 18). Australians are having fewer babies – experts say it could have more consequences than we realise. *ABC News*, https://www.abc.net.au/news/2024-04-18/australia-fertility-rate-could-predict-the-next-five-years/103692844

68 On the effect of these initiatives on the birthrate, see Pakaluk, C. (2024). *Hannah's children: the women quietly defying the birth dearth*. Regnery.

69 The traditional Latin Mass refers to the Mass as it was said in the Western Church before the reforms of Vatican II, which translated the Mass into vernacular languages like English and simplified its format considerably. The Novus Ordo refers to the post-Vatican II reformed rite of the Mass.

70 Paul VI, Pope. (1968, July 25). *Humanae vitae*, https://www.vatican.va/content/paulvi/en/encyclicals/documents/hf_p-vi_enc_25071968_humanae-vitae.html

71 Bertotti, A., & Christensen, S. (2012). Comparing current, former, and never

users of natural family planning: an analysis of demographic, socioeconomic, and attitudinal variables. *The Linacre Quarterly*, 79(4), 474–486. https://doi.org/10.1179/002436312804827154; Burge, R. (2023, January 13). Is Catholic teaching on birth control driving people from the pews? *National Catholic Reporter*, https://www.ncronline.org/opinion/catholic-teaching-birth-control-driving-people-pews; Kessler, G. (2012, February 17). The claim that 98 percent of Catholic women use contraception: a media foul. *Washington Post*, https://www.washingtonpost.com/blogs/fact-checker/post/the-claim-that-98-percent-of-catholic-women-use-contraception-a-media-foul/2012/02/16/gIQAkPeqIR_blog.html; Mauro, J-P. (2023, January 13). Survey: Catholic contraception use diverges from Church teaching. *Aleteia*, https://aleteia.org/2023/01/13/survey-catholic-contraception-use-diverges-from-church-teaching/; O'Loughlin, M. (2016, September 28). Poll finds many U.S. Catholics breaking with church over contraception, abortion and LGBT rights. *America: the Jesuit Review*, https://www.americamagazine.org/faith/2016/09/28/poll-finds-many-us-catholics-breaking-church-over-contraception-abortion-and-lgbt

[72] Martyr, P., & Bullivant, S. (2024). *The Catholics in Australia Survey 7 – Family planning*, https://papers.ssrn.com/sol3/papers.cfm?abstract_id=4856022

[73] Martyr & Bullivant, *Family planning*.

[74] Ibid.

[75] You might start with Fisher, S. (2014). *The sinner's guide to Natural Family Planning*. Our Sunday Visitor.

[76] Martyr & Bullivant, *Family planning*.

[77] Ibid.

[78] Royal Commission on Aged Care Safety and Quality. (2019). *Interim report: neglect*, (3 vols), https://www.royalcommission.gov.au/aged-care/interim-report is awful. Most of the recommended reforms will also not be achievable because of chronic staff shortages across all industry sectors across Australia.

[79] Catholic Voice. (2021, December 13). A culture of life shines in intergenerational living. *Catholic Voice*, https://www.catholicvoice.org.au/a-culture-of-life-shines-in-intergenerational-living/

[80] Hyndman-Rizik, N. (2010). At my mother's table: migration, (re)production and return between Hadchit, North Lebanon and Sydney. PhD Diss., Australian National University. https://openresearch-repository.anu.edu.au/bitstream/1885/49372/5/02whole.pdf.

[81] Clements & Bullivant, *Catholics in contemporary Britain*, 76.

[82] EWTN Global Catholic Network. (2022, July 15). New poll from EWTN News and RealClear Opinion research finds likely Catholic voters disagree with transgender ideology, support increased border security. *PR Newswire*, https://www.prnewswire.com/news-releases/new-poll-from-ewtn-news-and-realclear-opinion-research-finds-likely-catholic-voters-disagree-with-transgender-ideology-support-increased-border-security-301587505.html

[83] Fr Harrison, personal communication, 30 May 2024.

[84] Martyr, P. (2024, October 28). Don't forget to pray for the dead, *The Catholic Weekly*, https://catholicweekly.com.au/dont-forget-to-pray-for-those-in-purgatory/

Chapter 3

Parish life in Catholic Australia

If the family is the heart of the Church, then the parish is the skeleton that holds it together. In this chapter, we will talk about parish life in Australia, and naturally, we're going to focus a lot on the liturgy. The parish is sadly the place where many Catholics have also experienced their greatest sufferings in the Church in Australia today, and where the undeclared doctrinal and liturgical guerilla wars have been fought the hardest, with the most casualties. Today, two parishes right next door to each other may as well be in different Catholic Churches (and sometimes parallel universes).

Our parishes are where we are formed into the *synagōgē*, the 'great assembly', the *ekklesia* – the People of God. But we should remember that – as Vatican II reminded us in *Lumen Gentium* – this is a top-down process. As US theologian Dr Larry Chapp said:

> The Church is constituted as a sacramental reality and its entire existence is grounded first and foremost in this 'vertical' relationship with God. And as such the Church is also inherently hierarchical. And it is only after establishing this fundamentally sacramental and vertical constitution of the Church does *Lumen Gentium* discuss the Church as a pilgrim people of God.
>
> In other words, this 'people' is only what it is in virtue of baptism and inclusion in Christ's body. There is no hint here, therefore, of the Church as a mere voluntary society of like-minded people who come together in order to celebrate their like-mindedness and to establish a kind of ecclesial polity grounded in the sheer power of their collective wills.[1]

We're not the People of God in a kind of Marxist fist-waving way. We're the People of God because we are the lump of clay constantly at work in the hand of the Potter.

It's good to be reminded of this, because I think most Mass-going Catholics have found that their parishes are also very human entities. Many of us run the risk of sinking into a beige parish world of bourgeois squabbles about Pat taking over Kath's flower arranging while the music ministry tunes up in the background. St Peter calls us 'a people set apart' (1 Peter 2:9), but today we are a people increasingly disappearing into a comfortable and persuasively secular background. Without further ado, let's take the blinkers off.

What are our parishes like?

The numbers

There are currently 1,392 parishes in Australia (97 Eastern rite parishes and 1,295 Western rites parishes), and they're everywhere.[2] We already know roughly how many Western and Eastern rite Catholics go to Mass on Sundays, so we know that the 'average' parish community size in the Western rite in Australia is around 300 people, and in the Eastern rites and ordinariates, it's around 335 people. But obviously in reality, our parishes are all different shapes and sizes and with different populations. For example, the parish of Kalgoorlie-Boulder in the archdiocese of Perth covers a territory of 471,118 square kilometres – bigger than many Australian dioceses – but only around 5,000 Catholics live there.[3]

At the other end of the scale, there are just over 800 Catholics living in the of the parish of Buranda (St Luke's) in the archdiocese of Brisbane, where you could walk the parish boundaries in an hour or so.[4] Some parishes are a short walk from each other but in different dioceses and states, like Albury-Lavington (in the diocese of Wagga Wagga in NSW, with just over 4,000 Catholic residents)[5] and Wodonga (in the diocese of Sandhurst in Victoria, with around 10,000 Catholic residents).[6]

Officially, almost all of Australia's Catholics speak English, and only 3% are thought to be not proficient in it.[7] But ethnic makeup and first language also vary wildly from parish to parish. In the parish of Toongabbie in the diocese of Parramatta, there's around 5,000 Catholics resident, but only around 3,000 of them speak only English at home (59%).[8] In the parish of Casino in the diocese of Lismore, 95% of the 3,600 Catholics who live there speak only English at home.[9] Of the 100 Catholics living in the parish of Jabiru in the diocese of Darwin, 74 of them speak only English at home, and the rest speak Aboriginal and Filipino languages.[10]

But this data – produced by the National Centre for Pastoral Research (NCPR) from the 2021 Census data – only tells us about the people who identified as Catholics in the Census. That means that it's likely to be a bit different from the people you see at Mass on Sundays in these parishes. The apparent ethnic makeup of a parish is also not always a reflection of its linguistic abilities. For example, officially, just 71% of the parish of Willetton's Catholic population (archdiocese of Perth) speak only English at home. But I know that if I go to Mass in that parish, I'll see that it has a mostly subcontinental and Asian congregation – and the Mass is said in English with everyone enthusiastically participating.

The Catholics in Australia survey (CIA2022) produced some interesting data about our parishes as well. Almost two-thirds of the people who took part were what I called 'parish-dwelling': they lived in the parish where they attended Mass regularly. But that's because they were older and more likely to own their own home in a particular suburb of their choice – an increasing challenge for younger Catholics due to the high cost of real estate in Australia.[11]

Younger Catholics said in the survey that they were attending different churches for Sunday Mass mostly because of convenience, and many were also attending a specific chaplaincy, like a Latin Mass, migrant, or university chaplaincy.[12] Because they often can't afford to live near where they'd like to go to Mass, they travel long distances to attend Sunday Masses where they feel included and welcomed. In some parts of Australia, some families have re-located to places where they can attend Mass in peace and have formed what we increasingly call an 'intentional community' in the area. This is also happening in the United States.[13]

Those who lived in cities and urban areas showed the greatest variation in where they attended Mass, which is understandable – there are more options available. By contrast, those who lived in regional areas were more likely to live within the boundaries of the parish where they attended Mass, but that's probably because rural parishes tend to be much bigger than urban ones.[14]

When participants attended a Mass that wasn't in English, the highest rate of parish-dwellers was found among our Eastern rite Catholics. Some Eastern communities are long-established in Australia, meaning that many worshippers had more choice about where to buy their home. Eastern rite parishes are also quite stable once established, which makes people want to invest in living closer to them. That's why, for example, you find a lot of Maronite Catholics living in the (Western rite) parish of Bankstown in Sydney, because it gives them easy access to several Maronite churches nearby.[15]

Those who attended Novus Ordo Masses in languages other than English, and those who attended the Traditional Latin Mass (TLM), had higher numbers of floating parishioners. Many ethnic language chaplaincies and the TLM tend to be less firmly fixed in the one place, so there is less attraction in moving to an area permanently when your chaplaincy may be moved at any time. TLM attenders are much more likely to be younger as well, which is also associated with greater mobility when it comes to choosing a place to go to Mass.[16]

We also asked participants to tell us, 'In the last twelve months, have you served in any of the following roles in your church community?' We provided a list of common parish roles, and participants told us the ones we'd forgotten, so we ended up with a splendid list that includes everyone who isn't clergy (priests and deacons). People could nominate as many roles as they had filled in the last twelve months (Figure 2).

So who's doing all the work? Not surprisingly, it's the Weeklies – those who go to Mass at least every Sunday. There were slightly more women than men involved, but men and women appear to share many roles in Australian parishes. Even traditionally female roles – church cleaning, flowers, morning teas, hospitality, and children's liturgy – seem to be shared between men and women. The only roles which were reported to be almost exclusively male were acolyte, altar server, and men's ministry (Figure 3). It also looks like these many tasks are spread across a wide range of age groups. Younger Catholics who attend Mass are actively involved in their parishes and are filling roles that are appropriate to them, such as youth ministry.[17] You may not see this in your area, but it's happening elsewhere.

The CIA2022 study also turned up a very small number of people who described themselves as 'cohabiting' who were also acting as readers at Mass and Extraordinary Ministers of Holy Communion. If you're one of those people reading this: you're not supposed to be doing that. The Church formally discourages people whose lifestyles are not congruent with Catholic teaching, and/or who are not in full communion with the Church, to take part in certain roles at parish level.[18] You probably didn't know this, and maybe your parish priest didn't know it either. But you know it now.

Figure 2. Number of people undertaking different parish roles in the Catholics in Australia Survey 2022 (CIA2022).

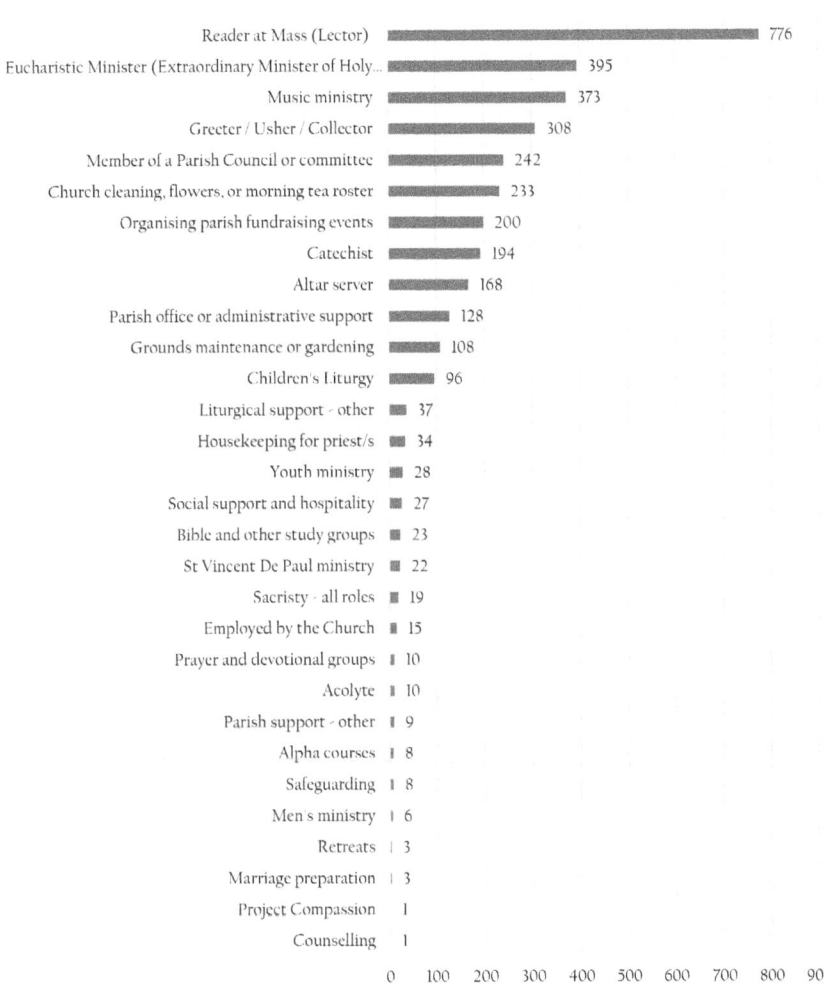

Figure 3. Gender balance of people undertaking different parish roles in the Catholics in Australia Survey 2022 (CIA2022).

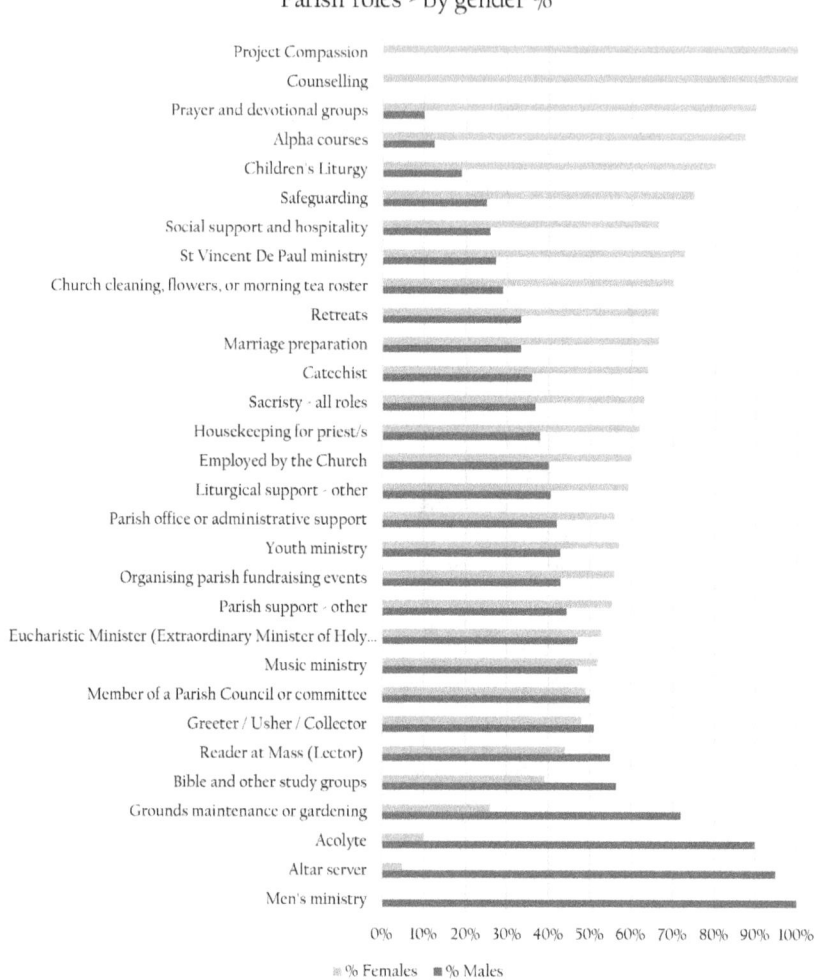

Boutique parishes, liturgical silos, and 'roaming Catholics'

As we know from Chapter 1, around half of all the Mass-going Catholics in Australia live in just four archdioceses – Melbourne, Sydney, Perth, and Brisbane. They mostly go to Mass in parishes located in relatively small areas. The exception to this is the Archdiocese of Perth, which is huge, but almost everyone lives in the city on the far west coast.

These archdioceses are also old, which means their urban areas – and parish networks – have grown organically over time. Many people have moved out of the city and live in the suburbs. It takes a long time to find some available land and build a church on it, so the local Church hasn't always kept up with these demographic movements. Because the churches are now not always where the Mass-going Catholics are, we have been left with what I call 'boutique parishes' – the inner-urban ones with tiny congregations and not much else. Fr Stephen, who has a large suburban parish to manage, has also noticed this: 'In my diocese, some of the small inner-city parishes probably need to be merged at some point. Quite apart from the question of fewer priests, there's just not a whole lot of life in some of them compared to the larger outer-suburbs parishes.'[19]

Parish priests who stay too long in one place can become a bit 'unique', and so can some lay people. For example, there are ten operational Catholic churches within about a five-kilometre radius of where I live. At least eight have congregations of perhaps 200-300 people across an entire weekend. They're also all liturgically different – and that's putting it mildly.

What does this liturgical difference look like? If you're a newcomer to any urban area in Catholic Australia, you might start by going to Sunday Mass at your nearest parish. There, you find that everyone says the words of consecration along with the priest and extends their right hands over the gifts, which makes it look a bit like a Nazi rally. You might (rightly) consider this a liturgical abuse, so you try another parish. But at the next one, you get treated with dark suspicion when you don't buy a chastisement survival kit with blessed beeswax candles and three days' worth of tinned beans at the piety stall. You might (rightly) consider this to be excessive devotion to a private revelation, so you try another parish.

Congratulations! You've joined the ranks of Australia's Catholic liturgical nomads: the 'roaming Catholics' who float between parishes in the hope of finding a bit of peace and quiet somewhere. Like-minded liturgically liberal Catholics tend to cluster together, and so do the traditional-minded Catholics. But the mobile ones are more likely to be younger Catholics, and they're also usually more traditionally minded. There are different reasons for this, as Isla, a young mother of three, pointed out.

> You have to be careful about where you attend Mass, or where you would take a friend inquiring about the faith, because most parishes do not truly reflect what the Church teaches. 99% of the families that I know drive further than their local parish because they are seeking reverent liturgies, fellow parishioners who know and love their faith, and priests who care about souls (eg: by offering inspiring, informative and sometimes challenging homilies, by offering Mass with reverence and devotion, by offering regular confessions etc). It is a privilege to have that option, and the ability to get there, but it is a shame that the local parish (for most people) doesn't cut it.[20]

Being a 'roaming Catholic' is even harder when you live in a regional or remote area, where your choices for Sunday Mass are much more limited. Katrina lives in one such regional area with her husband and their large family.

> Where do we belong? We are orthodox, traditionally inclined and prefer but don't attend the [Traditional Latin Mass], don't fit in well, do not attend the attached Catholic school, and are not quite *simpatico* with the locals. Finding other larger families such as ours is possible (just look for the twelve-seater Toyota HiAce, or 'Vatican Van'), but rare enough.[21]

She's also noticed some less positive trends in regional parishes.

> The further away from a large city centre ... the more lax a parish can become. ... we've had some doozies here in [our area], looking at you particularly, [Fr X]. The last-named priest actually did serious damage to the children's

faith development through the school, he haemorrhaged parishioners, removed the confessionals (they haven't returned), forbade anyone from addressing him as Father, and preached heresy. Repeated letters to [the local bishop] by concerned parishioners brought no response. We had the good fortune of at least being mobile enough to go elsewhere. Others were not so blessed.[22]

The tyranny of personal taste

Liturgical silos have been used as too-hard baskets by many bishops, because it's an easy way of stopping different groups of Catholics from annoying each other too much. But it also means that many parish priests don't hear complaints from the pews about how they say Mass, even if they're hopelessly out of touch with the mind of the Church. That natural corrective – people who think differently from you, and who are willing to say this to your face – is removed when everyone is carefully avoiding the Masses and priests they don't like.

How did we get here? I thought it was good to start this chapter with a reminder about the divine mission of the Church, because it's easy to forget this when we see the imposition of wildly varying personal tastes on the parish and the liturgy. How churches should be decorated was laid out very clearly by Vatican II in its constitution on the liturgy, known as *Sacrosanctum Concilium*, in chapter 7.[23] It's been largely ignored at parish level in Australia, where usually a series of determined individuals have imposed their personal tastes. Sometimes this is the parish priest, but very often it's lay people.

When you walk into a church, your eye is supposed to be drawn immediately to the tabernacle, because that's where Jesus lives, and it's his house, and you've come to visit him. But too often the interiors of Australian parish churches are smothered in synthetic fire-hazard fabrics, dusty or obviously artificial flowers, and felt banners that show their age in both design and quality. As different migrant communities move into a parish, they often put their own stamp on top of this.

Some of the problem is that many modern church buildings are poorly designed, with pitched ceilings, plain tinted glass windows, and vast expanses of exposed interior brick wall which are drab and depressing. It's natural that you'd want to brighten it up, but the results can be chaotic. The issue of poorly designed churches has been covered by other authors,[24] so I'll leave it for now – except to recommend to you the work of certain gifted priests and architects who have learned how to transform ugly boxes into beautiful churches.[25]

The rest of the problem comes from individual lay people who are misinformed about what is and isn't appropriate to the interior of the house of God. Rampant individualism has run unchecked because no one wanted to be labelled 'unkind' or 'un-Christian' for saying no to them. Sometimes a person's desire to fulfil their own artistic needs – even very spiritualised ones – has overridden everyone else, including the parish priest. When challenged, there are hurt feelings and sometimes tears, because the individual can't understand that what they found very theologically uplifting to create is not helpful for the people who have to look at it every Sunday.

Music ministry

Much the same can be said for the music ministry, which – I have discovered – is one of the most divisive topics that you can write about in the Church in Australia.[26] The role of music in the liturgy was also spelled out by Vatican II in *Sacrosanctum Concilium*. There's an entire chapter on it which should be mandatory reading for any parish music ministry. The idea was that parish congregations would be learning how to chant the parts of the Mass in Latin – chant, not sing. Liturgical chanting is where the words take priority over the melody, and the words should flow with the same cadences of natural speech (without people hanging on to that last note forever).

You can do this with minimal musical accompaniment. Have you ever heard a congregation chant the traditional version of the Our Father unaccompanied? There's a swell of human voices that ebbs and flows naturally, because everyone knows the words and the melody, and can sing it with confidence. Chant might also be the closest thing we have to the authentic voice of the early Church – it's thought to have come to us from the ancient Jewish tradition of worship.[27] Fr Vincent, who works in Victoria, thinks this would solve some problems.

> ... can we move past the pre-recorded tape music at Mass and actually bother to learn the prescribed music found in the Roman Missal, especially if there is no music ministry? ... The music settings found in the Roman Missal are sufficiently beautiful and exuberant, but I don't get why people opt for sub-par music that is not as ethereal?[28]

For the most part, *Sacrosanctum Concilium*'s excellent musical directives are ignored in Australian parishes in favour of combining a diverse range of musical talents and instruments in a small space, with varying results. I have found from attending Mass all over Australia for the last thirty or so years that too often we end up with a musical performance in which the musicians drown out the choir, who in turn drowns out the congregation, who stop singing and just listen. Then they clap at the end. When you hear applause, it's generally a sign that you've been attending a musical performance, rather than being led in worship.

I'm not just talking about the Hillsong-style ensemble with the emotional lead singer who sings about God with their eyes closed. The operatic soloist who belts out an incomprehensible responsorial psalm like it's the second act of *Tosca* is just as guilty. So is the overly fussy *schola* whose artistic director has the vapours if a baby cries through the polyphonic *Agnus Dei*. So is the tyrannical organist who insists that their four or five personal favourites are the only possible expressions of good taste in church music and refuses to play anything else.

Church music is not about you. It's about God. And this is where we get it hopelessly wrong, because we've made it all about us. One of the problems of the modern Church in Australia is that we have turned in on ourselves and tried to find God primarily in each other. However, God is in the tabernacle, and is consumed in the host, and we're meant to find him there first. Loving each other is meant to flow out of this.

Good music is important, but people are saps. We are romantic and easily carried away by powerful melody. This is how liturgical music has become about stirring up good feelings about God and the people around you. This is also how it becomes less about worshipping God, which is a different thing altogether. Having good feelings about God and each other is not the same as loving him and loving each other.

Too many of our hymns have become celebrations of ourselves, and of niceness and sentimentality. This isn't the stuff of which the Church is made, because no one goes to their death for niceness and sentimentality. They go out of love, which is real and strong and often painful. Sentimental, childish, and doctrinally flawed hymns don't build a strong faith community. They alienate people of real faith and are a sore trial to the people who really want to worship God.

Many modern hymns also have poor theological content. In 2010 the US Conference of Catholic Bishops (USCCB) warned that bad hymns 'would erode Catholic sensibility regarding the fullness of Eucharist teaching, on the Mass as sacrifice and eventually on the church, as formed by that sacrifice.'[29] Who knew that singing every Sunday about 'bread and wine and a special meal' would make people believe that Holy Communion was just bread and wine and a special meal?

You will find that many hymns have also now washed out

the words 'son' and 'man', replacing them with gender neutral language. If you want to know what the Australian Catholic Bishops Conference (ACBC) thinks are appropriate hymns, you can visit their website.[30] I don't agree with pretty much anything on their lists, but then again, that's a matter of personal taste. The difference is that I recognise that this is just my personal taste, and not some divinely revealed standard against which everything else must be measured.

What can we do right now about bad hymns and music? The first is to remember that you don't need to have hymns at Mass at all, and if your music ministry can't deliver anything other than a cocktail lounge experience, then you probably shouldn't. One of my acid tests for whether music ministry is effective or not is whether the congregation is singing along vigorously with minimal help. Does this happen in your parish?

There are brave priests who have disbanded their parish music ministries and now simply choose familiar hymns and lead off with the opening line as they process in and out of the church, without any musical accompaniment. This can be successful. Of course, then someone needs to explain to the music ministry that their regular Sunday gig has been cancelled. The ensuing recriminations can be a sign that it's become less about worshipping God and more about personal fulfilment. It's hard – but it's probably more important right now to reorient our parishes back to the worship of God and to liturgical order. There's a lot we can do about our poor church music, but it's going to take courageous priests and supportive lay people to do it.

The flipside of music is silence. Many parishes are discovering the benefits of silence in the church at least before Mass, allowing those present to pray without distraction.[31] If you want this, you will have to ask your parish priest for greater use of silence, and hope that you have a parish priest who is willing to speak from the pulpit (probably more than once) about the need to allow other people that peaceful time with God before and after Mass in the church. It doesn't happen overnight, but it *can* happen.

Most of the answers to our liturgical problems are in *Sacrosanctum Concilium* and the General Instruction of the Roman Missal. The trouble is getting everyone from the bishops downwards to (a) read them, and (b) take them seriously.[32] This includes the diocesan-level liturgy 'specialists' who have been avoiding both these documents for a long time in favour of their own preferred authorities, personal whims of iron, and occasionally the desire to market their own musical compositions.

A young people problem

Most parishes in Australia have a chronic young people problem, mostly caused by the lack of them. The smaller size of Catholic families I described in the previous chapter has really affected how parishes interact with and welcome young families. All my informants with children described this, and I'll share a sample of their experiences here.

Isla, a mother of three young children, lives in the archdiocese of Perth with plenty of parish churches within driving distance. Yet she's struggling to find 'a place where my kids see children their age, and older, practising their faith.'[33] It's a shame she lives on the other side of the country from Alan and his family, who are having a much better time in their urban diocese.

> We appear to have a great Catholic [inquiry] group, which produces results, and we have education sessions sometimes on a Monday night after Mass and supper. It's packed with young people, it's very social and very educational. Getting special speakers who are straight down the line but interesting is a must. There are so many different events & functions run by our parish almost every night of the week, there is something for everyone. It's great. There is a real buzz, it's a real community and the priests are an extension of our direct family. This is all parish clergy led.[34]

Leah, who has five children and lives in a rural diocese, has felt very exposed at times in her rural parish.

> For many years in our local parish, we were the only young family, and this was very difficult. The older people were very welcoming and loved seeing the children, but it was almost too much, and we felt like a spectacle. There were two families with older and teenage children, but it felt like they were on a different wavelength to us.[35]

An anonymous married female convert and mother in her 30s living in the Melbourne area said in CIA2022 that:

> It is a lonely experience being a Catholic compared to my prior experience in Protestant churches. I am deeply concerned about the absence of community, most significantly for my children whom I hope grow up and continue on in the faith. My local parish life is dead or targets elderly Catholics (which also deserve community life), but as a family with young children it is very difficult to find Catholic community support. While I entrust this to God, I grieve what the Catholic Church is not. While Catholicism possesses the truth, for this convert other Christian denominations possess family support and community.

Josh, who lives in another diocese again, has noticed something else missing.

> Many Christian churches have FREE playgroup sessions for parents and little ones to come and meet other toddlers and parents. The one Church which doesn't have anything like this? The Catholic Church, which is incredibly sad. There is a real lack of family events in [our local] parishes to unite families and help them to journey together in faith.[36]

Ben, a father of three young children who also lives in Alan's diocese, is finding it a struggle.

> Everything in society pushes against religious practice – social events are often scheduled for Sundays, sporting

competitions often occur then, kids' birthdays are often celebrated on Sunday mornings so the real things people sanctify their life with (kids' sport and the sacred Sunday afternoon rest) are protected.

To be a practicing Catholic in 2024 requires a good bit of compromise – you can't say no to your kids attending the birthday parties on Sunday mornings, or the sport, because that will just breed resentment. So instead, you attend Mass at a different time, all the while realising that this relegates it to the second most important thing you'll do that day. It's a true Catch-22 situation.[37]

Clearly there's a lot to unpack here, but I'd like to look at three areas that especially concern me at parish level: children's liturgy, the phenomenon of the 'Lying Mass', and youth ministry.

Children's Liturgy

Let's start with little children. I love seeing families with kids at Mass: I admire their efforts to keep them sitting still and paying attention. It all takes time and effort, and the rest of the congregation must be patient and cut them some slack, especially when the child is clearly going through an awful stage.

But I've never seen the point of children's liturgy, and I still don't. I think it's because my experience of it for decades now has consisted of seeing children – some of whom are quite large and capable of intelligent thought – trotting back into the church carrying a picture that they've coloured in. Lauren, a young mother of three children, said:

> Mediocre, superficial, and naff praxis pose a real threat to the faith of children. Boys are particularly at risk, as they are more likely to be put off by proceedings which lack gravitas. Boys need to be confronted by the immensity and grandeur of Our Lord's sacrifice to understand who they are and their place in the world.[38]

Like Lauren, I've also seen that making children the centre of attention at Mass creates certain expectations which are unlikely to be met in the adult Church, or indeed in adult life.

I've never seen a cost-benefit analysis of delivering children's liturgy in parishes, in terms of looking at the results. It seems to operate on the same 'hoping that something will stick' principle as those optimistic baptisms I described earlier in the chapter on family life. What is the purpose of children's liturgy, and does it achieve this aim? If the aim is to get the kids out of church for a bit, then it's working well. If the aim is to help them love God so that they'll keep coming to Mass, it doesn't seem to be doing a very good job. We still have a staggeringly low Mass attendance rate as our children's liturgy graduates turn into adolescents and adults.

'Lying Masses'

Some years ago, my sister and I attended the usual evening Mass at a local parish – we'll call it St Alpha's. The church car park was full to bursting, and the church was full of people who we'd never seen before, all loudly talking to each other. They were accompanied by children of varying ages, also loudly talking to each other. As Mass began, it was immediately obvious that none of these people – children included – knew any of the parts or words of the Mass, or when to sit, stand, or kneel.

Then just before the final dismissal, the parish priest invited everyone to stand and 'make their commitment'. That's when we finally figured out that this was the Mass for the Confirmation class from the parish school. All the parents and children stood up, and the children dutifully read the words projected on screens at the front of the church about how they were going to engage fully in the preparation process for receiving Confirmation, including attending Sunday Mass.

But the parish priest – whose former parish was 'St Ethelberga's' – had forgotten to update his Confirmation commitment Mass slides. This meant that all the parents then dutifully read out in unison that they would take part in the St Ethelberga's Confirmation preparation process and bring their children to Mass on Sundays.

I think it's safe to say that few of those parents knew *where* they were – St Alpha's, not St Ethelberga's – nor *why* they were there, except that the school told them to turn up at this Mass at this time. Certainly, we never saw any of these people again. The following week, there were the same 20 or 30 grey-haired people who were always at that Mass. It was like a king tide had come in and gone out.

Soon after that, we noticed that 'commitment Masses' for parishes in our area had switched to being held on weekend afternoons. Presumably this is so regular parish Mass-goers were no longer puzzled by this tide of strange people simply appearing and disappearing. Perhaps it's also so that these 'commitments' can be made in front of people who understand that this consists mostly of adults and children saying stuff with no real intention of following up on any of it.

As we left Mass that evening, my sister said reflectively, 'That wasn't a Commitment Mass. That was a Lying Mass.' Perhaps that's too harsh a word, but these very wobbly 'commitments' – which are probably made without malice – are nonetheless untruths told by parents in front of their children in a church. The children are mostly not stupid and already know that these parental commitments won't be honoured. To date, I know of only one local parish which has stopped this custom, because the parish priest said that he wanted to stop exposing the parents to an occasion of sin.

It's worth thinking about the impact this kind of ceremony has on children and their willingness to go to Mass, and why they grow up thinking that organised religion is hypocritical. It might help to explain why Catholic-origin schools seem to inoculate children against Catholicism, rather than plant a seed that grows into an adult believing Catholic. It might also explain why Catholic marriages break up so easily – after all, if you and your whole family can lie in church once and get away with it, why stop there?

Youth ministry

There's been a proliferation of parish-level youth ministries across the country for decades now. Again, I have never seen a cost-benefit analysis of any Catholic youth ministry at any level in the Church. What is the purpose of youth ministry? It provides paid employment for some young people, who can also indirectly support the Catholic education industry by engaging in training. But where are the other outcome measures? Right now, we seem to be asked to just trust that it's working.

Academic and educator Richard Rymarz has done some thorough research into youth ministry in Australia, at parish and diocesan level. He's found that most young people involved in it are the exception to the rule – they are Mass-going Catholics, usually with strong faith. So, they can minister to those who are like them – but it's much harder for them to reach those who *aren't* like them.[39]

Ethnic minority groups have their own struggles in youth ministry, as do the Eastern rite churches. In 2008, when World Youth Day was held in Sydney, the local Maronite community also held a youth forum. It identified real needs: wanting to be formed in a Maronite identity that could be reconciled with living in Australia, and an overall feeling that Maronites were drifting away from their culture, heritage and faith and needed re-evangelising. They wanted to get together more often, and to be more involved in their Maronite parishes – and they wanted more Masses in English.[40] Fr Vincent said the same thing.

> Attention needs to be given to the post-migration generations whose education and outlook are Australian because Australia is our homeland now. We may keep the best elements of our respective cultures, but at the end of the day, this is home, and our expression of Church must

adapt to the hopes and joys of the society that we live in, not where our parents or grandparents are from.[41]

Over time, I've heard many different criticisms of Catholic youth ministry, usually from its survivors. At parish level, it can be cliquey and insular. It doesn't always prepare young Catholics well for the rigours of leaving the 'Cathosphere' for the hostile secular world. Anecdotally, youth ministry also has less appeal for young people who have gone straight from school to work, or who are completing apprenticeships. This is partly a class issue: these young people may not feel represented or welcomed in their parish youth ministry because they don't fit in with more affluent youth who are attending private schools or going to university. Youth ministry can also become dominated by one ethnic group, which effectively excludes other young Catholics.

There are exceptions to this somewhat self-serving model, and they mostly seem to be in parishes where there's a feisty young(ish) priest who isn't afraid to talk directly to young people about life, God, and their future. These young people then tell their non-Catholic friends and bring them along to meet Fr Directo in person, if they dare. Young people – and the not-so-young – seem to respond well to this kind of high-fibre, full-fat Catholicism.[42] Miriam attends one such parish in her urban area:

> My children have strong and genuine faith. Our parish (well, if I am honest, the 6pm Sunday night mass) is extremely reverent. It is a prayerful place to be. The faith oozes out of the young adults that attend in particular. And they attend in good numbers, as do children and families. Because it is reverent. My children have found community, and that is so essential for teens and young adults still forming themselves in the faith and the practice of it.[43]

Leah also had good experiences when she was involved in youth ministry as a participant.

> I had a very positive and formative experience of youth ministry. This was immediately after World Youth Day

in Sydney, and I don't know if it still the case now. ... From [local youth ministry] I made strong Catholic friendships, and the networks have endured into marriage and parenthood. As I have said, we are spread far apart and so our association is not parish based, but many of those people I knew in youth ministry have chosen to homeschool, which has mitigated the geographical challenge.[44]

Lex orandi, lex credendi – and vice versa

The whole idea of liturgy is to worship God. During Mass we connect spiritually with everyone in the building, but also with the entire universal Church on earth, plus the saints in heaven, plus the souls in purgatory. However, it's quite hard to get that impression from the way Sunday Mass is said in many parishes.

Paradoxically, weekday Masses are often more reverent. You're more likely to find a priest who simply does his job (offering a sacrifice). The laity in turn do their job (participating in this sacrifice from the pews). There's no singing. There's quiet prayer. There's a sense of order and peace that helps us remember why we're there – to worship God.

On Sundays, it's the opposite. There's much more noise. There are bustling parish personalities organising everyone everywhere. The music ministry is tuning up the saxophones and slide guitars. There's constant chatter in the pews. There are extra non-ritual rituals – commentary, children's liturgy, special offertories – and talks and reminders and priestly dad jokes. The sanctuary is also suddenly full of people.

The liturgical reforms of the 1960s were meant to make the Mass simpler and more accessible to the people. Sometimes at Sunday Mass I yearn for another liturgical reform that would return it to the quietness and recollection that I experience during the week. Alternatively, I wish that all the extra fun and games could happen during weekday Masses, and then I could have peace and quiet on Sundays.

When the Mass is remade in the image of the local community and focused on them, it effectively shuts out anyone else. Any ordinary Catholic should ideally be able to go to Mass in any parish church and not need to be 'welcomed' to 'our liturgy'. Katrina has seen what a more God-focused parish can do, and who it can attract.

> Thanks to a husband with a background he is both a bit proud of and uncomfortable with, I have met several men particularly who have taken the scenic route to the Faith. They're divorced, alone, recovering alcoholics, one an ex-Freemason, and so forth, and I observed that these men seem to be drawn to the [Traditional Latin Mass], or at least a parish with a strong orthodoxy, unapologetic teaching, courageous priest and a congregation who doesn't look like what these men and women are striving to put behind them.[45]

It's a question of turning our more inward-looking parish communities outward – reorienting them back to the worship of God. Recapturing a sense of the sacred in the liturgy – that splendid and often surprising intrusion of God in his most loving form – will help to bring this about. It also makes your parish automatically more inclusive of people who are genuinely seeking God, including the very marginalised.

But what do all of us at Mass really believe? The Plenary Council did one thing superbly well: in its first 'Listening' stage, it accurately captured the level of confusion and disagreement about basic Catholic beliefs in the pews at parish level.[46] Many older Catholics struggle with the reality of the Eucharist, the validity of the ministerial priesthood, and the value of celibacy. They don't know why their children and grandchildren no longer attend Mass or the sacraments, even after twelve years of expensive Catholic schooling. They see them living lives that were unthinkable to an older generation of Catholics: divorce, children born out of wedlock, cohabitation, and same sex marriages and partnerships.

The Anglican communion has shown us what happens when you try to accommodate multiple different interpretations of Christianity in the one Church: an increasingly irrelevant and top-heavy organisation with lots of empty buildings. By contrast, the Catholic eparchies in Australia all have strong and coherent doctrinal identities and quadruple the rates of Mass attendance, even with their tiny numbers. Some of this may depend on cultural identity, but their clear sense of who they are and what they believe is a useful lesson to the rest of us.

At the very least, it's clear we must help this puzzled generation with sound catechesis on the authentic deposit of faith. Perhaps if we can get that right, we will be in a better position to help the even smaller number of middle-aged and younger Catholics in the pews as well. We can look at this more closely at the end of this book.

The sacrament of Reconciliation in the parish

Jesus preached repentance as a condition to salvation at least 18 times in the Gospels.[47] But it's hard to feel (or indeed to say) sorry if you are one of those splendid people who never does anything wrong. This might be why the sacrament of Reconciliation (Confession) has gone so much out of fashion in so many parts of Australia.

The CIA2022 study found that two-thirds of all the Catholics we spoke to went to Confession at least annually (which is what the Code of Canon Law states is the basic requirement for all Catholics; canon 989). Just over half went to Confession several times a year. We found that men went to Confession more than women, and that those aged under 40 went far more often than those aged over 40.[48]

The parish church is where most of us go to this sacrament, and individual confession of sins is the norm in the Catholic Church. It's between you and God, and you are both using the priest as

God's preferred go-between. It's often difficult – but if we really understood this sacrament, we'd be there a lot more often. It's not a counselling session, nor should it be. Instead, it's a brief ceremony that provides forgiveness of your sins, reconciliation with God, atonement, and purification. The best formula for a good confession is to be honest and thorough in your examination of conscience *before* you get in there. If you have prepared properly, then it's 'Be brief, be sorry, be gone'.

A good, honest confession rebuilds you from the inside out. It's more powerful than an exorcism. It regenerates the soul, so that even the deepest and most messy wounds can heal from the bottom up. It reconnects you with Jesus Christ himself because you must face your pain and shame with him. He can't heal your wounds unless you show them to him. If it were enough just to say sorry in our own heads to God, he'd have let us do that. But Christ the Physician is not content with putting a band-aid on emotional and psychological ulcers that go down to the bone. He wants to get in there and heal them.

Many parishes, especially post-COVID19, now only offer the sacrament of Reconciliation 'by appointment' which can be difficult for someone who's already struggling with shame and guilt. Encouraging priests to make themselves available at regular times for anonymous Confession, and sticking to those times, is a great start. Lay people can consolidate this by going to Confession regularly at those times to ensure that the priest knows that the need in his parish is real.

What is a parish meant to be?

After all this, it's time to remind ourselves again of what a parish actually is. The Code of Canon Law has an entire section on what parishes are, and how they are supposed to be run. It's in Book II, 'The People of God'.[49] Here's two key points – and I've added emphasis where I think it matters.

> A parish is a **certain community** of the Christian faithful stably constituted in a particular church, whose pastoral care is entrusted to a pastor (*parochus*) as its proper pastor (*pastor*) under the authority of the diocesan bishop. (Canon 515.1).
>
> As a general rule a parish is to be **territorial**, that is, one which includes all the Christian faithful of a certain territory. (Canon 518)

Let's add what the Catechism says (2179):

> A *parish* is a **definite community** of the Christian faithful established on a stable basis within a particular church; the pastoral care of the parish is entrusted to a pastor as its own shepherd under the authority of the diocesan bishop."[115]
>
> The parish initiates the Christian people into the ordinary expression of the liturgical life: it gathers them together in this celebration; it teaches Christ's saving doctrine; it practices the charity of the Lord in good works and brotherly love:
>
> 'You cannot pray at home as at church, where there is a great multitude, where exclamations are cried out to God as from one great heart, and where there is something more: the union of minds, the accord of souls, the bond of charity, the prayers of the priests'.[116]

Being a liturgical nomad has lots of advantages. Once you find a parish you like, you can be reasonably sure that Mass will be said in a way that doesn't set your teeth on edge or make you angry every week. You might find that you're going to Mass where your like-minded Catholic friends also worship, so you get to see them more often. You will be with a like-minded priest as well. If you have young children, they'll be less likely to hear unusual things taught in the homily at Mass.

But there are also disadvantages. You're not in the local area, so you aren't always available for things like working bees. Because you're there mainly for the Mass, it might take a long time for you to decide to say hello to anyone else. If you're there to join your friends at Mass, you may find that you rarely talk to anyone else, and if your friends don't go to the parish BBQ, you might skip it as well. Above all, you're not in any danger of hearing erroneous ideas about God and the Church – and thus you have no opportunities to correct error.

What I am saying here is not going to go down well with many younger Catholics who already feel unwelcome in Boomer parishes. I'm saying it because while I totally sympathise with their struggles, I – being a bit older and with no kids – have made myself attend a local parish consistently now for some years. I've met and gotten to know many different Catholics. We've managed to rub along together because we're all members of the Body of Christ. So have Steve and Helen and their eight children: 'We find help and support from our fellow parishioners, who, despite sometimes holding different opinions on Church topics, are united by a common generosity of spirit and charity, often going above and beyond to help each other out.'[50]

It takes time and patience, but if traditionally minded Catholics want these parishes back for themselves, they can have them – with a little effort and organisation, and a lot of patience and charity. Find a local parish that's not too egregious, start going there, and keep going there – even in the face of things that aren't being done your way. Get to know the other locals. Volunteer for things. You will soon find friends and even allies. You'll be ideally placed to do things like bring in speakers to provide formation evenings for anyone who's interested.

You and your friends may be the only ones at first, but you'll gradually win hearts and minds. Leah and her family have found some respite.

> ... we were asked to become the sponsors of a young family seeking to enter the Church in our local parish and we felt that we were being called to be present to support them. It made such a difference to our own experience to have just

one other family in our local parish and since then we have regularly attended our territorial parish.

It's still not ideal. The music is still bad and it's still difficult to access Confession. I worry about my children and if they will get what they need in this parish to grow in the faith. I am consoled that God has made it clear that this is where he wants us at the moment, and that my husband and I both attended less than ideal parishes and Catholic schools, yet by the grace of God we made it to the other side.[51]

In some places it's harder than others, partly because some of our parishes have become social clubs for like-minded and like-living people. Katrina speaks from the heart:

One of the challenges families such as ours face with is our own background. Mine is that of the respectable poor, and my husband's that of dysfunctional/disreputable poor. ... Efforts with varying degrees of success are made to welcome migrants of all sorts of backgrounds, but many of the working class are being lost to the Faith. It begins to look too 'gentrified'. ... Catholics with very dysfunctional backgrounds may never feel very welcome.

It may be that there needs to be a different focus on those battered members of society who find the Church, and enter it, but still with all the barnacles of these more difficult pasts attached. I have noticed over the years that men such as my husband don't get involved, struggle to form friendships, feel judged in spite of reassurances to the contrary, feel uncomfortable or are unduly sensitive.[52]

Some of the Plenary Council documents and contributions called for the Church to be more inclusive of marginalised people. But these were often pre-selected – for example, 'Those who do not feel welcome at the table of the Lord because of personal choices, lifestyle, sexual orientation, remarriage outside the Church, patriarchy, clericalist attitudes and dissent from Church teaching.'[53] I think the authors may have forgotten people like Katrina and her family. The most marginalised people are often right under our noses in our parish – they're the people who no-one talks to.[54]

Ultimately, if you think you have very little chance of making a difference – if you aren't prepared to take on the parish council, or the liturgy director, or the music ministry director, or the parish priest, or all of the above, consistently, and over a long period of time – then you might be better off going elsewhere. Leah understands this battle.

> Many of us are torn between wanting to build up our local parish but also feeling the pressure of a limited number of years in which to enculturate our children into all that is most beautiful in our faith tradition. Many families make the call that for their children's sake, they can't afford to stay in a parish where so few people seem to take the faith seriously and the liturgy is rendered banal.[55]

Does this make us C S Lewis' hated 'tasters of churches'?[56] Yes. But unfortunately, that decision was made for us decades ago when liturgical experimentation and individual taste were allowed to run riot.

Parishes that are already changing

The bottom line for our parish liturgies is to recapture a sense of the sacred. Thankfully there are bishops and dioceses in Australia already promoting genuine parish renewal.[57] How do you measure if it's working? I don't think it's by the number of discussion papers produced, or salaried staff employed. And I don't think it's what they've tried in the UK under the influence of the Anglican Alpha movement, which has some serious cracks in its façade of evangelical dynamism.[58]

Instead, I think the best measures are that in any given parish, Sunday and weekday:

1) Sunday and weekday Mass attendance increases,
2) the number of people in the Rite of Christian Initiation of Adults (RCIA) program grows, and

3) the queue for the sacrament of Reconciliation gradually gets longer each week.

These are core signs of people's renewed relationship with God that's changing their outward behaviours, and they're all measurable, and should be recorded. All the other things that we perhaps currently think are central to parish life – study groups, activities, charitable appeals, and social work – will then get much easier.

Fr Robert now works in an urban parish where tradition is welcomed and celebrated, and he's seeing a measurable increase in numbers, as well as the type of people attending Mass there.

> The younger generations are most noticeably represented, in particular young families. This generates substantial pastoral work, eg. spiritual direction and Confessions, weddings and baptisms, adult faith formation, etc.
>
> In the first fourteen years after ordination, I celebrated only one wedding of a young couple that intended to live the Catholic faith in its fulness in their married life and weren't co-habiting before marrying. In the last ten years I can remember only one instance of a cohabiting couple, the rest have all been firmly intent on being as Catholic as possible. This has been a cause of considerable joy to me personally.[59]

Dioceses and churches in Australia and around the world are already finding that small changes bring great rewards. Have you noticed that more and more people in your parish are now kneeling to receive Holy Communion? (I notice they're also young enough to have good knees.)[60] It doesn't really take any longer to distribute Holy Communion in this way – we're talking four minutes versus three minutes. And really, when we are physically eating God himself, I'm not sure why we have to rush things.

Does your parish have any times set aside for Adoration? This is growing like a secret wildfire in parishes all over Australia, and it's a powerhouse of prayer and graces for our increasingly interesting

Catholic future.⁶¹ Some parishes are adding Adoration chapels with 24-hour secure access and have healthy rosters for day and night Adoration. Another beautiful trend on the rise is seasonal devotions – really living the liturgical year and celebrating each seasonal change at home as well as in the parish church.

None of this is nostalgia: the Catholics driving these trends are too young to remember the pre-conciliar Church. Instead, for the first time they're plugging into an amazing spiritual heritage, and they're loving it.⁶² Miriam (in her late 40s) said, 'I love that so many parishes have Adoration available, it was not available to me growing up.'⁶³ Ben said:

> In many local parishes, there is a core group of younger families that are keeping the flame burning. By default, no one in this generation are 'cultural' Catholics only – you now have to make a conscious decision to attend Mass, and if you're going to be doing that, you're far more likely to be faithful than someone just apathetically following the crowd, as it were.⁶⁴

I'm also very encouraged to see the increase in men's ministries in our parishes. Katrina, the mother of quite a few sons, said:

> A place for young men: Best organised by the priest and older men of the parish, I would love to see a place where our single young men could be interacting with other men and forming genuine friendships at a personal level. Social media hasn't done our sons a lot of favours, where strong voices, ideologies and lazy analysis can turn young men into something that you wouldn't want to let any young women near.⁶⁵

Leah has noticed the same problem: 'It is unfortunately harder for the men, who don't have the same opportunities for regular catch ups, and I know my husband finds it harder to find fellowship with other Catholic men.'⁶⁶

Men have struggled more in recent decades than probably ever before in developed countries, especially with the epidemic of porn and fatherlessness. Building strong young Catholic men means better future priests and fathers, and it also provides a spiritual home for the increasing number of divorced Catholic men.[67] Oliver, a divorced father of three in his forties, said, 'I have also benefited from ... a monthly morning men's church service which I try to attend, and when I do attend, very much enjoy.'[68]

A reality that most of us are going to have to face in the coming years is parish restructuring at diocesan level. I've been watching diocesan reform in the US for a while now, where not everyone is happy about it and there's been some significant pushback.[69] The dioceses that stand out for me are Cincinnati and Chicago, where they're reducing numbers of parishes quite radically.[70] However, this model could work – or at least be given a good try – in our urban Church in Australia.

The idea is to create larger zones by consolidating several parishes – but just keeping one church open as the Mass centre for that zone. This will bring Mass-going Catholics out of the boutique parishes into one church where they'd have to meet each other and worship with each other. We're not talking mega-parishes. We're talking about taking four churches with Sunday congregations of around 200, closing three of them, and bringing those 800 people to the Sunday Masses at the biggest church instead. With three Masses on Sunday, that's only 267 people per Mass – a nice solid congregation. You could offer a couple more Sunday Masses if you were worried about being swamped.

Who will say all these Masses? The team of clergy that serves that Mass centre. Closing boutique parishes frees up priests who can then serve across a zone. They'd be rostered for Confession and Mass at the Mass centre and cover each other on holidays and sick leave. They'll share out the other tasks like baptisms, weddings, funerals, and hospital and aged care chaplaincy.

One objection is that different priests saying the Sunday Masses will be confusing. If Fr Relaxo has us all doing interpretative dance on the sanctuary one week, and Fr Apocalypto threatens us all with the coming chastisement the next week, that's going to upset people. But what you're worried about is already happening. It's just happening in different parishes, where you don't have to see it. So perhaps the real fear is that you'll have to put up with 'things you don't like' in your own church. But how did we arrive at such liturgical divergence in the first place?

We already know the answers – bad catechesis, bad priestly formation, and weak bishops. Allowing boutique parishes and liturgical silos to continue long past their use-by date has made the problem worse. If we can teach people what the Mass really is, standardise the way it is said, and stop laxity and abuses, we have a better chance of a new model of parish working as well. Without liturgical reform, the laity will simply choose their favourite clergy and follow them to their new Mass centre.

Bishops who have found their younger and more traditional-minded priests irritating might need to think again. These priests are the ones most likely to walk a liturgical middle path and appeal to the largest number of churchgoing Catholics. They are immune to the liturgical nonsense of the last few decades, but they have also had some scary conversations with Fr Apocalypto and know that he doesn't represent the future of the Church either.

No matter what, bringing parishioners and clergy out of their silos and into a larger Mass centre may cause frictions at first – but it's more likely to have an overall positive effect. Many priests and laity have become insensitive and stubborn from being in echo chambers for too long. They need a bit of fresh air to render them more flexible and open again. Of course, if any priest is unable to serve on a team because he feels terribly hurt by it all, he could always be given a round of rural and remote parishes instead. They'd love to see him every Sunday.[71]

Conclusion

I think that we need to try to respond generously to parish restructuring. Yes, there will be a lot of hiccups. The clash of the music ministries alone will produce a vale of tears. There will be frayed tempers, 'church rage', and many opportunities to practice the virtue of patience. But we need to try something, because the Church in Australia is in serious trouble at parish level. Part of the solution will also lie with our parish priests – of whom more in the next chapter.

---

[1] Chapp, L. (2024, May 21). True and false democracy in the Catholic Church. *National Catholic Register*, https://www.ncregister.com/commentaries/true-and-false-democracy-in-catholic-church

[2] Australian Catholic Bishops Conference (ACBC). (2022). *Catholic Australia: Pastoral Research – Statistics*, https://www.catholic.au/s/article/Statistics#:~:text=How%20many%20parishes%20are%20there,belonging%20to%20Eastern%20Catholic%20Churches.

[3] Archdiocese of Perth. *Parish boundaries*, https://www.perthcatholic.org.au/Parishes_Mass_Times.htm?cms%2Erm=Boundaries; National Centre for Pastoral Research (NCPR). (2023). *2021 Census parish social profile – Kalgoorlie-Boulder*, https://ncpr.catholic.org.au/2021-Parish-Social-Profiles/Perth/Kalgoorlie-Boulder.pdf

[4] Archdiocese of Brisbane. *St Luke's, Buranda*, https://brisbanecatholic.org.au/parishes-and-mass-times/parish/st-lukes-buranda/ and NCPR. (2023). *2021 Census parish social profile – Buranda*, https://ncpr.catholic.org.au/2021-Parish-Social-Profiles/Brisbane/Buranda.pdf This would not necessarily be a very enjoyable or safe walk, given that the Pacific Highway runs across this parish, but it could be done if you were very determined.

[5] NCPR. (2023). *2021 Census parish social profile – Albury-Lavington*, https://ncpr.catholic.org.au/2021-Parish-Social-Profiles/Wagga%20Wagga/Albury-Lavington.pdf

[6] NCPR. (2023). *2021 Census parish social profile – Wodonga*, https://ncpr.catholic.org.au/2021-Parish-Social-Profiles/Sandhurst/Wodonga.pdf

[7] NCPR. (2023). *2021 Census parish social profile – Willetton*, https://ncpr.catholic.org.au/2021-Parish-Social-Profiles/Perth/Willetton.pdf, 18.

[8] NCPR. (2023). *2021 Census parish social profile – Toongabbie*, https://ncpr.catholic.org.au/2021-Parish-Social-Profiles/Parramatta/Toongabbie.pdf

[9] NCPR. (2023). *2021 Census parish social profile – Casino*, https://ncpr.catholic.org.au/2021-Parish-Social-Profiles/Lismore/Casino.pdf

[10] NCPR. (2023). *2021 Census parish social profile – Jabiru*, https://ncpr.catholic.org.au/2021-Parish-Social-Profiles/Darwin/Jabiru.pdf

[11] Al-Akiki, G. (2024, June 19). Can Catholics afford to live near their parishes? *The Catholic Weekly*, https://www.catholicweekly.com.au/cost-of-living-catholic-parishes/

[12] Martyr, P., & Bullivant, S. (2024). *The Catholics in Australia Survey 1 – Mass attendance*, https://papers.ssrn.com/sol3/papers.cfm?abstract_id=4646161, 27.

[13] La Rosa, M. (2024, May 4). 'To find your people' – How Catholics are building intentional communities. *The Pillar*, https://www.pillarcatholic.com/p/to-find-your-people-how-catholics

14 Martyr, P., & Bullivant, S. (2024). *The Catholics in Australia Survey 10 – Parish life*, https://papers.ssrn.com/sol3/papers.cfm?abstract_id=4942224

15 NCPR. (2023). *2021 Census Parish Social Profiles: Bankstown (Archdiocese of Sydney)*. https://ncpr.catholic.org.au/2021-Parish-Social-Profiles/Sydney/Bankstown.pdf

16 Martyr, P., & Bullivant, S. (2024). *The Catholics in Australia Survey 9 – Traditional Latin Mass (TLM) attenders*, https://papers.ssrn.com/sol3/papers.cfm?abstract_id=4942220; Martyr & Bullivant, *Parish life*.

17 Martyr & Bullivant, *Parish life*.

18 See for example Archdiocese of Perth. (2022). *Extraordinary Ministers of Holy Communion: guidelines*, https://liturgy.perthcatholic.org.au/wp-content/uploads/2022/10/Guidelines-for-Altar-Ministers-EMHC-and-Acolytes-2022.pdf

19 Fr Stephen, personal communication, 30 August 2024.

20 Isla, personal communication, 7 June 2024.

21 Katrina, personal communication, 20 June 2024.

22 Ibid.

23 Catholic Church. (1963). *Sacrosanctum Concilium: on the sacred liturgy*, https://www.vatican.va/archive/hist_councils/ii_vatican_council/documents/vat-ii_const_19631204_sacrosanctum-concilium_en.html

24 Rose, M. (2001) *Ugly as sin*. Sophia Institute Press, and (2000). *The renovation manipulation*. Aquinas. See also Smith, R. (2007). Don't blame Vatican II: Modernism and modern Catholic church architecture. *Sacred Architecture*, 13, 12-18. https://www.catholicculture.org/culture/library/view.cfm?recnum=8000

25 Longenecker, D. (2017, April 29). Restoring beauty in church buildings. *Crux*. https://cruxnow.com/church-in-the-usa/2017/04/restoring-beauty-church-buildings includes a range of examples of restored churches.

26 Martyr, P. (2021, February 3). Condensed milk liturgical music. *The Catholic Weekly*, https://catholicweekly.com.au/philippa-martyr-condensed-milk-liturgical-music/; Martyr, P. (2021, February 16). Ditch the cha-cha and try a little chant. *The Catholic Weekly*, https://catholicweekly.com.au/philippa-martyr-ditch-the-cha-cha-and-try-a-little-chant/; Martyr, P. (2021, August 26). Liturgical fallout of the 70s, *The Catholic Weekly*, https://catholicweekly.com.au/dr-philippa-martyr-liturgical-fallout-of-the-70s/.

27 There is an interesting paper called 'The history of Gregorian chant' available online from St Cecilia's Abbey, Ryde, UK: https://stceciliasabbey.org.uk/wp-content/uploads/2022/07/CHANT-HISTORY-1.pdf However, this theory is contested by some historians of music, and given that we have no recordings or readable written music for ancient Jewish worship, it is impossible to prove. But the fact that chant was found in both the early East and West in Christianity, and persisted in both, might hint at common ancestors as well.

28 Fr Vincent, personal communication, 31 August 2024.

29 Catholic News Agency. (2010, December 20). 'All are Welcome' not a welcome hymn at Mass, USCCB committee says. *Catholic News Agency*, https://www.catholicnewsagency.com/news/46872/all-are-welcome-not-a-welcome-hymn-at-mass-usccb-committee-says

30 Australian Catholic Bishops Conference (ACBC). (2021). *Recommended hymns and*

songs approved by the Bishops Conference (liturgical documents), https://www.catholic.au/s/article/Recommended-Hymns-and-Songs

31 Staudt, R. (2024, August 8). The power of silence and the problem of sound in adoration. *Catholic World Report*, https://www.catholicworldreport.com/2024/08/08/299691/

32 The *General instruction of the Roman Missal* (GIRM) can usually be found in bound copies of the average Sunday Missal, and online at https://www.vatican.va/roman_curia/congregations/ccdds/documents/rc_con_ccdds_doc_20030317_ordinamento-messale_en.html

33 Isla, personal communication, 7 June 2024.

34 Alan, personal communication, 29 April 2024.

35 Leah, personal communication, 19 June 2024.

36 Josh, personal communication, 3 September 2024.

37 Ben, personal communication, 1 June 2024.

38 Lauren, personal communication, 7 August 2024.

39 Rymarz, R. (2019). Catholic parish-based youth ministers: a preliminary study. *Journal of Youth and Theology*, 18(1), 49–64; Rymarz, R. (2019). Youth ministers: Another Catholic narrative? *Australasian Catholic Record*, 96(4), 445–457. https://search.informit.org/doi/10.3316/informit.859283806894076

40 Taouk, Y., Ghosn, M., Steel, A., & Butcher, J. (2012). Maronite church and youth identity in Australia: at the crossroads. *Australasian Catholic Record*, 89(3), 299–310.

41 Fr Vincent, personal communication, 31 August 2024.

42 Hitchens, D. (2023, September 23). Inside the fastest growing – and shrinking – churches in the UK. *Spectator*, https://www.spectator.co.uk/article/inside-the-fastest-growing-and-shrinking-churches-in-the-uk/

43 Miriam, personal communication, 20 June 2024.

44 Leah, personal communication, 19 June 2024.

45 Katrina, personal communication, 20 June 2024.

46 Dantis, T., Bowell, P., Reid, S., & Dudfield, L. (2019). *Final report for the Plenary Council Phase 1 – Listening and Dialogue*, https://plenarycouncil.catholic.org.au/wp-content/uploads/2020/03/Diocesan-Final-Report-Phase-1-Sydney.pdf ; also Martyr & Bullivant, *Mass attendance* and *Believing* reports.

47 For the curious, they are: Matt 4:17, Matt 11:20, Matt 11:21, Matt 12:41, Mark 1:14, Mark 6:11, Luke 3:8, Luke 5:32, Luke 10:13, Luke 11:32, Luke 13:1, Luke 13: 3, Luke 13:5, Luke 15:7, Luke 15:10, Luke 17:3, Luke 17:4, and Luke 24:47, plus six times in the Book of Revelations.

48 Martyr, P., & Bullivant, S. (2024). *The Catholics in Australia Survey 5 – Behaving*, https://papers.ssrn.com/sol3/papers.cfm?abstract_id=4850676

49 Code of Canon Law, Book II, Title III, Chapter VI, Parishes, Pastors, and Parochial Vicars. https://www.vatican.va/archive/cod-iuris-canonici/eng/documents/cic_lib2-cann460-572_en.html#CHAPTER_VI

50 Steve and Helen, personal communication, 9 August 2024.

51 Leah, personal communication, 19 June 2024.

52 Katrina, personal communication, 20 June 2024.

⁵³ Plenary Council. (2020). *Thematic Discernment Paper 1: missionary and evangelising*, 6. https://plenarycouncil.catholic.org.au/wp-content/uploads/2020/05/PC2020-thematic-papers-1.pdf

⁵⁴ Martyr, P. (2024, October 23). Make room in your heart for the poor and the weird. *The Catholic Weekly*, https://catholicweekly.com.au/catholic-church-australia-present-and-future/

⁵⁵ Leah, personal communication, 19 June 2024.

⁵⁶ Lewis, C. (1952). *The Screwtape letters*. Geoffrey Bles, ch XVI, 81-85.

⁵⁷ Sydney's work recently has been impressive, Ang, D. (2024, May 29). Parish renewal is never a solo endeavour. *The Catholic Weekly*, https://www.catholicweekly.com.au/parish-renewal-is-never-a-solo-endeavour/. See also Archdiocese of Melbourne, https://melbournecatholic.org/live/parish-life/parish-leadership-and-renewal; and Diocese of Broken Bay, https://www.bbcatholic.org.au/mission/parish-renewal.

⁵⁸ Tomlinson, H. (2024, June 26). Potential pitfalls of Catholic Parish Summit's evangelising spirit. *Catholic Herald*, https://catholicherald.co.uk/potential-pitfalls-of-the-catholic-parish-summits-evangelising-spirit/

⁵⁹ Fr Robert, personal communication, 11 June 2024.

⁶⁰ For guidelines on how Holy Communion is to be received in Australia, see https://www.catholic.au/s/article/Guidelines-for-Reverent-Reception-of-Holy-Communion. The choice of receiving in the hand or on the tongue is made by the receiver, not the distributor.

⁶¹ For Australian locations, see https://adorationtinyhost.wordpress.com/adoration-chapels/. For Brisbane, see https://www.perpetualadoration.com.au/. For Western Australia, see https://whatsonperthcatholic.wordpress.com/eucharistic-adoration/, but I'm not sure how up to date this is. See also Al-Akiki, G. (2024, June 12). Watch and pray at two new perpetual adoration chapels. *The Catholic Weekly*, https://www.catholicweekly.com.au/perpetual-adoration-chapel-sydney/

⁶² Cleary, A. (2023, August 2). What World Youth Day means to Australians. *Catholic Herald*, https://catholicherald.co.uk/what-world-youth-day-means-to-australians/; Baker, J. (2024, June 14). A TikTok priest and a surfing nun: The new wave of conservative Christians. *Sydney Morning Herald*, https://www.smh.com.au/national/a-tiktok-priest-and-a-surfing-nun-the-new-wave-of-conservative-christians-20240610-p5jkmq.html

⁶³ Miriam, personal communication, 20 June 2024.

⁶⁴ Ben, personal communication, 1 June 2024.

⁶⁵ Katrina, personal communication, 20 June 2024.

⁶⁶ Leah, personal communication, 19 June 2024.

⁶⁷ For example, see https://www.sydneycatholic.org/maximus/maximus-resources/; https://menalive.org.au/; https://www.catholic.au/s/article/Catholic-Men-s-Ministry-and-Groups; Cox, V. (2024, April 8). Men's ministry helps restore lives and build community. *Catholic Voice*, https://www.catholicvoice.org.au/mens-ministry-helps-restore-lives-and-build-community/

⁶⁸ Oliver, personal communication, 17 August 2024.

⁶⁹ Pinedo, P. (2024, May 29). Diocese of Buffalo to merge a third of its parishes. *Catholic World Report*, https://www.catholicworldreport.com/2024/05/29/diocese-of-buffalo-to-merge-a-third-of-its-parishes/; McKeown, J. (2024, May 15). Vatican

halts some parish closures in St. Louis following appeals. *Catholic World Report*, https://www.catholicworldreport.com/2024/05/15/vatican-halts-some-parish-closures-in-st-louis-following-appeals/; Payne, D. (2024, September 11). 'Harsh realities': Diocese of Buffalo announces final list of parish mergers, closures. *Catholic World Report*, https://www.catholicworldreport.com/2024/09/11/harsh-realities-diocese-of-buffalo-announces-final-list-of-parish-mergers-closures/

[70] Chicago's program is called *Renew My Church*, https://www.renewmychurch.org/. Monk, D. & Christian, P. (2024, February 20). Beacons of Light backlash: Closures have begun and Catholics aren't happy about it. *WCPO Cincinnati*, https://www.wcpo.com/news/local-news/i-team/beacons-of-light-backlash-closures-have-begun-and-catholics-arent-happy-about-it ; Weber, K. (2024, April 18). What happens when a diocese takes a synodal approach to parish restructuring? *America: the Jesuit Review*, https://www.americamagazine.org/faith/2024/04/18/catholic-diocese-parish-closings-mergers-247747

[71] Martyr, P. (2022, September 8). Neither Fr Relaxo nor Fr Apocalypto. *The Catholic Weekly*, https://catholicweekly.com.au/dr-philippa-martyr-neither-fr-relaxo-nor-fr-apocalypto/

Chapter 4

The Catholic clergy in Australia

In the Catholic Church, 'clergy' are bishops, priests, and deacons. In the Acts of the Apostles (written before the end of the first century AD), we started out with just bishops (*episkopoi*, or 'overseers'). Deacons were then appointed to do what we might call the social work of the early Church so that the bishops didn't have to do it (Acts 6:1-7). By the time of St Ignatius of Antioch (c108-140AD) we know that these three clerical roles existed in a hierarchy in the Church.[1] Bishops came first, then priests who represented the bishop locally to ensure that everyone could get access to the sacraments, and then deacons.

'Clergy' comes from the Latin word meaning 'clerk' or someone with learning, who can read and write. It's also where we get our new favourite word in the Church today, which is 'clericalism'. This word means different things to different people. To some, it means the abuse of the clerical state when priests demand to be treated better than everyone else and exploit their office. To others, it means the fact that ordained ministers exist at all, which they find at best suspicious and at worst gravely offensive.

But the Catholic Church couldn't exist without bishops and priests. Without them, we don't have most of the sacraments, and without the sacraments, we don't have those direct channels of grace that draw us into the life of the Trinity. The seven sacraments are staked out firmly in the Church's foundations, and they've been doing their job ever since they were instituted.[2] Not all of them need a priest – lay people can baptise in emergencies if they've already been baptised themselves, and lay people normally administer the sacrament of Marriage to each other when they get married (the priest or deacon is just there to make sure it's done properly).

The other sacraments do need a priest, or a bishop (Reconciliation, the Eucharist, Confirmation, Holy Orders and Anointing of the Sick). Lay people can't administer these, and so we need our ordained brothers to help us out. Our clergy are not magicians, and they don't have woo-woo powers. We just need them to be a bridge between us and God so that we can touch Jesus Christ in person all over again.[3] As beings with bodies, we need to smell, hear, touch, and taste and see that the Lord is good.[4] We do that through the physical realities of the sacraments.

If you're a Catholic, you believe this is how Jesus Christ set the Church on earth up when he lived here, and after he rose from the dead. The descent of the Holy Spirit at Pentecost is the formal birthday of the Church, but the groundwork had already been laid with Jesus' three years of ministry, the Last Supper and everything that went with it, and everything that came after it.

Given that there seems to have been such an obvious element of deliberate choice in what Jesus did when he established the Church, and that we've been doing the same stuff consistently ever since, a Catholic will either accept all this, or not accept it and cut ties with God and the Church. Jesus chose, and so can you. You're free to do either.

But there's a group of people who want to stay within the Church and convince us to change the rules about ordination and the clergy to suit their personal preferences. So far, they haven't succeeded in changing the Church's teachings. However, their current activities have certainly contributed to the general low morale in the Catholic priesthood in many developed countries today, including Australia.

In this chapter we will look at clergy numbers and trends in those numbers in Australia in the last 50 years. We'll also look at data on laicisation and seminary numbers. We will look at the vexed question of overseas priests working in Australia, what our bishops have been up to, and where our permanent deacons came from. We will also look at the clergy abuse scandal and try to find some ways forward from this for a demoralised priesthood. Let's start at the top with our bishops.

Australia's bishops

According to Vatican II, bishops have three jobs: to teach doctrine, to lead sacred worship as a priest, and to minister to us through governing the Church. In this section, I'm going to try to look at the Australian bishops as individual men, rather than as a faceless and impersonal 'Australian Catholic Bishops Conference' (ACBC). To be honest, my experience has been that the ACBC is a good place for bishops to hide when things go wrong, and not much use otherwise.[5]

The reason I'm so jaundiced is that I've seen how the ACBC has very rarely stood against the prevailing tide. As Australian theologian Tracey Rowland points out, 'Group policy documents are rarely, if ever, the fruit of heroic sanctity. They represent the lowest common denominator agreement of a large number of people.'[6] Tori, a young mother of three children, said in exasperation:

> I want to be able to point to brave priests and bishops speaking out in the current Australian culture wars, but I can't see anyone actually delivering results on any major issues which my children will inherit ... contemporary witnesses to the faith, within the Church, are so rare within Australia that they begin to discredit the Faith because there is no one with actual skin in the game taking and giving a few punches at the broader cultural and political level.[7]

Paul, a divorced father of three in his forties, said:

> The Catholic Church I seek is the one that understands the way of Christ is the Cross and celebrates a God who embodied self-sacrifice, literally. My own individual faith is fused with this principle and it's becoming an unsettling thought to me that perhaps those who steer the ship on which our Holy Mother Church travels may see it a little differently.[8]

The Bishop Geoffrey Robinson case in 2008, when the retired bishop had to be publicly corrected for his forays into somewhat novel theology, stands out because of this.[9] Thankfully the ACBC has more recently produced some documents that have pushed back against secularism: examples are the 2015 paper *Don't Mess With Marriage*,[10] and the 2022 *Created and Loved*, a guide to help Catholic schools navigate issues of gender identity.[11]

But for the most part, the ACBC's public statements have been commonplace and unexceptional. Their social justice statements unwaveringly back a suite of centre-left, completely socially acceptable causes which are already well supported and often well-funded by different Australian governments.[12] These causes are safe as houses, about as radical as sliced white bread, and designed to play to an affluent Boomer audience.

I know it makes sense to have a national body to make decisions that involve the whole Church across diocesan and individual state borders, but I have some questions about value for money. That's probably because the ACBC's annual financial report is a masterpiece of opacity. When an organisation has a consolidated statement of financial position of nearly $34 million in 2022, I'm inclined to be curious about how it's spending money each year, and on what.[13] How many people does it employ, on what salaries, and what do they do?

So instead, let's look at bishops as individual overseers of the parochial-diocesan Church in Australia. We have a lot of bishops (and bishop-equivalents) for such a small number of Mass-going Catholics. At my last count, there were 32 active ones (archbishops, bishops, and auxiliary bishops) and 28 retired ones. If we just count the active ones, it's about 1 active bishop for every 13,000 Mass-going Catholics.

But what do bishops in Australia today do all day? I'm largely in the dark about this, but I've been reliably informed that they go to a lot of meetings – and many of those meetings could have been replaced by emails. Is this what you want in a bishop? I'm not sure that it is.

My favourite type of bishop likes to get out among his people, say Mass every Sunday in his cathedral where he can be seen and heard by everyone, and then make himself available outside so that everyone can come and talk to him if they want. He will also hear Confessions in his cathedral on a regular basis, but without any fuss or fanfare. At times, he will even answer his own phone. In a rapidly shrinking Church, we probably need more of this type of bishop, because if we keep shrinking like this, we're going to end up with one bishop each. Think seriously about the type of bishop you'd like to have over for dinner.

My least favourite bishops avoid doing anything but the minimum carefully curated meet-the-peoples and prefer hiding in an office behind several locked doors and a scary secretary.[14] Fr Vincent said, 'The chancery of a diocese is now a CEO's office with the [executive assistant] being the gatekeeper-in-chief.'[15] But the traffic goes in both directions, with some clergy avoiding their bishop because they simply don't trust him anymore. Fr Robert said:

> One can try and excuse the statements and actions of one's superiors for only so long before it becomes clear that one must simply protect oneself, and by extension the good one tries to accomplish for souls. If one gets oneself hobbled or cancelled, how many souls are affected adversely and left as sheep without shepherds?[16]

The Catholics in Australia 2022 (CIA2022) survey asked people two optional questions about how they rated church leadership – the Australian bishops generally, and their own local bishop. Over 90% of the over 2,000 participants chose to answer this question, so they clearly wanted to be heard.

Just 29% of them rated the Australian bishops' leadership as good, and 22% said it was reasonable – but 49% said it was poor.

There was almost no difference in the over-40s and under-40s, but the women tended to be a bit kinder than the men. No matter how I diced and sliced it, the data seemed to keep returning the same basic proportions. Close to half of all my participants thought the Australian Catholic bishops' leadership was poor.

When it came to rating their local bishops, the results were a bit different. In psychology there's a thing called in-group bias – we tend to be nicer to people who we think belong to us in some way. This means that rating 'my bishop' or 'our bishop' might look a bit different from rating a faceless group of bishops. And sure enough, people were kinder to their local bishop – but not by much.[17]

When I first shared this data in the pages of *The Catholic Weekly*, it touched a nerve. Some people thought that the data vindicated their view that the Church's whole structure needs overhauling. Other people thought it vindicated their view about the fallout from Vatican II (not in a good way).

I went through the written comments section of the survey to see if the 50 or so comments made about bishops provided any further clues. A handful of people said that we shouldn't comment on this topic at all. 'Who are we to criticise our shepherds?' asked one. However, most people didn't suffer from the same hesitancy and were happy to let rip.

'Bishops must be more politically involved', said someone who rated both the Australian bishops and their own bishop's leadership as 'poor'. But others complained about how the bishops acted during the COVID19 lockdowns, and one told them to butt out of politics unless they were willing to excommunicate then-Victorian premier Dan Andrews. There were multiple complaints about bishops covering up sexual abuse, manipulating the Plenary Council agenda, and being in the pocket of the late Cardinal Pell, Opus Dei, and traditionalists.

This would have come as a surprise to the more conservative participants, who said in their comments that they were shut out by weak and 'uncontactable' local bishops. They also complained that the bishops appeased the political left and didn't show enough leadership in liturgy, moral teaching, and life issues. Some participants tried to tread a middle path, and provided examples of what they thought was good and bad leadership by individual bishops. But one participant simply said I should have included a 'very poor' option, because 'poor' didn't cut it.

Some said a few good things about specific named bishops and dioceses. However, these same dioceses and bishops were harshly criticised by others who saw them as either bastions of the dark ages or havens of grotesque liberalism. For example, CIA2022 had 148 participants from the diocese of Parramatta. Of these, 43% rated their local bishop Vincent Long's leadership as 'good' and 45% rated it as 'poor'. These are roughly the same proportions that I found in most Australian dioceses. Yet just a year earlier, around 4,000 petitioners from this diocese asked the Pope to remove Bishop Long from his position on doctrinal grounds.[18] No one said anything about this case in the written comments, but it certainly makes for interesting background reading.

I never thought I'd start to feel sorry for our bishops, but after reading the comments in my survey, I did. It reminded me all over again that anyone who wants to be a bishop is already unsuitable for the job, because there's clearly something wrong with him.[19] You quite literally can't please anyone. So maybe it's better not to try – and just stick with teaching authentic doctrine, leading priestly worship, and governing the local church.[20]

The episcopal entourage

To be fair, because of the increasing corporatisation of the Church in Australia, it's now harder to be a good and effective bishop. Hans Urs von Balthasar described this process back in 1986 in the Church in Germany, and it will be instantly recognisable to any Australian Mass-going Catholic today.

> The 'decentralisation' of the Roman Curia has led directly to the curialisation of the diocese. In some countries, the diocesan machine has been inflated to an unprecedented degree, not to mention the pastoral councils, which since Vatican II have been added on all levels: that of the diocese, the deanery, and the parish.
>
> Dioceses in Germany are administered by approximately a hundred to five hundred employees, and I would say, without having seen the statistics, that the total number of ecclesiastical positions in the country approaches several thousand, all of them on full salaries which in all likelihood exceed by many times those of the Vatican.
>
> The bishop is severely hampered in his movements because he now is forced to avail himself of expert advice from all the proper organisations. Added to this are the permanent offices of the national conferences of bishops, which are supposed to free the individual bishop of much work. Alas, it is work proper to the individual bishop, responsibilities which have been withdrawn from him, a regrettable fact as far as the good of the Church is concerned.[21]

I think we also all know by now that the utter mismanagement of the clergy sexual abuse crisis was driven by a desire to save face and protect the Church's assets from lawsuits. There's a furphy that increased lay leadership would have exposed clergy sexual abuse in Australia a lot sooner. That's nonsense – abusive clergy had plenty of lay enablers in the Australian Church, well documented in Australian advocacy group Broken Rites' online databases.[22]

Cases of clergy sexual abuse in the English-speaking world have revealed any number of compromised lay people who helped with covering up and explaining away, either directly or indirectly. They were usually wealthy and influential, or employed by the Church, or in useful professions.[23] Predatory abusive clergy are also often highly charismatic individuals with male and female lay followers who will defend them to the death, even in the face of evidence showing that the priest or bishop was a repeat offender.[24]

What exposed the clergy sexual abuse crisis were determined lay people outside the Church, many of them secular journalists. They only began investigating because the victims had been ignored and treated badly by the Church authorities that they went to for justice. The sooner we acknowledge this – and stop trying to co-opt the clergy abuse crisis as a way of subverting or eliminating the episcopate and the ordained ministry completely – the better.[25]

I think it's fair to say that the Church in Australia has invested heavily in recent decades in avoiding bad publicity and maintaining good financial management. It seems to have developed a corporate heart at diocesan level, and suggestions that we make it even more corporate tend to alarm me.[26] Australian theologian Tracey Rowland describes this as the 'charismatic' versus the 'bureaucratic' model of Church authority.

> ... there is a tendency for bishops to behave ... like chief executive officers of modern corporations. They surround themselves with lawyers, accountants, and in some of the wealthier dioceses with professional 'spin doctors', alias public relations advisers. The lawyers encourage them to be risk-averse. ... The accountants tell them that they must conserve their capital and increase their capital fund ... The public relations agents tell them that they must 'market' the Church to the world as an agent of philanthropy and remain quiet about aspects of the Church's teaching likely to be unpopular with powerful interest groups.[27]

If I believed that an influx of mission statements, codes of conduct, and governance policies would make the average diocesan office more human, I'd embrace it. But I've worked in the public service, and I know that this stuff is mostly about covering one's nether regions in case of litigation.

Clergy sexual abuse in Australia

Which brings us to this painful area. Yes, most of our bishops failed hopelessly, and most of the obvious episcopal failures are also now dead. It's hard to talk about collateral damage, because there has already been so much damage of so many innocent people – both abuse victims who haven't been believed, and wrongly accused priests.

When Catholics try to tell me that the sexual abuse crisis is largely manufactured by enemies of the Church, I agree with them – but they think the enemies are outside, while I think the enemies are inside. I also usually direct them to a longstanding US-based website which has lots of horribly convincing global data.[28] In case you're wondering about terminology in sexual abuse cases: 'substantiated' allegations are those which have been investigated and the allegation is found credible or true, based on the evidence gathered. 'Unsubstantiated' allegations are those which have been investigated and the allegation was found not credible or false, again based upon the evidence. There's another category called 'Unable to be proven' where there has been an incomplete investigation because of a lack of information.

Within these categories is a whole spectrum of claims – from those where it's very likely the priest or bishop was guilty of everything he was accused of and more, right down to unjust speculations made by troubled fantasists. The same Catholics who tell me we are being persecuted by mysterious forces, rather than justly punished for our negligence, also tend to believe that most abuse allegations are malicious, made up for money, or fabricated by mentally unwell people. However, the 2004 US-based John Jay report on the scope of child sexual abuse by clergy found that out of 5,681 diocesan investigations of abuse allegations from 1950-2002, just 83 allegations (1.5%) were found to be false.[29]

The usual response of any bishop and diocese in Australia in the last five decades was to allow the accused priest – if he was still living – to simply retire or resign. Very few have gone to prison, been removed from the priesthood, or have sought laicisation. In fact, most accused priests in most developed countries had already gone to be judged by their creator by the time they were accused of sexual abuse.

We know that many clerical abusers in Australia got away with their crimes in this life. They were stood down, protected, allowed to die without trial, with no acknowledgement from their dioceses and religious superiors of what they had done. Their hundreds – possibly thousands – of victims have been left with no validation, no closure, and no justice from a Church that told them they were imagining things. So perhaps if God requires that a public atonement be made for this – and if someone accepts this injustice personally to make that public atonement – then I suppose that's the way it must be.[30]

We're now years on from the enormous wave of exposures of clergy sexual abuse in Australia in the late 1990s, and the case numbers appear to have diminished. It's also possibly affecting younger priests differently from older priests. Fr Harrison recalled:

> The scandal broke when I was still in high school – long before I even considered the priesthood. Naturally, I consumed the news 'from the pews,' as a member of the lay faithful, and I was frankly grateful that I hadn't been prey to the predators. (There were clergy abusers in my parish, but that was in my pre-school years.) I instinctively related to victims and survivors as peers: slightly older than me, but more or less the same generation. I never identified with the predator priests, not even when I joined the priestly ranks. I share the outrage and horror of older priests, but none of their self-reproach or shame.[31]

With this in mind, let's look at the state of the Catholic priesthood in Australia today. We'll focus mostly on diocesan clergy (priests ordained for a diocese) rather than religious clergy (those who are part of a religious order). Religious priests can be moved in and out of dioceses very easily, and their numbers fluctuate more than the diocesan clergy, so we'll talk more about them in the next chapter on religious life.

Diocesan priests in Australia today

What's it like to be a parish priest in Australia today? I asked Fr Stephen, who is working in a large suburban Australian parish, what his main challenges were.

> I must begin with my own personal faults, which in my case include time management, self-discipline, self-centredness, superficiality in prayer, laziness, the challenges of celibacy, etc. Church politics can get a bit disheartening at times – I generally ignore it as much as I can and focus more on the responsibilities I've been entrusted with. Adjusting to living in an increasingly secular/irreligious society, and the accompanying increase in hostility/incomprehension towards organised religion. The amount of administration/red-tape required on a parish level is significant for a largely volunteer-run organisation. Having to spend more time behind a desk than in face-to-face ministry. Fewer priests and the associated risks of burnout. The inevitable slowness of the Church's institutional framework to adjust to this new situation.[32]

It's a thorough summary, and one which is consistent with what other priests have told me (and may also have told you). There are challenges from the outside world, but just as many from the inside – from the local Church itself, especially its bureaucratic side. Fr Michael feels this very much.

> For me the toughest challenge comes from within the Church. It is the influence in the parishes and diocesan offices of people who do not truly love and believe in the Church. They may say they do, but they disagree with many Church teachings and think that attitude is compatible with faith.[33]

The numbers

As I demonstrated with data in Chapter 1, Australia doesn't have a priest shortage; we have a priest distribution problem. The immediate and most practical solution to this is for the ACBC to lead a national shakeup based on data from each diocese that would show how to redistribute Australia's priests more effectively. This will probably never happen, because the rules around **incardination** – the formal canonical relationship between the diocesan priest and his local bishop – are pretty rigid.[34]

According to the *Annuarium Statisticum Ecclesiae*, in 1970 there were 2,396 diocesan priests in Australia, and in at the end of 2021 (the last year for which I have data) there were 1,596. If you go by the *Official Directory of the Catholic Church in Australia*, there were 2,410 diocesan priests in 1970 and then just 1,742 in 2020-21. This is also a brief lesson in why we need consistent and probably centralised data collection about clergy numbers, as well as other things.

The *Annuarium* also tells me that since 1970, 596 diocesan priests have left the active ministry in Australia. I can't tell you how many of each ordination class every year eventually left, but I can tell you how many left in each calendar year – it's in the Appendices of this book. The peak year for what used to be called 'defections' was 1973 with 29, but since the year 2000, the number of priests leaving the active ministry has fallen to almost half of what it was before then. That's nothing compared to the number who have died in that time, which was 1,969. More are dying than are being ordained each year.

Thankfully the numbers of ordinations have also been reasonably steady over this period – there's never been a year when there were zero, although our lowest point was in 2004 with just 13 for the entire country (Figure 4). If the number of ordinations is now gradually increasing, and the number leaving the active ministry is decreasing, then these are both positive signs. We can't do much about the older priests dying, but if we have a smaller but stable and persevering group of younger clergy coming up in the ranks, then it's not all bad.

Figure 4. Priestly ordinations in Australia, 1970-2021, *Annuarium Statisticum Ecclesiae*

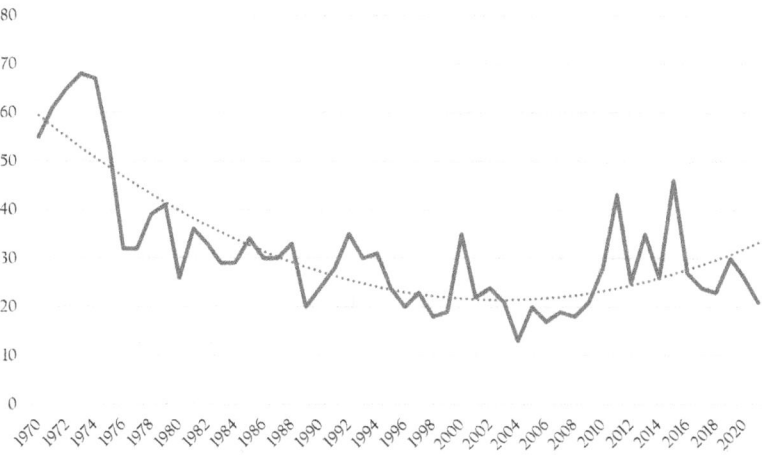

Ordinations to the diocesan priesthood in Australia per year, 1970-2021

Table 7. Diocesan seminaries in Australia

State	Seminary
Victoria	Corpus Christi College, Melbourne
NSW	Holy Spirit Seminary, Parramatta
NSW	Seminary of the Good Shepherd, Sydney
NSW	Vianney College, Wagga Wagga
Queensland	Holy Spirit Seminary, Brisbane
Western Australia	St Charles Seminary, Perth
NSW	Redemptoris Mater Seminary (Neocatechumenal Way)
Western Australia	Redemptoris Mater Seminary (Neocatechumenal Way)

Priests really come from two places: families (see Chapter 2) and seminaries. Both places are critical in the good formation of priests. There are currently eight seminaries in Australia (Table 7). Since 1990, the Church in Australia has formed 4,898 seminarians

(*Annuarium*), but only ordained 1,629 of them (*Official Directory*). That's around one-third – which just goes to show that many are called, but few are chosen.

My colleague Stephen Bullivant recently did an in-depth study with 13 priests in the archdiocese of Sydney – mostly aged between 30 and 34 and ordained in the last ten years.[35] Six were born and raised in Australia, and the rest overseas. Family formation in faith was hugely important for these future priests, as two of them shared:

> Brought up in a strong Catholic home. Mum and Dad both practiced the faith and we prayed every day at home. Almost all my entire large and very close-knit extended family practise their Catholic faith and therefore aunties and uncles and older cousins contributed to our formation in faith with our parents. Service to the local parish was strongly encouraged in our family (Priest 1).

> Growing up we prayed the Rosary every night, and all of us received the sacraments. We had grace before meals, and often we'd be pretty guarded about the things taught in schools. If (and when) the schools failed to teach the Faith, we'd get some kind of catechesis at home (Priest 2).[36]

But school and university were also vital. This is where these future priests formed strong networks with people like them – young, mostly middle class, normal, suburban Australians with highly committed Catholic families.[37] One of them said:

> That was very standard, that understanding that you're Catholic and committed, and that's normal because a lot of other people seem to do it and [their parents] have normal, stable jobs. They're not – they don't seem – very crazy. ... There was a significant number of people for who practice in the faith was normal, and so it was almost like the assumed position. So, when things undoubtedly get turbulent in the teenage years and you're working yourself out, you've got a strong group of friends for whom the faith is normal.[38]

Seminary formation by itself can't produce good priests if the foundations aren't strong. These young clergy also reflected on how their vocation was directly influenced by their own experience of priests as they were growing up. Another priest said:

> I sensed a de-clericalisation of priests in parishes where they were like 'Don't call me Father' or not wearing clerics. It was strange. Why would you try to hide this thing? We want you to be a priest because I can see from these other – a lot of these other priests, these Franciscans, or the [school chaplains], their visibility is part of the job, that people can see them and talk to them, and they make themselves available in that way. I didn't really understand why they wanted to diminish that aspect. That seemed to me very important.[39]

They identified the key drivers of their vocation as a love of Jesus in the Eucharist, a love of Adoration of the Blessed Sacrament, and good liturgy.

Sydney is one thing – this archdiocese has a strong formation program and lots of people and enthusiasm. But across Australia, the diocesan-level picture is different. According to the *Official Directory*, before 1998 every diocese in Australia had at least some young men in formation for the priesthood. But in 1999, four dioceses in Australia had no men in formation. In 2004 and 2005 we reached our lowest ebb when ten dioceses in Australia – over one-third of all our Western Catholic dioceses – had no men in formation (that was the year when we managed only 13 ordinations nationwide). But this has slowly reversed, and by 2021 we were back to just four dioceses with no one in formation. This is also a positive sign.

If you look in the Appendices, you'll see that two states have been consistently productive in terms of vocations – NSW and Western Australia. This is largely due to the presence of two seminaries created to form priests for the Neocatechumenal Way.[40] This is a vibrant international movement of re-evangelisation built around local parish communities and active lay re-catechesis by missionary priests.

The two Redemptoris Mater seminaries in Sydney and Perth train and ordain priests for this movement who are then available for parish work in the diocese, although they are primarily missionaries and can be moved around. Ordinations from these two seminaries have helped to significantly boost ordination and clergy numbers in both archdioceses.[41] Having said that, in early 2023 a record 17 men also entered the diocesan Seminary of the Good Shepherd in Sydney – a number not seen for around 40 years.[42]

The quality of our seminary formation is going to determine whether our future priests can go the distance, or not. In the US, in the wake of the clergy abuse crisis, seminary formation has been overhauled. More seminaries are now introducing a 'propaedeutic year' of pre-formation in which future seminarians learn how to fast from social media, how to pray the Liturgy of the Hours, and how to address other messier parts of their lives – like porn addiction – that will stand in the way of them being happy and fulfilled priests.[43]

Fatherhood is a key element of the Catholic priesthood, and it's suffered from the same crisis that secular fatherhood has in most Western countries in the last fifty years. Australian theologian Tracey Rowland has said that:

> fatherhood is an iceberg lying beneath contemporary debates in ecclesiology. That feminists want to replace the notion of God the Father with God the creator is further evidence that fatherhood is the pivotal issue around which these alternative understandings of the Church revolve, even if this is not always explicit in the debates. Bureaucratic committees can be gender neutral, but a father can only be a male.[44]

I've had interesting conversations over the past few years with Fr Thomas Berg of St Joseph's Seminary, New York and Fr Dominic Allain of the diocese of Southwark in the UK. Both have been involved in seminary formation and also the healing of people damaged by clergy sexual abuse. They both agreed that a real challenge of their work is forming candidates for the priesthood who haven't been fathered properly.

Young men should achieve a fuller maturity before ordination so that they can become effective spiritual fathers. In fact, Rowland has suggested that 'providing fathers for the fatherless could be construed as a high priority field hospital service.'[45] The best priests I know are like this. So are the best bishops. Many priests who have already been ordained, perhaps without this level of formation, may need to discover what it really means to be a spiritual father. Some of them – poorly fathered themselves – will take longer to get there. This is another reason why I welcome the rise of coherent and positive men's ministries in the Church today.

Bishops must be spiritual fathers to their clergy: to love them, be interested in them, and be available for them. But it's also their job to protect their flock from predators, starting with seminary formation. Anecdotally, the relationship between diocesan clergy and their bishops is a red-raw area in Australia today. Fr Robert, a priest working in an urban Australian diocese, said that:

> a vigorous if not heroic effort needs to be made to heal the profound distrust that presently exists between bishops and priests. The last thing needed in this matter is to implement yet another level of corporate inspired ... structure, which would only exasperate the already grave dissatisfaction and distrust on the part of priests. There must be a personal, face to face, individual building up of trust.[46]

But Fr Stephen, working on the other side of Australia, has had a different experience: 'I have a good relationship with my bishop. I get the chance for an extended conversation with him about once a year, but he has also been available at short notice when significant challenges have arisen. I also feel reasonably well-supported by the broader curia and church office.'[47] Fr Jason, in another part of

Australia, has also had a positive experience: 'I have been fortunate that my Archbishop, despite his challenges, is supportive and encouraging. Like anyone, it's important to have one's gifts (and zeal) at least recognised.'[48]

Mistrust of bishops by diocesan clergy has been documented in two major US studies of priestly life: the 2021 Survey of American Catholic Priests, and the 2022 National Study of Catholic Priests.[49] Both studies found that many younger diocesan clergy reported poor and mistrustful relationships with their local bishops. Some of this has come from mismanagement of clergy abuse cases where the pendulum has swung in the direction of assuming guilt until innocence was proven.

The only substantial recent survey of Australian priests has been the 2011 *Our Fathers* study by Chris McGillion and John O'Carroll, which surveyed 542 priests.[50] Most priests who took part in the *Our Fathers* study expressed liberal theological opinions, and more than half were aged over 60 years. (We found the same relationship between increased age and more liberal beliefs in our CIA2022 survey as well).

But even with this, it was possible to see a more conservative younger cohort of Australian priests emerging from their data. They were more optimistic about the future Church in Australia, less likely to see the Australian bishops as too conservative, more likely to want to be called 'Father', and more likely to support traditional Catholic core beliefs and teachings.[51] Both the major US studies I've referred to also identified an emerging cohort of younger and more conservative priests. So did a recent study of priests in Germany, which found that they also largely rejected the proposed 'synodal way' of liberalisation underway there currently.[52] The National Centre for Pastoral Research (NCPR) is at the time of writing conducting a national survey of Australian clergy, and the results will be forthcoming in 2025. It will be interesting to see what they find.

Overseas clergy

And of course, some of our parish clergy come from overseas. In Chapter 1 we looked at the increasing role of the Syro-Malabar community in supplying us with bi-ritual priests to help fill gaps, especially in regional areas. But we don't currently have much data on how many priests in Australia have come here from overseas as priests.

In 2016 the NCPR estimated that 41% of diocesan priests in Australia were born overseas, coming from 64 different countries. The top five countries of birth were India, Vietnam, the Philippines, Ireland (north and south), and Nigeria. However, around 16% of all of them grew up in Australia, and another 64% came to Australia already ordained. Just 20% came to Australia to be formed for the priesthood.[53] Following up on this, the NCPR – citing data from the Australian Catholic Migrant and Refugee Office – said that 727 overseas-born clergy arrived in Australia between March 2012 and September 2022.[54]

Some parishioners are grateful that they have a priest at all, even if his English isn't marvellous, but others find this very trying. One woman in her 30s (not a regular Mass-goer) complained in the CIA2022 comments section:

> I think one of the main changes that must occur is to change the rules regarding priests being allowed to marry. Originally the Catholic Church allowed this and there is a strong case to give priests this option to address a few issues we have at the moment. The main issues I speak of are 1) we are in desperate need of more priests in Australia and 2) we should be endeavouring to have more AUSTRALIAN priests and should not need to rely so much on foreign priests coming over to fill gaps. I really hope this change/reversion is considered as a high priority item.[55]

Why do priests from developing countries end up living permanently in Australia? It's not like their home countries don't need them. For example, Nigeria has a thriving and persecuted

Catholic population of around 30 million people,[56] of whom around 94% attend Mass on Sundays (28.2 million people),[57] but with only around 7,500 priests in 2022.[58] That's one priest per 3,760 practising Catholics – a far higher ratio than we currently struggle with in Australia.

It's hard to talk about this in the Church in Australia today. Liberals might decry this discussion as racist, and conservatives might decry this as a smear on the fidelity and orthodoxy of the Catholic developing world.[59] Having said that, I often find that those most angry about foreign-born clergy are liberal Catholics. This is because they are generally older and more set in their ways, and usually harder of hearing and less able to grapple with heavy accents. They usually also favour lay leadership of parishes, rather than having an overseas-born priest – and quite often they are the people who want to do the leading.

Katrina lives in a rural area in Victoria and has seen older liberal Catholics manipulating their overseas-born parish priest.

> ... the heterodox parish council is running rings around Fr X. He himself comes across as orthodox enough, but apologetic. His liturgical training is also sadly lacking, and the members of both the liturgical committee and parish council are taking upon themselves roles rightly reserved for the priest – particularly concerning the Blessed Sacrament, distribution of Holy Communion, modifications to various prayers to make them as inclusive as possible, and so on.[60]

Eloise, in another diocese, described the same thing happening in her parish with priests from a different ethnic group and members of a religious order.

> We have some beautiful priests who have arrived in our parish. Good. Smart. Holy [overseas born] priests from [a religious] order. They have been here a year and in Aus[tralia] for about 2. Our parish has been in something of a growth period for a few years. We have ... lots of solid

young(ish) people and families and some very faith filled older people.

ANYWAY, the old guard who have been very unhappy with all this... are flexing their muscles and safeguarding the priests into a corner. The priests have zero context for the Australian Church. They don't get why the younger set are literally flipping out over words like 'equal participation', 'life-giving liturgy', liturgy committees, and being asked to process in if they are the readers, and why the old guard are having nervous breakdowns over candles, Latin music and Eucharist processions and horror of horrors the unsafe practice of Communion on the tongue and UNSAFEST of all, kneeling to do so.[61]

And yet there are lots of charitable, practical, parish-based solutions to help a parish priest whose English needs polishing. Older parishioners with time on their hands can help Father to learn English by inviting him over for dinner and making conversation with him. You could practise his homily with him, help him to choose online pre-prepared homilies that are suitable, encourage him to read it out rather than preaching *extempore*, and get him to project the words of the homily on to the overhead screens during Mass. How's that for equal participation?

I personally don't care who's saying Mass or in what language, as long as he's properly ordained to do it. My argument against the constant importation of clergy is more like the one that decries the mass importation of Filipino nursing staff to work in Britain's National Health Service when those nurses are desperately needed in their own country's struggling hospitals.[62] We admit priests to Australia on religious visas, and sometimes that ends up being converted into permanent residency and eventually citizenship.[63] From one angle, it's positive: priests from developing countries are on a mission to the spiritually dying West. They will keep the Church alive here and hold off the incursion of irrelevant lay leadership.

At the other end of the spectrum, it's cynical. Some priests see better opportunities in affluent Western countries, and take them, preferably permanently. Some bishops also see ways of moving troublesome clergy offshore and making them someone else's problem. We are complicit in this: their presence here helps us to avoid the dramatic but unpopular restructuring and redistribution of local clergy, parishes and dioceses which the Church desperately needs. It also leaves us exposed to the possibility that a future hostile federal government could cancel all religious worker visas and neatly pull the rug out from under us. Something like this has recently happened in the US.[64]

We need to think seriously about whether we are depriving these countries of the clergy and religious they desperately need – especially in persecution – simply because we were too selfish for too long. Other dioceses in countries like France[65] and the US[66] are improving their home-grown vocation numbers by diligent prayer and hard work. Dioceses in Australia that strongly encourage Adoration for vocations, who are not ashamed of a male-only presence on the altar every Sunday, and who have sound formation programs, have no shortage of young men interested in the priesthood.

The bottom line is that if your diocese has an empty seminary, you already know who's responsible. That would be you. Too many of us didn't have enough children or didn't do enough Adoration for priestly vocations. We raised our (smaller) families with an unspoken belief that priests came from somewhere else – overseas, or other people's families. Not our sons.

As I write, the archdiocese of Melbourne is celebrating the appointment of two new auxiliary bishops: Father Thinh Nguyen (Vietnamese) and Father Rene Ramirez RCJ (Filipino). This is a reminder that the future of the Church in Australia is going to reflect far more diversity in culture than perhaps our Boomers are comfortable with. It's also a reminder that priests from these types of ethnic backgrounds will make up more of Australia's future episcopate.[67]

Permanent deacons

In June 1967 Pope St Paul VI opened the way for individual Western-rite dioceses and conferences of bishops to revive the permanent diaconate.[68] This is when men (married or single and celibate) discern a call to serve God as literally a 'servant, one who does as he is told' (*diakonos*). Permanent deacons are ordained and can perform baptisms, marriages and funeral services in the name of the Church. They can also read the Gospel at Mass and preach a homily. Most of Australia's permanent deacons are married.[69]

The 1967 mandate was designed to make it easier for mission territories to increase the numbers of ordained ministers to help support the local priests. Australia's first diocesan permanent deacons were ordained in the early 1980s for the Northern Territory, Western Australia, and Queensland, all of which have enormous territories and small numbers of people. By 1992, Western Australia's diocese of Bunbury – large and sparsely populated – had 12 permanent deacons, easily more than any other Australian diocese. It wasn't till around 2007 that the neighbouring archdioceses of Perth acquired a similar number of permanent deacons. By 2021 there were almost 200 permanent deacons in Australia.[70]

Permanent deacons have always been part of the Eastern Church's tradition, where they assist in specific liturgical roles and help distribute Holy Communion.[71] There have been small numbers of them in Australia for many years who assist with ministering to their communities. This is very noticeable within the Melkite community, which has had the largest number of permanent deacons of any Eastern Catholic community in Australia. The Military Ordinariate was another early adopter of the permanent deacon model (1994).[72] As a result, it now has the largest community of permanent deacons outside the regular diocesan structure in Australia, where they minister to Catholics in the armed forces spread across a wide range of places and situations.

I have seen permanent deacons at work at grassroots levels in different parishes. I can see how useful they can be in assisting a busy parish priest and relieving the burden of the work of baptisms, weddings and funerals, as well as visiting the sick for Holy Communion and leading services of Holy Communion in the absence of a priest. I was especially touched by the ministry of one permanent deacon in a large parish where the parish priest had committed suicide. The impact on the community was understandably appalling, but the deacon held things together in a way that only someone who really knew the parish and its people could do. This was an example of diaconal service at its very best.

There is no priest shortage in Australia. But because there is a priest distribution problem, permanent deacons are a traditional and suitable adjunct to the work of parish priests. They can't replace them, but they can certainly help them. It's a ministry that sits firmly within Catholic tradition, and it should be preferable to lay leadership of priestless parishes.

You will notice that I have not addressed the calls for women to be ordained to the priesthood or the diaconate in Australia. That's because neither is possible in the Church. It has never been possible and has never been carried out historically.

The New Testament 'deaconesses' had specific roles which assisted Christian women in very male-dominated cultures. This culture no longer exists in most Western countries – the Church in the West has literally outgrown its need for deaconesses. Intensive hands-on service in Catholic communities was instead taken up by consecrated women in active religious orders, and increasingly now by male and female lay people. The calls for female ordination also seem to mostly come from a small and privileged minority of older women in the Church in Australia, and they don't represent the views of most Mass-going Catholics here, especially younger people.[73]

Making things better

Every Christian is faced with the same challenge every day. You can surrender to the world, or you can fight back – and fighting back takes a lot of energy. Because of this, many of our clergy have preferred to become indistinguishable from everyone else. Priests, like laity, need to go back to being different. I know this is unpopular, especially when clerical reputations are at an all-time low, but it doesn't hurt to go out in public looking like a priest.

> An anecdote: I was walking down the street once with Fr X, and a colleague from [work] – some young bloke drove past and hollered out the window something about being a paedophile. Without missing a beat, my colleague turned to Fr X and said how wonderful it is to see people 'recognising his priesthood.'[74]

If the worst thing that happens is that someone's rude to you, then you're doing okay.

The parish priest is the human hub of the parish community – or at least, he should be. There's a good way and a bad way for a new priest to enter an established parish community, and the slow and steady way (rather than the new broom way) is usually the safest. The Code of Canon Law puts it this way:

> The pastor (*parochus*) is the proper pastor (*pastor*) of the parish entrusted to him, exercising the pastoral care of the community committed to him under the authority of the diocesan bishop in whose ministry of Christ he has been called to share, so that for that same community he carries out the functions of teaching, sanctifying, and governing, also with the cooperation of other presbyters or deacons and with the assistance of lay members of the Christian faithful, according to the norm of law. (Canon 519)

This entire section of the Code is quite beautiful: it lays out the priest's pastoral duties one by one. He must make sure we're being taught properly through the Word of God. He must foster works of the gospel in the parish. He must ensure that the Eucharist is our source and summit of life. He must get to know the families entrusted to his care. And he is to outsource work to lay people when he can, because keeping the parish going is also our job. No one in any parish – even a rural one – should have to go through what Katrina did.

> We had to face, my husband and I, burying our stillborn daughter. So we contacted the local parish priest, and it took us three days to track him down. He was at the golf club. He had nothing for us, just cheerfully told us he was a modern priest, so we shouldn't have been looking in the presbytery for him. I have no objection to him playing golf – good on him. I can't even hit the ball. But how about he has an answering machine or something? He certainly didn't offer counselling or prayers either. Maybe we should have asked. We weren't thinking very clearly though.[75]

How well do priests support one another? Fr Jason said that he's found good support for himself – but he's been willing to seek it out.

> Personally, I don't find any priests who go out of their way to show 'support', but I find support in connecting with priests who are, as I said, faithful and sincere. Support also comes from friends/families who are of a similar heart and mind. I would suggest that part of the calling to serve is to seek support that is needed (from peers and superiors) and not expect it to be handed to them.[76]

One change which I think would be beneficial – and which is becoming more likely as we face parish amalgamations – is for priests to live a common life together in the same house. I know from personal experience that living with other fallible people is the easiest way to become less selfish. We have a problem with 'bachelor priests' in Australia – growing more selfish and fussier as they age – which will not be solved by marriage. But it might be mitigated by having to share accommodation with their brother priests.

Many of them won't want to live together because they don't know or like each other very much. Some of them know each other too well (at least by reputation) and wouldn't feel comfortable sharing because of that. It's sad to think of diocesan priests not getting on with each other. It's an indictment of any diocese and shows neglect of this important dimension of priesthood. Infighting and playing favourites in the chancery office doesn't help. Sending out-of-favour priests to difficult postings or remote areas also doesn't help.

Then there are the priests living double lives, whether gay or straight. No one living this kind of life willingly gives it up, and they won't risk getting caught out by living in community. Living in community will expose the lazy – but also the alcoholics and porn addicts, who might then get the help they need. To me, these are all arguments in favour of diocesan priests living in common – but then again, I'm not a priest.

You can't reform parish structures properly without also working to restore trust between priests, and between priests and bishops. This is a great opportunity for healing if local bishops are prepared to be brave. And if you want parish reform, you will have to work on liturgical reform as well. I'm sure you can hear the weeping and gnashing of dentures from here. And it's true – most people absolutely hate change at the parish level, and especially change on this scale.[77]

Conclusion

We have a lot of work to do in the parochial-diocesan Church in Australia. Much of the heavy lifting must be done by our clergy – priests, bishops, and deacons. Thankfully we have plenty of them, if not always in the right places. The first thing that every Catholic in Australia must do is to pray for our clergy. Pray for new vocations, but don't forget to pray for the vocations we already have. Pray for them as if the future of the Church depended on them – because it does.

Our bishops must work much harder to rebuild years of broken trust with their priests, as well as with their lay people. There have been some fine personal examples of this in Australia – but sadly all too few of them. It will take years and a lot of apologising and a lot of humility, transparency, and consistency. There also needs to be more getting out of the office and among the people, and less hiding behind the Praetorian Guard of the chancery and the ACBC.

Our diocesan priests in Australia today aren't always the happiest bunch of men. The sexual abuse crisis has demoralised many of them. They've often been poorly formed, and sometimes their pastoral experiences have left them shattered. We read stories of priests struggling with pornography, addictions, theft, illicit affairs with men and women, and occasionally suicide. Some leave the active ministry after a long slow withdrawal from the very things that attracted them initially. Some become affluent 'bachelor priests' who do just enough and no more, staying safely in a not-too-demanding parish and enjoying their regular holidays. Some are often lonely and beset by doubts about their worthiness and the effectiveness of their ministry.

What else can the Church in Australia do to help its priests remember who they are, and who they were called to be? They need more time and encouragement to be priests – to be men who can summon God down from heaven and give him to other people. The engine and the fuel of this is prayer time. No priest should be so busy that he can't spend a lot of time in prayer, especially if he's doing things that lay people can do instead. Lay people: if you see your priest going under, step up and help.

Our priests are also demoralised because of the relentless secularisation of everything and everyone around them (including us). We need holy priests if we are to become holy ourselves, but we also need to help them to be holy. We can do that by taking the sacraments seriously and letting them soak through us and change us into what God wants us to be. A happy priest is one who can see that his ministry is making a difference – so be different.

---

[1] Ignatius of Antioch, *Letter to the Magnesians* 2, written around 110AD and available online at https://www.newadvent.org/fathers/0105.htm

[2] Norman, K. (2022, March 10). Why sacraments are important for your faith. *Crosswalk*, https://www.crosswalk.com/faith/spiritual-life/why-sacraments-are-important-for-your-faith.html

[3] Cardaronella, M. (2023, October 27). God's sacramental plan: why we need the sacraments and the Church. *Catechist*, https://www.catechist.com/gods-sacramental-plan-need-sacraments-church/

[4] Klein, J. (n.d.). A former Evangelical discovers why we need the sacraments. *Catholic Digest*, https://www.catholicdigest.com/faith/sacraments/a-former-evangelical-discovers-why-we-need-the-sacraments/

[5] The Pillar. (2021, January 22). What is a bishop's conference, anyway? *The Pillar*, https://www.pillarcatholic.com/p/what-is-a-bishops-conference-anyway

[6] Rowland, T. (2024). *Unconformed to the age: essays in Catholic ecclesiology*. Emmaus, 103.

[7] Tori, personal communication, 31 August 2024.

[8] Paul, personal communication, 29 May 2024.

[9] Catholic News Agency. (2008, May 14). Controversial retired Australian bishop reprimanded for his book. *Catholic News Agency*, https://www.catholicnewsagency.com/news/12635/controversial-retired-australian-bishop-reprimanded-for-his-book

[10] Australian Catholic Bishops Conference (ACBC) (2015). *Don't mess with marriage: a pastoral letter from the Catholic bishops of Australia to all Australians on the same-sex marriage debate*, https://www.sydneycatholic.org/pdf/DMM-booklet_web.pdf

[11] ACBC. (2022). *Created and loved: a guide for Catholic schools on identity and gender*. https://drive.google.com/file/d/1X11WeuMYfHeyMwVmMQMivzMZUnI6rOQQ/view

[12] You can read them here: https://www.catholic.au/s/article/Bishops-Statements.

[13] ACBC. (2023). *Australian Catholic Bishops Conference annual report 2023*, 58. https://s3.ap-southeast-2.amazonaws.com/acbcwebsite/Articles/Documents/ACBC/2024/ACBC%20Annual%20Report%202023%20FINAL.pdf

[14] Martyr, P. (2022, May 30). The bishops' Praetorian Guards. *The Catholic Weekly*, https://www.catholicweekly.com.au/philippa-martyr-the-bishops-praetorian-guards/

[15] Fr Vincent, personal communication, 31 August 2024.

[16] Fr Robert, personal communication, 11 June 2024.

[17] Martyr, P. (2023, August 18). How do Aussie Catholics rate their bishops' leadership? *The Catholic Weekly*, https://www.catholicweekly.com.au/philippa-martyr-how-do-aussie-catholics-rate-their-bishops-leadership/

[18] Pentin, E. (2021, May 3). Australian Catholics petition Vatican to remove their bishop over his stance on homosexuality. *National Catholic Register*, https://www.

ncregister.com/news/australian-catholics-petition-vatican-to-remove-their-bishop-over-his-stance-on-homosexuality

[19] Interestingly, St Gregory the Great took the same attitude to those with aspirations to church leadership in the opening of his *Pastoral rule*, written in the late 500s. You can read it online at *Documenta Catholica Omnia*, https://www.documentacatholicaomnia.eu/01p/0590-0604,_SS_Gregorius_I_Magnus,_Regulae_Pastoralis_Liber_[Schaff],_EN.pdf

[20] Martyr, P. (2023). We don't want bishops made in our own image, do we? *The Catholic Weekly*, https://www.catholicweekly.com.au/philippa-martyr-we-dont-want-bishops-made-in-our-own-image-do-we/

[21] Hans Urs von Balthasar (in conversation with Angelo Scola) (1986). *Test everything, hold fast to what is good*. Thanks to Dr Tom Gourlay for bringing this quote to my attention.

[22] Martyr, P. (2020, May 7). The lay role in covering up abuse. *The Catholic Weekly*, https://www.catholicweekly.com.au/the-lay-role-in-covering-up-abuse/

[23] Adolphe, J. (2020). Organisational culture and male-on-male sexual violence: a comparative study. In J. Adolphe and R. Rychlak, *Clerical sexual misconduct: an interdisciplinary analysis* (pp. 147-176). Cluny.

[24] Broken Rites. (2010, October 4). A recent cover-up: A church school failed to protect children from abuse. *Broken Rites*, https://brokenrites.org.au/drupal/node/129

[25] Since the initial wave of exposures, more clergy, religious, and lay people have become whistleblowers over abuse – see for example the US-based group Catholic Whistleblowers, https://www.catholicwhistleblowers.com/

[26] A good example of this is *The light from the Southern Cross: promoting co-responsible governance in the Catholic Church in Australia*, https://www.catholic.au/s/article/Church-Governance

[27] Rowland, *Unconformed to the age*, 100.

[28] This website is at https://www.bishop-accountability.org/. You will need a strong stomach.

[29] White, S. (2020, March 26). False allegations are rare – and real. *Ethics and Public Policy Center*, https://eppc.org/publication/false-allegations-are-rare-and-real/. See also John Jay College of Criminal Justice. (2004). *The nature and scope of sexual abuse of minors by Catholic priests and deacons in the United States 1950-2002*, 94, https://www.usccb.org/sites/default/files/issues-and-action/child-and-youth-protection/upload/The-Nature-and-Scope-of-Sexual-Abuse-of-Minors-by-Catholic-Priests-and-Deacons-in-the-United-States-1950-2002.pdf

[30] Martyr, P. (2023, January 12). Cardinal George Pell: Moments of true greatness. *The Catholic Weekly*, https://www.catholicweekly.com.au/cardinal-george-pell-moments-of-true-greatness/

[31] Fr Harrison, personal communication, 30 May 2024.

[32] Fr Stephen, personal communication, 30 August 2024.

[33] Fr Michael, personal communication, 5 August 2024.

[34] Catholic Church. (1983). *Code of Canon Law*, Book II, Part I, Title III, Chapter II, 265-272. https://www.vatican.va/archive/cod-iuris-canonici/eng/documents/cic_lib2-cann208-329_en.html#CHAPTER_II.

35 Bullivant, S. (2024). 'This is the greatest thing a man can do': vocational journeys of recently ordained Catholic priests in Australia. *Religions*, 15, 1-23. https://doi.org/10.3390/rel15080896

36 Bullivant, 'This is the greatest thing a man can do', 4.

37 Ibid., 6.

38 Ibid., 6.

39 Ibid., 10.

40 The movement's website is here: https://neocatechumenaleiter.org/en/. You can read about the purpose of the Australian seminaries here: https://www.vocations.catholic.org.au/s/seminaries I am not involved in this movement because I don't like guitars in church, but there is no doubt that they have impressive numbers.

41 Staff Writers. (2015, September 23). Redemptoris Mater: the seminary the little old ladies built. *The Catholic Weekly*, https://www.catholicweekly.com.au/redemptoris-mater-neocatechumenal-seminary-sydney/ ; O'Brien, J. (2024, August 22). Words of Deuteronomy fulfilled: Redemptoris Mater Seminary celebrates 30 years of the Lord letting us know the way forward. *The Record*, https://therecord.com.au/news/anniversaries/words-of-deuteronomy-fulfilled-redemptoris-mater-seminary-celebrates-30-years-of-the-lord-letting-us-know-the-way-forward

42 Cramsie, D. (2023, February 22). Super seventeen enter Sydney seminary. *The Catholic Weekly*, https://www.catholicweekly.com.au/super-seventeen-enter-sydney-seminary/ . See also Rodrigues, M. (2024, July 29). Seminary sees promising rise in future priests for regional Australia. *The Catholic Weekly*, https://www.catholicweekly.com.au/sydney-seminary-sees-regional-vocations-up/

43 Briscoe, P. (2023, September 5). New propaedeutic year offers spiritual detox to aspiring priests, *Our Sunday Visitor*, https://www.oursundayvisitor.com/new-propaedeutic-year-offers-spiritual-detox-to-aspiring-priests/; Meloy, D. (2024, April 14). First-year seminarians will unplug from technology starting in fall at Detroit seminary. *Catholic World Report*, https://www.catholicworldreport.com/2024/04/14/first-year-seminarians-will-unplug-from-technology-starting-in-fall-at-detroit-seminary/

44 Rowland, *Unconformed to the age*, 55.

45 Ibid., 55.

46 Fr Robert, personal communication, 11 June 2024.

47 Fr Stephen, personal communication, 30 August 2024.

48 Fr Jason, personal communication, 13 June 2024.

49 Vermurlen, B., Cranney, S., & Regnerus, M. (2021, October 28). *Introducing the 2021 Survey of American Catholic priests: overview and selected findings*. https://ssrn.com/abstract=3951931; Vaidyanathan, B., Jacobi, C., Kelly, C., White, S., & Perla, S. (2022). *Well-being, trust, and policy in a time of crisis: highlights from the National Study of Catholic Priests*. https://catholicproject.catholic.edu/wp-content/uploads/2022/10/Catholic-Project-Final.pdf

50 McGillion, G., & O'Carroll, J. (2011). *Our fathers: what Australian Catholic priests really think about their lives and their Church*. John Garratt.

51 McGillion & O'Carroll, *Our fathers*, 173-176.

[52] Coppen, L. (2024, May 21). Study: young German priests reject synodal way priorities. *The Pillar*, https://www.pillarcatholic.com/p/study-young-german-priests-reject

[53] My thanks to Dr Stephen Reid of the NCPR for providing me with this summary of the findings of this internal report, personal communication, 9 October 2024.

[54] NCPR. (2024). *A profile of Catholic clergy in Australia.* https://ncpr.catholic.org.au/a-profile-of-catholic-clergy-in-australia/

[55] Martyr, P., & Bullivant, S. (2024). *The Catholics in Australia Survey 8 – Irregulars and Nevers*, 33. https://papers.ssrn.com/sol3/papers.cfm?abstract_id=4912660

[56] There are multiple sources for this information online, most of them contradicting each other. For example, this source has no date, https://www.catholicsandcultures.org/nigeria, while this source says it's 30 million, Mares, C. (2023, February 14). Nigeria's newest cardinal shares secret behind the highest Mass attendance in the world. *Catholic News Agency*, https://www.catholicnewsagency.com/news/253640/nigeria-s-newest-cardinal-shares-secret-behind-the-highest-mass-attendance-in-the-world

[57] Mares, Nigeria's newest cardinal, has figures.

[58] Catholic Hierarchy.org – I counted them by diocese for 2022.

[59] Martyr, P. (2019, November 3). Righting the clergy imbalance. *The Catholic Weekly*, https://catholicweekly.com.au/philippa-martyr-righting-the-clergy-imbalance/

[60] Katrina, personal communication, 20 June 2024.

[61] Eloise, personal communication, 30 May 2024.

[62] Buchan, J. (2007). International recruitment of nurses: policy and practice in the United Kingdom. *Health Services Research*, 32, 1321–1335. https://www.ncbi.nlm.nih.gov/pmc/articles/PMC1955378/

[63] Agile Legal (2023, May 17). *Visa options for sponsoring a minister of religion or religious assistant to work in Australia.* https://www.agilelegal.com.au/visa-options-for-sponsoring-a-minister-of-religion-or-religious-assistant-to-work-in-australia; Rodrigues, M. (2024, April 18). I come from a land down Umbers. *The Catholic Weekly*, https://www.catholicweekly.com.au/i-come-from-a-land-down-umbers/ It was easier for Bishop Umbers because he came to Australia from New Zealand as a young man to attend university, and the rest was history.

[64] The Pillar (2024, August 15). NJ diocese and priests sue State Department over visa policy change. *The Pillar*, https://www.pillarcatholic.com/p/nj-diocese-and-priests-sue-state

[65] Silva, W. (2024, June 22). The Catholic Church in France will have 105 new priests in 2024. *Catholic World Report*, https://www.catholicworldreport.com/2024/06/22/the-catholic-church-in-france-will-have-105-new-priests-in-2024/

[66] *Catholic Herald*. (2024, April 17). Half of new priests ordained in US this year will be 31 years old or younger. *Catholic Herald*, https://catholicherald.co.uk/half-of-new-priests-ordained-in-us-this-year-will-be-31-years-old-or-younger; Rytel-Andrianik, P., & Zielenkiewicz, T. (2024, March 19). US Diocese of Columbus doubles number of seminarians in two years. *Vatican News*, https://www.vaticannews.va/en/church/news/2024-03/columbus-ohio-bishop-fernandes-doubles-vocations-two-years.html

[67] *Melbourne Catholic*. (2024, November 8). Two new auxiliary bishops appointed for Melbourne. *Melbourne Catholic*, https://melbournecatholic.org/news/two-new-auxiliary-bishops-appointed-for-melbourne

⁶⁸ Paul VI, Pope. (1967, June 18). *Sacrum diaconatus ordinem*, https://www.vatican.va/content/paul-vi/en/motu_proprio/documents/hf_p-vi_motu-proprio_19670618_sacrum-diaconatus.html

⁶⁹ Australian Catholic Diocesan Vocations Directors Conference. (2023). *The permanent diaconate*, https://www.vocations.catholic.org.au/s/news/resources-vocations-MCDIXQDUDEXFDRHL653MHTSNI3XU

⁷⁰ *Official directory of the Catholic Church in Australia*, various years. See Appendices.

⁷¹ Klesko, R. (2024, August 3). Deacons are emissaries of Jesus Christ. *National Catholic Register*, https://www.ncregister.com/blog/klesko-deacons-emissaries

⁷² *Official directory of the Catholic Church in Australia*, various years. See Appendices.

⁷³ Martyr, P. (2020, April 21). Women deacons misses the point. *The Catholic Weekly*, https://catholicweekly.com.au/women-deacons-misses-the-point/; Martyr, P. (2024, May 20). The reasons why we don't need women deacons. *The Catholic Weekly*, https://catholicweekly.com.au/philippa-martyr-the-reasons-why-we-dont-need-women-deacons/; Martyr, P. (2024, May 23). Pope Francis made it clear the church can't ordain women as deacons. *The Catholic Weekly*, https://catholicweekly.com.au/pope-francis-made-it-clear-the-church-cant-ordain-women-as-deacons-heres-why-some-people-will-always-disagree/. For the attitudes of younger Australian Mass-going Catholics to women's ordination, see Martyr, P., & Bullivant, S. (2024). *The Catholics in Australia Survey 3 – Believing*, https://papers.ssrn.com/sol3/papers.cfm?abstract_id=4723637

⁷⁴ Anonymous, personal communication, 22 November 2024.

⁷⁵ Katrina, personal communication, 20 June 2024.

⁷⁶ Fr Jason, personal communication, 13 June 2024.

⁷⁷ Martyr, P. (2022, September 8). Neither Fr Relaxo nor Fr Apocalypto. *The Catholic Weekly*, https://catholicweekly.com.au/dr-philippa-martyr-neither-fr-relaxo-nor-fr-apocalypto/

Chapter 5

Religious life and new apostolates in Australia

In this chapter, I'm going to look at religious life in Australia, and at new movements and ministries which I think may become more important to us in the future. The reason I've combined the two is that if I just wrote about the consecrated religious men and women in Australia, I would have a very short chapter. Some religious communities in Australia now have more and younger vocations, although not anything like the numbers that they used to. People – including some religious superiors – can get excited and talk about 'plenty of new vocations', but that usually just means 'more than one', and not all of those will persevere.

Religious life, for those of you who aren't sure, is the way of life lived by people called to be monks, nuns, brothers, or priests in religious communities, all living the **evangelical counsels** of poverty, chastity, and obedience under a rule of life. Most of Australia's religious orders are **active** – that is, they work in areas like education, social services, and health. Only a small number are **contemplative** – that is, their chief task is prayer for the Church and the world, and they often live in some form of **enclosed** community to minimise distractions from this.

Religious communities aren't little clubs for Catholics who want three square meals a day and lots of time for prayer. People in religious life also aren't just pious folks who dress oddly and do good works. If those two things defined religious life, a lot of lay Catholics would qualify, me included. I've heard many devout Catholic married women say, quite seriously, that if their husband died and their children were grown up, they'd enter religious life.

Having seen religious life up close, that sounds to me like a man approaching retirement who says he'd like to join the SAS now because he always loved playing soldiers as a kid.

Religious life is a powerful force for good in the Church when communities are founded through a carefully discerned, formal process built around a specific **charism**. The charism is the core spiritual gift that the religious community brings to the Church – for example, care for the poor, education of young girls at risk, or perpetual Adoration. It should be ordered towards helping the Church to flourish and carry out its mission. No religious community exists for its own sake, and they shouldn't try to see themselves as independent of or separate from the Church's authority or mission.

Making vows in a religious community **consecrates** a person to God in a unique and potent way, recognised by canon law and the spiritual tradition of the Church. They are 'set apart' for God's use in the Church.[1] But they don't undergo an **ontological change** – a change in the core of our being; a permanent change that can't be undone – as we all undergo when we are baptised, confirmed, or ordained. Religious consecration isn't a sacrament. But it doesn't need to be, because it's a public commitment to live your entire life as a sign of the future Kingdom of God – the future state where we will no longer need the sacraments.[2]

You could say that religious are like the lungs of the Church. Their consecrated lives breathe in all the daily awfulness and breathe out the purified breath of God. They're also rather like God's earthworms: they work often in silence, often hidden, and they break down the bad and turn it into good. You almost never see them, but you can see the results in the garden. Wise bishops know this, which is why they foster religious communities in their dioceses (spiritually it's the equivalent of buying a worm farm).[3]

The rise and fall of different religious orders is a normal part of the Church's history. Active religious orders are founded for a particular social need, and when that need is met – perhaps by a growing welfare state or by Catholic agencies run by lay people – then their work is done. By contrast, contemplative life never goes out of style: the Church will always need it.

Religious life is also very tough on the body and the soul because it's meant to be. You give up the exercise of your own will on a daily basis. Your day is extremely full, and it's all on someone else's schedule. This is hard work, and it is only transformative and healing and renewing in people who are very open to receiving and cooperating with God's graces. This is why only around a third of the applicants to a religious order will end up staying and making perpetual vows.

I spoke to the Australian community of the Dominican Sisters of St Cecilia about some of the challenges they face in forming young women for religious life today. In their response they focused on one particular element for obvious reasons.

> As a religious community, we have made a conscious and deliberate choice to pay close attention to how we use media and technology. Religious life is counter cultural. Religious are signposts of the life to come where God will be all in all. Thus, we use technology when necessary for our work and we limit its use outside of the essential. We do not have our own mobile phones, and we do not use social media. We do not surf the internet for recreational purposes. We write postal letters to our families rather than messaging or emailing. ...
>
> We are acutely aware of the effects that technology can have on the individual and on family dynamics, producing a false sense of self and relationships. Technology produces noise. This detachment from the world, from family, friends, and technology is often difficult, but bears much fruit in opening up a space where the Lord can speak, and we can listen.[4]

Religious life is in strange shape in Australia today. It's like we have two types of religious orders. One is a long-established congregation, elderly, often living outside of their original community or buildings, wearing lay dress, and not accepting new vocations. The other type is usually newer, younger, living in community life, wearing a habit, and accepting new vocations. Each group has its own problems and own joys, but it's fairly obvious which group is likely to be still around in 2050. It's also clear that these two groups don't always rub along together well. Sr Yvette, who heads a younger religious community in Australia, told me:

> I think there is something in the spiritual and Church environment of Australia which is hostile to new communities flourishing. A large part of the problem is Church politics. In Australia, many older religious congregations no longer wear the habit, and take a hostile view of communities that choose to wear it ... I see that the habit brings a witness, but I'm not opposed to people who don't wear it. They can be a witness to religious life just as we are, because it's the way we live it, not just what we wear. ... There are Sisters who wear their community's pin on their shirt who witness to Christ and really love God and love religious life and love being Sisters, and that's awesome.[5]

The decline of religious life in the Church both internationally and here in Australia since Vatican II has been well mapped.[6] The impetus to live according to the evangelical counsels of poverty, chastity, and obedience hasn't disappeared from the Church in Australia or anywhere else, but it might be taking new forms here. The Church renews itself and moves with the times far more than most people realise. With the decline in consecrated religious life, it's possible to see new movements (including some new forms of religious or quasi-religious life) beginning to take shape in Australia. I'm not sure that these will ever completely replace traditional religious life here – or anywhere – but it's worth thinking about.

The numbers

Thankfully, religious life in Australia is well documented, so that makes my job a lot easier. The first post-Vatican II study of religious life here was the *National Statistical Survey of Religious Personnel, Australia 1976*, which was commissioned and carried out by the Conferences of Major Superiors of Australia.[7] It's a dense and detailed report with very little commentary on the data – but what there is, is quite telling.

The report speculated that one of the reasons so many women had left religious life after the Council was because it had been made easier for them to do so: 'Many who had found it imperative to remain in religious life, now felt free to depart ... whereas earlier a number of constraints may have been operative.'[8] Certainly there was a social explosion of new job opportunities for women after World War II, so that now you could become a teacher or a nurse without also becoming a nun. It also gradually became possible for women to support themselves financially without getting married.

In 2009, Bob Dixon and the Pastoral Projects Office (as it was then) led a project commissioned by the National Council of Catholic Religious Australia to survey all Catholic religious institutes and societies of apostolic life in Australia. An impressive 161 societies and congregations took part. The study found that around a quarter of Australia's religious were born overseas, and about a third of these had come to Australia as a member of their congregation. Some very small countries were punching well above their weight in terms of religious vocations, including Papua New Guinea and Samoa.[9]

But otherwise, it's a grim picture: 30 congregations of women religious involved in the study reported that they had fewer than ten sisters left in Australia. The median age of all religious in Australia was 73 years. The two largest congregations in Australia were the Josephites or 'Brown Joeys', founded by St Mary Mackillop (794 members), and the Christian Brothers (416 members). From

1997-2008, 401 people made their first profession in religious life in Australia – their first commitment to vows, usually temporary, with perpetual profession following later. But in the same period, 483 people left religious life.[10]

Having seen the 2009 report, Catholic Vocations Ministry Australia then invited the same team back again to do a more in-depth study of religious life in Australia in 2014.[11] I've created a combined table from these two studies which shows the decline in religious community numbers over time. The 2009 study had predicted that by 2020, there would be as few as 6,000 religious in total in Australia – but it looks like we got there sooner. It's also interesting to note that in 1966 there were more nuns in Australia than there are now Mass-going Catholics in most Australian dioceses.

Table 8. Australian religious personnel, 1901-2016 [12]

	1901	1926	1951	1966	1976	2009	2016
Sisters	3,622	8,141	11,245	14,622	12,619	5,927	4,394
Brothers	388	837	1,532	2,163	2,089	884	680
Clerical religious	195	432	1,087	2,628	2,321	1,611	1,003
Total	**4,205**	**9,410**	**13,864**	**19,413**	**17,029**	**8,422**	**6,007**

This time around, 93 religious superiors and leaders took part in the study, representing around two-thirds of all Australia's religious men and women. Most of the religious communities surveyed said that they had very few or no applicants in the various stages of formation in religious life: **postulants** (a period of six months to a year), **novices** (after postulancy, a period of one to two years), and those in **temporary vows** (after novitiate, usually three years).

The communities with new vocations had attracted them through hard work and innovative approaches. They had invested resources into this, and usually had a director or team in charge of vocations. They were offering short-term live-in experiences for those discerning religious life in their community, they were using social media, and they were making themselves visible and available in person to young people through schools, chaplaincies, and retreats.[13]

But there was still a retention problem. Those sampled reported that a total of 439 people had joined a religious institute since 2000, but 185 of these (42%) had left by 2015. A community needs a proper formation program that supports new members spiritually and intellectually. It's also important that no one is pressured to stay or leave, and the communities needed to find new ways to support and accompany those who decided to leave or who were asked to leave.

Some communities handle exits from religious life better than others: the Dominican Sisters of St Cecilia in Sydney responded to my question about this.

> Women do leave the community, especially in the eight years of formation prior to perpetual profession. This is a sign of a healthy community. When this happens, she is supported in a way that is unique to her situation. She is given what she needs to return to her family and to support herself as she begins her new life outside the convent.[14]

Sadly, I know several women in Australia who left religious life in different communities after the year 2000 whose transition was mismanaged to the point of abuse. Some of this flowed from abuses already existing within their religious community, which is why they left in the first place.

The study also looked at admission checks for candidates (Table 9). The low level of what I would consider thorough checks of candidates for female communities is worth noting. A religious superior or community can always decide about admissions on a case-by-case basis once they have all the information – but it's really helpful to have all the information first.

Table 9. Use of admissions checks by religious communities in Australia, 2014[15]

Type of check	% Female	% Male	% Average
Medical assessment	91	96	93
Referee check	83	86	84
Psychological testing	68	89	76
Police check	47	79	59
Behavioural assessment	47	64	53

This 2014 study also surveyed 55 new members of religious communities and held focus groups with some of them. Most were born in Australia, but most also had at least one parent born outside Australia. Almost three-quarters were born after 1970, and most were cradle Catholics. Some of their comments are fascinating. One male in perpetual vows said that what attracted him to his community was:

> the charism and life of the founder and other saints of the institute, as well as the way it was being lived out by the current members. [I was attracted to] the great balance between prayer and ministry in the institute, the members' love for the Church, for prayer and their wearing of the habit. The fact that they had Australian vocations.[16]

A female in perpetual vows said, 'The sisters wore a habit, lived in a convent with each other. They take their religious life seriously. They are not out to get vocations but help girls know and do God's will, with regards to their vocation.'[17]

But being attracted and staying are two different things. One female postulant said that what she found hard was, 'Giving over my control on my living arrangement and the possibility of being "judged" negatively by other members.'[18] One male religious who took part in a focus group reflected on, 'The fact that the existing members were older meant you knew that in the future the order would shrink and you would be required to look after them. That is daunting.'[19]

The 2014 study cleared up two common misconceptions. The first is that only traditional communities are getting new vocations in Australia: the authors said that they surveyed a wide range of communities, many of whom were not traditionalist at all, and yet they had new vocations. The other misconception is that religious life is something that only appeals to people born overseas – that it's part of a more conservative Catholic outlook that no longer thrives among the locals. In fact, of those still choosing religious life, plenty are Australian born.[20]

Another predictable but less welcome change has also come to religious communities which accepted a higher number of younger vocations from different parts of the world, often with different values from Anglo-Celtic Australia. Younger Catholics, including religious, are also often more traditionally minded, and often prefer wearing the habit and engaging in traditional devotions like the rosary and Adoration. It's been very challenging for older superiors and religious to yield control to these younger people, especially when their attitude in the past might have been more patronising than they realised.[21]

Religious priests

Religious clergy – the priests – are the survivors in this scenario. That's because they are an important part of the parochial-diocesan Church in Australia. Their presence in a diocese shares the pastoral load and provides some relief for the diocesan clergy. In some dioceses, like Darwin for example, they make all the difference: in 2021 there were just three diocesan priests, but 18 religious priests to minister to the 4,000 Mass-going Catholics in this large diocese – that's 86% of the Darwin clerical workforce.[22] The second highest rate was in Broken Bay, where 60% of its priests came from religious orders and communities. On average across Australia's dioceses, it's around 30% religious priests, but some – like Port Pirie – didn't have any religious clergy in 2021.

It's hard to keep track of religious clergy when you're trying to map out Australia's priests, because they're a lot more mobile than diocesan clergy. In the days when clergy and religious sexual abuse was much more common, offenders in religious communities could be easily moved across state and national borders without explanation, which was a key enabler of ongoing abuse. Today, a religious superior can still tell a priest in his community that he's being sent somewhere else tomorrow. (Ideally the superior should also let the local bishop know before he does this, especially if this priest has been given a parish).

Our eparchies in Australia also have the tradition of religious orders and religious priests. The Maronite community internationally has around 14 religious orders for men and women.[23] In Australia the Antonine Maronite Order runs the St Charbel Monastery in Melbourne,[24] while the Lebanese Maronite Order is active in Sydney.[25] The Maronite Lebanese Missionaries (Kreimists)[26] are also active in NSW. The Syro-Malabar community has a flourishing group of almost 50 religious communities worldwide,[27] and there are Syro-Malabar priests who are members of their Vincentian community active in the archdiocese of Perth, where they do parish work and hospital chaplaincy.[28]

Ministerial Public Juridic Persons

Obviously with the huge decline and increasing age of Australia's religious, those congregations that own a lot of property and businesses – such as hospitals, schools, and nursing homes – have to decide what to do with it all. The most common form of governance for these communities is now the **Ministerial Public Juridic Person** (MPJP). Canon law permits the establishment of entities called 'Public Juridic Persons' to carry out specific functions. It's a way of ensuring that the property and funds that the congregation owns will continue to be used for the purposes for which they were set up.

'Ministerial' PJPs are the same as other kinds of PJP under

canon law, but they are called 'ministerial' to distinguish them from PJPs that are parishes or dioceses.[29] An MPJP usually comes with a group form of stewardship, like a board or a college, usually made up of lay people. If you were wondering what happened to many of those old religious communities in Australia, have a look at this table and you can see what they're doing now. I will say more about these organisations in the chapter on the business arm of the Church.

Table 10. MPJPs operating in Australia and their original communities[30]

Original community	Current MPJP
Little Company of Mary, Province of the Holy Spirit	**Calvary Ministries**
Sisters of Charity Sisters of St Joseph of the Sacred Heart, NSW Province St John of God Brothers St John of God Sisters Little Company of Mary Sisters of Mercy, Singleton Brigidine Sisters, NSW Province Institute of the Sisters of Mercy Australia and Papua New Guinea Little Company of Mary – Region of the Southern Cross Trustees of Sisters of Mercy North Sydney Sisters of Perpetual Adoration	**Catholic Healthcare**
Congregation of the Dominican Sisters of North Adelaide Holy Cross Congregation of Dominican Sisters, Adelaide Congregation of the Dominican Sisters of Eastern Australia and the Solomon Islands	**Dominican Education Australia**

Christian Brothers	**Edmund Rice Education Australia**
Congregation of the Sisters of the Good Samaritan	**Good Samaritan Education**
Brigidine Congregation, New South Wales Province Brigidine Congregation, Victorian Province Presentation Congregation of Victoria	**Kildare Ministries**
Sisters of Charity	**Mary Aikenhead Ministries**
Institute of the Blessed Virgin Mary (Loreto)	**Loreto Ministries**
Sisters of Mercy	**MercyCare**
Institute of Sisters of Mercy of Australia and Papua New Guinea (15 Mercy congregations)	**Mercy Ministry Companions**
Sisters of Mercy Rockhampton Sisters of Mercy Townsville Sisters of Mercy Brisbane Presentation Sisters of Queensland Institute of the Missionary Franciscan Sisters of the Immaculate Conception Sisters of Mercy Parramatta Sisters of Mercy North Sydney Carmelite Province of Our Lady Help of Christians, Australia and Timor Leste	**Mercy Partners**
Sisters of St John of God Hospitaller Order of St John of God	**St John of God Australia Limited**
ANZ Province of the Society of the Sacred Heart of Jesus	**Sophia Education Ministries**

Everything old is new again

The social and cultural impact of the loss of religious life across Catholic Australia over fifty years has been considerable. While most of the Boomers grew up used to seeing nuns and brothers teaching at their schools, the current generation of Catholics may never encounter a religious at all. Traditional religious habits have become Halloween costumes. The abuse of children in Catholic institutions in Australia wasn't just carried out by priests; religious brothers and sisters of the era were also implicated, which also doesn't help the public perception of religious life today.

This public loss of face has weakened what should have been a powerful force for good. This came about through some factors that the communities couldn't control, like major social changes. But they also made plenty of mistakes as well. Some women's communities, gradually edged out of their teaching roles by lay people, became instead hotbeds of spiritualised anticlerical feminism and eventually neo-paganism.[31] Men's communities concealed the sexual abuse of adults and children.

This is why many good Catholic families today are not terribly enthusiastic when their son or daughter discerns a religious vocation. It's all right for other families, but it can be a bit of a concern or even an embarrassment in your own. There's lots of reasons for this: people have smaller families and are less willing to lose a possible source of grandchildren. Sometimes they're scared that our religious orders are corrupted and no longer living in a way that's faithful to their original charism, and their child will be at risk of spiritual or physical abuse.

The Dominican Sisters of St Cecilia in Australia discussed this openly with me.

> Another barrier that young women sometimes encounter is misunderstanding from their family. For a variety of reasons, there are misconceptions about this way of life. Some families think their daughter is joining a cult. Some

families cannot understand how she could be happy living a life of poverty, chastity, and obedience. Some can't fathom their daughter living on the other side of the world.[32]

Formation of religious locally is also challenging. Sr Yvette found that overseas resources were better for her needs than local.

> In America there are two associations for religious communities, and one of them – the [Council of Major Superiors of Women Religious] – is a great support. It has very good resources on religious life, formation for novice mistresses, workshops for superiors, formators – and all these [are] supporting religious life that is faithful to the Church's vision for religious. They have amazing courses on Church documents, canon law and papal homilies.
>
> I haven't found Catholic Religious Australia to be a good source of formation for religious life. This is a tough challenge for new communities like ours.[33]

One of the ways in which we could renew the Church in Australia is to welcome religious life back to our dioceses, parishes and families. The Church is full of new religious movements, most of them flourishing overseas in both English-speaking and other countries.

Wise bishops welcome these communities and keep an eye on them, but otherwise let them work out their mission. Bishops in Australia should also inform themselves better about religious life and its governance. This has been an ongoing problem in the Church's history anyway, and in an age when religious are few and far between, it's only gotten worse. Sr Yvette has found that:

> ... bishops don't know much about religious life. You have to explain things to them. St John Paul II realised this and he invited bishops and cardinals and religious together so that they – bishops and cardinals – could understand religious life. The document *Vita Consecrata* came out of that.[34]

I'll review below a sample of 'old' religious communities that are 'new' again in Australia, as well as some genuinely new ones. (If I've left yours out, it's not that I don't care about you; I'm sure you're doing a great job).

Benedictines

The oldest Western religious family is the Benedictine community – individual congregations living according to variations on the rule of St Benedict of Nursia (480-547AD). There are already men's Benedictine communities in Australia at New Norcia, WA[35] and Tarrawarra, NSW (Trappists),[36] and there is a women's community at Jamberoo.[37]

From 2007 a thriving traditional French Benedictine community at Abbaye St Joseph de Clairval regularly loaned out one of its English-speaking priests, Dom Pius Mary Noonan OSB, to travel to Australia and lead spiritual retreats. In 2017, Archbishop Julian Porteous invited Dom Pius and his community to make a foundation in the archdiocese of Hobart. Notre Dame Priory has been growing as a men's community in the Benedictine tradition ever since, attracting young Australian vocations.[38]

Carmelites

The Carmelites are another ancient religious community, and there are several thriving Carmelite women's communities in Australia, notably at Lismore, NSW and Launceston, Tasmania. There are also several men's communities active in Australia.[39] In 2019, Bishop Columba Macbeth-Green (himself also a religious, of the Order of St Paul the First Hermit) invited Carmelites from a community in Lincoln, Nebraska, to set up a foundation in his diocese of Wilcannia-Forbes. Two Australian-born sisters already in the Lincoln community and two others made the foundation at Mathoura, NSW, which at the time of writing was also receiving new local vocations.[40]

Religious Sisters of Mercy

The Sisters of Mercy, founded by Venerable Catherine McAuley in Ireland in 1831, have always been very active in Australia. Today the congregation's numbers have fallen dramatically, and many communities have allied their work with MPJPs. In the United States, however, another branch of the same religious family was formed in 1971 as the Religious Sisters of Mercy of Alma, Michigan. They live religious life in a way that's closer to the pre-conciliar life of the Sisters of Mercy, including wearing a habit with a veil, and living in common.[41] They now have a convent, St Joseph Home of Mercy, in Sydney.[42]

Dominican Sisters of St Cecilia

The Dominican Sisters of St Cecilia in Nashville, Tennessee, have been one of the more astonishing English-speaking religious success stories of the post-conciliar era. This is partly because they had a far-sighted superior during Vatican II who urged them to authentic renewal grounded in stability and continuity.[43] The community has grown by 64% since 2000, with around 300 sisters at present with a median age of 36, and 58% of the entire community aged under 40. They have an average of 18 new postulants a year, and an average novitiate size of around 50 sisters.[44]

The late Cardinal George Pell and then then-auxiliary bishop of Sydney, Anthony Fisher OP (another Dominican religious), invited the sisters to Sydney to help prepare for World Youth Day in 2008, and they've remained in Australia ever since. In Sydney the Dominicans of St Cecilia teach at two schools and are involved in chaplaincy work at the University of Sydney, the Centre for Evangelisation, and the Seminary of the Good Shepherd. They're also now working in Melbourne at a primary school and the archdiocesan university chaplaincy.[45]

Sisters of the Immaculata

Bishops can also oversee the formation of entirely new religious communities in their dioceses. In Hobart again, Archbishop

Porteous oversaw the formation of the Sisters of the Immaculata in 2013, a community whose charism was spiritual renewal through Adoration and faith formation, particularly in parishes and with young people. From 2021 the community moved to the Australian mainland.[46]

Missionaries of God's Love

In 1986, Ken Barker and a group of young men, all members of the Disciples of Jesus Covenant Community (see below), were discerning priesthood but wanted to remain part of their covenant community. They shared a common life and engaged in contemplative prayer and active ministry for the poor and marginalised. The community was eventually established in Canberra as the Missionaries of God's Love. A women's consecrated religious community was formed shortly afterwards.[47]

Other ways of witnessing

In Australia today, there are many options for Catholics who are looking to deepen and formalise their relationship with God, perhaps beyond the exclusively lay state. Ethan, a father of four, said that:

> I am constantly impressed by the various new ecclesial movements: the Neocatechumenal way, Communion and Liberation ... even Opus Dei (in specific instances, such as family activities like camps etc), even the various charismatic groups. The strong intentionality that characterises these groups is praiseworthy, and I have seen many instances of parents raise children in these contexts who actually come out with the faith intact, and meaningful for their children personally. This, of course, is not universal – but it does seem to me the best thing out.[48]

I'm going to outline some of them below. I don't belong to any of these organisations, and I have no vested interests in any of them. If I didn't mention your organisation, it's because I simply don't have space, and not because I don't think you're doing a wonderful job.

Religious associates, tertiaries and oblates

The oldest form of alliance with religious life for lay people has always been joining an existing community as a **tertiary** or **oblate**. Many men and women throughout the Church's history have followed this path, including St Catherine of Siena and St Rose of Lima, both of whom were lay women who became Dominican **tertiaries**, belonging to the 'third order' – the first and second orders being the male and female religious communities.

Many religious communities in Australia offer this form of lay association and have regular meetings to help form them in the charism of the community and live this out in their daily lives as lay people. The Josephite community in Australia has taken this a step further and has introduced 'associates' – lay women who make a covenant with the community but live in their own homes and keep their jobs.[49] This has now expanded into the Josephite Companions program which is open to both men and women.[50]

Consecrated virgins and hermits

One of the oldest forms of religious life is that of the consecrated virgin, which dates to the apostolic era when women could choose to dedicate their lives to God perpetually and permanently in virginity. At the time this was radical and unprecedented, and it still startles many people today. As time passed and consecrated virgins began to live in community with each other for safety and economy, women's enclosed religious life developed instead. In some religious orders, women would make vows in the community but also make a separate vow of perpetual virginity.

The Rite of Consecration of a Virgin for women living in the world was restored by Vatican II in 1970. Consecrated virgins must undergo careful formation under the authority of the local bishop, and they also continue to live in the world and provide for themselves completely. They don't wear a habit or a veil or have a special title or letters after their name. They pray the Liturgy of the Hours daily, like a priest or a religious, and their job is to pray especially for the diocese.[51]

The United States Association of Consecrated Virgins says that in 2015, there were eight consecrated virgins in Australia.[52] In 2020, the NCPR did a survey of consecrated virginity in Australia, to mark the 50th anniversary of the revival of this form of life. They found a total of 13 consecrated virgins in Australia, with an average age of 56, and an average age for beginning formation of 40. The dioceses had very little information on these women that they could share.[53]

Hermits are another ancient form of religious life that has been revived in the post-conciliar era. When you have a bad day, it's often tempting to think of becoming a hermit just to get a bit of peace and quiet. But St Benedict, the author of a supremely sensible monastic rule, noted that the only kind of monk who might be called to be a hermit is one who has been thoroughly tested by living in community first.[54] In other words, wanting to get away from other people is not a sign that you have a vocation to be a hermit; it's a sign to work on your community living skills. A true vocation as a hermit (male or female) is rare and quite specific.

There have always been hermits in the Church, and in medieval England there were some famous and saintly anchorites and anchoresses like Julian of Norwich. A hermit lives the essence of consecrated life on their own under the authority of the diocesan bishop (canon 603), and in strict separation from the world. That strict separation is a key element, along with a life of prayer and penance for the Church and the world.[55] You are unlikely to find a hermit in your diocese, because they usually don't want to be found, but you can always ask if there are any on the diocesan books. There's at least one in the archdiocese of Perth, and one in Hobart.[56]

Opus Dei

Opus Dei is a movement founded in 1928 by St Josemaria Escriva in Spain, which eventually became a **personal prelature** in 1982. A personal prelature has clergy and lay members, and a specific ministerial purpose. It's like an ordinariate (see Chapter 1) in that it can minister to people across a wide geographical area. The 'personal' part refers to the fact that the prelature has authority over the persons in it, rather than a specific territorial area. Opus Dei remains today the only personal prelature in the Catholic Church.

The charism of Opus Dei is basically the sanctification of daily life and work through ordinary activities. There's a clear emphasis on the practical means to achieving this through prayer and sacrifice, regular reception of the sacraments, spiritual reading, and regular small sacrifices for others. It aims to build up integrity of your spiritual and temporal life, so that you're not – for example – a pious Catholic on Sundays but a ruthless workaholic on Mondays to Saturdays.

Opus Dei has a bad reputation in some corners of the Church. In Australia it's especially noticeable among older Anglo-Australians from an Australian Labor Party background because Opus Dei was thought to be on the 'wrong' (winning) side of the Spanish Civil War. Thanks to dedicated local and international conspiracy theorists, it has been woven by some people into a complex pattern of malevolent conservatism in the Church in Australia, alongside Bob Santamaria, the late Cardinal Pell, and the traditional Latin Mass movement.[57]

This mindset found its way into some of the Catholics in Australia survey (CIA2022) written responses, and two of these stood out for me because they mentioned Opus Dei specifically.

> I am certainly not a conservative Black and White Catholic and have very little time for the far right Opus Dei wing of the Church. I truly believe that Women deserve to have a greater voice in Church matters and pray that one day we will see women leaders in the Church! (a woman in her 60s in Sydney who was a weekly Mass-goer)
>
> I think this a critically needed survey and it is my [hope] it will attract a vast range of views to make it valid. My

fear is it will be skewed by the "right" (Opus Dei et Al) who will make it their mission to get people to advocate for their view of religion. (a second woman in her 60s in Sydney who identified as a schoolteacher with 40 years' experience, and who was a monthly Mass-goer)

The Sydney element might reflect the fact that Opus Dei runs several schools there. It's easy to find out more about these schools because the ABC did some investigative journalism into them in 2023.[58] The bulk of the complaints seem to be that children at the schools were taught that porn was harmful to them, and that being gay was going to make their life very difficult. This is surely what you'd expect at schools that are openly advertised as Catholic and associated with Opus Dei. I'll say more about this kind of thing in the chapter on the business arm of the Church.

Opus Dei is exactly like any other Catholic group, ministry, or movement – or indeed parish – in Australia. The sanctification of its members depends on God's work in their individual souls, and their response to this. It's equally prone to abuses of its structure and spirituality, and like any other movement in the Church, it would do well to recognise and address these as they arise. Opus Dei as a movement is also a lot smaller than people think. I don't think the Church, or the country, are in any danger from it taking over everything.

Catholic Charismatic Renewal

Charismatic renewal – a movement based on powerful personal experience of the **charisms** associated with the presence of the Holy Spirit – is part of a broader global Christian subculture that exists across many different denominations. Catholic charismatic renewal began as a movement in the US in the 1970s, and one of the first places it spread to was Australia.[59] It led to the foundation of charismatic communities and experiments in collective living like the Emmanuel Community[60] and the Disciples of Jesus Covenant Community.[61]

The focus of these movements and communities is more intense prayer and immersion in the scriptures, healing of physical and mental disorders, and 'deliverance ministry' which seeks to relieve people of common 'spiritual bondages' such as addictions and compulsions. I've been to quite a few charismatic events, but I must admit that it's not really my thing, although I know people who say they have benefited from it. The international Catholic Charismatic Renewal movement co-operates with the Holy See and is managed by a body called CHARIS through the Dicastery for the Laity, Family and Life.[62]

Neo-Catechumenal Way

I mentioned this new movement in the earlier chapter on clergy, because it's been a significant contributor to diocesan priest numbers across Australia since it arrived here. Like Opus Dei, it was founded in Spain – but in 1964 in one of Spain's poorest areas of shanty towns around Madrid. Francisco Argüello (known as Kiko) and Carmen Hernández both wanted to bring a real experience of Jesus to these largely uncatechised communities. Together they developed a model of adult evangelisation that became known as the Neocatechumenal Way.[63]

The model was successful and effective, and welcomed by some Spanish bishops who found that it was helping to revitalise their dioceses. The movement began to attract young men seeking formation for the priesthood, and the first Neocatechumenal seminary was established in Rome in 1986. Its arrival in Australia was not greeted with universal acclaim; there is a website called *NeoCats No!* which outlines all the reasons why its author thinks that the movement will cause harm to the Church in Australia.[64]

The Neocatechumenal Way is strongly parish-based, but with an outward missionary focus. Their model of formation has also undergone changes and improvements over time to align it more closely to Catholic teaching and practice in areas like the Eucharist and the reception of Holy Communion.[65] I've not had a lot to do with them personally, but I know people who have experienced their parish life and have good things to say about it.

Risks and blessings

Like everything in the Catholic Church – which is made up of sinners – things can go wrong in religious life and new movements. With some groups, including prayer groups, experiments in communal living, or groups that are trying to discern if they're going to become a formalised religious order, it's possible for spiritual abuse to weave into this. The Little Pebble is an egregious example,[66] but there are others who have operated on a more minor scale.

There's a dysfunctional model of spiritual abuse which involves an 'un-worldly' leader who is in fact selfish and manipulative, and who uses spirituality to control people and bend them to their personal will. This can often be accompanied by a lot of *faux-*humility, manifestations of what look like charisms, visions, and **locutions** – hearing the voice of God or the saints directly – and so on. This can also happen in long-established religious orders, where investigations into spiritual abuses are now beginning to take place more frequently.[67]

Also, not all new religious orders and movements will get beyond the planning stage. For example, in 2008, Archbishop Hickey of Perth oversaw the formation of the Missionaries of the Gospel, a diocesan-based nascent women's religious community whose charism was to follow Jesus through the teachings of Pope John Paul II, with lay associates.[68] After 2012, his successor Archbishop Timothy Costelloe SDB (another religious, this time of the Salesians of Don Bosco) asked the community to slow down its planned development to allow for more discernment. The two postulants in formation left, and at the end of 2016 the community was wound up.

The local Church can do a lot to keep an eye – and a steadying hand – on new movements, and it should. That's where the rebuilding of trust between bishops and their lay people really needs to happen, because otherwise well-meaning lay people will do things in secret that are potentially dangerous for them and for the Church. Doing good work when it's aligned with the Church's mission and under obedience to local authority – that is, the bishop – enhances the good of the work that you do.

It's also good for local dioceses to be transparent when things go wrong with movements or religious communities in their diocese. I know from experience that too often, the burden is thrown on to the laity to do their own fact-finding, whereas sunlight is usually the best disinfectant. A frank and open statement on the diocesan website can work wonders and stop the rumour mill.

Conclusion

When religious life goes right, it's the happiest you can be on earth. When it goes wrong, it can be a source of terrible misery to its members and to the wider Church. We will probably never see the huge numbers of religious in Australia again that we had in the 1960s, but that may be a good thing. Given the numbers who left once it was made easier for them, it's likely that many of these were 'social vocations' rather than actual callings to a lifetime of consecration. I could be wrong; I don't know the insides of people's hearts and souls.

But what's taking its place is worth welcoming. We have an abundance of new ways in which lay people can live their lives as Catholics with help from the people around them, because there's always more strength – and greater accountability – in numbers. There are lots of options in Australia and overseas for men and women who don't feel especially called to marriage right now, or who are wondering if their inability to find a spouse might be indicating a call to a different way of life. We still have so many willing souls who are ready to do great things for God, and to live the evangelical counsels. We need them like never before.

[1] Diocese of Parramatta. (n.d.). Consecrated religious life. *Diocese of Parramatta*, https://parracatholic.org/contribute/discern-my-vocation/consecrated-religious/

[2] John Paul II. (1996, March 25). *Vita consecrata*, https://www.vatican.va/content/john-paul-ii/en/apost_exhortations/documents/hf_jp-ii_exh_25031996_vita-consecrata.html

[3] Grantham, J. (2018, May 16). Hildegarde of Bingen, part 2. *Catholic Outlook*, https://catholicoutlook.org/part-two-hildegard-bingen/

[4] Dominican Sisters of St Cecilia, Sydney, personal communication, 15 August 2024.

[5] Sr Yvette, personal communication, 20 August 2024.

[6] See for example McCallum, J. (1987). Secularisation in Australia between 1966 and 1985: a research note. *Australian and New Zealand Journal of Sociology*, 23(3), 407–422. https://doi.org/10.1177/144078338702300306

[7] Sisters State Advisory Research Groups. (1977). *National statistical survey of religious personnel, Australia 1976*. Conferences of Major Superiors of Australia.

[8] Sisters State Advisory Research Groups, *National statistical survey*, 76.

[9] Dixon, R., Reid, S., & Connolly, N. (2011). 'See I am doing a new thing': The 2009 survey of Catholic religious institutes in Australia. *Australasian Catholic Record*, 88(3), 271–283; 276.

[10] Dixon, Reid, & Connolly, 'See I am doing a new thing', 274-275.

[11] Dixon, R., Webber, R., & Reid, S. (2021). Contemporary approaches to religious vocations in Australia. *Australasian Catholic Record*, 98(3), 335–348. The full report can be found at: Dixon, R., Webber, R., Reid, S., Rymarz, R., Martin, J., & Connolly, N. (2018). *Understanding religious vocation in Australia today: report of a study of vocations to religious life 2000-2015 for Catholic Vocations Ministry Australia*. ACBC Pastoral Research Office, https://ncpr.catholic.org.au/wp-content/uploads/2021/07/CVMA-Report-Final-report-Feb-2018-Rev.pdf

[12] Dixon, Reid, & Connolly, 'See I am doing a new thing'; Dixon, Webber & Reid, Contemporary approaches, 336, reporting on https://ncpr.catholic.org.au/2018-survey-of-religious-congregations-in-australia/

[13] Dixon, Webber, & Reid, Contemporary approaches, 339.

[14] Dominican Sisters of St Cecilia, personal communication, 15 August 2024.

[15] Dixon, Webber, & Reid, Contemporary approaches, 342.

[16] Ibid., 342-343.

[17] Ibid., 343.

[18] Ibid.

[19] Ibid., 344.

[20] Ibid., 348.

[21] This is discussed with courage and aplomb in Dixon, Reid, & Connolly, 'See I am doing a new thing', 282. A local parish near me is run by a male religious order, and the younger (non-white) members tend to wear the traditional habit, while the older ones (a mix of white and non-white) don't.

22 This was compiled from the data in Catholic Hierarchy.org plus data from the 2021 National Count of Attendance.

23 Maronite Heritage. *Orders*. https://www.maronite-heritage.com/Orders.php

24 St Charbel Melbourne. *The Antonine Maronite order*, https://www.saintcharbel.org.au/monastery/the-antonine-maronite-order/

25 St Charbel's Monastery and Parish. *History of our mission*, http://www.stcharbel.org.au/our-parish/history/

26 Our Lady of Lebanon. *The Congregation of Maronite Lebanese Missionaries*, https://www.ololb.org/content/congregation-maronite-lebanese-missionaries

27 Roberson, R. (2024). *The Eastern Christian Churches*. Catholic Near East Welfare Association, https://cnewa.org/eastern-christian-churches/the-catholic-eastern-churches/from-the-assyrian-church-of-the-east/the-syro-malabar-catholic-church/

28 My office is located at the QEII Medical Centre in Perth, and I have attended weekday Masses here and at St Aloysius Shenton Park since around 2016, all said by Syro-Malabar Vincentian priests.

29 Australian Catholic Bishops Conference (ACBC). (2022). *Public juridic persons*, https://www.catholic.au/s/article/Public-Juridic-Persons; Association of Ministerial Public Juridic Persons (AMPJP). (2024). *About MPJPs*, https://ampjp.org.au/about-mpjps/

30 AMPJP, *About MPJPs*.

31 For a brief explainer, see Longenecker, D. (2019, October 29). Pachamama, witchcraft and women's ordination. *Dwightlongenecker.com*, https://dwightlongenecker.com/pachamama-witchcraft-and-womens-ordination/

32 Dominican Sisters of St Cecilia, personal communication, 15 August 2024.

33 Sr Yvette, personal communication, 20 August 2024.

34 Ibid.

35 *New Norcia Benedictine Community*, https://www.newnorcia.com.au/

36 *Tarrawarra Abbey*, https://www.cistercian.org.au/

37 *Jamberoo Abbey*, https://www.jamberooabbey.org.au/

38 *Notre Dame Priory*, https://www.notredamemonastery.org/about/

39 *Carmelite Spirit*, https://carmelite.com/friars/

40 *Carmel of Elijah*, https://carmeljmj.org.au/history

41 *Religious Sisters of Mercy of Alma, Michigan*, https://www.almamercy.org/our-history

42 *Saint Joseph Home of Mercy*, https://www.almamercy.org/sydney

43 *Dominican Sisters of St Cecilia*, https://www.nashvilledominican.org/community/congregation-history/the-years-of-the-second-vatican-council/

44 *Dominican Sisters of St Cecilia*, https://www.nashvilledominican.org/community/congregation-history/the-fruits-of-the-new-springtime/

45 *Dominican Sisters of St Cecilia*, https://www.nashvilledominican.org/apostolate/where-we-serve/dominican-sisters-in-australia/

46 *Sisters of the Immaculata*, https://hobart.catholic.org.au/vocations/lay-religious-orders/sisters-of-the-immaculata/ and https://immaculata.org.au/

47 *Missionaries of God's Love*, https://www.mglpriestsandbrothers.org/ourstory; https://www.mglsisters.org/aboutus

48 Ethan, personal communication, 30 May 2024.

49 Dixon, Webber, & Reid, Contemporary approaches, 346.

50 *Sisters of St Joseph*, https://www.sosj.org.au/become-involved/josephite-companions/

51 *United States Association of Consecrated Virgins*, https://site.consecratedvirgins.org/whatis. For an example of what this can look like, Farrow, M. (2024, November 5). 'Boots on the ground' – Catholic life for a consecrated virgin. *The Pillar*, https://www.pillarcatholic.com/p/boots-on-the-ground-catholic-life

52 *United States Association of Consecrated Virgins*, https://site.consecratedvirgins.org/whoarewe

53 My thanks to Dr Stephen Reid of the NCPR who provided me with this summary from the internal report on this project, personal communication, 9 October 2024.

54 Rule of Benedict, Chapter 1, https://archive.osb.org/rb/text/rbejms1.html#1

55 St Cuthbert's House, Hermitage of the Diocese of Nottingham. (n.d.). *How to be a hermit*, http://www.stcuthbertshouse.co.uk/howtobeahermit.html.

56 Rosengren, P. (2008, October 29). Alone, but not lonely: A new hermit for Perth. *The Record*, https://therecord.com.au/news/local/alone-but-not-lonely-a-new-hermit-for-perth/; Porteous, J. (2022). Consecration of canonical hermits: hidden with Christ in God. *Archdiocese of Hobart*, https://hobart.catholic.org.au/2022/04/20/consecration-of-canonical-hermits-hidden-with-christ-in-god/

57 See for example Lockwood, G. (2011, February 21). *The Catholic right in SA Labor*. Australasian Society for the Study of Labor History. https://labourhistorycanberra.org/2015/04/the-catholic-right-in-sa-labor/

58 Australian Associated Press. (2023, January 31). Sydney schools linked to conservative Catholic group Opus Dei investigated over 'broad' curriculum concerns. *SBS News*, https://www.sbs.com.au/news/article/sydney-schools-linked-to-conservative-catholic-group-opus-dei-investigated-over-broad-curriculum-concerns/0zck5hb4y; Smith, A., & Carroll, L. (2023, January 28). War of words erupts between Opus Dei schools and the ABC. *Sydney Morning Herald*, https://www.smh.com.au/national/nsw/war-of-words-erupts-between-opus-dei-schools-and-the-abc-20230127-p5cfvs.html; Milligan, L., Fallman, M., & Zillman, S. (2023, January 31). Federal government writes to regulators investigating Opus Dei-affiliated schools that former students say caused 'pain and suffering'. *ABC News*, https://www.abc.net.au/news/2023-01-31/government-investigation-considered-over-opus-dei-schools/101910228

59 A good brief history is Maiden, J. (2019). The emergence of Catholic charismatic renewal 'in a country': Australia and transnational Catholic Charismatic Renewal. *Studies in World Christianity*, 25(3), 274-296.

60 *Emmanuel Community*, https://www.emmanuelcommunity.com.au/about

61 *Disciples of Jesus Covenant Community*, https://dojcommunity.com/about/

62 *Catholic Charismatic Renewal International Service* (CHARIS) International, https://www.charis.international/en/about-charis/

63 *NeoCatechumenal Way*, https://neocatechumenaleiter.org/en/history/#inicio

64 Arbuckle, G. (2024). *NeoCats No!*, https://neocatsno.org/

[65] Zenit. (2006). On liturgical norms for the Neocatechumenal Way. *Zenit/EWTN*, https://www.ewtn.com/catholicism/library/on-liturgical-norms-for-the-neocatechumenal-way-4286

[66] Drewitt-Smith, A. (2023, June 22). Paedophile cult leader 'Little Pebble' William Kamm granted bail after alleged breach of court orders. *ABC News*, https://www.abc.net.au/news/2023-06-22/paedophile-cult-leader-faces-court-alleged-breach-of-bail/102509370

[67] De Lassus, D. (2020). *Risques et derives de la vie religieuse*. Cerf; available in English as *Abuses in the religious life and the path to healing*. Sophia Institute Press; Cernuzio, S. 2021. *Il velo del silenzio*. San Paolo.

[68] *The Record*. (2008, October 22). New religious vows in Perth. *The Record*, https://therecord.com.au/news/local/new-religious-vows-in-perth/; The Record. (2009, January 7). New community to throw open its doors. *The Record*, https://therecord.com.au/news/local/new-community-to-throw-open-its-doors/

Chapter 6

THE BUSINESS ARM: CATHOLIC-ORIGIN ORGANISATIONS IN AUSTRALIA

I started this book with an analogy about the Catholic Football Club (CFC), which was rapidly running out of active members, players, and football fixtures. However, it was also making lots of money through its government subsidised CFC casino, hotel, and spa complex which anyone could access, whether they were club members or not. We've spent most of this book so far talking about the CFC's few remaining players and active club members who still attend the fixtures in the increasingly draughty grandstands that were built for the good old days. Now it's time to look at the casino, spa, and hotel complex down the road.

Obviously, it's not a real casino, hotel and spa complex. Instead, it's an independent educational network of Catholic-origin schools, universities, hospitals, health care, and welfare agencies. Most of these were originally set up to provide affordable services for Catholics who were often very poor. But that was a long, long time ago. Today, perpetuating this multi-billion-dollar Catholic industrial complex is what many people think is the chief purpose of the Church in Australia. And they don't really care about the 'Catholic' thing; they just want the subsidised services to continue without interruption.

The relationship of these organisations with the different levels of Australian government needs closer examination. For example, a lot of the parochial-diocesan Church's wealth sits in property ownership – churches and schools. But Catholic schools, hospitals, and charities would collapse without substantial recurring government funding. We've also been reading quite a lot about the scandalous stonewalling in Australia of payouts to clergy abuse victims,[1] and more recently the recurring exposes of Vatican fiscal corruption.[2]

I would love to see a public, Catholic-led conversation about what it means to be a Church whose founder owned almost nothing, but which now seems to prioritise protecting its assets over anything else. These topics have been common in private conversations among the Catholics I have known for around thirty-five years now. But I have never seen these topics really grappled with in print or in any form, and especially not in the Catholic media. That's why this chapter is also going to examine the decline and fall of independent Catholic journalism in Australia, and its replacement with 'strategic communications' which no one reads, nor is expected to read.

Corporate soteriology

Does working for an organisation with the word 'Catholic' in its name make it more or less likely that you will go to heaven?

This is the question I have been chewing over as I've been writing this chapter.[3] **Soteriology** is the name given to the study of salvation as a theological concept. To answer my question, I must strip everything back to the basic purpose and mission of the Church, which is to save souls by drawing people into a direct personal relationship with the Holy Trinity. There are certain important actions that are part of this process: things like feeding the hungry, clothing the naked, and observing the golden rule. All this social teaching builds on the welfare provisions already laid out in Deuteronomy and Leviticus – and on the scathing prophetic reminders to observe these that make up such a lot of the Old Testament.

Countless holy men and women, and almost every founder of an active religious order, did this work themselves. They nursed, housed, and taught the most vulnerable. They did this at great personal cost, and they did it for the sake of the Kingdom. Their followers did the same, right up to the mid- to late twentieth century. But gradually the religious stopped doing the work, and lay people started picking up the slack. Professions like nursing and teaching became professionalised, better paid, and better resourced. Social workers took the place of good hearted and charitable people who saw a need and met it, however imperfectly.

But not all our Catholic charitable work has become professionalised – and nor should it. This is why the Missionaries of Charity, Mother Teresa's religious order, still attract so many vocations. Mother Teresa copped a lot of flak for not using her donations to set up high-end medical facilities in poor areas.[4] But she was wiser than most, because she realised that they'd quickly become facilities for the middle class and rich, and the poor would be crowded out. There are arguments about safety and quality here, but fundamentally, Mother Teresa chose to make ten destitute and dying people comfortable for the short remainder of their lives, rather than giving one person more expensive and life prolonging treatment.

So where does that leave our current Catholic-origin health care system? Most of the Catholic-origin facilities began with nuns and brothers delivering care directly themselves, which was their vowed intention for the rest of their lives. But now they're living in retirement, sitting atop multimillion dollar corporations run by Ministerial Public Juridic Persons (MPJPs). To what extent do these businesses and corporations form part of the Church's mission? Are they really part of the Church? What if most of their employees aren't Mass-attending Catholics? Are they explicitly serving the Church's mission on earth? The parochial-diocesan part of the Church serves this end quite clearly – but outside of that, what makes a 'Catholic' organisation?

I don't have answers to all these questions, but I found help from an unexpected person – Fr Charles E Curran, a famously dissident theologian on sexual issues.[5] Back in 1997, he wrote a thorough treatment of these questions, mapping out what would eventually become known in the Catholic world as 'identity and mission'. He is writing about the US scene, but much of what he says is also applicable to Australia.

Curran notes that 'One question that never comes up in the recent literature is: Are these institutions the best way for the Church to carry out its mission?' It's true that the Church in developed countries doesn't usually need to spend a lot on health care, higher education, and some social services, because that's already taken care of by the government or they're self-funded. So that's a plus. But then Curran adds: 'However, there is a downside to this, which again is not frequently recognized. The Church as such, as the people of God, does not have any real sense of ownership with regard to these institutions or functions.'[6]

Curran looks at the fraught question of 'Catholic' health care provision. This began as a way of ensuring that poor Catholics were able to access free or low-cost health care. But with the rise in government spending on health care, many Catholic-origin health care facilities have metamorphosed into private health care providers that are only accessible to those who can afford the private health insurance premiums, or who want to pay directly for their care.

> Traditionally health-care institutions were not-for-profit; they were seen as serving the needs of the community. Will for-profit institutions with an emphasis on the bottom line lower the quality of health care and destroy the physician-patient relationship? Can and should Catholic health-care institutions continue to exist in this environment? ... in light of this situation Catholic hospitals have an impossible mission. The mission statements of these institutions are beautiful and inspiring, but the culture of the Catholic hospital prevents the fulfillment of the stated mission in the present circumstances.[7]

What about Catholic-origin charities? Many of these began as very small local operations to help address specific needs like food, shelter, and clothing for those in need who could least afford it.[8] But again, with the incursion of government funded welfare programs, the charities now employ salaried staff, so that when you donate to them, a certain percentage of what you give is going to support a growing infrastructure.[9] You are also paying for these charities already out of your taxes.

In 1997, Curran used the example of the organisation Catholic Charities USA, which is an umbrella for a nationwide network of agencies.[10]

> ... Catholic Charities, as the largest private human-service network in the U.S., receives almost two-thirds of its budget from tax money ... As additional services are funded through block grants, intense competition will exist at both state and local levels to determine which agencies will receive the funds available. And to complicate matters further, more for-profit corporations will apparently be vying for a share of these funds. Without doubt some existing programs in Catholic Charities will be cut or even eliminated.[11]

It's an interesting and clear-sighted perspective, and one which should give us a lot to think about in terms of Catholic-origin corporations and organisations.

Curran also notes that there's no real impediment to any of these organisations employing non-Catholics. They can be 'committed to the mission of the agency and act according to its basic values and principles.'[12] But what happens if, as a non-Catholic, they can't see a problem with their business or company engaging in certain actions that Catholics find immoral? I suppose they could stop working there. But if they formed the majority of, say, the governing board, it would be easier for them to sanction the immoral actions, especially if pressure was being applied from a funding body like a state or federal government.

And here is the rub. In the chapter on religious life, we saw that a great many religious orders in Australia have now placed their assets in the hands of MPJPs. In this way, they hope to safeguard the Catholic patrimony of their organisation. But what if the MPJP governing body is made up mostly of non-Mass-going Catholics? We have already seen that these don't think or believe like Mass-going Catholics. Can they be relied upon to resist a hostile government incursion over matters of Catholic faith and morals? We'd all like to think so – but we have yet to find out.

Diocesan bureaucracies

We'll start where we are on slightly safer turf: the diocesan bureaucracy. You will find one of these in every diocese in Australia, usually based in and around the chancery office. There's no argument that these people serve the core business of the Church, because they're supporting the local bishop in keeping the local show on the road. They help to keep the diocesan parish structure solvent and operational, and the churches open and insured, and the priests housed and occasionally fed. It's just that there seems to be more and more of them all the time, which is inevitable in any bureaucracy – especially when there's increasing regulation involved.

The numbers and the balance sheet

There's more financial transparency at diocesan level than most people realise, although there's always room for more. There's a table in Appendix 2 of how our dioceses publicly report their annual financial activities, with the most recent figures I could find. The total equity for all the dioceses where I could find this information was approximately $1 billion in 2023.

Before you get excited, this isn't cash. It's **equity** – so the current value of all the property owned, plus any other assets owned, plus cash, and minus all the expenditure, debts, loans, and outgoings. For example, in December 2023, the archdiocese of Perth had assets worth nearly $708 million, but outgoings of nearly $658 million.

What's left over once you subtract these from the assets is your equity (in Perth's case, around $50 million).

These numbers can be affected by all sorts of things. Most dioceses in Australia today show eye-watering asset values, reflecting the fact that they bought land up to two hundred years ago that's massively appreciated in value. Current events are also important: if your diocese is in the middle of a real estate boom, your assets will be valued much more highly than if you're a diocese where no one especially wants to buy property.

This money is also what's keeping the show on the road – and this relates directly to the offertory collections taken up at Mass in your diocese. The offertory collection represents a gift in monetary terms of your labour. You aren't growing the wheat and making the hosts or the wine, so you make a substitute gift of money. The first collection in a Catholic parish traditionally goes to support the priest in the parish.

Today the money usually goes back to the diocese where it's used to offset priests' stipends (their income). The stipend is not huge – but he usually gets a house, a car, and a superannuation fund with the job, so his major outgoings are taken care of. This also allows wealthier parishes to help support the poorer ones with smaller first collections.

The second collection is supposed to go to the upkeep of the parish. This can vary hugely, from paying off a mortgage on a new building like a hall or parish centre, to simply keeping the lights on. But many Catholic parishes in Australia run at a loss, mostly because people with well-paying jobs are still putting a handful of loose change in the collection each week. A full-time employed person should be giving a sum that's closer to the price of a half-tank of petrol or an office lunch (including a coffee). In Australia today, this is somewhere between $20 and $50. If you have very limited means, it's different – you give what you can.[13]

Right now, our parish collections aren't nearly enough to keep the local Church going, and everything is more expensive with each passing year. Dioceses have salaried employees who need to be paid and loans that need to be serviced. Investments are another way of keeping the coffers topped up, so dioceses will try to invest money to ensure they have ongoing income.

Trouble in paradise

So yes, all this needs governance and administration. But there's a dark side to diocesan bureaucracy, as with every organisation. The Royal Commission into Institutional Responses to Child Sexual Abuse (2012-2017) rightly pointed out that clericalism is linked to a sense of entitlement, superiority, exclusion, and abuse of power. However, there's sometimes a kind of 'lay clericalism' among people who occupy privileged Church-related positions, often working in dioceses alongside bishops (and bishops' conferences).

We all know that diocesan and other forms of Catholic employment sometimes depend not on what you know, but who you know, and who you're related to. There are longstanding networks of Catholic 'old boys' of both sexes everywhere in Australia: men and increasingly women who know each other from their private Catholic school, Catholic community social and welfare organisations, and countless other Catholic networks. I will return to this point later in this chapter.

They all do good work, I'm sure, but the people in these organisations are only human. The same Royal Commission found that Cardinal Pell's claim to have been misled by the local Catholic Education Office in Melbourne on the extent of Fr Peter Searson's abuse was 'implausible'.[14] Being a lifelong Mass-going Catholic with ample experience of Catholic officialdom, I found it entirely plausible. Clericalism has sometimes infected lay people in diocesan bureaucracies of all kinds to the point where they minimised or excused a lot of bad clerical behaviour.[15]

The diocesan bureaucracies that expanded in Australia from the

1980s were also increasingly headed by lay people, mostly men, some of whom were demonstrably both hard-headed and hard-hearted. I suspect this is still going on, because I keep meeting people who have left Australian Catholic diocesan employment under acrimonious conditions. It's terrible to witness the heartbreak of a person who was excited to go to work for the 'Church', only to find that they're actually working for a well-protected narcissist boss.

And it's not just here. Tim Glemkowski is a layman who led the successful US Eucharistic Congress team from 2022 to its conclusion in Indianapolis in July 2024. He said in a later interview that:

> I remember one corporate executive who came to work for the Church telling me that she had never encountered as much nastiness in corporate America as she had working for the Church and, furthermore, if her organization had operated the way the Church did it would have closed decades before.[16]

As we know, narcissists tend to do well in corporate environments. They can make quite good 'leaders' because they lack empathy, meaning that they can sack people easily and do ruthless deals that benefit their organisation. I agree that the chancery or diocesan office should not be a sheltered workshop for incompetent cronies – but it's also not Wall Street.

A few years ago, I came across a series of articles by Australian Protestant pastor Stephen McAlpine about the problems of narcissistic leadership and spiritual abuse in churches today.[17] Bad and dangerous people in church leadership positions can damage people spiritually – but they are often rewarded for it, because they get the results, the influence, or the numbers that their employer wants.

It's easy to see how this has come about, because you'll also find it in the Acts of the Apostles and the letters of St Paul. While the Church was surrounded with enemies on the outside, there were also plenty of nightmares on the inside. Their problems – and ours – really arose from personalities, people, and sin, with individuals jockeying for power and influence and using whatever means necessary to achieve this.

But when this affects a Catholic workplace, the environment can become just as toxic as a secular workplace, but with a crucifix on the wall. McAlpine says: 'For many people who are bullied – or experience a toxic work environment at church, before being let go – it's the cognitive dissonance between how they are being treated and what is being said from the front – often by the perpetrator – that is most troubling.'[18] In many churches, including the Catholic Church in Australia, non-disclosure agreements are also a binding part of any severance package, which often allows harm to continue because it's never publicly exposed.

So what's the solution? For McAlpine, a Christian organisation must be able to mitigate risk, but 'the key must be serving the interests of those involved in the organisation, not the brand in and of itself.'[19] The Church as employer must not use ideas of corporate safety and asset protection to justify workplace mistreatment, especially of those who are there because they love God and want to help build up the Body of Christ.

I've spent quite a bit of time looking at Australian diocesan websites, and I see a lot of job titles, many of which seem very straightforward. Others are less so. I think a good acid test of any diocesan role, position, or agency is to ask: if this were shut down tomorrow, how would it affect the lives of ordinary parishioners in this diocese? I think in many cases the answer would be 'not at all'.

What these offices and agencies do provide is employment for quite a lot of people. Like Ronald Reagan, I believe the best welfare program is a job. But some of the work is about developing policies, procedures, and compliance with an increasing range of secular and ecclesiastical governance demands. And some of it – like Catholic offices for ecology, the environment, or climate change – is just window-dressing.

Today, directors of Catholic diocesan agencies are now persons of importance in the local Church and are summoned to deputise at ribbon-cuttings for bishops who are presumably busy elsewhere. They are told to do things like 'develop an alignment between mission, strategic priorities and positive organisational culture.' We now have directors of something called 'mission and identity' in the Church in Australia. We didn't have these fifty years ago, because back then we could assume that everyone working for the Church was a Mass-going Catholic who understood what the Church's mission was, and what their Catholic identity was.

Who are these people? There's a thing called social network analysis which allows us to map interrelationships of people – who's marrying who, who is supervising who, and who is promoting who. For example, Australian journalists and media workers tend to marry each other, with interesting results.[20] My colleague Stephen Bullivant collaborated on a social network analysis of the wide-ranging influence of former cardinal Theodore McCarrick in the United States.[21] I suspect that a social network analysis of diocesan employees in any Australian diocese would be very revealing – and another good research project – because anecdotally a lot of them seem to be related to each other, or related to people who work in Catholic-origin education and health care.

This is why Pope Francis has recently introduced anti-nepotism rules in the Vatican curial offices – it's too easy for married couples and relatives who work together to turn a blind eye when corruption is sneaking in.[22] In small communities – and Catholic communities are quite small – there can be many overlapping and potentially conflicting interests. Personally, I'm also curious to know if people who work for the Church in Australia are more or less likely to go to Mass regularly on Sundays. I think this would make another excellent research project.

Don't rock the boat

The trouble with being comfortably employed in a setting like this is that you're much less likely to rock the boat if you see things going wrong inside the organisation. In 1972, sociologist Irving Janis came up with a concept that he called – in Orwellian terms – groupthink.²³ It has eight defining characteristics (Table 11).

Table 11. Irving Janis's eight characteristics of groupthink

Illusion of Invulnerability	Over-optimism and willingness to take risks.
Rationale	Ignoring and discounting warnings and negative feedback.
Morality	'We are good people, so whatever we do is morally right and justifiable.'
Stereotypes	The group reduces opponents to crude stereotypes, branding them stupid or weak.
Pressure	This is applied to anyone in the group who expresses concern about the proposed line of action.
Self-censorship	Group members keep quiet about their doubts or minimise them.
Illusion of Unanimity	'Silence is consent. Therefore, we all agree.'
Mind Guards	Self-appointed enforcers who help to minimise dissent.

Groupthink is a dangerous way to run any organisation because it means that the organisation becomes deaf to feedback from within its own ranks – which is actually the safest and most effective form of feedback. Internal feedback is much better than waking up to a camera crew on your doorstep after a whistleblower goes to the media.

How does this work in practice in the Church? Let's say you work for a diocesan marriage counselling agency. It's a nice job with nice people. One evening, you attend a parish-based information session on the annulment process that's delivered to a large audience. During that presentation, the speaker – a priest from your local marriage tribunal – admits that his preference is to ensure that everyone who presents a case gets an annulment from the tribunal to the point of him offering to 'fix it for you' if necessary.

You are troubled by this, because you know that's not how marriage tribunals are supposed to work. What do you do? You can tell your line manager – but what will she do? Will she take it up with the local bishop? How likely is it that the bishop will do anything? He's a bit scared of Fr Fixit, who is a highly trained moral theologian of many years' standing in the diocese. The bishop has also said that he doesn't like Catholics who are too conservative because they're all troublemakers. And what if you tell your line manager, only to find out that she agrees with Fr Fixit and has had two annulments in her family through his helpful intervention?

The person most likely to get in trouble in this scenario is you. So, you say nothing. And this is exactly what happened at the first rumours of clergy sexual abuse. Fr Charm is an old friend of the bishop. Your husband heads a local chapter of the Knights of the Southern Cross where Fr Charm is chaplain. Everyone loves Fr Charm – he's such a wonderful priest – and no one will believe his victims. And no one will believe you either. And if you don't believe *me*, the 2018 case of Siobhan O'Connor in the (now bankrupt) US diocese of Buffalo shows exactly what happens to diocesan employee whistleblowers at the mercy of a public-relations/financial-protection model of diocesan administration.[24]

We are back at the point where I began this chapter – the question of how much any of this is serving the Church's mission and saving the souls of those involved as well. If the people who work for the Church at close quarters are weak and corruptible, then what hope has the structure as a whole? The solution to these problems is partly more transparent and disinterested governance, but also personal conversion of heart. Without becoming holier people in the church workplace, we will struggle to become a better Church – no matter how many Catholic offices for fashionable causes we have.

Catholic-origin schools in Australia today

For a school to be called 'Catholic', the Code of Canon Law states that it should be 'under control of the competent ecclesiastical authority or of a public ecclesiastical juridical person, or one which in a written document is acknowledged as Catholic by the ecclesiastical authority' (canon 803). Fair enough. But going back to the question of corporate soteriology: what part do Catholic-origin schools really play in the mission of the Church in Australia?

Catholic-origin schools in Australia started as tiny and very poor ventures, often founded and staffed by religious communities, with minimal fees and designed to allow even very poor families to access faith-based schooling. Everything changed in the 1960s at the end of a long and protracted battle between Catholic education authorities and the federal government to extend government funding to Catholic and other independent schools.[25]

Have you ever asked yourself: What would have happened if these schools hadn't gotten state aid? They would have remained small and poor, like the little Catholic school my elder brothers and sisters attended in the 1960s. But would that have been a bad thing? If our Catholics in the pews were so hungry for social advancement, those who could afford it would have sent their children to non-Catholic private schools. But not all of them – some of them would have funded good small Catholic private schools out of their own pockets.

Then, as the tide of Mass-goers went out slowly over the 1970s and 1980s, more and more parents would have sent their increasingly limited numbers of children to the posher non-Catholic private schools. Would this have been such a bad thing, given that they'd already stopped coming to Mass in our churches?

Who would have been left in the Catholic schools? The children of the poor and the children of the Mass-goers – in other words, the Church's preferential option, and the traditional demographic of our religious orders' schools, hospitals, orphanages, and other charitable works. What a different Church we would have been in this country without state aid for Catholic schools.

Of course, none of this happened, and with state aid secured, Catholic-origin schools in Australia began a long and prosperous climb upwards. But it's questionable as to whether this climb has really served the Church's mission as effectively as it could have. It may also be that Catholic-origin education in Australia now exists more for its own sake than for the sake of the Church's mission.

The numbers – and the balance sheet

Catholic-origin schooling today is a huge business in Australia. In 2022 there were almost 800,000 students enrolled in 1,759 schools, and the system employed around 104,500 staff.[26] There are also different types of Catholic-origin school in Australia: **systemic** schools, which were set up by dioceses, and **non-systemic** schools, which were set up by religious orders, some of which are now run by MPJPs. State governments in Australia manage the provision of schools, so Catholic-origin schools in each state sit under local legislation, but also under the governance of local and state-level Catholic education offices. On top of all of that is a National Catholic Education Commission.

You can read any number of annual reports from the many different governing bodies overseeing Catholic-origin education in Australia, and their reporting across many key performance indicators is very impressive. However, there are only two things that I am interested in. One is how these schools are funded, and the other is how they are measurably contributing to the Church's mission.

The funding part is easy to find out about, and we'll look at that in a moment. But if you've read this far in this book, you'll see that I have quite a specific measure of whether something is contributing to the Church's mission. Is this entity, program, agency, or whatever, supporting the parochial-diocesan structure and helping it to grow?

We can best measure that by looking at the number of Mass-going Catholics in Australia today and which way this is trending. I think this is a very fair measure of the effectiveness of Catholic-origin school system in any state. The reason I think it's fair is that so many of the annual reports tell me that the Catholic-origin school system is part of the Church's mission and is evangelising and forming future Catholics. Let's see how that's working out in action.

First, the finances. The National Catholic Education Commission said that in 2022, 58.4% of all funding for Catholic-origin schools came from the federal government, and a further 15.7% from state governments. That's a total of 74.1% – in other words, around three-quarters of all funding for Catholic-origin schools came from the government, in one form or another.[27] The remaining 25.9% came from other sources of income. Not all states and dioceses are equal in this respect (see Table 12 for a selection), and Catholic education authorities report their finances slightly differently from state to state. But no matter how you slice it, it's clear that taxpayers' money is keeping the Catholic-origin school system afloat.

Table 12. Proportions of government and other funding in the income of Catholic-origin schools in Australia, 2022-24 – examples

Authority	Identifiable government funding (state and federal)	Other funding (including student fees)
Brisbane Catholic Education[28]	78%	22%
Catholic Education NT[29]	–	–
Catholic Education South Australia (CESA)[30]	48%-95%	5%-52%
Catholic Education Tasmania[31]	93%	7%
Catholic Education WA (CEWA)[32]	75%	25%

Catholic Schools New South Wales (CSNSW)[33]	85%	15%
Diocese of Maitland-Newcastle Catholic Schools Office[34]	81%	19%
Melbourne Archdiocese Catholic Schools[35]	78%	22%
Victorian Catholic Education Authority (VCEA)[36]	98%	2.4%

Second, who is actually using the Catholic-origin school system? In 2023, the National Catholic Education Commission reported that 58.5% of all students enrolled in Catholic-origin schools were Catholics, and 41.5% were not.[37] But remember that these Catholics are nominal Catholics only; we don't have much data on the Sunday Mass attendance rate among Catholic school students. In 2015, Richard Rymarz and Anthony Cleary collected data from Catholic-origin schools in the archdiocese of Sydney that showed around 19% Sunday Mass attendance in years 5 to 11, which is very high. But at the time Sydney had an average Mass attendance rate across all age groups of 15% – one of the highest in Australia.[38]

A 2013 study also found that around 60% of students in Australian Catholic-origin schools come from middle and upper middle-class backgrounds, while only a third of Catholics from disadvantaged backgrounds attend Catholic-origin schools.[39] You will see from their annual reports that Catholic-origin education authorities in each state are working on improving performance indicators like the number of admissions with a disability or from an Aboriginal or Torres Strait Islander background. However, it's harder to find data on the socioeconomic indicators of the other children.

So quite a good proportion of the children at Catholic-origin schools are non-Catholics. No one has an issue with this, because the schools are open to everyone, and they are affordable private education, so they're popular with non-Catholics. Catholic-origin schools like to say that this is a plus because they can potentially evangelise all the non-Catholics.

But there are two major problems with this argument. The first is that the surest measure of the impact of any form of Catholic evangelisation is whether a person decides to become a Catholic, either now or later. There is no data anywhere – at least that I can find – showing that Catholic-origin schooling in Australia helps to make non-Catholics into Catholics.

What we do have is the Catholics in Australia study (CIA2022), which measured people's conformity with core beliefs of Catholicism, asked whether they were converts, and asked them about their schooling. This study found that the more Catholic-origin schooling a participant had, the less they conformed with core Catholic beliefs and practices, including going to Confession and choice of family planning practices. The less Catholic-origin schooling a participant had – especially if they were under 40 years of age – the more they conformed with the Church's teaching on a wide range of issues and practices. It also turns out that 79% of the 297 converts we spoke to didn't attend Catholic-origin schools.[40]

The second problem is that data from the national censuses of 2016 and 2021 shows that while the number of enrolments in Catholic-origin schools is rising, the rate of nominal Catholic enrolments in Catholic-origin schools in Australia is falling. There's a table in Appendix 2 which will show you this by state and diocese. Between 2016 and 2021, the national percentage of Catholics enrolled in Catholic-origin primary schools dropped by 8%, and in Catholic-origin secondary schools by 7%. In some states, the drop was even higher: in Western Australia, the number of Catholics enrolled in Catholic-origin primary schools dropped by 10% and in secondary schools by 13%.

Figure 5. Percentage of non-Catholic students enrolled in Australian Catholic-origin primary and secondary schools [41]

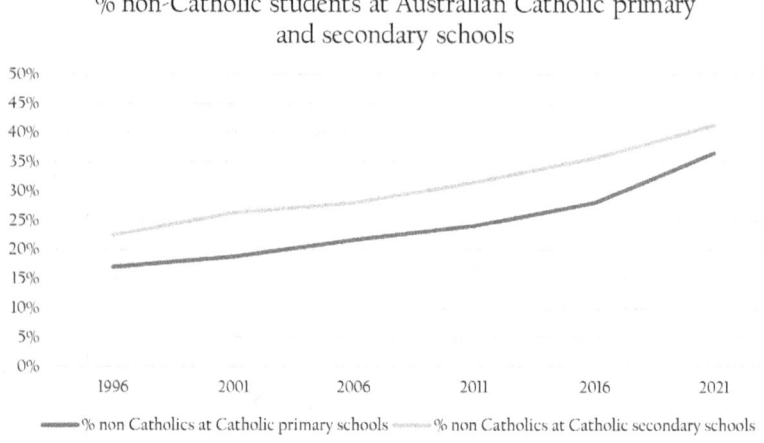

What might this look like in real life? In Australia in 2020, the national average enrolment in a Catholic-origin primary school was around 320 children, with 63% nominal Catholics (that's 202 children). Let's assume the pre-COVID19 national Mass attendance rate of around 11% applied to this school. That means that around 22 Catholic children in the entire school are being taken to Mass on Sundays by their parents. If the school has grades 1 to 6, that's around 4 children in each year group. The other 300 or so aren't going anywhere except school Masses.

The average national Catholic-origin secondary school in the same period had an enrolment of around 1,055 students, and 59% on average were Catholics, so that's 623 students. Unfortunately, the Mass attendance rate in this age group in 2021 was estimated at around 6.5%.[42] That means that only around 41 students in the entire school are going to Sunday Mass on a regular basis. If the school has grades 7 to 12, that's around 7 students per year level.

Imagine being one of the Mass-going kids in that school. You'd feel very isolated. Isla, a young mother of three and a former Catholic-origin school teacher, confirmed this from her own experience.

> In the large school that I worked at (approx 100 teaching staff), there were 3 of us practising the faith. Barely any families in a school of over 1000 kids practised the faith. So, if you put your teen into the local Catholic high school, the odds of them finding a friend who is also striving to become a saint are EXTREMELY low. And positive peer influence is a big factor for teens, so having friends who share your faith throughout your teen years is helpful (in my opinion).[43]

This could be another reason why many Mass-going Catholic parents are choosing to educate their children elsewhere. You also don't have to be a mathematical genius to predict what will happen soon if this rate of decline in Catholic enrolments continues: we will end up with a Catholic-origin education system with almost no Catholics enrolled in it. The schools will be full to bursting and financially solvent, but it's arguable as to whether they would still be 'Catholic'.

Fr Stephen, whose work takes him to several Catholic-origin schools in his large urban parish, has noticed the same thing.

> Almost all the serious young Catholics I know who are starting to marry and have children are wondering what they should do regarding their children's schooling. They see the very poor rate of church participation among those with twelve years of Catholic schooling. Some are choosing home-schooling, others public schooling, and others Catholic schooling but keeping a close eye on things. As a result, many Catholic schools will likely become even more nominally Catholic than they currently are, and eventually bishops may wonder if the effort of maintaining such a system is worth it.[44]

It also helps to explain certain recent events in Australia, such as the visit of US Catholic speaker Jason Evert. Three Catholic-origin schools in the Diocese of Broken Bay in NSW cancelled Evert's planned visit after a backlash from students and parents who made it plain that they didn't agree with the Church's teaching on human sexuality.⁴⁵ Undeterred, Evert spoke at several Sydney Catholic-origin schools instead.⁴⁶ Something similar happened in 2023 with a media investigation of Sydney's Opus Dei-run schools, where investigative reporters uncovered the startling fact that these Catholic-identifying schools were teaching the Catholic religion.⁴⁷ That this made them stand out among other Catholic schools is worth noting.

It's clear that the much-vaunted evangelisation effect on non-Catholics in Catholic-origin schools is not working as planned.⁴⁸ Rymarz and Cleary found that: 'In terms, though, of a strong reinforcing mechanism that helps sustain a distinctive worldview, Catholic schools have little impact once demographic factors are controlled for and most Catholic youth [have] weak affiliation and generic worldviews.'⁴⁹ It's almost as if these parents simply see Catholic-origin schools as a way of getting affordable quality private education for their children. And that's exactly what's happening, according to a 2009 report from Brisbane Catholic Education. This found that middle class and upwardly socially mobile parents were enrolling their children in Catholic-origin schools 'for predominantly pragmatic rather than religious reasons [with a resulting] marked decline in religious commitment'.⁵⁰

And who can blame them? Ethan, who has worked in Catholic-origin education, said:

> I think there is so much more that could be offered if the Catholic schools had some awareness of the rich intellectual and formational traditions that have animated the history of the Church, but that all seems to have been sold up the river so as to allow Catholic schools the dignity of offering a palatable education to those in Australian society who want a (relatively) cheap private education, and who are prepared to put up with some Jesus sprinkles on top (from time to time).⁵¹

Sometimes you hear the argument that people who use the Catholic-origin education system are also subsidising the state education system with their taxes, so everyone should lay off criticising them.⁵² This is fallacious. You could just as easily argue that the remaining 64% of people who send their kids to government schools are paying taxes to support a private, heavily subsidised Catholic-origin sector that they'll never use.⁵³ Isla, who now homeschools her children, also said that she feels excluded from what should be her own school system.

> ... in an ideal world, the teachers and kids at the local Catholic school would know and love the faith, the curriculum would be Catholic, and I would happily be able to send my kids there. As a Catholic parent, I feel like I have been almost forced out of what is rightfully ours as Catholics – our Catholic education system – as it has been taken over and leaves a lot to be desired [when] it comes to an actual Catholic education.⁵⁴

Catholic-origin schoolteachers

If the comments in CIA2022 were anything to go by, participants who identified as teachers in the Catholic-origin system were as unhappy with the state of the Church in Australia as I am, but for different reasons. Like this young man, for instance:

> The right-wing and church leadership in Australia is so worried about trying to hold people by the throat if you don't follow their outdated preachings, that you're neglecting the real people of the church. You could have so many more people involved in the church if you stopped trying to crucify every modern issue as being anti church. I've lost count how many times the church 'leaders' here have not followed the teachings of Jesus Christ. The hypocrisy is absolutely astounding. Stop trying to control women, people of the lgtbq+ family and immigrants and actually follow the teachings of Jesus Christ. Signed, a secondary teacher in the Sydney Catholic Schools system. (male, 30-39, brought up as Catholic, attended all Catholic schooling, goes to Mass intermittently)

What do we know about our Catholic-origin schoolteachers

and their personal faith? And does this matter? In the first chapter of this book, I talked about the need to know who we're listening to when we gather information about the Church from random Catholics. Knowing how often they go to Mass is a critical part of that information, so yes, it does matter.

Fr Michael, a priest in his fifties with many years of pastoral experience, explains why.

> Some [people] do not attend Mass regularly but fill positions of influence in the diocesan chancery and schools' office and schools. They are the ones who prepare children to receive the Most Blessed Eucharist for the first time, and they often lack the faith in this sacrament which would motivate them to attend Mass every Sunday. They prepare children for Confession but don't believe in it enough to go regularly or ever. They help children prepare for Confirmation but do not witness to their being on fire with the Holy Spirit and loving the Church.[55]

Leah, who lives in a rural diocese, has noticed a disturbing trend in her parish: 'We get quite a few teachers coming across from the Catholic school to be baptised for "career purposes". We have never seen them before their baptism, and we never see them again.'[56]

There is also a turf war taking place in Catholic-origin schools in Australia that goes something like this: religious education teachers are responsible for the faith formation part of Catholic education, not the rest of the staff. But the religious education teachers respond that it's not fair to give them the whole load – surely all teachers at a Catholic-origin school should be taking part in the students' faith formation?[57] Ethan has worked in Catholic-origin education and can give us an indication of which side is winning: 'Religious Education and any other religious elements seem to operate within the school in a manner that resembles them simply being tacked on to the educational model that operates elsewhere (i.e. in conventional state schools).'[58]

However, I think most Catholics who take their faith seriously would be hoping that in a Catholic-origin school, all the staff would be Mass-going Catholics whose lifestyles aren't openly at odds with the Church's teaching on sexuality and marriage. For example, Fr Michael is really happy with his situation.

> I have a wonderful Catholic RE coordinator in our parish school, a regular Mass attender who is also rostered for an hour of Adoration weekly. She has endeavoured to have practicing Catholic teachers teach Year 4 so that the children preparing for first Holy Communion would be taught by believers. She has a collection of about 50 donated First Communion dresses dry cleaned and ready to be borrowed each year.[59]

But I suspect he's in the minority. We don't really know what's going on in the staff room in terms of these issues, even though they're all easily measurable. Some local Catholic-origin education authorities have tried to find out about the level of faith formation in their teaching staff, but this data doesn't seem to have been made public.[60]

There's also a question of who's teaching the teachers. Fr Michael was less happy about a woman religious in a neighbouring diocese: 'Sr X in the Y diocese has been teaching new Catholic school teachers for 40 years that Jesus is not present in the Blessed Sacrament. Because she has been tolerated, many thousands of children have been taught a corrupted version of the Faith.'[61]

Richard Rymarz has presented exemplars of Catholic-origin schoolteachers which may be recognisable if you've been in the system yourself.[62] 'Marcus' is concerned about recruitment and retention as well as teacher quality:

> ... we just can't get enough RE teachers, nowhere near enough! ... Being an RE teacher begins with having a knowledge base, and that is becoming increasingly rare. ... they're just not connected, good authentic witnessing teachers with a sense of an active, committed faith, and most of them have never had it![63]

Then there is 'Siobhan', another participant in Rymarz's studies.

> She had a positive experience of being a student in Catholic schools and was very enthusiastic about her job. She was not an active member of a worshipping community but saw what she called the 'whole sacramental system' as being an important part of Catholic education. When she was visiting her mother, she went to Mass with her and regarded this as a perfectly natural and proper thing to do. She described her Catholic affiliation as being associated with having certain values, which she acknowledged were embraced by a wide range of people including many who were explicitly not religious.[64]

'Winona' is teaching the sacramental units at her school because 'it was important that children know more about this'. But Winona herself is a None – someone who says in the census that they have no religion at all.

> Winona did not come from a family with any real religious roots; she never attended faith-based schools, and all her tertiary education was in secular institutions. She was teaching at the school to fill a need for teachers. ... In addition, one of the attractions of taking on this position was that, if she remained at the school for a number of years, she was guaranteed a permanent position in a more attractive part of the diocese.[65]

In many parts of Australia, children at Catholic-origin schools are now given some form of religious literacy testing at intervals in primary school. However, the data from these tests is generally not made public, although it may be shared with the schools and parents. Teachers in Catholic-origin schools have mixed feelings about the administration of religious literacy tests – much as many secular teachers feel about the National Assessment Program-Literacy and Numeracy (NAPLAN).[66] Part of this comes from the feeling that the test results are – rightly or wrongly – a reflection on their performance as teachers.

Again, we're back where we started. What is the purpose of the

Catholic-origin education system? Is it to advance social mobility among the aspirational middle classes? Is it to create social capital and keep most of its graduates out of prison? Or is there a deeper purpose to it all?

I'm not saying there aren't pockets of good Catholic-origin education available. I am certain that there are. But for the most part, I see the system being used as cheap private schooling for aspirational people. This would be great if they were subsequently being drawn into the life of the Church and joining our parish communities. But they're mostly not. Otherwise, our Mass-going demographics would look rather different.

There are tentative moves now in some areas for the schools to try to re-engage parents as well as their children during preparation for the sacraments. However, given that there is no guarantee that the teachers in any Catholic-origin school are themselves properly formed in their faith, this may be a case of the blind leading the blind. Fr Stephen also wonders if he's doing any good at all.

> Our schools, for instance, constitute such a large institutional footprint, and take up a significant amount of my time as a parish priest, with seemingly little fruit emerging as a result. The glass-half-full view would be that it gives us a chance to plant seeds with folks whom we otherwise would have little-to-no contact with. The glass-half-empty view might be that many students are being presented with a rather lukewarm and uncompelling version of the faith, which in most cases will be swiftly abandoned.[67]

The school Mass

School Masses – at schools or at parishes – can be heartbreaking for Mass-going Catholic parents and others. They're not dissimilar to Lying Masses (see my earlier chapter on parish life). Earlier this year, I was listening to local radio as I drove to work. A group of DJs were in fits of laughter over the fact that one of their number, a parent, had gone to a school Mass that week at his child's Catholic-origin school. He said, 'I had to go to my kids' school Mass, right, [laughter] and you know, when I go up to get Communion …' At that point I switched off the radio. Isla had a sad experience of her own.

> As I overheard one exasperated mother say at church after a vigil Mass (that she had to attend in the lead-up to her child's First Holy Communion) 'Why do they make us do this? As if we haven't got anything better to do!' Her and her friends were then all eye-rolling about the church attendance that the school requests of them. My heart broke at that moment for Our Lord in the Eucharist… most likely just received by this mother 10 minutes earlier, and if not by her, then by most of the other parents there.[68]

It's clear that the Catholic-origin school in question had given no guidelines to anyone on the conditions for the reception of Holy Communion at these school Masses. Perhaps this is where we could start if we want to change things for the better.

In 2024, I attended an All Saints Day parish-based school Mass. Mass opened with a song that told the children present 'We are all saints' already, which made it sound super-easy and fun. Into my head came an image of Blessed Jerzy Popiełuszko, beaten and drowned in communist Poland in 1984. Not super-easy or fun for him – or indeed for any real saint I can think of, canonised or not.

In the homily, the deacon asked how many of the children had been trick-or-treating the night before, and there was a forest of raised hands. None of them could remember the responsorial psalm that they'd just recited, including the children who'd just read it at the lectern. Later they sang another song about having a 'meal with Gard' – the teacher leading the hymn sang it with an American accent, so all the kids did as well.

I tried to see the experience through the eyes of a non-Mass-attending child of that age group. The whole thing was boring, weird, not joined up, and certainly not a religion I'd be the slightest bit interested in. It also helped me to understand why Mass-going parents who take their faith seriously are deserting the Catholic-origin school system in droves.

Catholic-origin universities and chaplaincies in Australia

If Rymarz and Cleary are right, and school students show a slump in their Catholic belief and practice in high school, then Catholic-origin tertiary institutes should be casting out nets to bring them back to the Church as young adults. There are several Catholic-origin tertiary education providers in Australia today, including Australian Catholic University, the University of Notre Dame Australia, the Catholic Institute of Sydney, Catholic Theological College, and Campion College. They cater for different demographics: the universities and Campion College are mostly for school leavers, while the other institutes tend to have smaller footprints and deliver specific theological formation courses.

I would like to tell you how these institutions and their chaplaincies are working very hard to bring lapsed and cynical Australian Catholic-origin high school graduates back into the active practice of their faith. But I can't, because there is very little publicly available data on what proportion of any one institution's enrolments are Catholics, and whether they are regular Mass attenders or not, and few evaluations of the effectiveness of their chaplaincy services and programs.[69]

An informant told me:

> 'University Chaplaincies', who operate the chaplaincy programs in the state universities in Sydney, is doing really good work, funded by the archdiocese of Sydney (no surprises here). I doubt that they are keeping stats and if they are, they're certainly not publishing them, but they have a relatively organised operation – a happy hangover from Pell and [World Youth Day 2008] – and they (as well as the good folks at UNDA in Sydney) run

[Rite of Christian Initiation of Adults] programs that are welcoming a number of 20-somethings into the Church each year. The Melbourne archdiocese has redirected some focus to this end also in the past few years. Again, no stats.[70]

One exception to this is the *In Altum* program developed and rolled out by the University of Notre Dame Australia at its Sydney and Fremantle campuses – but the numbers involved in this program are tiny.[71] I also know anecdotally from my two visits there that Campion College has many Mass-going Catholic students, including those from the home-schooling community, and an active chaplaincy program.

I can definitely tell you that nationally in 2021, some 213,242 nominal Catholics were enrolled in higher education in Australia, with an additional 113,460 enrolled in technical or other forms of advanced education.[72] Do you ever think about Catholics who are enrolled at TAFE or doing apprenticeships? Most people don't, which is why you might struggle to find chaplains on the TAFE campuses. Anecdotally, apprentices and TAFE students who are working also don't always fit well into existing Catholic youth ministries. This means that we're potentially missing an entire section of the young Catholic Mass-going population who are vital for the Church's future.[73]

What I can also tell you is that Catholic-origin higher education is in the black financially. Every one of the organisations I have listed above except Campion College has publicly available financial reports, and they all showed very healthy equity in 2023. Higher education is a profitable business in Australia if you can obtain federal government supported places for your students, and these are no exception. And yet Mass attendance in this age group is very low in Australia. This suggests that perhaps our Catholic-origin institutes of higher education are not doing a very good job revitalising the faith of these young Catholic adults, even though they have access to their hearts and minds for at least three years.

And it seems they have the same problems as some Catholic-origin schools in Australia. When former union leader Joe de Bruyn, himself a Catholic, spoke at an Australian Catholic University graduation ceremony in October 2024, he described abortion as 'the deliberate killing of unborn human beings'. He also said that most human communities throughout history had regarded marriage as something that took place between a man and a woman.

De Bruyn was being given an honorary doctorate at the same ceremony and had provided his speech to ACU a week in advance.[74] Yet his speech triggered walkouts from some of the graduands and staff present. The *Daily Mail* reported:

> As people left the exhibition centre in droves – including some who had been sitting beside him on the stage – Mr de Bruyn encouraged students to preserve their Catholic faith in the years to come.
>
> 'My experience is that many Catholics cave in to peer pressure. They think their professional lives will be harmed if they promote the teachings of the church.
>
> 'My experience is that this is not so,' he said.[75]

ACU later offered free and confidential counselling services to graduates and staff who attended the ceremony, with their spokesperson saying without any hint of irony that, 'ACU is committed to providing a safe, inclusive and respectful environment for students and staff of all beliefs ... Education, faith, respect and acceptance are at the heart of our mission as a Catholic university.'[76]

All of this raises some interesting questions. What factors make a Catholic in Australia choose a particular university? Are Catholics distinguishable from non-Catholics in this respect? Is it pragmatism or proximity or other factors? Do Mass-going Catholics prefer Catholic-origin universities and institutes of higher education? And does this matter to any Catholic-origin institute, if their enrolments are high enough for them to break even financially?

We don't seem to know the answers to any of these questions, but I'm very curious about all of them, which means they might make good future research projects. I would also love to see more data shared and published on Australian university chaplaincy programs that measurably work to re-engage disaffected young Catholic adults. Meanwhile, I will let Ethan, who works in Catholic education, have the last word.

> I would love to see more care taken to the 'spiritual accompaniment' of young adults in the years after high school – only one university in [my state] has a regular chaplain ... there is no chaplaincy to any TAFE or other training institution. I think that this is a serious misstep for the Church ... at this crucial time, and work done with young people during this time will pay serious dividends for the Kingdom, and likely save a great deal of pain for any number of individuals.[77]

Catholic-origin hospitals and health care in Australia today

So far, my picture of the Catholic industrial complex is pretty grim, and Catholic-origin health care provision is no exception. How does it serve the parochial-diocesan part of the Church in Australia? Let me refresh your memory about what Fr Charles Curran said back in 1997: 'in light of this situation Catholic hospitals have an impossible mission. The mission statements of these institutions are beautiful and inspiring, but the culture of the Catholic hospital prevents the fulfillment of the stated mission in the present circumstances.'[78]

It's true that some Catholic-origin health care services help to subsidise free or low-cost services via different initiatives that help people experiencing disadvantage of all kinds. But the bulk of their income and expenditure is in delivering health care services in a semi-private collaboration with state governments and the Commonwealth government, who need their hospital and aged care beds to relieve pressure on the public health and aged care systems.

In 2011, Archbishop Anthony Fisher of Sydney described two fictional Catholic hospitals, St Mary Magdalene and St Norbert's, which he had invented as far back as 1997 as models of how Catholic-origin health care was evolving.

> My purpose was to highlight some of the challenges for Catholic identity presented by modern institutionalized medicine and to outline two kinds of response: one has been to offer top-quality healthcare on competitive terms but at some cost to 'Catholic identity'; another maintains religious traditions and particular, often fairly low-tech, forms of care but at the risk of becoming rather marginal.[79]

Health care is good. We all need it. But how is this any of this specifically Catholic health care? Is there anything more to it than a mission statement?

The numbers – and the balance sheet

In my previous chapter on religious life, I described the active religious orders whose multi-million dollar corporations are now run by MPJPs.[80] Billions of dollars are churned through Catholic-origin health care and related organisations in Australia every year. I don't want to labour the point, but we are once again faced with questions of how any of this helps to build up the parochial-diocesan structure of the Church. What I see here are successful health corporations that have at best a historic relationship with the local Church and are now operating in their own right and for their own ends.

One thing did leap out at me when I was reading the Calvary Health Care Bethlehem Kooyong Precinct annual report for 2023. What started life in 1941 as a Catholic private hospital in Victoria has now become a publicly funded health service, run as part of an MPJP. After a recent overhaul of the site, they relocated the chapel in the new complex.

> A Catholic mass and Anglican mass are held monthly in the space as well as other significant services in the Chapel and adjoining Mary Potter Courtyard. A sacred space for everyone in the heart of the Calvary Kooyong Precinct, the Chapel is accessible for anyone seeking quiet reflection, prayer and spiritual solace.[81]

My local secular public hospital also has Mass once a month in its chaplaincy – the same rate as this Catholic-origin hospital. But my office is located on another secular public hospital campus, where Mass is usually offered at the chaplaincy three days a week and on Sundays. I am better served as a Mass-going Catholic by working on a secular hospital campus in Perth than I would be working at Calvary Health Care Kooyong.

The recent case of Calvary Hospital in the ACT is worth looking at in more detail. In June 2023, the ACT government basically gave itself legislative permission to acquire Calvary Hospital's operations and staff, with no compensation to the original owners.[82] By May 2024 the ACT government had paid $23 million for associated costs but were waiting for Calvary to make its formal claim before paying any more.[83]

Catholic media presented this as a shameless land grab, which it may well have been. Having said that, the ACT government already owned the land on which the hospital was built, and always did.[84] Calvary and the ACT government had been negotiating about the future use of the site for at least a year beforehand.[85] Calvary Public Hospital Bruce, the hospital in question, was also already operating as a public hospital. I can't find the detailed funding arrangements, but I assume from the title 'public hospital' that most of the work being carried out there was already being funded by taxpayers.

The legislative grab was sneaky, but there was also a reasonable business case behind it. If it's already a public hospital in everything but name – and in this case, in name – then why can't the local government take over the whole enterprise? And this is what every Catholic MPJP and Catholic-origin health care and social services organisation, business, and corporation should look out for. The more government funding you take for your operations, and the more you come to rely on this, the greater the risk of this happening to you one day. It's also harder to take the moral high ground when you don't own the ground in question.

Catholic-origin charities

We know the Church in Australia has a robust history of charitable welfare work, mostly carried out by heroic religious and committed lay people. But what's the story today – are these charities still running on cash donations from good Catholic people? Or are Catholic charities in Australia today mostly made up of government-funded salaried workers who provide goods and services to the disadvantaged?[86]

The Catholic Church is not alone in Australia in receiving government funding for charitable enterprises; other mainstream churches do the same. I decided to look at some representative Catholic charities, just in NSW.[87] You can see that the proportion of government funding for each varies considerably. Some of these charities have bigger investment portfolios than others, so they can raise more revenue from these sources instead. You can also see here what proportion of the charity's expenses came from the cost of employing paid staff.

Table 13. NSW Catholic charities, government revenue and donation revenue, December 2023

Charity	% revenue from government	% revenue from donations and bequests	% employee expenses
Marist Youth Care Ltd[88]	98%	<1%	82%
CatholicCare Wilcannia-Forbes[89]	95%	1%	58%
CentreCare SouthWest NSW[90]	85%	2%	71%
CatholicCare Social Services Hunter-Manning[91]	78%	2%	54%
CatholicCare Diocese of Wollongong[92]	66%	<1%	72%
St Agnes Care and Lifestyle[93]	63%	<1%	68%
CatholicCare Diocese of Broken Bay[94]	60%	1%	72%
CatholicCare Sydney[95]	56%	7%	78%
Dunlea Centre (Boys Town)[96]	48%	39%	73%
Marymead CatholicCare Canberra Goulburn[97]	47%	<1%	73%
St Francis Social Services[98]	38%	43%	63%
Daughters of Charity of St Vincent de Paul – Rosalie Rendu[99]	0%	1%	20%
Trustees of Mary Aikenhead Ministries[100]	0%	34%	19%

What does all this mean for what we used to think of as 'Catholic charity' – as a moral action performed by one individual to benefit another? Fr Charles Curran said back in 1997 that in some ways, getting government funding for Catholic charities is a good thing because it relieves the Church of the burden of having to fund these charities themselves. But he also said that this reduced the sense of ownership of these services by the Church as the people of God. Can we as Catholics really pat ourselves on the back for the wonderful work our Church is doing for the poor and marginalised, when it's actually doing it on the taxpayer dollar?

It's also risky. When most of your funding comes from a secular government, how are you allowed to spend it? Can you deliver authentically Catholic social services within the moral framework of the Church? For example, what about providing condoms for street prostitutes who might be using your drop-in service, or referring pregnant homeless women for abortions if they want them? Should you abandon even trying, and have an open-doors policy for all comers with no moral judgement? And if you go down that path, can anyone then distinguish between a Catholic charity and a secular charity?

Bear in mind, too, that it's not like these charities are handing out fistfuls of government cash to disadvantaged people. Most of the government funding that goes to charities is to pay salaries for staff to deliver goods and services. So perhaps we can also see this as a Catholic-adjacent job creation scheme operating within a charity framework. Like the Catholic-origin schools, this currently works for everyone – the staff get paid, the poor get the services, and the Church gets the credit.

Finally, this poses some interesting questions about where and when Catholics – especially struggling families – might choose to give charitable donations from what's left after they've paid their taxes and superannuation. For example, in the 2023-24 financial year, 40% of the taxes I paid became government welfare payments to people in greater need than I: aged care, disability care, families, the unemployed, and 'other'. I am already more than tithing to help the poor in this country via a range of agencies, probably including many Catholic charities. The next time a Catholic charity asks me for a donation, I could say quite honestly that I already gave at the office.

But isn't it better that the government gives all this money to the Church, rather than frittering it away on wicked projects of its own? This response usually comes from people whose Catholicism has devolved into the football club supporter mentality: better us than them. Really? If they can show me how most Catholic charity work is really all that different from secular government-funded projects, I'll think again. In the meantime, it seems increasingly that the least confusing form of Catholic charity might be simply to give food or groceries to a homeless person on the street. It's direct, it's local, and you're connecting immediately and personally with Christ in disguise. Or, donate in kind to a small local organisation with minimal overheads and no government funding. They do exist, if you're prepared to look for them.

Whatever happened to the Australian Catholic media?

Once upon a time, most dioceses in Australia had at least one print newspaper, and possibly some magazines as well.[101] Today, most diocesan publications – and with them, authentic Catholic journalism in Australia – have disappeared. They have been replaced by tightly controlled lay-led diocesan communications offices and directors. We also now have mostly websites, and very few print media periodicals remain.

And yet outside Australia, genuine Catholic journalism is thriving. In the UK and the US, there are many quality publications, all available online with at least some free content, that now form part of many Australian Catholics' daily media digest (including mine). The *Catholic Herald* (UK), *Crux*, *America*, *Catholic World Report*, and *The Pillar* are just a few that come to mind.

Catholic journalism occupies a tricky space in the Church – it sits between the Church's revealed teachings and mission and what's going on in the world. When Catholic journalists exercise their vocations responsibly, readers begin to trust them. The CIA2022 study found that when Catholics had to make important moral decisions, one of the primary sources of information they accessed were Catholic media websites – but not diocesan websites.[102]

Trustworthy Catholic journalists serve at the coalface of the Church where it's living and too often bleeding. Adam Wesselinoff, past editor of *The Catholic Weekly*, described his job in these terms.

> Editorial work also involves endless micro-judgments about everything from conforming copy to house style, to interacting with readers. ...
>
> For instance: the other day we had a reader call to complain that there was too much Maronite content in the newspaper. What do you do about such a complaint? Is it the paper's fault that Maronites are among the most vigorous and organised Catholics in Sydney?
>
> What happens when someone pitches you a story about having been abused by a priest or calls to complain about our coverage of Cardinal Pell based on their past experiences of abuse – both interactions I've had more than once.
>
> What about church politics? Last year we had a stoush with the papal biographer Austen Ivereigh over some columns we syndicated by George Weigel about Francis' 10th anniversary. How do you resolve a disagreement between duelling papal biographers?[103]

My experience as an opinion columnist in the same publication has been similar. People have read my column and unburdened themselves via email to me about all sorts of things because they trust that I will listen, and they hope that I will respond (and I always do). You will find the same thing happening in the comments box of any Catholic online publication that offers real journalism and real opinion. Other Catholics respond and share, building up conversations, airing grievances, and seeking solace.

Do they do this to diocesan communications directors? I doubt it. I'd guess that trust in Australian Catholic institutional media releases and strategic communications is at an all-time low. Communications in the corporate sense is mostly about gatekeeping, influencing, or plausible deniability. It's largely anonymous. You may find articles on a diocesan communications website written by named individuals who may be described as journalists, but these stories will have been edited to conform with a predetermined and acceptable spin.

This is just public relations. Everything is always rosy in the diocese; everyone is smiling in the photos; there are no crises and no dramas. The few remaining print journals survive by selling advertising to Catholic-origin schools, universities, aged care providers, and funeral directors, so it's hard to imagine them running any hard-hitting exposés of the Catholic industrial complex. There are no different voices – and I suspect fewer and fewer readers. Most diocesan Catholic communications in Australia are now so bland that it's like they don't expect – or even want – anyone to read them.

I will give you an example of how this can work in practice against the actual communication of information, and what message this really sends to ordinary Catholics. In May 2024, the NCPR released its 2021 report on Sunday Mass attendance which showed a catastrophic drop in national Mass attendance numbers from around 600,000 to around 400,000. The ACBC media release headline? 'National survey shows Australia's Catholics are online and multicultural.'[104]

This was not an accident or an oversight. Whoever wrote the media release had chosen to ignore the obvious bad news story that was front, centre, and unavoidable. Instead, they chose to zoom in on something much, much less scary than the fact that we'd lost nearly a quarter of a million Mass-going Catholics in just five years. This approach does not build trust in church leadership, because what it really communicates is a preoccupation with face-saving and an unwillingness to tackle the hard stuff that's shaping our future as a Church.

And yet I understand why they might feel this way. The Church in Australia right now is politically weak and exposed. We can't summon up a scary voting bloc to influence any party in any election. We have no wide-ranging support base in the Australian population, who are increasingly hostile to organised religion. We have a lot of tax-free organisations which absorb billions of dollars of government funding. We own a lot of property.

One thing only is currently keeping an aggressive State at bay. If we closed all the Catholic-origin agencies, schools, and hospitals, no government in any state in Australia has the wherewithal to accommodate the people who would then need rescuing, housing, and schooling. Right now, it works for everyone that the business arm of the Church is allowed to continue in its present form.

But that may change, especially if the State decides it could do just as good a job of running all this by itself – after all, it's paying for almost everything. Threatening to close Catholic-origin organisations in protest worked in 1962 in the battle for state aid for schools. It would not work in 2024 as part of a campaign to secure religious freedom for schools to teach the Catholic religion and employ Catholic teachers – mostly because the staff (who don't care either way) would almost certainly refuse to go on strike.[105]

Conclusion

This has been a difficult chapter to write. I have spent most of my life on the government payroll, and I know how comfortable it can be. There is also nothing wrong with making money, or making a profit, or 'not making a loss' if you're a not-for-profit organisation. Catholic-origin schools, universities, health care, and charities are providing goods and services to people who need them. They're probably doing it quite well, because they're held accountable by government – their principal funder – for what they do.

But is this part of the Church's mission? Does any of this support the parochial-diocesan structure of the Church? I'd suggest that most of this business – and it is mostly business, with a sprinkling of charity – is indistinguishable from similar secular businesses and non-government organisations in Australia. They're doing the same job. They're even doing charity or philanthropy in the same way as most non-Catholic businesses in Australia, because there are now hearty tax incentives for corporations to give back to the community in many ways.

I believe that there is only one way in which the Catholic industrial complex really gives back to the parochial-diocesan structure in Australia. That's in the silent work of holy people who just happen to be employed by these Catholic-origin businesses and corporations. I have said before that the Catholic-origin education system in Australia is the great employer of the nation's brothers-in-law, and I still mean it (having had two brothers-in-law employed by it).[106] If the people working in these organisations are growing in grace with the Mass and the sacraments and daily prayer and sacrifice, or just plain offering it up, then that's all to the good.

But these holy people could just as easily do this essential work of building up the Body of Christ by working for a secular organisation or corporation. Any one of us can do this work, and in fact we're all called to it. We should all try to turn our paid work into something that sanctifies us. And you can do that driving a forklift, running a mine site, teaching at a secular school, swiping groceries through a checkout, cleaning offices at 5am every weekday, or moving large amounts of stuff around through an import-export business.

I would also argue that these Catholic-origin businesses,

corporations, and charities now exist for themselves, rather than for the Church. They are self-sustaining – as long as the government funding continues. They don't need the Church, and their relationship with the Church is now mostly sentimental, like memories of a teenage romance when you reach retirement age.

This sentimentality is also probably the greatest risk. Given that so few Catholics in Australia go to Mass on Sunday, and fewer and fewer believe in its core teachings, it's statistically likely that those who are now sitting on the MPJP boards and governing bodies of charities aren't regular Mass-goers at all. They're also mostly from the Boomer generation – the one with the lowest levels of Catholic belief in Australia.[107]

These organisations are also employing thousands of people who would be very disgruntled if they suddenly lost their jobs in the Catholic business arm. They are the people least likely to put up a fight if the government starts exercising a heavier hand, like introducing sex education programs at odds with Catholic teaching or demanding that hospitals offer procedures that aren't consistent with Catholic morality. William, who has experience in this area, thinks this model is already outdated.

> I'll be really blunt – I'd like to see a formal end to the PJP model of governance. I'd like to see that end – it's not working. We've got boards that have no understanding of Catholic faith and they're running institutions with a framed mission statement stuck to the wall that isn't lived. It's embarrassing for all of us who are trying to work and lead with a mission mindset to have people around who are well remunerated, leading organisations on the government dollar with the word 'Catholic' everywhere. It's not honest.[108]

But without government funding, most of these Catholic-origin organisations would collapse completely. They are unlikely to survive the imposition of any real government sanctions – and an unsympathetic government is only an election away. I am not sure it's realistic to expect this amount of money with no conditions attached.

So where can we go from here? It's probably time for a palate cleanser, so please join me in the final chapter where we can try to make sense of all of this and find some constructive ways forward.

---

[1] There have been some successful civil cases brought against Australian dioceses, most recently Burke, C. (2023, November 19). Multi-million Catholic Church payout 'massively important' for future sexual abuse cases. *ABC News*, https://www.abc.net.au/news/2023-11-19/catholic-church-payout-important-future-sexual-abuse-cases/103118822. In an earlier case in the archdiocese of Perth, the complainant had been offered $50,000 compensation by the archdiocese. He successfully sued in a civil case and was awarded $2.45 million in 2021, McNeill, H. (2021, January 21). Catholic Church makes record payout in child sex abuse case. *WA Today*, https://www.watoday.com.au/national/western-australia/catholic-church-makes-record-payout-in-child-sex-abuse-case-20210120-p56vng.html

[2] The Cardinal Becciu case is extraordinary, mostly because it proceeded to a trial and conviction, despite substantial efforts in many mainstream Catholic media sources to minimise and explain away what was going on over several years beforehand. AFP. (2023, December 17). Vatican court convicts cardinal Angelo Becciu of embezzlement. *The Guardian*, https://www.theguardian.com/world/2023/dec/16/vatican-court-convicts-cardinal-angelo-becciu-of-embezzlement. *The Pillar* is the best source of continuous and detailed reporting on this scandal.

[3] I re-read the entire section in the Catechism on the human condition and salvation (1877-2051), and Leo XIII's encyclical 1891 *Rerum Novarum*, https://www.vatican.va/content/leo-xiii/en/encyclicals/documents/hf_l-xiii_enc_15051891_rerum-novarum.html, before writing this chapter.

[4] The best-known complainant here was the late Christopher Hitchens. See for example (2003, October 20). Mommie dearest: The pope beatifies Mother Teresa, a fanatic, a fundamentalist, and a fraud. *Slate*, https://slate.com/news-and-politics/2003/10/the-fanatic-fraudulent-mother-teresa.html. You can read a summary of common complaints about St Teresa by Taylor, A. (2016, September 1). Why Mother Teresa is still no saint to many of her critics. *Washington Post*, https://www.washingtonpost.com/news/worldviews/wp/2015/02/25/why-to-many-critics-mother-teresa-is-still-no-saint/

[5] Editors. (1986, March 29). The Charles Curran case: From March 29, 1986. *America: the Jesuit Review*, https://www.americamagazine.org/issue/100/charles-curran-case

[6] Curran, C. (1997). The Catholic identity of Catholic institutions. *Theological Studies*, 58, 90-108; 93. Available from https://www.xavier.edu/jesuitresource/online-resources/documents/Curran.pdf

[7] Curran, Catholic identity, 97.

[8] Australian Catholic Historical Society. (n.d.). *Australian Catholic charities*, https://australiancatholichistoricalsociety.com.au/history-resources/australian-catholic-charities/

⁹ How much' is a complex question and there's no simple formula for working it out – but it's something you should ask about before you donate to any charity. For a good summary of why, see Seedling. (n.d.). How much should a charity spend on admin? And what else you should ask to make sure your donation isn't wasted. *Seedling*, https://seedlinggiving.com.au/blog-article/how-much-should-a-charity-spend-on-admin See also St Vincent de Paul Society. (2011). *Submission to Treasury review of not-for-profit governance arrangements (Jan 2011)*, https://treasury.gov.au/sites/default/files/2019-03/St-Vincent-de-Paul-1.pdf; also Australian Charities and Not-for-Profits Commission. (n.d.). *Charities and administration costs*, https://www.acnc.gov.au/for-public/understanding-charities/charities-and-administration-costs

¹⁰ *Catholic Charities USA*, https://www.catholiccharitiesusa.org/

¹¹ Curran, Catholic identity, 102-103.

¹² Ibid,, 92-93,102.

¹³ Martyr, P. (2024, May 11). Money and ministry: Are we serving the right master? *The Catholic Weekly*, https://catholicweekly.com.au/money-and-ministry-are-we-serving-the-right-master/

¹⁴ Piotrowski, D. (2020, May 7). What George Pell knew: Bombshell report reveals Cardinal failed to remove a notorious paedophile priest who 'repeatedly sexually abused children in the confession booth'. *Daily Mail*, https://www.dailymail.co.uk/news/article-8294783/Cardinal-George-Pell-Redacted-royal-commission-report-released.html

¹⁵ Broken Rites. (n.d.) The Marist Brothers recycled an offender to a new position of trust. *Broken Rites*, https://brokenrites.org.au/drupal/node/80. See also Martyr, P. (2020, May 7). The lay role in covering up abuse. *The Catholic Weekly*, https://catholicweekly.com.au/the-lay-role-in-covering-up-abuse/

¹⁶ The Pillar. (2024). Glemkowski: Why the National Eucharistic Congress worked. *The Pillar*, https://www.pillarcatholic.com/p/glemkowski-why-the-national-eucharistic

¹⁷ McAlpine, S. (2021, February 6). Clerical bullying and spiritual abuse: Are they the same thing? *Stephen McAlpine*, https://stephenmcalpine.com/clerical-bullying-and-spiritual-abuse-are-they-the-same-thing/. See also: (2017, November 7). Does your church have a spiritual Spacey? *Stephen McAlpine*, https://stephenmcalpine.com/does-your-church-have-a-spiritual-spacey/;

¹⁸ McAlpine, S. (2019, October 14). Bully vol. 3. *Stephen McAlpine*, https://stephenmcalpine.com/bully-vol-3/

¹⁹ Ibid.

²⁰ Crikey. (2005, July 25). Hundreds of journalistic couples. *Crikey*, https://www.crikey.com.au/2005/07/25/hundreds-of-journalistic-couples/; Crook, A. (2010, March 17). Journalism media couples: an updated Crikey list. *Crikey*, https://www.crikey.com.au/2010/03/17/journalism-media-couples-an-updated-crikey-list/ ; Crikey. (2016, January 14). Media couples: a (significantly updated) Crikey list. *Crikey*, https://www.crikey.com.au/2016/01/14/media-couples-a-significantly-updated-crikey-list/

²¹ Sadewo, G., Bullivant, S., & Cranney, S. (2021). McCarrick, the kingmaker? A social network analysis of episcopal promotion in the Roman Catholic Church. *Catholic Social Science Review*, 26, 247-261. https://www.pdcnet.org/cssr/content/cssr_2021_0026_0247_0261

[22] The Pillar. (2025, September 5). *Newlywed IOR employees fall foul of nepotism rule*. The Pillar, https://www.pillarcatholic.com/p/newlywed-ior-employees-fall-foul

[23] Janis, I. (1971). Groupthink. *Psychology Today* (magazine), November, 84-89. Available in reprint at https://agcommtheory.pbworks.com/f/GroupThink.pdf

[24] O'Connor, S. (2018, November 22). Confessions of a Catholic whistleblower. *First Things*, https://www.firstthings.com/web-exclusives/2018/11/confessions-of-a-catholic-whistleblower

[25] You can read about the history of state aid here: National Museum Australia. (2022). *Aid for non-government schools*, https://www.nma.gov.au/defining-moments/resources/aid-for-non-government-schools

[26] National Catholic Education Commission (NCEC). (2022). *National Catholic Education Commission annual report 2022*, 3. https://ncec.catholic.edu.au/wp-content/uploads/2023/08/2022-NCEC-Annual-Report.pdf

[27] NCEC, *Annual report 2022*, 18.

[28] Brisbane Catholic Education. (2024). *Annual report 2023*, https://www.bne.catholic.edu.au/aboutus/AnnualReports/Documents/2023%20BCE%20Annual%20Report.pdf

[29] This report does not provide data on income but does provide a pie chart showing the proportions of different types of income with no data labels, Catholic Education Northern Territory. (2023). *Catholic Education Northern Territory 2022 annual report*, 81. https://os-data-2.s3-ap-southeast-2.amazonaws.com/ceont/bundle3/catholic_education_nt_-_annual_report_2022.pdf

[30] CESA has five separate funds, all of which report separately. The Special Purposes Account annual report from 2022 reports grant income as 95% of all income in that report. However, if we sum all the income from all five reports, grant funding falls to 48% of all income in that year. Catholic Education South Australia, https://report.cesa.catholic.edu.au/statistics-and-financials/financial-reports

[31] Catholic Education Tasmania. (2023). *Catholic Education Tasmania annual report 2022*, https://tascathed.schoolzineplus.com/_file/media/2680/20231212_annual_report_2022.pdf

[32] Catholic Education WA (CEWA). (2024). *Catholic Education WA annual report 2023*, https://www.cewa.edu.au/wp-content/uploads/2024/06/AnnualReport2023_v2_Web.pdf

[33] Catholic Schools NSW (CSNSW). (2024, September 9). *How Catholic schools are funded*, https://www.csnsw.catholic.edu.au/funding-of-nsw-catholic-schools-system/; Catholic Schools NSW. (2023). *Catholic Schools NSW annual report 2023*, https://www.csnsw.catholic.edu.au/sites/default/files/2024-10/CSNSW-Annual-Report-2023.pdf; projected 2024 funding – CSNSW, *How Catholic schools are funded*, https://www.csnsw.catholic.edu.au/funding-of-nsw-catholic-schools-system/

[34] Diocese of Maitland-Newcastle Catholic Schools Office. (2023). *Financial report 2022*, https://www.acnc.gov.au/charity/charities/3223f2a8-38af-e811-a963-000d3ad244fd/documents/

[35] Melbourne Archdiocese Catholic Schools. (2023). *Financial report 2023*, https://www.acnc.gov.au/charity/charities/35e4116b-1596-ed11-aad1-0022489733de/documents/

36 Victorian Catholic Education Authority. (2023). *Victorian Catholic Education Authority annual report 2023*, 32-33. https://vcea.catholic.edu.au/about-us/governance/#annual-reports

37 NCEC. (2024). *National Catholic Education Commission annual report 2023*, https://ncec.catholic.edu.au/wp-content/uploads/2023/04/NCEC-2023-Annual-Report_Final.pdf

38 Rymarz, R., & Cleary, A. (2016). Some religious beliefs and behaviours of Australian Catholic school students. *Journal of Beliefs and Values*, 37(1), 68–77. https://doi.org/10.1080/13617672.2016.1141530; National Centre for Pastoral Research (NCPR). (2021). *Australian Catholic Mass attendance report 2016*, https://ncpr.catholic.org.au/wp-content/uploads/2021/07/Mass-attendance-in-Australia-2016-Revised-July-2021.pdf

39 McLaughlin, D., & Standen, P. (2013). The rise and demise of Australian Catholic education? Unpublished paper read at Australian Catholic School Leadership Conference, Sydney, August 12. Cited in Gleeson, J., & O'Neill, M. (2018). Student-teachers' perspectives on the purposes and characteristics of faith-based schools: an Australian view. *British Journal of Religious Education*, 40(1), 55–69; 57-58. https://doi.org/10.1080/01416200.2016.1256266

40 Martyr, P., & Bullivant, S. (2024). *The Catholics in Australia Survey 11 – Catholic schooling*, https://papers.ssrn.com/sol3/papers.cfm?abstract_id=5016420

41 Data taken from the National Centre for Pastoral Research (NCPR) *Diocesan social profiles* for 2016, https://ncpr.catholic.org.au/2016-diocesan-social-profiles/, and 2021, https://ncpr.catholic.org.au/2021-diocesan-social-profiles/

42 NCPR. (2024). *Australian Catholic Mass attendance report 2021*, https://ncpr.catholic.org.au/wp-content/uploads/2024/05/Mass-attendance-in-Australia-2021-FINAL.pdf

43 Isla, personal communication, 7 June 2024.

44 Fr Stephen, personal communication, 30 August 2024.

45 Staff Writers. (2024, May 20). Conservative American 'chastity speaker' Jason Evert's visits to NSW schools cancelled after backlash. *ABC News*, https://www.abc.net.au/news/2024-05-20/schools-cancel-visit-by-us-chastity-speaker-jason-evert/103868358

46 Al-Akiki, G. (2024, May 21). Evert a success with students and parents. *The Catholic Weekly*, https://catholicweekly.com.au/jason-evert-a-success-with-students-and-parents/

47 See Chapter 5 on religious life.

48 Rymarz, R., & Cleary, A. (2016). Some religious beliefs and behaviours of Australian Catholic school students. *Journal of Beliefs and Values*, 37(1), 68–77. https://doi.org/10.1080/13617672.2016.1141530

49 Ibid.

50 Dowling, A., Beavis, A., Underwood, C., Sadeghi, R., & O'Malley, K. 2009. *Who's coming to school today? Final report*. Brisbane: ACER, Brisbane Catholic Education. Cited in Gleeson & O'Neill, Student-teachers' perspectives, 58. https://doi.org/10.1080/01416200.2016.1256266

51 Ethan, personal communication, 30 May 2024.

52 Donnelly, K. (2019). Danger: the threats to Australia's Catholic schools. *The Catholic Weekly*, https://catholicweekly.com.au/danger-the-threats-to-australias-catholic-schools/ I'm hoping Kevin has had a come-to-Jesus moment, quite literally, since then.

53 Australian Bureau of Statistics (ABS). (2023). *Schools*. https://www.abs.gov.au/statistics/people/education/schools/latest-release

54 Isla, personal communication, 7 June 2024.

55 Fr Michael, personal communication, 5 August 2024.

56 Leah, personal communication, 19 June 2024.

57 Poncini, A. (2024). Formation fit for purpose: empowering religious educators working in Catholic schools. *Religions*, 15(6), 665-. https://doi.org/10.3390/rel15060665. See also O'Shea, G. (2017). Confronting dualism in religious education. *Journal of Religious Education*, 64, 197-206. https://link.springer.com/article/10.1007/s40839-017-0044-6

58 Ethan, personal communication, 30 May 2024.

59 Fr Michael, personal communication, 5 August 2024.

60 The Catholic education system in Western Australia has commissioned two recent studies into faith formation needs among its staff – in 2015 and again in 2023. Poncini, Formation fit for purpose.

61 Fr Michael, personal communication, 5 August 2024.

62 Rymarz, R. (2023). A narrative approach to discerning some key issues for Catholic education in a more synodal Church. *Religions*, 14, 1121. https://doi.org/10.3390/rel14091121

63 Ibid.

64 Ibid.

65 Ibid.

66 Australian Education Union Victorian Branch. (n.d.) *National teacher survey gives thumbs down to NAPLAN*, https://www.aeuvic.asn.au/national-teacher-survey-gives-thumbs-down-naplan This cites a 2018 survey.

67 Fr Stephen, personal communication, 30 August 2024.

68 Isla, personal communication, 7 June 2024.

69 See also Haddad, R. (2023). George Cardinal Pell's contribution to tertiary chaplaincy reform: a personal recollection. *Journal of the Australian Catholic Historical Society*, 44, 154-.

70 Anonymous, personal communication, 7 November 2024.

71 Topliss, J., Gourlay, T., & Chua, R. (2024). In Altum – 'Put Out into the Deep': a formation program for missionary discipleship for students at the University of Notre Dame Australia. *Religions*, 15(2). https://doi.org/10.3390/rel15020147 See also Wesselinoff, A. (2022, September 23). New campus approach goes for discipleship. *The Catholic Weekly*, https://catholicweekly.com.au/new-campus-approach-goes-for-discipleship/

72 NCPR. (2024). *Social profile of the Catholic community in Australia*, 20. https://ncpr.catholic.org.au/wp-content/uploads/2023/04/2021-Social-Profile-of-the-Catholic-Community-in-Australia-R.pdf

73 Martyr, P. (2024, October 23). Make room in your heart for the poor and the weird. *The Catholic Weekly*, https://catholicweekly.com.au/catholic-church-australia-present-and-future/

74 Cassidy, C. (2024, October 22). Former union head Joe de Bruyn's speech condemning abortion and same-sex marriage sparks walkout at Catholic university.

The Guardian, https://www.theguardian.com/australia-news/2024/oct/22/joe-de-bruyn-speech-acu-walkouts-abortion-same-sex-marriage-ntwnfb

75 Collins, P. (2024, October 22). Graduation address sparks mass walkout at major Australian university. *Daily Mail*, https://www.dailymail.co.uk/news/article-13985447/Graduation-speech-walkout-abortion-killer.html

76 Collins, Graduation address.

77 Ethan, personal communication, 30 May 2024.

78 Curran, Catholic identity, 97.

79 Fisher, A. (2012). *Catholic bioethics for a new millennium*. Cambridge University Press, 275-301.

80 See also McMullen, G., & Laverty, M. (2020). Learnings from the development of new lay-led church entities in Australia. *Australasian Catholic Record*, 97(2), 131–143.

81 Calvary Health Care Bethlehem Kooyong Precinct (2023). *Annual report 2022-23*, 40. https://www.calvarycare.org.au/public-hospital-bethlehem/wp-content/uploads/sites/5/2023/11/2023_CHCB_AnnualReport_FINAL.pdf

82 Fisher, A. (2024, June 9). Religious freedom in a secular world: Doomed or doable? *The Catholic Weekly*, 12-13. The full statement can be found here: https://www.sydneycatholic.org/addresses-and-statements/2024/religious-freedom-in-a-secular-world-doomed-or-doable-31-may-2024/

83 CathNews. (2024, May 13). Talks continue on Calvary hospital compensation. *CathNews*, https://cathnews.com/2024/05/13/talks-continue-on-calvary-hospital-compensation/

84 Bajkowski, J. (2023, May 11). ACT nationalises Canberra's second hospital as Barr removes Catholic operator. *The Mandarin*, https://www.themandarin.com.au/219970-calvary-hospital-stealthily-nationalised-by-act-government/

85 Australian Capital Territory Health Directorate. (2023). *Annual report 2022-23*, 60. https://www.act.gov.au/__data/assets/pdf_file/0007/2302387/ACT-Health-Annual-Report-2022-2023.pdf

86 St Vincent de Paul Society. (2024). *Frequently asked questions*, https://www.vinnies.org.au/about-us/frequently-asked-questions; MacKillop Family Services. (2024). *2023 – 2024 Financial Report Collaboration*, https://www.mackillop.org.au/uploads/About-MacKillop/Publications/Annual-reports/2024_MacKillop_Financial-Report.pdf

87 Catholic Social Services Australia. (2024). *About our members*, https://cssa.org.au/our-members/about-our-members/?state-NSW/members-list

88 Marist 180 (Marist Youth Care Ltd). (2024). *Financial overview (2023)*, https://www.acnc.gov.au/charity/charities/096d6c8a-38af-e811-a962-000d3ad24a0d/profile

89 CatholicCare Wilcannia-Forbes. (2024). *Financial overview (2023)*, https://www.acnc.gov.au/charity/charities/068192b3-3aaf-e811-a963-000d3ad24077/profile

90 CatholicCare South West. (2024). *Financial overview (2023)*, https://www.acnc.gov.au/charity/charities/250c1b7c-3aaf-e811-a961-000d3ad24182/profile

91 CatholicCare Social Services Hunter Manning. (2024). *Financial overview (2023)*, https://www.acnc.gov.au/charity/charities/c251023d-38af-e811-a963-000d3ad24077/documents/

92 CatholicCare Diocese of Wollgongong [Catholic Family Welfare Services]. (2024). *Financial overview (2023)*, https://www.acnc.gov.au/charity/charities/8c76733e-39af-e811-a963-000d3ad244fd/profile

[93] St Agnes Care and Lifestyle. (2024). *Financial overview (2023)*, https://www.acnc.gov.au/charity/charities/cf3426dd-2daf-e811-a963-000d3ad24077/profile

[94] CatholicCare Diocese of Broken Bay. (2023). *Financial overview (2023)*, https://www.acnc.gov.au/charity/charities/4c868520-39af-e811-a961-000d3ad24182/profile

[95] CatholicCare Sydney. (2024). *Financial overview (2023)*, https://www.acnc.gov.au/charity/charities/af461e89-3aaf-e811-a962-000d3ad24a0d/profile

[96] Dunlea Centre. (2024). *Financial overview (2023)*, https://www.acnc.gov.au/charity/charities/ad0f75b9-38af-e811-a960-000d3ad24282/documents/

[97] Marymead CatholicCare Canberra & Goulburn. (2024). *Financial overview (2023)*, https://www.acnc.gov.au/charity/charities/5a8843db-39af-e811-a960-000d3ad24282/profile

[98] St Francis Social Services. (2024). *Financial overview (2023)*, https://www.acnc.gov.au/charity/charities/fb86ed2c-39af-e811-a95e-000d3ad24c60/profile

[99] Daughters of Charity of St Vincent De Paul, Rosalie Rendu. (2024). *Financial overview (2023)*, https://www.acnc.gov.au/charity/charities/19d0bada-39af-e811-a961-000d3ad24182/profile

[100] Trustees of Mary Aikenhead Ministries. (2024). *Financial overview (2023)*, https://www.acnc.gov.au/charity/charities/503bf532-38af-e811-a962-000d3ad24a0d/profile

[101] Australian Catholic Historical Society. (n.d.) *The Catholic press in Australia*, https://australiancatholichistoricalsociety.com.au/history-resources/the-catholic-press/

[102] Martyr, P., & Bullivant, S. (2024). *The Catholics in Australia Survey 5 – Behaving*, https://papers.ssrn.com/sol3/papers.cfm?abstract_id=4850676

[103] From a speech given by Adam Wesselinoff to staff of the Sydney Centre for Evangelisation following his resignation from the editorship of *The Catholic Weekly*, 20 August 2024; reproduced here with permission.

[104] Catholic Australia. (2024, May 24). National survey shows Australia's Catholics are online and multicultural. *Catholic Australia*, https://www.catholic.au/s/article/National-survey-shows-Australia-s-Catholics-are-online-and-multicultural

[105] See for example Independent Education Union of Australia, NSW Branch (2024, June 4). Union rejects Catholic Archbishop of Sydney's threat to close schools. *MediaNet*, https://newshub.medianet.com.au/2024/06/union-rejects-catholic-archbishop-of-sydneys-threat-to-close-schools/51749/

[106] Martyr, P. (2021, March 5). Stranded under the Southern Cross: news from a shrinking Church. *Gaudium et Spes 22*, https://gaudiumetspes22.com/blog/stranded-under-the-southern-cross-news-from-a-shrinking-church

[107] Martyr, P., & Bullivant, s. (2024). *The Catholics in Australia Survey 3 – Believing*, https://papers.ssrn.com/sol3/papers.cfm?abstract_id=4723637

108 William, personal communication, 17 October 2024.

Chapter 7

Making it all work

Have you ever read the Code of Canon Law from start to finish? I don't recommend it, but it's almost worth it for the wonderful closing line – canon 1752, which relates to the transfer of pastors. It concludes 'the salvation of souls, which must always be the supreme law in the Church, is to be kept before one's eyes.'

And that's it right there. That's the point of all the rules, regulations, warnings, and infrastructure. The salvation of souls is the supreme law in the Church. We must keep coming back to this all the time, every day, or we start sinking in the quicksand of parish feuds, diocesan rumblings, bogus mysticism,[1] and international Church politics.

I was talking to someone about this book, and they wondered if I was taking too functional an approach to the Church. They said they personally were more interested in helping people realise their vocation in the Church today as a charism, rather than as a function. God has given the Church everything it needs to flourish. If it's not flourishing, it's because the baptised are not using their charisms. They don't even know they have them.

This sums up exactly what I want to say to everyone who is reading this book. You personally are part of the solution (unless you've chosen to be part of the problem, but repentance is always an option). And what's important is **who you are**, first and foremost. It's about becoming more and more the mature Christian who God created you to be and living out your divine filiation as his beloved child.

Hans Urs von Balthasar also reminds us about the cost of witnessing:

> The 'one thing necessary' is for people to bear witness to the glory of God's love for the world .... Witnesses who put their whole lives into their vocation of bearing witness, and whose *raison d'etre* is simply to testify to the light on the mountain, the city set on a hill, the mountain's God-given freedom. Being a witness of this kind is more of a burden than a dignity. It calls for a life familiar with the air of the mountain, the air of the heights, and prepared to extend it to others. There is no substitute ... to replace holiness. It is either genuine or not there at all.[2]

Having said that, it's also about what you can do for the parochial-diocesan Church, and when and why and how. The Church in Australia needs people who are deeply rooted in Christ through the sacraments and the gospel, and who are also willing to let all this follow them out of Mass and into the world.

We know it's going to be hard, and all my informants recognised that. Lauren said that it's becoming 'increasingly harder to be a Catholic in polite society.'[3] Josh noted that 'It will be tough for Catholic families in the next decade or two to raise their families in a culture so hostile to Christianity, an underwhelming Catholic education system and if the government in office remains hostile to the faith.'[4] But there are also signs of hope. William, who works for the Church, said:

> I suspect that by then – we are in the early stage now – we will have stepped beyond the left/right divide in these issues in the Church. I can't imagine that Catholics will care as much about whether you're liberal or conservative – a bit more of a richer lived orthodoxy is emerging instead. Commitment to the poor will be a natural part of being Catholic.[5]

A young male frequent Mass-goer in the 18-29 age group said in CIA2022's open comment section:

> It doesn't matter what year it is or what social media platform or shiny logo promotes a certain ideal (both traditional and liberal Catholics are guilty of this). It

is allowing people to have a sincere relationship with Jesus through the church he established. And as a young Catholic, any form of liturgy that calls people into this relationship is needed. Because it seems the people making [these] decisions will die and join Our Lord long before the consequences are reaped by this generation of Catholics who face an increasingly hostile world to Jesus and the love he offers all people. ... young Catholics are the ones going to pay for the Church for the next 60 years. It's fair that they have a chance to hear their views and place them into action.

The bottom line for everyone I have spoken to is roughly the same: Recapture the sacred; the sense of the supernatural in our faith. St Peter calls us 'a people set apart' (1 Peter 2:9), and he's right, but this sense has been largely lost in the Church in Australia today. Australian Catholics are almost invisible because we no longer carry around that sense of eternity and of sacredness – consecration – that used to set us apart. We don't set the bar very high anymore. And yet our young people have shown us over and over that they can rise to a challenge. The Church can offer the high and serious demands of living a truly good life, and this should be at the front of how we relate to the world.

Our part in our downfall

But first, some owning up. In the Biblical parable, Jesus described a shepherd with a flock of 99 faithful sheep and one rogue sheep. In the Church in Australia today, we have the reverse: around 92 missing sheep for every eight sheep safely in the sheepfold – or at least going to Mass every Sunday.

Are they lost? Yes. A Catholic who doesn't believe in God any longer, or who half-believes and goes to Mass once in a blue moon, is in real spiritual trouble. I am all in favour of going after lost sheep. I'm also happy to have an honest conversation about how the sheep got lost in the first place. This stuff didn't just happen. As a Church, we made individual and collective decisions that brought us here.

Those with the greatest responsibility in the Church let us down badly. But we were all in it together.

Some people think the solution is to send out more clergy so that they can retrieve the lost sheep. But Vatican II told us that it was actually *our* job – ordinary lay people. Most of the lost sheep are other ordinary lay people in our own families, schools, and workplaces. They will listen to us a lot sooner than they'll listen to some random priest who they don't even know (or trust, because they think he's a paedophile).

We had *Humanae Vitae* given to us by a Pope who is now a saint. We could have taken it seriously. We could have built a more generous and creative Church which pushed back against a selfish and materialist culture, welcomed larger families, and actively supported them. We didn't, so now we face the demographic winter that's setting in. Often our personal example has also been lousy. If being a Catholic makes you unhappy, then you're doing it wrong. You don't have to embrace charismatic renewal and clown Masses, but you could try cheering up a bit.

If you're really concerned about lost sheep, there are three things you can do immediately without anyone needing to create a program or spend any money. You can let them go, pray for them, and give them a good lived example. God likes us to make a free choice in religion – Vatican II made that very clear.[6] The best way to convince someone of the truths of the faith is not to nag them or try to terrify them into believing (what US theologian Dr Larry Chapp calls 'Hell-cowbell').[7] Instead, you need to expose them to the possibilities of a Catholic life well-lived, mainly by living that life yourself.

Too many people in the Church have actively taught the idea that Catholicism is a set of nice aspirations which can't really be lived out in practice. Many lapsed Catholics have also been taught their religion as a subject in school which made them dislike it – taught in an empty, facile, or disconnected way. They've never really joined the dots between theory and practice because they've never really seen it lived out or heard someone explain with authority how to join those dots.

It takes exposure to personal good examples to bring the faith home – and those personal examples must start with you. This happens best in confident and open relationships where you learn how to love the sinner but hate the sin. Any Mass-going Catholic, including you, should also be able to explain your lived faith easily and simply to another person in everyday language, out of a deep inner conviction in its truth. There's a much-overused word for this – 'authenticity' – but this is a situation when authentic faith shines through.

People hate it when I write about this stuff. They love it when I can point to a clear external enemy and say that they're responsible for everything that's wrong in the Church. But when I start suggesting that the solution lies with each one of us working harder on our personal holiness and good example, they tend to go off me a bit.

This is what too much Church politics can do to a Catholic, whether they're arch-liberal or archconservative. It can leave you very calloused and cynical, and less capable of hearing God's still, small voice. In some tragic cases, people have left the Church altogether when God refused to conform himself to their preferred religio-political agenda.[8] Please don't be this person.[9]

There's no doubt that a lot of what's currently dying in the Church needed to. Tori, a mother of three young children, said of the future that, 'I hope to be standing in the smouldering remnants of Catholic Inc, built by vainglorious Australian boomers who literally swayed, clapped and fiddled as almost 2000 years of Catholic moral leadership and teachings on faith, family and marriage was squandered in the post sixties era.'[10] So what can we rebuild in the smouldering remnants?

As far as I can see, there are two major areas we need to focus on as a future Catholic community in Australia. The first is to consolidate and unite – as best as possible – the Mass-going community that we've still got. This is mostly in the urban areas, although there are some noteworthy outposts in the regions. The second is to work on bringing back as many of the lost sheep as we can. This is also the order in which I think we should do these things.

I've already made recommendations or described positive changes in some of my earlier chapters, especially the chapter on parish life. This chapter will not repeat these – or will try not to, anyway – and will try instead to get us all to look forward to other future changes we can make that might be positive for the Church in Australia. So let's see where and how we can rebuild.

Changing our families

Obviously, conversion begins at home in the individual human heart, by rebuilding close personal relationships with God through a strong prayer life and regular use of the sacraments. God owes us nothing; everything is gift, and remembering this daily helps to reorder the universe, putting us back in our rightful place.

Our parents and grandparents' generations found that being a Catholic in Australia meant that they were often treated as second-class citizens. This led them to work hard to blend in with non-Catholics who were often more affluent and socially acceptable. It seems that they worked too hard, in that Australian Catholics are now largely indistinguishable from everyone else. So perhaps a small, simple step we can take is to start to differentiate ourselves again at the family level.

This doesn't involve us all running away to rural enclaves or wearing mysterious outfits either at Mass or at home. I am certain that some people would enjoy this as well, and please feel free to do this if you really want. But as much as it's fun when you're young, Catholic cosplay isn't sustainable.[11] Instead, I was thinking more of simple things that we can do that used to be a part of Catholic culture which we have lost, and we can regain.

Some of them are re-arising spontaneously because younger Catholics are very attracted to them. One of these is Friday abstinence from meat. You don't have to eat fish, but you can make the effort to have a meat-free day and explain why if you're asked. Meat-free days are currently fashionable which makes them easy to adopt without too much struggle. It would help if church leadership could start talking about this as well, but there's nothing stopping you from starting now.[12]

Consolidation also begins at the authentic grass roots level – in families who connect with other families. Younger families with children have shown real expertise in this area. Many Mass-going younger Catholics have already formed loose 'intentional communities' which socialise with each other on a regular basis (and often at parks with fences so that the many children present can't run out into the road).[13]

Tori has found this very consoling and helpful.

> What's going right exists in informal networks on an ... ad hoc basis of Catholic families – the majority of whom include immigrants and/ or converts – who have come to Australia and/or into the Church and brought the fire and passion with them to create webs of families and friends almost by chance. ... It is these families whose witness in the daily struggles of life, almost in isolation of any local parish or diocesan support, that inspire and reassure that a Catholic culture exists in spite of the local archdiocese.[14]

You should also meet these people. You really should; they'd restore your faith in the future Church. I went to a clothing swap at one such household in January 2024 which moved me so much that I wrote an article about it for *The Catholic Weekly*.[15] The hostess had invited not just her Catholic friends, but also a friendly female neighbour who was the right age. The harvest is rich, but the labourers are few. If we don't do this work – each one of us, when we can, even in tiny ways – how can we hope to fulfil our mission?

If you're Mass-going but also going a bit domestically insane, this might sound like manna from heaven. Why not start something like this of your own? Just meet up with one other family somewhere. It doesn't have to be fancy or expensive – after Mass, or in a park, or at someone's house. Bring the children. Get to know each other and bolster each other's faith and life choices. Let the women all gather in one corner and the men in another if that's what works for you – and it works for lots of people. It's especially good for men to gather and socialise with other Mass-going Catholic men; iron sharpens iron, and they draw strength and also correction from it.

Sometimes you might be unable to find your tribe in rural or regional areas, so you might be more reliant on online communities. Petra is in a very small parish community on the edge of a larger city, and they're now using WhatsApp to good effect.

> ... our small Catholic community has created a WhatsApp group so that we can communicate with each other. Through this group, people can mention if they are sick or need a lift, ask for prayers for themselves or relatives, share photos from their Camino Pilgrimage, share new hymns that we would like to introduce, or announce changes of times and venues for Masses. All of this helps to create a sense of community and family. This was a lay initiative (actually my own) and the priest seems to be happy to use it for his own announcements.[16]

Katrina and her family have similarly found help online.

> Most help, whether for faith development, encouragement, home education, Bible studies, prayer groups: it's in online communities or in the small interest groups which spring up around a focus (such as home school support and activity groups).
>
> ... I would say that finding websites such as the St Paul Centre (Scott Hahn), Fr Mike Schmitz, and various Catholic home school/education sites such as Look to Him and Be Radiant, Kendra Tierney and similar mums who blog is one of the things which I have found very valuable.
>
> All these online resources and many more have been a

boon in the life of Catholics everywhere, and have allowed me to be connected in ways that aren't available through many parishes. Suddenly spiritual development is in the hands of a laity who previously may not have had access to many of these materials, and most vitally, many of the thinkers who have spent years learning and practising their faith. It means that I have been significantly less likely to be influenced by well-meaning but fanatical fringe-dwellers, which is always one of the dangers in any group of believers.[17]

But as Katrina said, there are also risks when zeal, the desire for orthodoxy, and poor formation all meet the internet. Leah, who lives in a rural diocese, explained:

A typical story might go like this. A young mother finds a community or friendship group where it seems Catholicism is being taken seriously and really lived out – and indeed, there are many good Catholic things happening in that space. But there are also other beliefs prevalent in the community that are not part of the deposit of faith but that seem so enmeshed in the culture of the group that the young mother feels they are part of the package and must be accepted in order to really belong.

These could be beliefs concerning: the roles of men and women in marriage and public life, education of children, vaccination, young vs old earth theories, heliocentrism. ... but the one that I really struggle with is watching my educated friends trying to claim that dinosaurs never existed. A very small number even go so far as to claim that the earth is flat. They generally quote the Bible and Catholic websites that have taken Protestant views on these matters and given them a Catholic veneer.

It baffles me seeing my friends tie themselves in knots to explain away scientific theories or facts that in no way conflict with the Catholic faith and which have been supported by the Magisterium and doctors of the Church. I really hope that this is a short-lived trend but many of these women are homeschooling their children![18]

It's hard to know how to address this when you encounter it, because 'saying the wrong thing' in the hope of introducing a bit more balance can send some very fervent people further down rabbit holes. However, this is a problem which is probably best overcome by a lot of patience and some sounder catechesis.[19]

When you're having your real-life face-to-face get-togethers, it's natural that married couples will choose other married couples to socialise with at first. But don't be afraid of extending your social group to include some single Catholics as well, or widowed, or divorced ones, or even clergy if they're willing. These people often get left out or forgotten in the mix. Kind people have included me in their families for years now and it's transformed my world view and made me very happy.

If you are an unattached Mass-going Catholic, here also is your opportunity to actively seek and find your tribe of like-minded, like-living Catholics. Some of you may want to meet future spouses; some will be happy just the way you are. Figure out which type of Catholic you are and choose your tribe accordingly.

We can also seriously improve our chances of lasting, faithful and happy Catholic marriages with better marriage preparation. It must absolutely offer the same full-fat, high-fibre catechesis that we really need right now – but it must also be realistic about the practicalities. Diane, who divorced in her late fifties, said:

> I think more honest and adult conversations need to take place about abuse, marriage roles, children, responsibility, family planning as they fit in a Catholic context of marriage. I think the best Catholic material is not popular with Catholic marriage prep because it is solidly clear about the need for appropriate chastity, the limits of family planning and sexual freedom within marriage.[20]

Katrina also offers a sobering reflection.

> Without wanting to crap heavily over choices and regrets, one of the challenges I face personally is a deep feeling of complete inadequacy in the face of children now ranging

in age from nine through to 34. I wish I had known what a slog it was going to be – I mean genuine, sympathetic advice from an older mother who has had a large family. I get a little tired when I get advice from women with five children. It isn't the same.[21]

We need to take responsibility for not helping larger families by fighting for fairer family taxation, improved social services, and more affordable housing. That's a social justice campaign that all of us could have gotten behind. If the Church had gone in hard on this topic, we might have had more equitable choices now available about having a parent return to work or not when there are young children who need care. But it's not too late to start pushing back hard, and now is the time to do it. The chattering classes in Australia are just starting to notice that we're having some population issues with the baby drought, plus our national child care budget has completely blown out.[22] This is also where we can possibly find some common ground with them.

As I said in the chapter on family life, I would love to see more of our younger Catholic families living in multi-generational households if they can. With the decline in the quality of institutional aged care, I think this is a humane and practical way forward. It's going to vary from family to family, and there are lots of variations on this theme, but they all involve children caring physically and spiritually for elderly parents as much as they can in the parents' own home. Parents: your job is to start thinking of this now as well and having conversations with your adult children about the future.

Changing our parishes

Location, location, location

Things in the Church have a way of turning around. For example, in the 1990s, we were told that the future Church in Australia would consist of lay led priestless parishes unless we started ordaining married men and women immediately. In Ballarat in the

2000s, two regional parishes began to experiment with a lay-led parish model in the place of regular Masses where a single priest had to minister to a large area.[23] One of the case studies was St Mary Mackillop parish, Western Border. But the current (late 2024) Mass schedule indicates that there are now three priests hard at work in the parish, providing far more Masses, and there is very little lay-led worship.[24] So sometimes our dire predictions don't come true.

That said, our parishes in Australia should be in for a few surprises. Some dioceses have begun reshuffling and consolidating theirs, and others desperately need to. Some of our parishes are going to have to merge or be closed to allow all Mass-going Catholics access to a priest and the sacraments. We can get by on fewer priests in urban dioceses, which will free them up for work in rural areas. Most Catholics in urban areas can drive. If they can't, their dioceses can buy buses and organise shuttle runs to parishes that have become Mass centres.

This will be hard for those of us who are used to being liturgical nomads. However, if you can join a parish and invest in it, you are more likely to stay and try to help build it up. As the number of Mass-goers shrinks, these 'bigger' parishes may not be all that big after all. No one should fear getting lost in a mega-parish, and people should be encouraged to attend their local parish church as much as possible.

The parish is a spiritual reality as well as a physical one.[25] One way of building up parishes again is the formation of house groups, in which Mass-going Catholics get together in small groups within the parish to get to know each other, and to study the faith together. As our parishes shrink and are amalgamated, it will shake a lot of us out of our comfort zones. We will have to socialise with people outside the parish silo that we're used to.

Fr Michael would take this even further.

> I would like to see the Latin rite Catholic Church copy some

of the structural practices of the Syro-Malabar Catholics. They form groups of families within their parishes who have an elected leader who is then on the parish council. These groups help to coordinate regular home visitations and blessings, care for the sick and other pastoral care. This happens in a similar way in Saigon, where parishes are divided into districts with a committee. If a priest is called to visit the dying, one of the committee comes with the priest and can get him up to speed about the family situation and introduce him. This really extends the priest's pastoral outreach.[26]

Religious life can also help parishes to expand their reach, especially in rural and regional Australia. Sr Yvette said:

> ... so many parishes are in need of support, especially the country parishes. This has meant that we are able to run parish missions, evangelise through doorknocking and outreaches, and we have seen many little ones that wouldn't have been outreached come to God. We have also been able to support priests who are struggling with being alone with very little support and it has been a privilege and blessing to be able to help them.[27]

This may involve crossing all sorts of boundaries like ethnicity which often divide a parish socially. This is currently a sensitive area in some parishes, as Ethan, a father of four young children who lives in an urban area, has found.

> Parish life is difficult as there are few families with children around the same age as ours who are local. Those families with children of the right age are mostly from recent migrant communities, which are beautiful and close knit, but very difficult to participate in as an 'Anglo-Aussie'. I do not begrudge that, but it is a real struggle.[28]

Leah has noticed this as well in her rural diocese.

> We are seeing increases in our Filipino population, and I think they will form a far higher proportion of the parish and the whole diocese in 30 years. The rate of attrition

of their children unfortunately seems to be similar to the local population however, so only time will tell how this will play out. Most of our priests are missionaries from the Philippines and India and I think this trend will also continue.[29]

This will also require open-minded and loving priests who can remind us frequently that we're all worshipping the same God, who calls us all to love one another. Anyone who wants Mass-going Catholic grandchildren would be wise to welcome kind, devout, solvent Mass-going spouses into the extended family, no matter what their ethnic background is.

Rearranging parish Mass times to suit a young family demographic, if that's what your parish seem to be attracting, might also help make opportunities for young families to meet each other. Weekday Mass times might also need reviewing, because right now it's often quite challenging for a working person to get to a weekday Mass. Katrina said:

> When we first arrived in [our town], there was a 7am Mass which was very well attended by parents ready for work bringing children in school uniform, young adults off to work, the elderly ... The priest at the time certainly had his faults, but he wasn't wrong on this one. Possibly he holds the record for the fastest Mass ever, I'm not real sure. He'd give the title holder a run for his money anyhow. I was genuinely surprised though at how many were at the 7am Masses he offered.[30]

This is going to vary from area to area, but it should be possible to open a discussion with the parish priest about this – and be prepared to turn up to the Masses you've asked him to say.

Parishes may need to up their social game – although many parishes are often better at this than at promoting devotional life. All parishes should have a decent parish hall with a working kitchenette and plenty of chairs, and ideally a safe and secure play area for small children. This makes it much easier for mothers at home raising young families to bring their children along to social events at the church – and they should be encouraged to do this.

Young people also need a place and space in the Church to socialise with and encourage each other, and that can work at parish level. Miriam, a mother of three children who have benefited from a parish-level well-managed youth group, said:

> I sincerely hope that all or most parishes take seriously the idea that teen and then young adult groups at a parish level are essential. That age group needs to feel part of something. They need to feel part of a community for themselves within the bigger parish life. So they can simply socialise, while being faithful and coming to mass every Sunday. It is hard to be countercultural, they need support in that age bracket.[31]

Other Catholics have voted with their feet and their mortgages and are forming intentional communities. Couples and families may move house to an area where there's a good parish and some of the people they already know. Often these are on the outskirts of expensive metropolitan areas, where young families on a single income can buy more room to grow. They may begin sharing homeschooling opportunities or using the local government school and supplementing this with faith-based activities for groups of their children.

This kind of networking and consolidation will be easier for those Catholics living in the archdioceses of Sydney, Melbourne, Brisbane and Perth. Outside of that, it's going to be a painful witness for our increasingly isolated rural Mass-going Catholics. Leah reflected sadly:

> I've realised from writing these responses how little my parish has to do with how I live my faith from day to day. I go there for the sacraments, try to be involved and do good to people there, but it's not a place I feel I can trust to help me grow in the faith or to form my children (beyond the reception of the sacraments).[32]

The very least we should be doing is providing Mass and the sacraments to these outlying areas on a weekly basis using a roster of priests. We have enough priests to do this; it just needs better organisation within each diocese and across diocesan boundaries.

The liturgy

As liturgical silos and boutique parishes break down, and priestly formation improves, we will hopefully see fewer and fewer priests who feel the need to make themselves the centre of attention at Mass. Working on standardising the way in Mass is said across a diocese is a project well worth pursuing. There will always be ageing radicals who refuse to conform, but in time, we should see some real improvements. Any ordinary Catholic should ideally be able to go to Mass in any parish church in Australia and not need to be 'welcomed' to 'our [version of the] liturgy'. There are obvious pitfalls here in that everyone is going to have a different idea of what 'renewal' might look like, so it calls for cool heads.[33]

There can and should be room for traditional practices like the priest saying Mass 'facing God' and offering the laity the option of kneeling for Holy Communion in a way that's inclusive of older adults and those with disabilities, such as using a kneeler or the front pews for this. All liturgical changes should always be introduced after education and explanation for all those who attend Mass at the parish. Too-zealous clerical and lay 'new brooms' tend to score own goals when they rush the reform of the liturgy in a parish. Leah can tell you what that looks like.

> When we first moved to our town, we tried hard to become a part of our local parish, but it was hard work. I was still very young, on fire for the faith and did not yet have the life experience that helps me to make peace with what I see as less than ideal in the liturgy, which I have limited power [to] change. My attempts to influence and help with the music in our parish were very well meant but overzealous. They bemused and, I think, annoyed a

subset of the community. They just weren't ready for 'Let all mortal flesh keep silence'![34]

Now that we're on the other side of COVID19, it's also time to revisit the use of extraordinary ministers of Holy Communion and the chalice for the congregation. Many parishes don't need extraordinary ministers at Sunday Mass, and they definitely don't need them at weekday Masses. They are very much needed, though, to help take Holy Communion to the sick and housebound in the parish and at special-event Masses like Easter and Christmas. It would be good to see the introduction of a diocesan-level rule for only the priest and acolytes to distribute Holy Communion at Mass unless the congregation is larger than 200 people at a single Mass.

I used to love receiving Holy Communion under both forms. But I am also aware that reception from the chalice as it's done in many parishes – or was done before COVID19 – is often sloppy and careless. 'Dunking' of a host into the chalice is not permitted by the Australian Catholic Bishops Conference,[35] and yet I see it happening, and I have seen more spillage on carpet than I care to remember.

I am glad that COVID19 stopped this practice in many places. I don't know how many parishes have re-introduced it, but it's not necessary. You receive the whole Jesus, body, blood, soul and divinity, in the host alone. If people are keen on both species, the priest can use an intinction set, but this will mean that people will have to receive Holy Communion on the tongue. Again, this needs proper education, explanation, and catechesis before anything is changed.

The revival of Adoration across Australia is one of the most beautiful signs of the living Church (John 4:24).[36] Parishes should be encouraging this and, where possible, building or adapting Adoration Chapels. There's been a recent resurgence in public Eucharistic processions, another very Catholic tradition which also helps to put us literally on the front foot, instead of retreating.

While we're at it, we also need an extensive parish-level catechesis on the sacrament of Reconciliation and its relationship with the reception of Holy Communion. Leah said:

> I would like the Bishops to encourage all their priests to preach about confession from the pulpit, to teach people about mortal vs venial sin, to let them know it's actually a mortal sin to miss Sunday Mass without a serious reason, to let them know what their obligations are with regard to Confession and then also to teach them about the mercy of God, how much he wants them to come to Confession and how much it will help them to grow in their spiritual life. These were all things I had to learn as an adult, because 14 years of Catholic school and going to Mass every Sunday didn't teach them to me.[37]

Mass-going Catholics in Australia form a spectrum of belief and worship preferences. The Traditional Latin Mass (TLM) communities are part of that spectrum – they are not weird outliers to anyone except certain diocesan diehards and the secular media. People who attend the TLM are measurably similar in Catholic belief and practice to Novus Ordo-attending Catholics who go to Mass during the week as well as Sundays.[38] Yet the suspicion with which they are sometimes treated is real. Ethan, who works for the Church, noted that:

> While I do not attend any more, when I did, I found that working in a Church context meant that I had to keep my TLM attendance under wraps – any affiliation I could have been seen to have had with a TLM community would have been severely career limiting (which is my experience).[39]

Either way, if your diocese is going to offer the TLM, it should have a stable parish of its own to help the community maintain the social supports that are one of the real blessings that often go with it. There are other good reasons for this, described in detail by US journalist Kevin Tierney.

> Due to the past strategy of intentionally ostracizing these

communities, they lack that relationship of trust built up over the years the way a parish does with the diocese. When you combine this with the general crisis of authority in the Church (where she has trouble using her influence among those most receptive to her), you have a movement that can potentially go off the rails without a lot of corrective mechanisms in place.

Yet the growth is often undeniable. How the Church encourages the dynamic growth of this movement while balancing out its excess will be a great challenge in the years and decades to come. But, in order to engage with it and help it, one must understand it.[40]

Colin, a father of four, has had positive experiences with his local TLM community.

I've been involved in youth evangelisation ministry for decades but I have never seen anything like this. And it's not a flash in the pan. The days of the grumpy old Trad with the chip on the shoulder are over. You see young families with lots of children; the optics of this is beautiful but sadly it is being suppressed and/or discouraged.[41]

But John has been to the TLM on and off for many years in the Eastern States and has had more mixed experiences.

The TLM has its own issues. The TLM does, at times, come across as aloof and less accommodating to those who do not 'fit'. The TLM has all the outward appearances of Catholicism with the hidden 'us & them' mentality. It is difficult to mention that you accept the Novus Ordo without receiving rebukes and judgements.[42]

Fr Robert thinks it will depend on how the Australian bishops respond to the changing profile of the Australian Catholics who are actually attending Mass, where they can expect to see an increasing number of so-called 'trads'.

If the bishops begin to look on the 'trads' as an opportunity to be cultivated, then ... the renewal of the life of faith I have been privileged to witness taking place will not only continue but increase exponentially. ... it is among the 'trads' that the strongest and most astonishing growth is taking place. Every movement has its problems, and the 'rad-trads' constitute the problems in the traditional movement – though, in truth, there aren't, in my observation, all that many of them. The majority of 'trads' are 'glad trads', not 'rad-trads'. The latter are moderated in their more radical tendencies by competent and balanced pastoral care.[43]

Slow and patient work to rebuild trust between local bishops and these communities would go a long way to reintegrate them into the local Church, where they can do a lot of good if they're allowed to.

Sacramental preparation

In my chapter on parish life, I noted the troubling phenomenon of 'Lying Masses'. Right now, we run Catholic school-based sacramental programs that put non-Mass-going children and their parents through a sort of sacramental sausage machine until they pop out the other end as functional atheists. Sometimes the experience of catechising children in government schools is just as unrewarding. Miriam, a mother of three, explains:

> I am a PREP catechist for state school children (Parish Religious Education Programme). ... that program is woefully lacking (supplied by the Catholic Ed Department, so not surprising). And I struggle preparing children from families who never come to Mass, never go to Confession, live lives contrary to the teachings of the Church. That system is lacking.[44]

But what if we tried doing it the other way around? What if we focused on the children of Mass-going Catholic families, and did our sacramental preparation through the parish church, where the children and families are known to the priest and the community?[45]

I have seen this work very well locally. The First Holy Communion group is small – perhaps just six or seven children –

but everyone in the church knows them and their families, and their First Holy Communion day becomes a parish celebration. It's very unifying and very joyous. Those children also continue to attend Mass with their families, and in time will be confirmed in the same parish, and again, it's joyful and unifying – especially if families are encouraged to celebrate with the parish afterwards, rather than having a private party at home.

To do this requires a parish catechist. There are already many Mass-going Catholics who are qualified catechists, or who teach religious education. It would also work well with existing homeschooling programs and parents. Katrina said:

> The NACF (National Association of Catholic Families – just in case you don't know, although you probably do) has produced some good booklets for Confession, the Eucharist and Confirmation which are well-edited and a solid foundation for me to adapt them as needed. They also reproduced a lot of the artwork from previous generations, so that they are not revoltingly cartoonish.[46]

The parish priest can and should be involved in this process and should be present at most or all of the classes as well. Parents should be encouraged to attend parish catechism classes if they want, so that they can hear and see what their children are being taught, and perhaps learn something themselves. This reconnects elements of the Church in Australia that have become largely disconnected: the parish priest, sacramental preparation, and the parents and families. It was the strength of these connections at the local level that built the Church up in the past, and it can do so again.

Changing our dioceses

Location, location, location – again

If you've been watching the Church internationally, you will have seen Pope Francis making changes to diocesan administration in the UK and Ireland. They have the same problems we do – too many dioceses, not enough priests in the right places, and shrinking Mass attendance rates. This calls for diocesan mergers and sometimes unusual episcopal appointments.[47]

I think this is also needed in Australia. I have no idea who recommended that we have a new bishop for the diocese of Broome, with barely 600 Mass-goers there. But Broome has also been a public relations disaster due to alleged abuses by the previous local bishop and there are potentially also some years of financial confusion that need to be sorted out by someone on the ground.[48] An administrator could do the management, but the public relations disaster is best solved by an actual bishop. With so few Mass-goers, he will soon know them all by name. Maybe this is a good thing.

I believe that our diocesan boundaries should be redrawn to reflect the reality of Mass attendance in Australia. This would also mean that more priests were incardinated in larger dioceses and would be able to be deployed better across larger areas. I hate this idea, because part of me loves the idea of having more and smaller dioceses where you could really get to know your bishop. But I think in Australia this isn't going to work – not with the very long distances people have to travel. Right now, we have bishops who care for a few thousand Mass-going Catholics and those who care for tens of thousands, and we need to rebalance that.

This kind of restructure will be excruciating just from an administrative point of view, with the rules around incardination. It would be especially excruciating when it became clear how many of Australia's priests are unwilling or unable to move from, say, the comfortable suburbs to the red dirt interior. There are all sorts of options here. I have long thought that the archdiocese of Hobart should actually be managed by a rotating team of clergy from Melbourne. Rural circuits in many dioceses can also be managed by regularly rotated teams. Every priest in Australia should have some experience of going bush and working in rural and remote areas, even if it only makes him very grateful when he gets back to the city.

What it shouldn't look like

There are two possible ways to save the Church in Australia. The first way is to accept reality: around 400,000 Mass-going Catholics in total, and most of our dioceses with less than 10 per cent Mass attendance. We could reorganise diocesan and parish boundaries for a proper distribution of priests, which would mean a bit more driving for some of us (especially the priests). This protects our core business, which should be to provide the sacraments to the Catholics who want them and need them. Then we can re-catechise our flock and equip them for effective evangelisation.

The second way is to ignore all this and instead try to remodel the Church into a middle-class job creation scheme. Our recent Plenary Council's governance and discernment papers thought the second way sounded like a winner. These documents were hopelessly out of touch with the Church on the ground in Australia. They were also an obvious blueprint for a completely different future Church that would work best for a small and select group of people who like working in offices on salaries.

The discernment paper, *Missionary and Evangelising* at least touched on the fact that most Australian Catholics are poorly catechised and can't evangelise yet.[49] But *Prayerful and Eucharistic* (Paper 3) managed to write almost 7,000 words without once mentioning the Real Presence or transubstantiation. There's a lot about meals, but no mention of who we're eating. Adoration is mentioned once in passing, and the word 'Mass' is relegated to a reference. I will leave you to think about that.

A Joyful, Hopefilled and Servant Community (Paper 5) touts the merits of a lay-led Church, preferably with no foreign clergy. I agree that we should stop stealing priests from developing countries, but we don't need to replace them with salaried white Boomer ladies.

Instead, our more than adequate numbers of local priests need to get out of their endless meetings and administrative work, and back into priesting.[50]

What it could look like instead

So instead of this flabby agenda, I'm looking for fat to trim, and I think I'll start in the diocesan chancery office. Back in 2020 I guesstimated the size of the diocesan and agency workforce in Australia. Having been told that the Church in Australia employed almost 200,000 people at that time, I subtracted the 83,000 health care staff and the 100,000 education staff and was left with around 17,000 people.[51] That's around 600 people per diocese.

I don't think we need Catholic offices for peace, justice, social justice, ecology, the environment, or anything of that ilk, with salaried staff. As far as I can see, the world is in just as big a mess as it was before these offices existed, and their disappearance will make zero difference to outcomes in the local Church. It will directly affect a small number of professional Catholics who have made a living this way, but that's all. I've also made a case earlier for disbanding unevaluated diocesan youth ministries which have done nothing to stem the exodus of young people from the Church.[52]

The Church must always be committed to charity, but it doesn't have to be on a corporate scale. Nor does it have to be simply a conduit for redistributing government money. It can be much smaller, more local, and more direct.[53] This is going to look different in every diocese, city, or parish. Small and local should be the new way forward for our Church, and this needs to replace the big and expensive offices and layers of management of a bygone era.

So what about our diocesan charitable agencies? I think we can certainly look much more closely at what they're providing, and to whom. In Australia today, there is a lot of relative poverty but little actual poverty. Our charities also seem to churn a lot of government funding and duplicate a lot of existing services. If any agencies or charities were managing to self-fund from donations and income from ventures like charity shops, I'd let them keep going. But if they want to keep calling themselves 'Catholic', then they won't be allowed to have, say, a Pride display in the shop window every year. Katrina notes:

> Some of my older children have volunteered at the local Vinnies shop front, but they aren't the same anymore, tending now to give unaffiliated and often dysfunctional adults a place to go. Not so bad in and of itself, but there usually isn't a Catholic working there within cooee, and it became increasingly clear that my daughters could not work with some of the more 'marginalised' men who volunteered there.[54]

While I'm on the subject, I'd close almost all the second-hand clothing shops – and it kills me to say this, because I've bought most of my clothes from them over the years. But it's become apparent now that most charity shops only sell on average about 17% of their donated clothing to people like me. The rest of the clothing is either being ragged locally, or going to landfill, or being shipped overseas to pollute other people's countries.[55]

It might be time for any Catholic who's read *Laudato Si'* to divest from the second-hand clothing industry altogether, because it's not really part of the 'circular economy' – it's mostly a one-way, highly polluting trip for fast fashion that will never really be recycled. Either that, or the Catholic charity shops need to start working on a different model: being much more selective about the clothing they accept, giving more clothing away in in-store 'clothing swap' events, and automatically binning all donated metal and glass items for recycling.

I also want to ask here about the role of all nominally Catholic charitable agencies in each diocese, and what they're providing, and to whom, and whether it's authentically Catholic. They receive government funding from a lot of different sources,[56] and I've never been convinced that they had a strong Catholic identity, despite the work of various 'Mission and Identity' staff over the years. I've talked to Mass-going Catholics who've used their services, and they've had mixed experiences.

I love cheap counselling resources to whom I can send all sorts of people – but is this really core business for the Church in Australia? Is this really the right kind of charitable work for a local Church that's rapidly shrinking? I'm not sure that our smaller, poorer future Church will be able to afford to provide these services. I'd look seriously at offloading them now if what they're providing is equivalent to secular assistance, mostly funded by government, mostly to non-Catholics, and with no authentically Catholic content.

But if we want to deliver authentically Catholic counselling and family services as a charitable work, we could instead create and subsidise smaller and authentically Catholic counselling services, with psychological, marital, and financial counselling services under one roof. There are Mass-going Catholic mental health care professionals of all kinds who would relish the chance to work with Mass-going Catholic clients, most of whom are very hesitant to consult secular mental health services. There are also openings here for fruitful partnerships with local clergy who are spiritual directors and exorcists.

At the diocesan level it would be good to see more open support of family-friendly policies for diocesan employees, but also for ordinary Australians. This is somewhere where the ACBC could also be more vocal. Catholics are feeling the pinch just as much as everyone else, especially with housing, as Ethan notes.

> Another major factor is simply the exorbitant nature of housing and living costs. While we are fortunate that one of us (me) is able to earn enough to allow for one of us (my wife) to stay home with our young children, and for us to live relatively comfortably, the very likely prospects of having to go into tremendous debt in the near future for a house that will be big enough for our growing family

is a source of stress. Especially if we are to stay in the area where we currently are (which, I might add is not particularly flashy!) where we have been trying to establish some semblance of community.[57]

All of the above changes need to take place at diocesan level. They are local changes, informed by the principle of subsidiarity and the idea that the people on the ground know the area and the local problems best.[58] Each diocese could make at least some of these changes and save itself some money.

Adult faith formation

So far, we've looked at ways of helping the shrinking Church in Australia to rediscover its sense of the sacred in the liturgy and faced some financial realities about its possible future. Thankfully there are good bishops and good dioceses where genuine lay renewal is already being promoted actively. Prayer groups flourish, and public devotions give people an opportunity to witness publicly. But there are other ways we can rediscover exactly what it means to be a Catholic in this brave new world. This means cultural changes – changes in how we live and how we evangelise.

And the fact is that not all of us are ready for it. Miriam, a mother of three, has noticed this.

> The other thing that I feel the Church isn't doing well, is catechism. I am shocked at the basic lack of knowledge about the faith among church goers. I don't have an answer for that one, it needs a major overhaul. School cannot be held responsible for it, because they have failed for long enough. Homilies are not the ideal place for catechism lessons, because we miss too many of the faithful due to lack of attendance, language barriers etc. But if we don't know the faith, why will we continue to practice it?[59]

Thankfully there is a wealth of wonderful programs available out there – international and home-grown – for genuine, uncompromising adult faith formation. There are good books, podcasts, and websites that can provide material for years of formation. Steve and Helen have used them: 'We have access to a huge amount of resources, most of them American unfortunately, to help us grow the faith in our families and communities. There is growth, however slow, in solid Australian resources as well. Much of it is encouraging and helpful'.[60]

Katrina also noted that, 'The St Paul Centre and Parousia Media here in Australia have really solid Bible study programs, Lenten retreats and Advent preparation which could become parish initiatives, rather than top-down imposition of things such as the devastating Renew program from some years ago.' The work of Gerard O'Shea and the Catechesis of the Good Shepherd is a good place to start locally for children's formation.[61] We also need excellent catechesis for the 'reverts' – those people who in later life decide to renew their relationship with the Church – as well as adult converts.

Our idea of what the Church is has been quite damaged in the last fifty years. We've seen a heavy focus on the Church as the People of God. There's nothing wrong with that; it's perfectly true. But it's not a democracy, or a bureaucracy, or quasi-Marxist construct, or a lump of plasticine for us to play with and mould into our preferred shapes, and it's also not the whole story. Knowing what the Church is and what it isn't is essential to any discussions we have about its future shape and direction. If we all have different ideas about what the Church is, we will get nowhere.

We can only move forward by accepting and using a fully Catholic understanding of the Church. This simply won't allow major doctrinal changes like women's ordination or allowing people to receive Holy Communion if they've chosen behaviours and ways of living that are directly contradictory to the Gospel and the Church's teachings. We need to be very clear about where the Church can change, and where it can't. And you can't arrive at that without understanding what the Church is: how it's divinely founded, the Bride of Christ, and the thing that saves the world.⁶²

We also must be realistic about what we can and can't achieve. For example, Sydney has a growing Centre for Evangelisation which is starting to get some real traction going in that archdiocese. But it's not its director's job to convert all of Sydney; it's the job of the increasing numbers of well-formed and re-catechised Mass-going Catholics in that diocese. And ultimately, it's down to God's personal wrestling match with each soul – this is where conversion of heart takes place, and it's an act of grace. We can do a lot to set up the right conditions for this 'heart speaks to heart' connection, but we can't force the outcome.

There are also wider opportunities. Some years ago, two groups of Catholics in two different states almost simultaneously founded Christopher Dawson-based organisations, in Perth and Hobart respectively (Perth first). For those of you who've never heard of him, Christopher Dawson (1889-1970) was a Catholic scholar who worked all his academic life to get the Church to meet the modern intellectual and cultural world half-way. The Dawson Society in Perth and the Dawson Centre in Hobart (now moved to Melbourne) have both run exciting programs of talks and mini-conferences with a range of excellent and sometimes controversial speakers.⁶³ These gatherings are part-academic and part-social, are great for networking, and we always have a good time (I've spoken at various events run by each group). The Anima Network and other Catholic women's networks have also done much to help like-minded Catholic women to connect with each other over talks and retreats.⁶⁴

We also need to keep an eye on the Eastern rites and the Ordinariates. As our numbers shrink, they will come to greater prominence, but only if they maintain their own numbers. The Maronite community suffered real losses of Mass attenders during COVID19, but the Syro-Malabar community is rapidly increasing in numbers. These communities will face their own problems with falling interest from the younger generation. I don't think it's realistic to expect these small communities to save the Church, but we can certainly work more closely with them in many ways.

Data collection

You've seen in this book how rubbery some of our figures are when it comes to the Church. I think we can do a lot better at parochial-diocesan level, because in a climate where, for example, the ABS is no longer distinguishing Catholic marriages from other types in its reports, our internal data collection must be taken more seriously.

For example, I heard a story about a leisurely Australian bishop who instructed his staff for years simply to 'add a few more' to last year's total before sending the baptism data to wherever it was meant to go. There were also stories about priests concocting baptism data which didn't correlate with the parish registers, and then being unable to explain the disparity in numbers, with amusing consequences. I will not reveal the names of these clergy or my sources, but these stories are all too believable.

This might mean that a diocese has to employ more staff in data collection and maintenance, and I would heartily endorse that – especially if they are scary and independent and can go round to parishes frightening the laxer clergy into keeping accurate parish records themselves. Doing some ongoing clergy formation on this would also help. I have always found when I want to collect data that it's easiest first to explain to the people involved why it's important to get it right. I also like to show them how the data will be used, and what it all means. Once the clergy have more buy-in on its collection, it should all get a lot easier and with less resistance.

I would love to see that data also made much more available at a local level. It's a form of increased transparency which would cost the diocese nothing, and it's consistent with the growing 'open science' movement that's combatting bad and fraudulent research globally. While we're at it, it would be great to see better diocesan websites with really useful information that's kept up to date. I would also like the *Official Directory of the Catholic Church in Australia* to continue to be available in print form, because it's much more user-friendly for quick access to formatted data than the online version.

Changing our clergy

Support your local bishop?

We've already seen that priestly numbers are good in Australia compared to the number of Mass-going Catholics, but that priestly morale is low. Ordinary Mass-going Catholics are crying out for strong episcopal leadership. The Church in Australia needs fewer corporate types and more pastoral, hands-on bishops who are unafraid of their diocesan bureaucracies and their clergy (the older of whom sometimes bully their bishop as well). There is a marked lack of trust now between priests and bishops, as well as between lay people and bishops, and we all need to work harder to heal this.

William said as much when I asked him about what lay people could do here and now to help the Church. He said he's seen a lot of the correspondence that comes across bishops' desks from the laity, and it's really discouraging.

> My ask of fellow sisters and brothers who are lay people in the Church is: pray for your bishop and support him. I don't care if he's conservative or liberal; support him anyway; pray for him regularly. But also, just offer your prayerful support. When he says something good, or ordains a good priest, or reforms something, write a letter and tell him how thankful you are and tell him you're praying for him. Encouragement and support.[65]

At the same time, ordinary lay Catholics want to see real

support from their bishops in a rapidly changing and sometimes dangerous world. Steve and Helen point out that, 'Lay Catholics have lost their jobs and livelihoods standing up for the truth, and I would like to see our bishops standing strong in a similar way when faced with criticism or media-led attacks.'[66] Tori adds, 'How do I convince my kids to take the faith seriously when ... the Archdiocese is constantly hitting me up for cash for various projects but has never asked "how can we help" with regards to the cost-of-living crisis, now arguably within its fourth year?'[67]

But Fr Michael thinks that some bishops are starting to realise that the future of the Church lies in a different place, and to recognise the value of living witnesses.

> The best thing is, as I suppose it has always been, the resilience of the laity who believe in and love the Church. ... I think they are beginning to influence bishops because they are the ones who regularly turn up for ordinations and other non-school related diocesan events, with their often-large families. And only they are providing new vocations. Bishops see them at daily Mass.[68]

Our future Mass-going communities will be small, but the people in them will really want to be there. They're already building up Adoration, support groups, and catechetical networks. The bishops in Australia need to identify these and invest in them if they want the Church to have a future beyond 2050. We're probably going to be more dispersed than we thought – but that's how leaven in the lump is supposed to act.

I would add to bishops and future bishops: Be visible. Be present. Hear Confessions in your Cathedral regularly, without fanfare. Don't hide in expensive offices away from your people. Make hard decisions. Sack the seminary rector if you need to. You will have to deal with clerical dead wood left over from your weaker predecessors. Leave your diocese in a better state than you found it. You need to connect with your Mass-going under-40s, who are founding young families and will be your backbone going forward to 2050, if you do this properly. Find them and make friends with them. You won't regret it.

People and priests – a two-way relationship

I've already described in the chapter on clergy how I think things could start to improve here. Rebuilding trust between clergy and local bishops is important, and that's only done through face-to-face relationships and consistent, transparent episcopal leadership behaviours. The bullying of younger clergy and occasionally the bishop himself by older Boomer priests needs to be shut down, no matter how useful these priests are to the local bishop as his occasional enforcers. I also think that more priests should live in common; it's protective and a great antidote against becoming a fussy, selfish bachelor.

So what else can we do? I started this section by thinking of all the ways in which the laity could help and support their priests. It took Petra to show me another perspective.

> As far as finding 'help and support' in the Church goes, my mind is discombobulated by the idea that the Church is there to give me help and support! For the last ever-so-many years, we have had priests who seem to think it is the duty of the parishioner to give them help and support and not the other way round. Where am I finding the help and support I need? For spiritual formation, I have to find resources for myself – fortunately not too hard to do these days.[69]

And yet when given chances to get lay help, some of them don't seem to know where to start.

> I have been astounded over the past 20 years to find out that none of our recent priests has had the slightest interest in my work life or any skills I can use for the benefit of the parish. The only priest who seemed to care and delegate jobs to those who had appropriate skills, was [Fr X], who in his former life was an accountant. If I were a priest, and running the parish like a business, I would first of all find

out about my 'human resources': all of the parishioners who have so much to contribute to parish life (not talking about money here).[70]

Fr Jason, a younger priest from another part of the country, confirmed this.

> My observation is that even amongst the 'good' priests there is a sense (whinging) that things should be done FOR them. Yes, I understand the need for support for priests etc, but I often hear in the criticisms of the way things are in the Church a sense of needing to be given support as opposed to, 'this is the situation we're in, and I'm going to serve and be faithful to the Lord in these often difficult circumstances because that is what He has called me to do'.[71]

Clearly this needs to be a two-way relationship, and perhaps we haven't gotten the balance right in some places.

Tori has noticed that local friendly family networks can attract clergy who need community: 'Occasionally, a "lone wolf" priest who has not had his faith crushed out of him by the banality of Church leadership, becomes part of these informal networks and is very beloved and embraced by those who can see the challenges that this poor padre faces.'[72] Ben can see smaller and more authentic parish communities becoming safe havens for good priests as well.

> I think certain changes will happen organically anyway – parishes will close, those that produce a liturgy that is appealing will attract the families, there will be a 'return to tradition' in some respects. Good, faithful priests will be looked after by these communities (and may well need to be protected from the institutional church and secular society at certain points).[73]

I've seen this work well in practice. It gives the priests a soft place to land on their days off, allows them to reach a wider community who needs them, and fosters future vocations to the priesthood. Being around priests who are normal men doing a supernatural thing, day in and day out, helps the laity and the priest to remember who he is, and what he's called to do.

What can priests do better at parish level (apart from say Mass and make the other sacraments available in a more reverent way)? Fr Jason provides his own antidote to the problem he noted above.

> ... a change I would like to see is a greater call (from leadership) to service/sacrifice. My sense is that in order for that call to be clearer, is a greater ability to name the enemy. We are generally so fearful to name the enemy (those in and out of the Church) and I think that results in lukewarmness. If there is no challenge/battle/crisis then then is no need to confront that challenge/battle/crisis. I could say more about the feminised priesthood we see, but I think the men we need as priests/leaders of the Church are able to recognise the enemy, and in imitation of Christ, lay down their life for the Church.[74]

I will give the last word to Fr Harrison, who has his own take on what the future might look like for him.

> God chose for me to be born in a season of epochal decline. None of this discourages me, and I am not pessimistic. I strive to be cheerful and serene. My faith is deeply personal; my relationship with Jesus is intimate. He is always sending me out, but it's on a soul-by-soul basis. I am not an important priest. I will always and happily tend to small flocks. My horizon is limited.[75]

This might also be a good way for all parish priests to recalibrate and get their sense of proportion back when they're feeling overwhelmed.

Changing our business arm

> The year is 2035, hopefully my last as archbishop. I've just emailed my draft homily for Sunday to the Religious Safety Commissioner for her approval. She's the independent regulator charged with ensuring that faith groups spread

> no discriminatory and otherwise harmful messages. With the help of [artificial intelligence], she vets all planned sermons and spiritual talks to be given in Australia each week, catching any inappropriate words or themes before they are spoken.
>
> Our school system also meets each month with Departmental officials to monitor what's taught in our schools and ensure this accords with contemporary expectations. The Department itself now appoints Catholic school principals, SERECs (Secular Ethics and Religious Education Coordinators), and other staff in accord with [diversity, equity, and inclusion] policy and approves all curriculum.
>
> Hospitals like St Vincent's [in Sydney] are no more. Because these institutions so stubbornly refused to provide 'the full range of services', such as abortion, euthanasia and sex-change surgery, the Greens-Teals Coalition nationalised the faith-based public hospitals in 2033, following the precedent of Calvary Hospital Canberra a decade before.
>
> Charitable status is no longer granted to faith-based education, health, aged care or welfare, and state subsidies have been declining, while secular bureaucratic interference and taxes on former charities have been increasing, making some of these institutions unsustainable. The Census people and the Productivity Commission, egged on by sections of the media, have decided religion no longer warrants recognition.[76]

This is Archbishop Anthony Fisher's recent grim prediction for the not-too-distant future of the Church's business interests in Australia. He goes on to say that he's just exaggerating for dramatic effect – but then provides several recent concrete examples of why his prediction is probably pretty much accurate. (I'm appalled that he sees himself caving in to these people by emailing his homilies to them, and instead I would encourage him to tell the Religious Safety Commissioner politely that he won't be playing).

But in principle, I agree with Archbishop Fisher; I think it's probably going to get ugly. So does Tori, who can see how hard it's going to be to clear out the dead wood.

> It's hard not to see most current Australian Catholic organisations and professional bodies as sheltered workshops staffed by unproductive, cafeteria Catholics who perpetuate a banality of evil characterised by petty fiefdoms, professional jealousies and endless 'busy work' to justify bloated salaries. Where are their results? What is the interest they have returned on the treasures bestowed upon them?[77]

So what can we do instead? We can get in first. We can start offloading functions and businesses which the Church was not founded to carry out, and which are holding it back from its true missionary work at parochial-diocesan level. These things are not assets; they are liabilities. I'd make a lot of changes to the Catholic-origin education system and the hospitals and health care system.

Catholic-origin schools

Catholic-origin school systems across the country, in every State, are mostly no longer supporting the mission of the Church in Australia. They're operating alongside it and employing a lot of people. But they're adding no value to the Church at all – in fact, I'd argue that they're weighing us down and may well be successfully inoculating children against Catholicism for the rest of their lives.[78]

I've already said that I think the solution is to cut ties – and cut them soon.[79] The Church in each State should look at brokering deals with their State government to sell and/or transfer school buildings and land. Most of them could be transformed into independent government schools quite easily. Many or most of the teaching staff will probably stay on if offered the opportunity. Most of the students probably will as well, once the parents realise they no longer have to pay high fees for basically the same education.

The media spin on this will be interesting, because people will want to know why the Church is doing this. There will be suspicious atheists who think we're selling dodgy land with sinkholes, and conspiracy theorists who think Dan Brown is right and that we're preparing for the mother ship to arrive. Telling the truth about why we're selling some of the schools will involve some public eating of humble pie by our bishops. But I think it's better to be honest and say, 'We've found that our community has moved to the outer suburbs, and these schools are no longer in the right places for our community.'

Is this selling the family silver? Yes, some of it. That's what family silver is for, when you're about to be persecuted. You sell it and sew the cash into your underwear and hope that you make it across the border. It would be great if we could sell these schools to State governments at market rates. I think leasing them is fraught with just as many problems as we currently face in our messy relationship with secular governments. It also prolongs the agony.

We don't have to sell all the Catholic schools. But we can certainly start with the ones which are built on land which is now worth a lot of money and where there are no young people living nearby. We can also find out which schools have now been thoroughly colonised by non-Catholics and are in effect already just cheap fee-paying independent schools with Catholic building names. I think we could start with the schools where the parents made the biggest fuss about Jason Evert's visit.

The money raised from their sale should go into providing diocesan-funded, modest fee-paying Catholic schools, at least at primary level, for the children of Mass-going Catholics. These aren't quite parochial schools, and they're likely to be built in unfashionable areas, but that's where our young Mass-going Catholics are living now. I can see these schools working alongside and at times with a second and third generation homeschooling network, in collaboration rather than opposition.[80] Steve and Helen think that this is where we will find the future of the parochial-diocesan Church in Australia:

> Those centres where there is a solid independent Catholic school or large homeschooling areas will have vibrant parish life and they will revitalise the Church in Australia eventually. But throughout most of the country and particularly in rural areas many churches will close and parishes die out. I think this decline is already fairly obvious.[81]

Home-schooling isn't for everyone, but Mass-going Catholics who want a different type of education for their children will struggle to set up their own schools, train teachers, and register everything under the current system. Again, we have to flip things around. Reviving a genuinely local Catholic school model – a Catholic primary school for children whose families are active in a particular parish or group of parishes – would be a lot smaller, but also a lot cheaper to run. It would offer a functional alternative to home-schooling for many young Mass-going Catholic families.

A Church which takes subsidiarity seriously should re-invest in schools like this. These schools will be entirely privately funded and will not take any government money. I'd love to see them run by governing boards made up of parents of children who attend the school, and the school chaplain. I'd also like to see the local bishop do a visitation to each of these schools once a year and have a good look at the kids, the parents, and the account books.

Who will oversee the new Catholic schools on a day-to-day basis? I'm so glad you asked, because we'll be closing most of each State's current Catholic education authority. The new Catholic schools will be privately funded and independently run by boards, so that doesn't leave a lot to do at this level. With fewer schools, there will be less to do, and we probably won't notice the disappearance of most of the middle-management jobs.

I think overseeing the new smaller Catholic system – which would be mostly reporting to the local bishop – could be done competently by a very small, younger, well-organised team. They can also do any educational authority compliance work to keep the school open under State law as an independent faith-based school. But I'm sure each State government's education department will need people who have experience with all their new ex-Catholic-origin schools, and I'd gladly see most of the management and administrative staff transfer from one form of government payroll to another.

Catholic-origin health care

I would also recommend cutting government ties in health care. I think we're well on the way to doing that anyway – but not in the way we should be. It will be done for us. Ministerial Public Juridic Persons (MPJPs) are, as I've said, only as good as their human members. As these governing boards and bodies become more saturated with people who are Catholic in name only, they will naturally cave in quite willingly to government demands.[82]

Once all the surviving members of their original religious orders have died, I suspect this will happen quite quickly. We'll also see what happens when the first requests for voluntary assisted dying start coming from individuals in Catholic-origin aged care facilities. That will be a good guide to how willing that organisation's leadership is to uphold the Church's teaching and preserve the dignity of the human person to natural death.

What would replace Catholic-origin health care? Catholic health care, I hope. But it will mostly take the form of primary health care – Catholic GPs and medical clinics who will be known and used by Mass-going Catholics. In our brave new future Church, we'll hopefully have more priests doing hospital and nursing home rounds, rather than lay people doing quite as much as they're doing now. It's a useful gig for a retired priest who's still steady on his pins, or a young priest who's too green for a parish just yet. Many Mass-going Catholics still don't realise that they need to be proactive in asking for chaplaincy support when they're in hospital, or their relatives are in hospital. Most hospitals – even the Catholic ones – will wait for the patient to ask for a priest.

As in the days of the Roman Empire, our care of our elderly and weak needs to look different from that of the mainstream. We need to become known again for the fact that we don't kill unwanted children and the elderly, and we genuinely care for each other because each of us bears the image of Christ. I would love to see new religious orders forming – even associations of lay faithful – who would provide community-based in-home care to older Catholics ageing in place, with or without family support.

This kind of work is already funded by the Commonwealth government through individual aged care packages. This is somewhere where I have no objection to people taking government funding, because it's about as subsidiary as it gets. A Catholic provider could set up and employ a small team of Mass-going Catholic support workers and pay them properly to work with Mass-going Catholic clients in their own homes. This could also extend to the ancillary services they provided: there are Mass-going Catholic occupational therapists, gardeners, nurses, and palliative care workers who might love this option. This provider could also liaise with parish priests to come and visit and anoint the person in their own home, and even offer Mass for them there sometimes.

Conclusion – the season of the furrow

Prophecy is a risky business, so this book is really just me and some other people sticking our necks out and trying to see where we might go in the absence of a new Pentecost (which I don't rule out either, of course). I think it's clear that we're in the season of the furrow, rather than the harvest. That doesn't mean that Catholic life in Australia won't be without its consolations, but it won't be all enjoyable. Children will leave homeschooling networks and Opus Dei and claim as young adults to have been abused. Some of them will be telling the truth. This will increase soft persecution of the Church in the media. There will also be humiliating reckonings with the heavy hand of the State in return for taking all those billions of dollars of taxpayers' money for so long.

But there is also a lot of hope. At the beginning of Lent in 2024, George Weigel offered the following roundup of the good news from the Church in the United States:

> **Seminaries.** In the main, US seminaries today are in better shape than they've ever been. The seminary reforms mandated by John Paul II in the 1987 apostolic exhortation *Pastores Dabo Vobis* have taken hold, and while there is still hard work left to be done – not least in inculcating the art of preaching – seminary rectors and formators in many North Atlantic countries marvel at what they see here and hope to imitate it.
>
> **Catholic Colleges and Universities.** Some of these are, indeed, Catholic wastelands. In others, there is a continual battle over sustaining a vibrant Catholic identity that prepares young men and women for missionary discipleship.
>
> Still others, however, are set firmly on the path of fostering intellectual rigor in an environment that supports ongoing and ever-deeper conversion to Christ. To name but a few, in alphabetical order: Thomas Aquinas College, Belmont Abbey College, Benedictine College, the Catholic University of America, Christendom College, the University of Dallas, the Franciscan University of Steubenville, the University of Mary.
>
> **Catholic Campus Ministry.** We are in a Golden Age of Catholic campus ministry, evident in what some might regard as surprising places like Texas A&M University and North Dakota State University. The Fellowship of Catholic University Students (FOCUS), a direct outgrowth of World Youth Day-1993 in Denver, now sends 980 young missionaries, recent college graduates, to 202 campuses in six countries for peer-to-peer evangelisation and catechesis.
>
> A high percentage of 21st-century vocations to the priesthood and consecrated life are nurtured by participation in on-campus FOCUS programs, and the number of fine Catholic marriages and families that

FOCUS and other excellent Catholic campus ministries have nurtured is incalculable.

The Thomistic Institute, run from the Dominican House of Studies in Washington, brings high-octane Catholic content to campuses from sea to shining sea, challenging wokery with truth.

Adult Catechesis and Formation. Here, too, the church in the United States is a global leader. The Word on Fire ministry created by Bishop Robert Barron goes from strength to strength and has now developed a first-class publishing program to extend the work done by Ignatius Press and other premier Catholic publishers.

The FORMED program of the Augustine Institute makes quality evangelisation and catechetical materials available to parishes that take adult formation seriously. The Catholic Information Center in downtown Washington, DC, is the heart of the New Evangelisation in the nation's capital. Then there is the work of intellectual and spiritual formation done by Legatus, the association of Catholic CEOs and professionals, and the Napa Institute.

The Reform of Consecrated Life. Vibrantly and joyfully orthodox American religious communities of women are growing: the Nashville Dominicans, the Dominican Sisters of Mary Mother of the Eucharist, the Sisters of Mercy of Alma, Michigan, and the Sisters of Life are but four examples. The Dominican Province of St Joseph is arguably the most dynamic religious congregation of men in the world.

Parishes and Schools. These have been the pastoral bedrock of US Catholicism for over two centuries. They still are, and they have a vitality unmatched elsewhere. Moreover, our inner-city Catholic schools are likely the most effective anti-poverty program in the country.[83]

Admittedly, the Catholic Church in the United States has more money, more people, and thus more critical mass. But why can't we aim for the same quality here in proportion to our numbers? There are other dioceses in the Anglosphere with worse problems that are turning things around, like Southwark in London and South Carolina in the US.[84] It's amazing what God can do when we let him.

The Church in Australia can go forward from its current messes – perhaps much smaller, humbler, and poorer, but perhaps much more like salt, light, and yeast for a country that really needs it. It will be made up of a group of witnesses of all ages who will have grown closer to God and to each other than perhaps they expected, and who will grow in joy as they find themselves being drawn each day into the heart of the Trinity. We don't know how this story ends with the Catholic Church in Australia, but I think it's worth sticking around to find out.

---

[1] This is a topic I've tried to steer clear of in this book, but if you want to know more, Martyr, P. (2021, July 19). A conversation about bogus mysticism and the rule of fear. *Gaudium et Spes 22*, https://gaudiumetspes22.com/blog/a-conversation-about-bogus-mysticism-and-the-rule-of-fear

[2] von Balthasar, H. (1982). What is required in witnesses. *You crown the year with your goodness: radio sermons*, trans G. Harrison. Ignatius.

[3] Lauren, personal communication, 7 August 2024.

[4] Josh, personal communication, 3 September 2024.

[5] William, personal communication, 17 October 2024.

[6] Catholic Church. (1965). *Dignitatis humanae: declaration on religious freedom*. https://www.vatican.va/archive/hist_councils/ii_vatican_council/documents/vat-ii_decl_19651207_dignitatis-humanae_en.html

[7] Chapp, L. (2021, May 12.) Universalism, Balthasar, the *massa damnata*, and the question of evangelization. *Gaudium et Spes 22*, https://gaudiumetspes22.com/blog/universalism-balthasar-the-massa-damnata-and-the-question-of-evangelization

[8] Steve Skojec, founder of the Catholic blog One Peter Five, is the example that comes most readily to my mind. Skojec, S. (2021, July 26). It's time to pass the torch. *One Peter Five*, https://onepeterfive.com/its-time-to-pass-the-torch/

[9] Martyr, P. (2024, June 14). Who's responsible for bringing back the church's lost sheep? *The Catholic Weekly*, https://catholicweekly.com.au/lay-evangelisation/

[10] Tori, personal communication, 31 August 2024.

[11] Lane, S. (2024, March 6). Tradwife ideology won't save you. *The American Mind*, https://americanmind.org/salvo/tradwife-ideology-wont-save-you/; Keating, A. (2017, October 2). The perfect family is an idol. *Church Life Journal*, https://churchlifejournal.nd.edu/articles/the-perfect-family-is-an-idol/

[12] Becklo, M. (2024, November 14). A layman's case for restoring the Friday meat fast.

Catholic World Report, https://www.catholicworldreport.com/2024/11/14/a-laymans-case-for-restoring-the-friday-meat-fast/

[13] La Rosa, M. (2024, May 4). 'To find your people' – How Catholics are building intentional communities. *The Pillar*, https://www.pillarcatholic.com/p/to-find-your-people-how-catholics

[14] Tori, personal communication, 31 August 2024.

[15] Martyr, P. (2024, January 29). Reject romance, return to clothes-swaps. *The Catholic Weekly*, https://catholicweekly.com.au/philippa-martyr-reject-romance-return-to-clothes-swaps/

[16] Petra, personal communication, 25 August 2024.

[17] Katrina, personal communication, 20 June 2024.

[18] Leah, personal communication, 19 June 2024.

[19] Martyr, A conversation about bogus mysticism.

[20] Diane, personal communication, 20 May 2024.

[21] Katrina, personal communication, 20 June 2024.

[22] Campbell, R. (2023; January 9). One for the country: do we need another baby bonus? *Sydney Morning Herald*, https://www.smh.com.au/national/ageing-population-falling-birth-rate-do-we-need-another-baby-bonus-20230108-p5cblr.html; Murphy, H. (2024, April 18). Australians are having fewer babies – experts say it could have more consequences than we realise. *ABC News*, https://www.abc.net.au/news/2024-04-18/australia-fertility-rate-could-predict-the-next-five-years/103692844

[23] Hughes, P. (2013). Organization of leadership in rural parishes: Some Australian Catholic case-studies. *Rural Theology*, 11(1), 3–14. https://doi.org/10.1179/1470499413Z.0000000003

[24] This can be found at: https://westernborder.church/mass-times/western-border-parish-mass-sawc-times/

[25] Vatican, Congregation for Clergy. (2020, July 20). *Instruction 'The pastoral conversion of the parish community in the service of the evangelising mission of the Church', of the Congregation for the Clergy*, https://press.vatican.va/content/salastampa/en/bollettino/pubblico/2020/07/20/200720a.html

[26] Fr Michael, personal communication, 5 August 2024.

[27] Sr Yvette, personal communication, 20 August 2024.

[28] Ethan, personal communication, 30 May 2024.

[29] Leah, personal communication, 19 June 2024.

[30] Katrina, personal communication, 20 June 2024.

[31] Miriam, personal communication, 20 June 2024.

[32] Leah, personal communication, 19 June 2024.

[33] Tomlinson, H. (2024, June 26). Potential pitfalls of Catholic Parish Summit's evangelising spirit. *Catholic Herald*, https://catholicherald.co.uk/potential-pitfalls-of-the-catholic-parish-summits-evangelising-spirit/

[34] Leah, personal communication, 19 June 2024.

[35] Australian Catholic Bishops Conference. (n.d.). *Guidelines for reverent reception of Holy*

Communion (Liturgical Documents), https://www.catholic.au/s/article/Guidelines-for-Reverent-Reception-of-Holy-Communion

[36] Martyr, P. (2020, March 5). Secret wildfire of Adoration. *The Catholic Weekly*, https://catholicweekly.com.au/philippa-martyr-secret-wildfire-of-adoration/

[37] Leah, personal communication, 19 June 2024.

[38] Martyr, P., & Bullivant, S. (2024). *The Catholics in Australia Survey 9 – Traditional Latin Mass (TLM) attenders*, https://papers.ssrn.com/sol3/papers.cfm?abstract_id=4942220

[39] Ethan, personal communication, 30 May 2024.

[40] Tierney, K. (2024, May 19). Opinion: The dynamism and challenge of 'DIY Traditionalism'. *Catholic World Report*, https://www.catholicworldreport.com/2024/05/19/opinion-the-dynamism-and-challenge-of-diy-traditionalsm/

[41] Colin, personal communication, 20 May 2024.

[42] John, personal communication, 12 August 2024.

[43] Fr Robert, personal communication, 11 June 2024.

[44] Miriam, personal communication, 20 June 2024.

[45] Fisher, S. (2024, April 26). Restored order of sacraments and family catechesis: a combination that works. *The Catholic Weekly*, https://catholicweekly.com.au/restored-order-of-sacraments-and-family-catechesis-a-combination-that-works/

[46] Katrina, personal communication, 20 June 2024.

[47] Coppen, L. (2024, April 11). How Pope Francis is reshaping the Church in western Ireland. *The Pillar*, https://www.pillarcatholic.com/p/how-pope-francis-is-reshaping-the; Coppen, L. (2024, September 12). Pope merges two Welsh dioceses. *The Pillar*, https://www.pillarcatholic.com/p/pope-merges-two-welsh-dioceses

[48] Osborne, P. (2024, October 14). Bishop Timothy Norton SVD appointed to Diocese of Broome. *ACBC Media Blog*, https://mediablog.catholic.org.au/bishop-timothy-norton-svd-appointed-to-diocese-of-broome/

[49] Martyr, P. (2019, July 18). A catechesis Australia needs. *The Catholic Weekly*, https://www.catholicweekly.com.au/phillipa-martyr-a-catechesis-australia-needs/

[50] Martyr, P. (2020, June 17). Precisely which Church? A response to the Plenary Discernment papers. *The Catholic Weekly*, https://catholicweekly.com.au/precisely-which-church-a-response-to-the-plenary-discernment-papers/

[51] Martyr, Precisely which Church?; Wilson, T. (n.d.). *Good works: the Catholic Church as an employer in Australia*, https://s3.ap-southeast-2.amazonaws.com/acbcwebsite/Articles/Documents/ACBC/nla.obj-1766235550-1.pdf; Catholic Health Australia. (2020). *Annual report 2019*, https://cha.org.au/wp-content/uploads/2021/04/CHA-Annual-Report-2019_final-compressed.pdf; National Catholic Education Commission. (2020, November 4). *2019 annual report*, https://ncec.catholic.edu.au/resource-centre/2019-annual-report/

[52] Ally, D. (2024, June 20). The secret to a thriving youth ministry. *The Catholic Weekly*, https://catholicweekly.com.au/youth-ministry-parish-renewal-conference/

[53] Martyr, P. (2024, May 4). Should Catholics reconsider their financial habits? *The Catholic Weekly*, https://catholicweekly.com.au/should-catholics-reconsider-their-financial-habits/

[54] Katrina, personal communication, 20 June 2024.

55 MRA Consulting Group. (2021). *Measuring the impact of the charitable reuse and recycling sector: A comparative study using clothing donated to charitable enterprises*, https://www.charitablerecycling.org.au/wp-content/uploads/2021/06/Charitable-Recycling-Australia-Recycled-Clothing-Impact-Assessment-240521.pdf; Samie, Y., Maldini, I., & Vladimirova, K. (2024, November 21). Overwhelmed by ever more clothing donations, charities are exporting the problem. Local governments must step up. *The Conversation*, https://theconversation.com/overwhelmed-by-ever-more-clothing-donations-charities-are-exporting-the-problem-local-governments-must-step-up-243709

56 Centrecare. (2024). *Support and funding*, https://www.centrecare.com.au/about-centrecare/support-and-funding

57 Ethan, personal communication, 30 May 2024.

58 Martyr, P. (2021, April 25). Small is beautiful for this particular age. *The Catholic Weekly*, https://catholicweekly.com.au/philippa-martyr-small-is-beautiful-for-this-particular-age/

59 Miriam, personal communication, 20 June 2024.

60 Steve and Helen, personal communication, 9 August 2024.

61 O'Shea, G. (2017). A comparison of Catechesis of the Good Shepherd and Godly Play. *British Journal of Religious Education*, 40(3), 308-316. https://www.tandfonline.com/doi/full/10.1080/01416200.2017.1292209; *Association of the Catechesis of the Good Shepherd Australia*, https://cgsaust.org.au/

62 Rowland, T. (2024). *Unconformed to the age: essays in Catholic ecclesiology*. Emmaus.

63 For the Perth site, https://dawsonsociety.org.au/. For the Hobart/Melbourne site, https://www.dawsoncentre.org/

64 *Anima Women's Network*, https://animanetwork.org/

65 William, personal communication, 17 October 2024.

66 Steve and Helen, personal communication, 9 August 2024.

67 Tori, personal communication, 31 August 2024.

68 Fr Michael, personal communication, 5 August 2024.

69 Petra, personal communication, 25 August 2024.

70 Ibid.

71 Fr Jason, personal communication, 13 June 2024.

72 Tori, personal communication, 31 August 2024.

73 Ben, personal communication, 1 June 2024.

74 Fr Jason, personal communication, 13 June 2024.

75 Fr Harrison, personal communication, 30 May 2024.

76 Fisher, A. (2024, June 9). Religious freedom in a secular world: Doomed or doable? *The Catholic Weekly*, 12-13. The full statement can be found here: https://www.sydneycatholic.org/addresses-and-statements/2024/religious-freedom-in-a-secular-world-doomed-or-doable-31-may-2024/

77 Tori, personal communication, 31 August 2024.

78 Martyr and Bullivant, *Catholic schooling*.

79 Martyr, P. (2018). Let's call the whole thing off? God, truth, and Buckminster Fuller. In D. Daintree (Ed.), *Creative subversion: The liberal arts and human educational fulfilment*. Connor

Court. Audio at: https://cradio.org.au/cradiotalks/talk-lecture-series/dawson-centre/lets-call-whole-thing-off/

[80] Figge, J. (2024, October 12). Homeschooling: 'Super weird,' or future of the Church? *The Pillar*, https://www.pillarcatholic.com/p/homeschooling-super-weird-or-future

[81] Steve and Helen, personal communication, 9 August 2024.

[82] Martyr, P. (2019, August 17). Fault lines for Catholic agencies. *The Catholic Weekly*, https://catholicweekly.com.au/philippa-martyr-fault-lines-for-catholic-agencies/

[83] Weigel, G. (2024, March 17). The good news is that the bad news isn't all the news there is. *The Catholic Weekly*, https://catholicweekly.com.au/the-good-news-is-that-the-bad-news-isnt-all-the-news-there-is/

[84] Coppen, L. (2024, July 25). 'Some definite service': How an English diocese is unleashing growth. *The Pillar*, https://www.pillarcatholic.com/p/some-definite-service-how-an-english; Duncan, G. (2024, July 2). The rise of South Carolina's Catholic population. *Catholic World Report*, https://www.catholicworldreport.com/2024/07/02/the-rise-of-south-carolinas-catholic-population/

Appendix 1

Possible research projects

These are all the possible research projects I identified throughout this book. If you'd like to be an honours or postgraduate student somewhere, or if you have the money to set up a lavishly appointed Catholic think-tank, one or more of these might suit you.

1. Surveying Catholics in the pews who disagree with the Church's teaching on key issues like birth control and asking them why they still go to Mass.
2. Mapping and collecting data on Australia's adult converts, ideally from the last 10 years if possible, using RCIA and other data from dioceses.
3. Analysing the published annulment data sets in the *Annuarium Statisticum Ecclesiae* for Australia from 1970 onwards.
4. Surveying or interviewing self-identified Catholics on what they believe about Confession, how often they go to Confession, and why they go, or don't go.
5. Surveying or interviewing Mass-going Catholics who don't send their children to Catholic schools – asking them what forms of education they've chosen instead, and the reasons why.
6. Is there an 'NFP-adjacent' group of Catholics – those who are doing 'mostly' NFP but occasionally using unapproved methods of birth control as well? How is NFP working for real-life users of it in Catholic Australia?
7. Assessing and evaluating belief in Purgatory among Australian Catholics – who still believes, and what do they believe, and why?
8. A social network analysis of the links between people employed in diocesan bureaucracies and other Catholic agencies and Catholic-origin businesses in a diocese.

9. What is the Mass attendance rate and conformity with core beliefs of Catholics who are currently in diocesan employment in Australia?
10. What factors make a Catholic in Australia choose a particular university – are Catholics distinguishable from non-Catholics in this respect? Is it pragmatism or proximity or other factors?
11. Do Mass-going Catholics prefer Catholic universities and institutes of higher education?

Appendix 2

Data sets on the Catholic Church in Australia

These are included here for those who like to flip to the back and look at things. If you want to use the Excel version, visit: Martyr, Philippa (2024), 'Australian Catholic Statistics 1970-2021', Mendeley Data, V1, doi: 10.17632/x23npr3cm9.1 (https://data.mendeley.com/datasets/x23npr3cm9/1)

Table 14. Baptisms in Australia, *Annuarium Statisticum Ecclesiae*, 1970-2021.
Cells have been left blank for the years where volumes were missing from the runs I accessed.

Year	Under 5-7 years	Over 5-7 years	Total
1970	74,853	3,601	78,454
1971	76,533	3,417	79,950
1972	76,035	2,963	78,998
1973	74,621	2,891	77,512
1974	76,844	2,583	79,427
1975	75,051	3,139	78,190
1976	72,084	2,704	74,788
1977	69,602	2,553	72,155
1978	69,775	2,540	72,315
1979			
1980	66,294	3,372	69,666
1981	66,384	3,714	70,098
1982	67,891	3,629	71,520
1983			
1984	70,290	4,634	74,924
1985	70,278	4,850	75,128
1986			
1987	68,554	4,003	72,557

1988			
1989	72,091	4,756	76,847
1990	75,010	4,696	79,706
1991	73,703	5,211	78,914
1992	72,370	3,922	76,292
1993	71,055	4,223	75,278
1994	71,065	4,802	75,867
1995	70,359	4,815	75,174
1996	63,524	4,445	67,969
1997	65,334	5,161	70,495
1998	62,471	4,854	67,325
1999	63,473	5,176	68,649
2000	61,917	4,872	66,789
2001	60,878	4,935	65,813
2002	58,386	4,603	62,989
2003	59,954	4,985	64,939
2004	60,139	5,266	65,405
2005	60,261	6,154	66,415
2006	61,844	6,428	68,272
2007	62,990	5,494	68,484
2008	62,607	5,665	68,272
2009	62,864	5,619	68,483
2010	62,379	6,286	68,665
2011	59,446	5,061	64,507
2012	63,793	5,282	69,075
2013	62,927	5,536	68,463
2014	59,083	5,243	64,326
2015	55,770	4,967	60,737
2016	53,231	4,876	58,107
2017	50,480	4,735	55,215
2018	47,625	4,138	51,763
2019	45,993	4,212	50,205
2020	40,541	3,686	44,227
2021	38,343	3,777	42,120

Table 15. Catholic marriages in Australia, *Annuarium Statisticum Ecclesiae*, 1970-2021

Cells have been left blank for the years where volumes were missing from the runs I accessed.

Year	Both Catholic	'Mixed'	Total	% both Catholic	% 'Mixed'
1970	15,540	15,259	30,799	50.5%	49.5%
1971	14,449	16,579	31,028	46.6%	53.4%
1972	14,404	15,858	30,262	47.6%	52.4%
1973	15,085	16,304	31,389	48.1%	51.9%
1974	15,134	15,783	30,917	49.0%	51.0%
1975	13,933	14,520	28,453	49.0%	51.0%
1976	12,547	13,793	26,340	47.6%	52.4%
1977	11,347	12,765	24,112	47.1%	52.9%
1978	11,069	12,914	23,983	46.2%	53.8%
1979					
1980	10,788	12,205	22,993	46.9%	53.1%
1981	11,180	12,546	23,726	47.1%	52.9%
1982	11,203	12,688	23,891	46.9%	53.1%
1983					
1984	11,905	12,799	24,704	48.2%	51.8%
1985	11,639	12,700	24,339	47.8%	52.2%
1986					
1987	11,824	11,776	23,600	50.1%	49.9%
1988					
1989	12,812	12,446	25,258	50.7%	49.3%
1990	12,276	12,685	24,961	49.2%	50.8%
1991	12,357	11,692	24,049	51.4%	48.6%
1992	11,230	21,615	32,845	34.2%	65.8%
1993	10,997	11,162	22,159	49.6%	50.4%

1994	10,832	11,395	**22,227**	48.7%	51.3%
1995	10,702	10,920	**21,622**	49.5%	50.5%
1996	9,923	8,327	**18,250**	54.4%	45.6%
1997	9,505	9,742	**19,247**	49.4%	50.6%
1998	9,184	9,643	**18,827**	48.8%	51.2%
1999	9,342	9,310	**18,652**	50.1%	49.9%
2000	8,907	8,803	**17,710**	50.3%	49.7%
2001	8,180	7,835	**16,015**	51.1%	48.9%
2002	8,006	7,353	**15,359**	52.1%	47.9%
2003	7,814	7,473	**15,287**	51.1%	48.9%
2004	7,897	6,915	**14,812**	53.3%	46.7%
2005	7,955	7,339	**15,294**	52.0%	48.0%
2006	8,043	6,942	**14,985**	53.7%	46.3%
2007	7,135	7,123	**14,258**	50.0%	50.0%
2008	7,196	6,785	**13,981**	51.5%	48.5%
2009	7,147	6,115	**13,262**	53.9%	46.1%
2010	6,984	6,043	**13,027**	53.6%	46.4%
2011	6,458	5,823	**12,281**	52.6%	47.4%
2012	6,245	5,443	**11,688**	53.4%	46.6%
2013	5,470	4,916	**10,386**	52.7%	47.3%
2014	5,355	4,393	**9,748**	54.9%	45.1%
2015	4,987	4,004	**8,991**	55.5%	44.5%
2016	4,534	3,632	**8,166**	55.5%	44.5%
2017	4,458	3,437	**7,895**	56.5%	43.5%
2018	4,069	3,198	**7,267**	56.0%	44.0%
2019	4,070	2,801	**6,871**	59.2%	40.8%
2020	4,065	1,773	**5,838**	69.6%	30.4%
2021	3,315	2,145	**5,460**	60.7%	39.3%

Table 16. Annual variations in diocesan clergy numbers, Australia, *Annuarium Statisticum Ecclesiae*, 1970-2021

Cells have been left blank for the years where volumes were missing from the runs I accessed. The data from these years was obtained from summary tables published in other volumes. This data is shown in italics and is not complete for each year.

Numbers of priests who left the priesthood are shown by year of laicisation, not year of ordination (year of ordination data is unavailable).

'Absent – other' are diocesan priests who are absent from their diocese for other reasons (eg. they have not died or left the priesthood). This might include study interstate or overseas, or temporary placement in another diocese.

Year	1 Jan	Ordained	Left	Died	Absent – other	Change	31 Dec
1970	2,396	55	22	34		-1	2,395
1971	2,395	61	14	25	5	17	2,412
1972	2,412	65	25	29	0	11	2,423
1973	2,423	68	29	31	65	-57	2,366
1974	2,366	67	26	41	7	-7	2,359
1975	2,359	53	16	31	45	-39	2,320
1976	2,320	32	19	24	18	-29	2,291
1977	2,418	32	24	37	12	-41	2,377
1978	2,374	39	22	30	2	-11	2,363
1979	2,332	41	17	47			2,356
1980	2,356	26	12	40	14	-12	2,344
1981	2,344	36	16	29	4	-5	2,339
1982	2,339	33	9	30	1	-7	2,332
1983	2,291	29	13	30			2,347
1984	2,347	29	11	37	1	-20	2,327
1985	2,327	34	15	26	13	-20	2,307
1986	2,190	30	19	34			
1987	2,261	30	10	49	8	-37	2,224
1988	2,174	33	8	32			

1989	2,224	20	12	45	9	-28	2,196
1990	2,196	24	7	25	15	7	2,203
1991	2,203	28	10	32	8	-22	2,181
1992	2,181	35	11	32	22	-30	2,151
1993	2,151	30	14	42	1	-25	2,126
1994	2,126	31	9	38	19	3	2,129
1995	2,129	24	6	50	7	-39	2,090
1996	2,090	20	10	34	4	-20	2,070
1997	2,070	23	10	39	9	35	2,035
1998	2,035	18	12	39	11	-44	1,991
1999	1,991	19	12	47	10	-30	1,961
2000	1,961	35	11	51	3	-30	1,931
2001	1,931	22	7	46	15	-16	1,915
2002	1,915	24	15	47	2	-36	1,879
2003	1,879	21	11	22	19	7	1,886
2004	1,886	13	9	41	2	-35	1,851
2005	1,851	20	7	40	23	-50	1,801
2006	1,801	17	11	38	3	-29	1,772
2007	1,772	19	7	34	5	-17	1,755
2008	1,755	18	6	43	8	-23	1,732
2009	1,732	21	11	25	10	-5	1,727
2010	1,727	28	6	37	5	-10	1,717
2011	1,717	43	8	48	45	32	1,749
2012	1,749	25	4	51	4	-25	1,724
2013	1,724	35	9	31	16	11	1,735
2014	1,735	26	2	45	32	-53	1,682
2015	1,682	46	4	50	7	-15	1,667
2016	1,667	27	5	49	13	-14	1,653
2017	1,653	24	3	56	7	-28	1,625
2018	1,625	23	4	40	1	-22	1,603
2019	1,603	30	4	35	4	-13	1,590
2020	1,590	26	8	40	22	0	1,590
2021	1,590	21	4	41	10	-14	1,576

Table 17. Western-rite Catholic seminarians in formation in Australia by state, *Official Directory of the Catholic Church in Australia*, 1990-2021

Data from the Archdiocese of Canberra-Goulburn has been aggregated to the NSW total.

Year	NSW/ ACT	Vic	Tas	SA/ NT	WA	Qld	Total
1990-1	101	52	3	15	19	49	239
1992-3	84	29	6	19	20	36	194
1994	60	23	2	11	18	31	145
1995	64	24	4	6	16	33	147
1996	58	22	5	6	51	41	183
1997	53	17	6	7	46	40	169
1998	53	18	6	7	45	22	151
1999	59	33	6	6	40	21	165
2000	56	31	6	6	53	16	168
2001	49	32	2	3	49	15	150
2002	52	34	1	3	42	18	150
2003	43	35	0	4	36	18	136
2004	40	36	0	4	40	15	135
2005	40	36	0	4	40	15	135
2006-7	66	36	0	3	44	7	156
2007-8	81	34	0	3	51	6	175
2008-9	80	37	0	4	38	11	170
2009-10	108	42	1	3	49	9	212
2010-11	96	40	1	3	48	17	205
2011-12	128	38	1	4	48	15	234
2012-13	127	42	3	4	56	19	251
2014-15	111	37	1	2	35	36	222
2016-17	104	46	5	5	32	17	209
2017-18	91	34	6	5	30	16	182
2018-19	108	47	7	5	29	21	217
2019-20	101	41	5	4	29	24	204
2020-21	102	39	5	4	23	21	194

Table 18. Western-rite permanent deacons in Australia by state, *Official Directory of the Catholic Church in Australia*, 1981-2021

Data from the Archdiocese of Canberra-Goulburn has been aggregated to the NSW total.

Year	NSW/ACT	Vic	Tas	SA/NT	WA	Qld	Total
1981-2				1	2	1	4
1983-4				1	2	2	5
1985-6		1		1	8	2	12
1988-9	2	1		2	8	2	15
1990-1	2	1	0	2	7	2	14
1992-3	4	1	0	4	13	2	24
1994	5	2	0	5	14	2	28
1995	5	1	0	7	14	3	30
1996	5	1	0	7	14	4	31
1997	7	1	0	7	13	4	32
1998	10	1	0	7	14	3	35
1999	11	0	0	7	11	3	32
2000	11	0	0	7	11	3	32
2001	12	0	0	6	10	3	31
2002	18	2	1	7	9	2	39
2003	22	2	0	6	10	2	42
2004	27	3	0	7	11	2	50
2005-6	27	3	0	7	11	2	50
2006-7	26	3	0	7	12	8	56
2007-8	26	5	1	6	27	11	76
2008-9	25	7	1	9	28	16	86
2009-10	31	6	0	10	27	15	89
2010-11	38	6	1	12	27	17	101
2012-13	37	7	2	14	26	18	104
2014-15	39	13	3	19	29	18	121
2016-17	43	22	3	16	27	18	129
2017-18	51	22	3	16	27	21	140
2018-19	59	24	2	16	25	23	149
2019-20	57	25	4	16	25	25	152
2020-21	63	25	4	18	24	24	158

Table 19. Eastern-rite and Ordinariate permanent deacons in Australia, *Official Directory of the Catholic Church in Australia*, 1992-2021

Year	Maronite	Melkite	Chaldean	Military Ordinariate	Our Lady of the Southern Cross	Total
1992-3		2				2
1994		3		1		4
1995		5		1		6
1996		5		4		9
1997		2		4		6
1998		3		4		7
1999		3		4		7
2000		3		4		7
2001		3		4		7
2002		3		4		7
2003		1				1
2004	1	4		2		7
2005-6	1	4		2		7
2006-7		3		5		8
2007-8			1	2		3
2008-9		2	1	1		4
2009-10		2	1	2		5
2010-11	1	7		3		11
2012-13	1	7	2	4		14
2014-15	2	7	3	4		16
2016-17	2	7	5	5	1	20
2017-18	2	8	5	6	1	22
2018-19	2	8	5	7	1	23
2019-20	2	8	5	7	1	23
2020-21	5	9	5	5	1	25

Table 20. Australian Catholic dioceses – estimated financial position (equity), 2023

Some dioceses did not have any information publicly available, and some only had older information available at time of writing. Earlier years than 2023 are shown in italics. The estimated total equity shown here is approximately $1 billion.

Eleven Australian dioceses currently participate in a CDF Community Fund: Ballarat, Bunbury, Hobart, Parramatta, Melbourne, Rockhampton, Sale, Sandhurst, Townsville, Wagga Wagga, and Wollongong. This is overseen by the Catholic Development Fund (CDF) in the Archdiocese of Melbourne.[1]

Diocese	Report	Year ended	Equity at end of financial year
Adelaide	Catholic Church Endowment Society Special Purpose Consolidated Financial Report[2]	December 2023	$203,971,490
Armidale	Armidale Diocesan Investment Group report[3]	December 2023	$47,448,925
Ballarat	CDF annual report[4]	December 2023	$15,453,421
Bathurst	CDF annual report[5]	June 2023	$20,992,818
Brisbane	Archdiocesan Development Fund annual report[6]	December 2023	$149,759,000
Broken Bay	CDF annual report[7]	June 2023	$ 9,391,259
Broome	No current report available		
Bunbury	No current report available		
Cairns	No current report available[8]	December 2022	$10,729,690

Canberra-Goulburn	No current report available[9]	December 2021	$18,484,708
Darwin	No current report available[10]	June 2020	$9,481,887
Geraldton	No current report available		
Hobart	No current report available[11]	June 2022	$15,986,095
Lismore	Diocesan Investment Fund report[12]	March 2024	$39,116,688
Maitland Newcastle	No current report available[13]	June 2021	$26,842,000
Melbourne	CDF annual report[14]	June 2023	$218,301,000
Parramatta	Diocesan Development Fund report[15]	June 2023	$38,158,131
Perth	CDF annual report[16]	December 2023	$49,790,587
Port Pirie	CDF annual report[17]	June 2024	$11,181,658
	Diocesan Development Fund report[18]	December 2023	$29,233,060
Sale	No current report available		
Sandhurst	Development Fund report[19]	June 2023	$26,068,098
Sydney	CDF annual report[20]	June 2023	$85,823,200
Toowoomba	Diocesan Development Fund report[21]	June 2023	$2,393,484
Townsville	Diocesan Development Fund report[22]	December 2023	$15,462,973
Wagga Wagga	No current report available[23]	June 2022	$16,168,747
Wilcannia Forbes	Part of Armidale Diocesan Investment Group[24]		
Wollongong	CDF annual report[25]	December 2023	$17,227,942

Table 21. Catholic-origin schools and enrolments in Australia, 1981-2021
Data taken from the *Official Directory of the Catholic Church in Australia*, various years.

Years	Primary Schools	Secondary Schools	Combined School	Other	Total	Students – primary	Students – secondary	Other	Total students
1981-2	1,313	473		19	1,805	317,354	195,697		513,051
1983-4	1,340	455		23	1,818	326,462	217,426		543,888
1985-6	1,303	450		30	1,783	332,691	233,877		566,568
1988-9	1,308	412		64	1,784	365,699	238,399		604,098
1990-1	1,344	433		60	1,837	336,372	246,238		582,610
1992-3	1,313	435		69	1,817	344,476	253,773		598,249
1994	1,298	411		74	1,783	342,987	243,601		586,588
1995	1,305	420		101	1,826	347,969	254,827		602,796
1996	1,295	394		132	1,821	353,175	257,920		611,095
1997	1,297	405		117	1,819	355,003	264,508		619,511
1998	1,254	362		115	1,731	358,925	272,454		631,379
1999	1,259	358		103	1,720	358,155	272,306		630,461
2000	1,261	363		125	1,749	363,175	280,355		643,530
2001	1,292	398		120	1,810	366,170	272,812		638,982
2002	1,255	343		119	1,717	343,520	245,096	67,371	655,987
2003	1,245	338		60	1,643	344,017	249,069	67,336	660,422
2004	1,241	329		128	1,698	368,539	295,299	637	664,474
2005-6	1,241	340	97	17	1,695	370,735	299,535		670,270
2006-7	1,236	340	100	17	1,693	373,474	304,187		677,661
2007-8	1,777	346	111	12	2,246	376,645	309,162		685,807
2008-9	1,226	349	112	10	1,697	378,059	312,561		690,620
2009-10	1,225	350	114	10	1,699	380,011	316,343		696,354
2010-11	1,222	325	141	10	1,698	383,917	320,138		704,055
2011-12	1,222	316	147	10	1,695	387,944	322,679		710,623
2012-13	1,229	317	148	10	1,704	395,156	327,561		722,717
2014-15	1,238	333	131	10	1,712	409,339	333,645		742,984
2016-17	1,235	349	137	10	1,731	403,468	360,791		764,259
2017-18	1,249	343	133	11	1,736	404,443	361,401		765,844
2018-19	1,245	350	139	11	1,745	405,515	360,749		766,264
2019-20	1,252	357	138	11	1,758	402,852	361,665		764,517
2020-21	1,254	347	148	12	1,761	402,072	366,219		768,291

Table 22. Catholic students enrolled in Catholic-origin schools as a percentage of all enrolments by state and diocese, 2016 and 2021

Data taken from the *Diocesan Social Profiles 2016 and 2021*, National Centre for Pastoral Research. Does not include data from the Diocese of Darwin, which is anomalous because of small numbers. The Archdiocese of Canberra-Goulburn is here aggregated to NSW.

Diocese/State	Catholic primary students, 2016	Catholic primary students, 2021	% loss	Catholic secondary students, 2016	Catholic secondary students, 2021	% loss
NSW						
Armidale	62%	57%	-5%	61%	53%	-8%
Bathurst	76%	69%	-7%	70%	63%	-7%
Broken Bay	86%	77%	-9%	74%	68%	-6%
Canberra-Goulburn	67%	59%	-8%	60%	54%	-6%
Lismore	65%	57%	-8%	56%	51%	-5%
Maitland-Newcastle	70%	60%	-4%	66%	56%	-10%
Parramatta	77%	70%	-7%	69%	64%	-5%
Sydney	77%	73%	-4%	71%	68%	-3%
Wagga Wagga	74%	67%	-7%	71%	64%	-7%
Wilcannia-Forbes	70%	62%	-8%	66%	57%	-9%
Wollongong	82%	75%	-7%	66%	62%	-4%
Queensland						
Brisbane	71%	61%	-10%	62%	56%	-6%
Cairns	60%	51%	-9%	55%	50%	-5%
	62%	55%	-7%	54%	47%	-7%
Toowoomba	63%	53%	-10%	59%	52%	-7%
Townsville	66%	58%	8%	60%	54%	-6%
South Australia						
Adelaide	57%	45%	-12%	51%	45%	-6%
Port Pirie	51%	37%	-14%	49%	43%	-6%

Tasmania						
Hobart	52%	40%	-12%	45%	38%	-7%
Victoria						
Ballarat	67%	60%	-7%	57%	55%	-2%
Melbourne	77%	70%	-7%	70%	65%	-5%
Sale	68%	58%	-10%	59%	49%	-10%
Sandhurst	65%	54%	-11%	58%	51%	-7%
Western Australia						
Broome	59%	59%	-0%	71%	53%	-18%
Bunbury	67%	53%	-14%	65%	50%	-15%
Geraldton	72%	58%	-14%	61%	49%	-12%
Perth	78%	68%	-10%	67%	61%	-6%

Table 23. Selected Australian Catholic-origin school authorities – estimated financial position (equity), 2022-2023

Agency	End of year	Equity
Brisbane Catholic Education[26]	December 2023	$1,969,905,000
Catholic Education NT[27]	December 2021	$837,124
Catholic Education South Australia (CESA)[28]	December 2022	$15,571,000
Catholic Education Tasmania[29]	December 2022	$3,964,321
Catholic Education WA (CEWA)[30]	December 2023	$1,434,829,555
Catholic Schools New South Wales (CSNSW)[31]	December 2023	$17,181,098
Diocese of Maitland-Newcastle Catholic Schools Office[32]	December 2022	$464,744,600
Melbourne Archdiocese Catholic Schools[33]	December 2023	$2,860,109,000
Queensland Catholic Education Commission[34]	December 2023	$11,632,267
Victorian Catholic Education Authority (VCEA)[35]	December 2023	$5,206,175

[1] Catholic Development Fund. (2024). *CDF annual report FY23*, https://irp.cdn-websitecom/787db205/files/uploaded/CDF%20Ann%20Rep%20Final 171123-39f3595f.pdf

[2] Catholic Church Endowment Society. (n.d.). *Special purpose consolidated financial report for the year ended 31 December 2023*, https://adelaide.catholic.org.au/_files/f/175732/CCES%202023%20Audited%20Financials.pdf

[3] Armidale Diocesan Investment Group. (2024). *Annual report 2024*, https://adig.com.au/wp-content/uploads/2024/07/ADIG-Annual-Report-2024.pdf

[4] Catholic Development Fund – Diocese of Ballarat. (n.d.). *Annual report 2023*, https://www.ballarat.catholic.org.au/wp-content/uploads/2024/06/2024-annual-report-web.pdf

[5] Roman Catholic Diocese of Bathurst Catholic Development Fund. (n.d.). *Financial statement for the year ended 30 June 2023*, https://cdn.prod.website-files.com/6181fbcf194a7c60ab81c6a8/650b9651063c7194288b1f72_Signed%2030%20June%202023%20CDF%20Financial%20Statements.pdf

[6] Archdiocesan Development Fund. (n.d.). *Annual report for the year ended 31 December 2023*, https://adf.brisbanecatholic.org.au/assets/uploads/signed_adf-annual-report-2023.pdf

[7] Catholic Development Fund Diocese of Broken Bay. (n.d.). *Annual report: general purpose financial statements for the year ended 30 June 2023*, https://www.bbcatholic.org.au/ArticleDocuments/1055/20230630-Broken%20Bay%20Audited%20Accounts.pdf.aspx

[8] Diocese of Cairns Catholic Development Fund. (n.d.). *Special purpose financial statements for the year ended 31 December 2022*, https://cairns.catholic.org.au/files/media/original/313/522/cab/CDF-Financial-Statements-31.12.2022-Final-Signed.pdf

[9] Catholic Development Fund Archdiocese of Canberra-Goulburn. (n.d.). *Annual financial statements – financial year ended 31 December 2021*, https://cdf.cg.catholic.org.au/wp-content/uploads/2022/04/220217_AnnualReport2021_Signed_Final.pdf

[10] Darwin Diocesan Development Fund. (n.d.). *Special purpose report year ended 30 June 2020*, https://static1.squarespace.com/static/602f24d61f1de445374ae9fd/t/602f386b97cbab7fdd5cb77a/1613707375400/S3.+DDDF+Annual+Financial+Statement+FY20.pdf

[11] Roman Catholic Church Trust Corporation of the Archdiocese of Hobart, trading as Catholic Development Fund Tasmania. (n.d.). *Financial report for the year ended 30 June 2022*, https://www.cdftas.com/wp-content/uploads/2022/11/Signed-2022-Financial-Statements.pdf

[12] Trustees of the Roman Catholic Church for the Diocese of Lismore as Trustee for Diocesan Investment Fund. (n.d.). *Concise financial report for the year ended 31 March 2024*, https://dif.au/important/uploads/2024/07/DIF_AnnualReportWeb2024.pdf

[13] Catholic Development Fund Diocese of Maitland-Newcastle. (n.d.). *Annual report for the year ended 30 June 2021*, https://myccf.com.au/wp-content/uploads/2021/12/30062021-CDF-Annual-Report-signed_FINAL.pdf

[14] Archdiocese of Melbourne Catholic Development Fund. (n.d.). *General purpose financial report for the financial year ended 30 June 2023*, https://irp.cdn-website.com/787db205/files/uploaded/CDF%20Annual%20Financial%20Statement%2030%20June%202023%20(Signed).pdf

[15] Diocese of Parramatta Diocesan Development Fund. (n.d.). *Financial report for the*

financial year ended 30 June 2023, https://parracatholic.org/wp-content/uploads/2023/09/DDF-Annual-Report-Financial-Year-2023.pdf

[16] Archdiocese of Perth Catholic Development Fund. (n.d.). *Annual report 2023*, https://www.cdfperth.org.au/wp-content/uploads/2024/06/2023-CDF-Financial-Statements-2023.pdf

[17] Catholic Development Fund Diocese of Port Pirie. (n.d.). *Annual report 30 June 2023*, https://ppcatholic.org/about-us/finances/ – choose 'CDF Audited Accounts' and then 'CDF-2023-Audit.pdf'

[18] Diocesan Development Fund. (n.d.). *Special purpose annual report for the year ended 31 December 2023*, https://www.ddfrockhampton.com.au/wp-content/uploads/DDF-AUDITED-ANNUAL-FINANCIAL-STATEMENTS-2023-FINAL.pdf

[19] DDF Diocese of Sandhurst Development Fund. (n.d.). *Special purpose financial report for the year ended 30 June 2023*, https://www.sandhurst.catholic.org.au/diocese-of-sandhurst-publications/2036-ddf-annual-financial-report-30-june-2023/file

[20] Catholic Development Fund Archdiocese of Sydney. (n.d.). *2023 annual report*, https://sydneycdf.org.au/wp-content/uploads/2023/12/CDF-Annual-Report-2023.pdf

[21] Roman Catholic Diocese of Toowoomba Diocesan Development Fund. (n.d.). *Financial statements for the year ended 30 June 2023*, https://www.twb.catholic.org.au/site/wp-content/uploads/2023/10/20230630-Financial-Report-and-Audit-Report-Diocese-of-Toowoomba-Diocesan-Development-Fund.pdf

[22] Townsville Diocesan Development Fund. (n.d.). *Financial statements for the year ended 31 December 2023*, https://os-data.s3-ap-southeast-2.amazonaws.com/tsv-catholic-org-au/bundle31/signed_financial_report_31.12.23.pdf

[23] Diocesan Provident Fund Diocese of Wagga Wagga. (n.d.). *Financial statements as at 30 June 2022*, https://wagga.catholic.org.au/wp-content/uploads/2022/09/2022-DPF_Financials-Signed.pdf

[24] Armidale Diocesan Investment Group. (2024). *Annual report 2024*, https://adig.com.au/wp-content/uploads/2024/07/ADIG-Annual-Report-2024.pdf – see https://www.wf.catholic.org.au/assistus/adig/

[25] Catholic Development Fund Diocese of Wollongong. (n.d.). *Financial statements as at 31 December 2023*, https://www.dow.org.au/wp-content/uploads/CDF-Financial-Statements-2023-signed.pdf

[26] The Corporation of the Trustees of the Roman Catholic Archdiocese of Brisbane. (n.d.). *Financial report year ended 31 December 2023*, https://www.acnc.gov.au/charity/charities/11a03e5e-38af-e811-a963-000d3ad24077/documents/

[27] Catholic Education Northern Territory. (n.d.). *2022 annual report*, https://os-data-2.s3-ap-southeast-2.amazonaws.com/ceont/bundle3/catholic_education_nt_-_annual_report_2022.pdf This report does not provide an equity balance. Instead, I have used the unexpended revenue remaining at the end of 2021.

[28] Catholic Education South Australia. (n.d.). *Financial reports 2022*, https://report.cesa.catholic.edu.au/statistics-and-financials/financial-reports CESA has five separate funds, all of which report separately. I added up the equity from all five in 2022 and subtracted the one deficit I found (in the Long Service Leave Fund), to produce this figure.

[29] Catholic Education Tasmania. (n.d.). *Annual report 2022*, https://tascathed.schoolzineplus.com/_file/media/2680/20231212_annual_report_2022.pdf

[30] Catholic Education Western Australia. (n.d.). *Annual report 2023*, https://www.cewa.edu.au/wp-content/uploads/2024/06/AnnualReport2023_v2_Web.pdf This figure includes property, plant, and equipment valued at $1.52 billion.

[31] Catholic Schools New South Wales. (2024, September 9). *How Catholic schools are funded*, https://www.csnsw.catholic.edu.au/funding-of-nsw-catholic-schools-system/ ; Catholic Schools New South Wales. (n.d.). *Annual report 2023*, https://www.csnsw.catholic.edu.au/sites/default/files/2024-10/CSNSW-Annual-Report-2023.pdf

[32] Diocese of Maitland-Newcastle Catholic Schools Office. (n.d.). *Financial report 2022*, https://www.acnc.gov.au/charity/charities/3223f2a8-38af-e811-a963-000d3ad244fd/documents/

[33] Melbourne Archdiocese Catholic Schools Ltd. (n.d.). *Financial report 2023*, https://www.acnc.gov.au/charity/charities/35e4116b-1596-ed11-aad1-0022489733de/documents/

[34] Queensland Catholic Education Commission. (n.d.). *2023 annual report*, https://qcec.catholic.edu.au/wp-content/uploads/2024/05/QCEC-2023-Annual-Report-FINAL-web-version.pdf

[35] Victorian Catholic Education Authority. (n.d.). *2023 annual report*, https://vcea.catholic.edu.au/about-us/governance/#annual-reports

Bibliography

Adolphe, J. (2020). Organisational culture and male-on-male sexual violence: a comparative study. In J. Adolphe and R. Rychlak, *Clerical sexual misconduct: an interdisciplinary analysis* (pp. 147-176). Cluny.

Agence France-Presse. (2023, December 17). Vatican court convicts cardinal Angelo Becciu of embezzlement. *The Guardian*, https://www.theguardian.com/world/2023/dec/16/vatican-court-convicts-cardinal-angelo-becciu-of-embezzlement

Agile Legal (2023, May 17). *Visa options for sponsoring a minister of religion or religious assistant to work in Australia.* https://www.agilelegal.com.au/visa-options-for-sponsoring-a-minister-of-religion-or-religious-assistant-to-work-in-australia

Al-Akiki, G. (2024, June 12). Watch and pray at two new perpetual adoration chapels. *The Catholic Weekly*, https://www.catholicweekly.com.au/perpetual-adoration-chapel-sydney/

Al-Akiki, G. (2024, June 19). Can Catholics afford to live near their parishes? *The Catholic Weekly*, https://www.catholicweekly.com.au/cost-of-living-catholic-parishes/

Al-Akiki, G. (2024, May 21). Evert a success with students and parents. *The Catholic Weekly*, https://catholicweekly.com.au/jason-evert-a-success-with-students-and-parents/

Ally, D. (2024, April 24). Sydney's baptism boom has us beaming with pride. *The Catholic Weekly*, https://www.catholicweekly.com.au/sydneys-baptism-boom-has-us-beaming-with-pride/

Ally, D. (2024, June 20). The secret to a thriving youth ministry. *The Catholic Weekly*, https://catholicweekly.com.au/youth-ministry-parish-renewal-conference/

Altenburger, M. (2017, November 29). Single life is more fundamental for Christianity than both married and religious life. *Church Life Journal*, https://churchlifejournal.nd.edu/articles/single-life-is-more-fundamental-for-christianity-than-both-married-and-religious-life/

Ang, D. (2024, June 7). National study to investigate reasons for decline in Mass attendance. *The Catholic Weekly*, https://www.catholicweekly.com.au/national-study-to-investigate-decline-in-mass-attendance/

Ang, D. (2024, May 29). Parish renewal is never a solo endeavour. *The Catholic Weekly*, https://www.catholicweekly.com.au/parish-renewal-is-never-a-solo-endeavour/

Archdiocesan Development Fund. (n.d.). *Annual report for the year ended 31 December 2023*, https://adf.brisbanecatholic.org.au/assets/uploads/signed_adf-annual-report-2023.pdf

Archdiocese of Brisbane. *St Luke's, Buranda*, https://brisbanecatholic.org.au/parishes-and-mass-times/parish/st-lukes-buranda/

Archdiocese of Melbourne Catholic Development Fund. (n.d.). *General purpose financial report for the financial year ended 30 June 2023*, https://irp.cdn-website.com/787db205/files/uploaded/CDF%20Annual%20Financial%20Statement%2030%20June%202023%20(Signed).pdf

Archdiocese of Perth Catholic Development Fund. (n.d.). *Annual report 2023*, https://www.cdfperth.org.au/wp-content/uploads/2024/06/2023-CDF-Financial-Statements-2023.pdf

Archdiocese of Perth. (2022). *Extraordinary Ministers of Holy Communion: guidelines*, https://liturgy.perthcatholic.org.au/wp-content/uploads/2022/10/Guidelines-for-Altar-Ministers-EMHC-and-Acolytes-2022.pdf

Armidale Diocesan Investment Group. (2024). *Annual report 2024*, https://adig.com.au/wp-content/uploads/2024/07/ADIG-Annual-Report-2024.pdf – see https://www.wf.catholic.org.au/assistus/adig/

Association of Ministerial Public Juridic Persons (AMPJP). (2024). *About MPJPs*, https://ampjp.org.au/about-mpjps/

Australian Associated Press. (2023, January 31). Sydney schools linked to conservative Catholic group Opus Dei investigated over 'broad' curriculum concerns. *SBS News*, https://www.sbs.com.au/news/article/sydney-schools-linked-to-conservative-catholic-group-opus-dei-investigated-over-broad-curriculum-concerns/0zck5hb4y

Australian Bureau of Statistics (ABS). (2022). *2021 Census, Religious affiliation in Australia*, https://www.abs.gov.au/statistics/people/people-and-communities/cultural-diversity-census/2021/Census%20article%20-%20Religious%20affiliation%20in%20Australia.xlsx

ABS. (2022, November 10). *Marriages and divorces Australia*, https://www.abs.gov.au/statistics/people/people-and-communities/marriages-and-divorces-australia/2021#marriages

ABS. (2022, October 18). *Births, Australia*, https://www.abs.gov.au/statistics/people/population/births-australia/latest-release

ABS. (2023). *Schools*, https://www.abs.gov.au/statistics/people/education/schools/latest-release

ABS. (n.d.) *Population projections Australia (2022-2071)*. https://www.abs.gov.au/statistics/people/population/population-projections-australia/latest-release

Australian Capital Territory Health Directorate. (2023). *Annual report 2022-23*, https://www.act.gov.au/_data/assets/pdf_file/0007/2302387/ACT-Health-Annual-Report-2022-2023.pdf

Australian Catholic Bishops Conference (ACBC). (2015). *Don't mess with marriage: a pastoral letter from the Catholic bishops of Australia to all Australians on the 'same-sex marriage' debate*, https://www.sydneycatholic.org/pdf/DMM-booklet_web.pdf

ACBC. (2021). *Recommended hymns and songs approved by the Bishops Conference (liturgical documents)*, https://www.catholic.au/s/article/Recommended-Hymns-and-Songs

ACBC. (2021, November 8). *Who can be baptised?* https://www.catholic.au/s/article/Who-can-be-baptised

ACBC. (2022). *Catholic Australia: Pastoral Research – Statistics*, https://www.catholic.au/s/article/Statistics

ACBC. (2022). *Created and loved: a guide for Catholic schools on identity and gender*, https://drive.google.com/file/d/1X11WeuMYfHeyMwVmMQMivzMZUnI6rOQQ/view

ACBC. (2022). *Public juridic persons*, https://www.catholic.au/s/article/Public-Juridic-Persons

ACBC. (2023). *Australian Catholic Bishops Conference annual report 2023*, https://s3.ap-southeast-2.amazonaws.com/acbcwebsite/Articles/Documents/ACBC/2024/ACBC%20Annual%20Report%202023%20FINAL.pdf

ACBC. (n.d.). *Guidelines for reverent reception of Holy Communion (Liturgical Documents)*, https://www.catholic.au/s/article/Guidelines-for-Reverent-Reception-of-Holy-Communion

Australian Catholic Diocesan Vocations Directors Conference. (2023). *The permanent diaconate*, https://www.vocations.catholic.org.au/s/news/resources-vocations-MCDIXQDUDEXFDRHL653MHTSNI3XU

Australian Catholic Historical Society. (n.d.). *Australian Catholic charities*, https://australiancatholichistoricalsociety.com.au/history-resources/australian-catholic-charities/#Social_justice_advocacy_and_theory

Australian Catholic Historical Society. (n.d.). *The Catholic press in Australia*, https://australiancatholichistoricalsociety.com.au/history-resources/the-catholic-press/

Australian Charities and Not-for-Profits Commission. (n.d.). *Charities and administration costs*, https://www.acnc.gov.au/for-public/understanding-charities/charities-and-administration-costs

Australian Education Union Victorian Branch. (n.d.). *National teacher survey gives thumbs down to NAPLAN*, https://www.aeuvic.asn.au/national-teacher-survey-gives-thumbs-down-naplan

Bajkowski, J. (2023, May 11). ACT nationalises Canberra's second hospital as Barr removes Catholic operator. *The Mandarin*, https://www.themandarin.com.au/219970-calvary-hospital-stealthily-nationalised-by-act-government/

Baker, J. (2024, June 14). A TikTok priest and a surfing nun: The new wave of conservative Christians. *Sydney Morning Herald*, https://www.smh.com.au/national/a-tiktok-priest-and-a-surfing-nun-the-new-wave-of-conservative-christians-20240610-p5jkmq.html

Baker, M. (2011, May 24). *Paul Brazier*, https://www.superflumina.org/brazier_tribute.html

von Balthasar, H. (1982). What is required in witnesses. *You crown the year with your goodness: radio sermons*, trans G. Harrison. Ignatius.

von Balthasar, H. (1989). *Test everything, hold fast to what is good*. Ignatius.

Becklo, M. (2024, November 14). A layman's case for restoring the Friday meat fast. *Catholic World Report*, https://www.catholicworldreport.com/2024/11/14/a-laymans-case-for-restoring-the-friday-meat-fast/

Benedict, St. (c.530). *Rule of Benedict*, https://archive.osb.org/rb/text/rbejms1.html/1

Bennett, J. (2017). *Singleness and the Church: a new theology of the single life*. Oxford University Press.

Bertotti, A., & Christensen, S. (2012). Comparing current, former, and never users of natural family planning: an analysis of demographic, socioeconomic, and attitudinal variables. *The Linacre Quarterly*, 79(4), 474–486. https://doi.org/10.1179/002436312804827154;

Bonacci, M. (1999, February 1). Love and the single Catholic. *Crisis Magazine*, https://crisismagazine.com/vault/love-and-the-single-catholic

Brisbane Catholic Education. (2024). *Annual report 2023*, https://www.bne.catholic.edu.au/aboutus/AnnualReports/Documents/2023%20BCE%20Annual%20Report.pdf

Briscoe, P. (2023, September 5). New propaedeutic year offers spiritual detox to aspiring priests. *Our Sunday Visitor*, https://www.oursundayvisitor.com/new-propaedeutic-year-offers-spiritual-detox-to-aspiring-priests/

Broken Rites. (2010, October 4). A recent cover-up: A church school failed to protect children from abuse. *Broken Rites*, https://brokenrites.org.au/drupal/node/129

Broken Rites. (n.d.) The Marist Brothers recycled an offender to a new position of trust. *Broken Rites*, https://brokenrites.org.au/drupal/node/80

Brown, A. (2020, August 20). A profile of single Americans. *Pew Research Center*, https://www.pewresearch.org/social-trends/2020/08/20/a-profile-of-single-americans/

Buchan, J. (2007). International recruitment of nurses: policy and practice in the United Kingdom. *Health Services Research, 32*, 1321–1335. https://www.ncbi.nlm.nih.gov/pmc/articles/PMC1955378/

Bullivant, S. (2024). 'This is the greatest thing a man can do': vocational journeys of recently ordained Catholic priests in Australia. *Religions, 15*, 1-23. https://doi.org/10.3390/rel15080896

Burge, R. (2023, January 13). Is Catholic teaching on birth control driving people from the pews? *National Catholic Reporter*, https://www.ncronline.org/opinion/catholic-teaching-birth-control-driving-people-pews

Burge, R. (2023, October 12). The Catholic Church is in trouble in places where it used to dominate. *Graphs About Religion*, https://www.graphsaboutreligion.com/p/the-catholic-church-is-in-trouble

Burke, C. (2023, November 19). Multi-million Catholic Church payout 'massively important' for future sexual abuse cases. *ABC News*, https://www.abc.net.au/news/2023-11-19/catholic-church-payout-important-future-sexual-abuse-cases/103118822

Calvary Health Care Bethlehem Kooyong Precinct (2023). *Annual report 2022-23*, https://www.calvarycare.org.au/public-hospital-bethlehem/wp-content/uploads/sites/5/2023/11/2023_CHCB_AnnualReport_FINAL.pdf

Campbell, R. (2023; January 9). One for the country: do we need another baby bonus? *Sydney Morning Herald*, https://www.smh.com.au/national/ageing-population-falling-birth-rate-do-we-need-another-baby-bonus-20230108-p5cblr.html

Cardaronella, M. (2023, October 27). God's sacramental plan: why we need the sacraments and the Church. *Catechist*, https://www.catechist.com/gods-sacramental-plan-need-sacraments-church/

Cassidy, C. (2024, October 22). Former union head Joe de Bruyn's speech condemning abortion and same-sex marriage sparks walkout at Catholic university. *The Guardian*, https://www.theguardian.com/australia-news/2024/oct/22/joe-de-bruyn-speech-acu-walkouts-abortion-same-sex-marriage-ntwnfb

CathNews. (2024, May 13). Talks continue on Calvary hospital compensation. *CathNews*, https://cathnews.com/2024/05/13/talks-continue-on-calvary-hospital-compensation/

Catholic Australia. (2024, May 24). National survey shows Australia's Catholics are online and multicultural. *Catholic Australia*, https://www.catholic.au/s/article/National-survey-shows-Australia-s-Catholics-are-online-and-multicultural

Catholic Church – Congregation for Clergy. (2020, July 20). *Instruction 'The pastoral conversion of the parish community in the service of the evangelising mission of the Church'*, of the Congregation for the Clergy, https://press.vatican.va/content/salastampa/en/bollettino/pubblico/2020/07/20/200720a.html

Catholic Church Endowment Society. (n.d.). *Special purpose consolidated financial report for the year ended 31 December 2023*, https://adelaide.catholic.org.au/_files/f/175732/CCES%202023%20Audited%20Financials.pdf

Catholic Church. (1963). *Sacrosanctum Concilium: on the sacred liturgy*, https://www.vatican.va/archive/hist_councils/ii_vatican_council/documents/vat-ii_const_19631204_sacrosanctum-concilium_en.html

Catholic Church. (1965). *Dignitatis humanae: declaration on religious freedom*, https://www.vatican.va/archive/hist_councils/ii_vatican_council/documents/vat-ii_decl_19651207_dignitatis-humanae_en.html

Catholic Church. (1983). *Code of canon law*, https://www.vatican.va/archive/cod-iuris-canonici/eng/documents/cic_lib2-cann460-572_en.html

Catholic Church. (1994). *Catechism of the Catholic Church*. Vatican.

Catholic Church. (n.d.). *General instruction of the Roman Missal (GIRM)*, https://www.vatican.va/roman_curia/congregations/ccdds/documents/rc_con_ccdds_doc_20030317_ordinamento-messale_en.html

Catholic Church. *Annuarium Statisticum Ecclesiae*. Central Office of Church Statistics.

Catholic Development Fund – Diocese of Ballarat. (n.d.). *Annual report 2023*, https://www.ballarat.catholic.org.au/wp-content/uploads/2024/06/2024-annual-report-web.pdf

Catholic Development Fund Archdiocese of Canberra-Goulburn. (n.d.). *Annual financial statements – financial year ended 31 December 2021*, https://cdf.cg.catholic.org.au/wp-content/uploads/2022/04/220217_Annual-Report2021_Signed_Final.pdf

Catholic Development Fund Archdiocese of Sydney. (n.d.). *2023 annual report*, https://sydneycdf.org.au/wp-content/uploads/2023/12/CDF-Annual-Report-2023.pdf

Catholic Development Fund Diocese of Broken Bay. (n.d.). *Annual report: general purpose financial statements for the year ended 30 June 2023*, https://www.bbcatholic.org.au/ArticleDocuments/1055/20230630-Broken%20Bay%20Audited%20Accounts.pdf.aspx

Catholic Development Fund Diocese of Maitland-Newcastle. (n.d.). *Annual report for the year ended 30 June 2021*, https://myccf.com.au/wp-content/uploads/2021/12/30062021-CDF-Annual-Report-signed_FINAL.pdf

Catholic Development Fund Diocese of Port Pirie. (n.d.). *Annual report 30 June 2023*, https://ppcatholic.org/about-us/finances/

Catholic Development Fund Diocese of Wollongong. (n.d.). *Financial statements as at 31 December 2023*, https://www.dow.org.au/wp-content/uploads/CDF-Financial-Statements-2023-signed.pdf

Catholic Development Fund. (2024). *CDF annual report FY23*, https://irp.cdn-website.com/787db205/files/uploaded/CDF%20Ann%20Rep%20Final-171123-39f3595f.pdf

Catholic Education Northern Territory. (2023). *Catholic Education Northern Territory 2022 annual report*, https://os-data-2.s3-ap-southeast-2.amazonaws.com/ceont/bundle3/catholic_education_nt_-_annual_report_2022.pdf

Catholic Education South Australia. (n.d.). *Financial reports 2022*, https://report.cesa.catholic.edu.au/statistics-and-financials/financial-reports

Catholic Education Tasmania. (2023). *Catholic Education Tasmania annual report 2022*, https://tascathed.schoolzineplus.com/_file/media/2680/20231212_annual_report_2022.pdf

Catholic Education WA. (2024). *Catholic Education WA annual report 2023*, https://www.cewa.edu.au/wp-content/uploads/2024/06/AnnualReport2023_v2_Web.pdf

Catholic Health Australia. (2020). *Annual report 2019*, https://cha.org.au/wp-content/uploads/2021/04/CHA-Annual-Report-2019_final-compressed.pdf

Catholic Herald. (2024, April 17). Half of new priests ordained in US this year will be 31 years old or younger. *Catholic Herald*, https://catholicherald.co.uk/half-of-new-priests-ordained-in-us-this-year-will-be-31-years-old-or-younger

Catholic News Agency. (2008, May 14). Controversial retired Australian bishop reprimanded for his book. *Catholic News Agency*, https://www.catholicnewsagency.com/news/12635/controversial-retired-australian-bishop-reprimanded-for-his-book

Catholic News Agency. (2010, December 20). 'All are Welcome' not a welcome hymn at Mass, USCCB committee says. *Catholic News Agency*, https://www.catholicnewsagency.com/news/46872/all-are-welcome-not-a-welcome-hymn-at-mass-usccb-committee-says

Catholic Schools New South Wales. (2023). *Catholic Schools NSW annual report 2023*, https://www.csnsw.catholic.edu.au/sites/default/files/2024-10/CSNSW-Annual-Report-2023.pdf

Catholic Schools New South Wales. (2024, September 9). *How Catholic schools are funded*, https://www.csnsw.catholic.edu.au/funding-of-nsw-catholic-schools-system/

Catholic Social Services Australia. (2024). *About our members*, https://cssa.org.au/our-members/about-our-members/?state=NSW/members-list

Catholic Voice. (2021, December 13). A culture of life shines in intergenerational living. *Catholic Voice*, https://www.catholicvoice.org.au/a-culture-of-life-shines-in-intergenerational-living/

CatholicCare Diocese of Broken Bay. (2023). *Financial overview (2023)*, https://www.acnc.gov.au/charity/charities/4c868520-39af-e811-a961-000d3ad24182/profile

CatholicCare Diocese of Wollgongong [Catholic Family Welfare Services]. (2024). *Financial overview (2023)*, https://www.acnc.gov.au/charity/charities/8c76733e-39af-e811-a963-000d3ad244fd/profile

CatholicCare Social Services Hunter Manning. (2024). *Financial overview (2023)*, https://www.acnc.gov.au/charity/charities/c251023d-38af-e811-a963-000d3ad24077/documents/

CatholicCare South West. (2024). *Financial overview (2023)*, https://www.acnc.gov.au/charity/charities/250c1b7c-3aaf-e811-a961-000d3ad24182/profile

CatholicCare Sydney. (2024). *Financial overview (2023)*, https://www.acnc.gov.au/charity/charities/af461e89-3aaf-e811-a962-000d3ad24a0d/profile

CatholicCare Wilcannia-Forbes. (2024). *Financial overview (2023)*, https://www.acnc.gov.au/charity/charities/068192b3-3aaf-e811-a963-000d3ad24077/profile

Centrecare. (2024). *Support and funding*, https://www.centrecare.com.au/about-centrecare/support-and-funding

Cernuzio, S. 2021). *Il velo del silenzio*. San Paolo.

Chapp, L. (2020, December 11). The choice: bourgeois well-being or conversion to Christ: beige Catholicism and the challenges of the young priest. *Gaudium et Spes 22*, https://gaudiumetspes22.com/blog/the-choice-bourgeois-well-being-or-conversion-to-christ-beige-catholicism-and-the-challenges-of-the-young-priest

Chapp, L. (2021, May 12.) Universalism, Balthasar, the *massa damnata*, and the question of evangelization. *Gaudium et Spes 22*, https://gaudiumetspes22.com/blog/universalism-balthasar-the-massa-damnata-and-the-question-of-evangelization

Chapp, L. (2024, May 21). True and false democracy in the Catholic Church. *National Catholic Register*, https://www.ncregister.com/commentaries/true-and-false-democracy-in-catholic-church

Cleary, A. (2023, August 2). What World Youth Day means to Australians. *Catholic Herald*, https://catholicherald.co.uk/what-world-youth-day-means-to-australians/

Clements, R. & Bullivant, S. (2022). *Catholics in contemporary Britain*. Oxford University Press.

Collins, P. (2024, October 22). Graduation address sparks mass walkout at major Australian university. *Daily Mail*, https://www.dailymail.co.uk/news/article-13985447/Graduation-speech-walkout-abortion-killer.html

Cook, M. (2021). 'Naked to mine enemies': Cardinal George Pell and the media. *Church, Communication, and Culture*, 6(1), 80-98. https://doi.org/10.1080/23753234.2021.1882317

Coppen, L. (2022, July 7). A day of drama at Australia's Plenary Council. *The Pillar*, https://www.pillarcatholic.com/p/a-day-of-drama-at-australias-plenary

Coppen, L. (2024, April 11). How Pope Francis is reshaping the Church in western Ireland. *The Pillar*, https://www.pillarcatholic.com/p/how-pope-francis-is-reshaping-the;

Coppen, L. (2024, July 25). 'Some definite service': How an English diocese is unleashing growth. *The Pillar*, https://www.pillarcatholic.com/p/some-definite-service-how-an-english

Coppen, L. (2024, May 21). Study: young German priests reject synodal way priorities. *The Pillar*, https://www.pillarcatholic.com/p/study-young-german-priests-reject

Coppen, L. (2024, May 23). Is Italy's *in persona episcopi* experiment for diocesan mergers ending? *The Pillar*, https://open.substack.com/pub/thepillar/p/is-italys-in-persona-episcopi-experiment

Coppen, L. (2024, September 12). Pope merges two Welsh dioceses. *The Pillar*, https://www.pillarcatholic.com/p/pope-merges-two-welsh-dioceses

Corporation of the Trustees of the Roman Catholic Archdiocese of Brisbane. (n.d.). *Financial report year ended 31 December 2023*, https://www.acnc.gov.au/charity/charities/11a03e5e-38af-e811-a963-000d3ad24077/documents/

Cox, V. (2024, April 8). Men's ministry helps restore lives and build community. *Catholic Voice*, https://www.catholicvoice.org.au/mens-ministry-helps-restore-lives-and-build-community/

Cox, V. (2023, December 19). 10,000 Christmas Mass invites go out to Queanbeyan residents. *Catholic Voice*, https://www.catholicvoice.org.au/10000-christmas-mass-invites-go-out-to-queanbeyan-residents/

Coyne, B. (2008, June 28). What lessons can we learn from the Bethel Covenant Community? *Bishop Accountability*, https://www.bishop-accountability.org/news2008/05_06/2008_06_28_Coyne_WhatLessons.htm

Cramsie, D. (2023, April 28). On God's beat: police officer among 200 new Catholics welcomed into the church. *The Catholic Weekly*, https://www.catholicweekly.com.au/on-gods-beat-police-officer-among-200-new-catholics-welcomed-into-the-church/

Cramsie, D. (2023, February 22). Super seventeen enter Sydney seminary. *The Catholic Weekly*, https://www.catholicweekly.com.au/super-seventeen-enter-sydney-seminary/

Crikey. (2005, July 25). Hundreds of journalistic couples. *Crikey*, https://www.crikey.com.au/2005/07/25/hundreds-of-journalistic-couples/

Crikey. (2016, January 14). Media couples: a (significantly updated) *Crikey* list. *Crikey*, https://www.crikey.com.au/2016/01/14/media-couples-a-significantly-updated-crikey-list/

Crockett, A., & Voas, D. (2006). Generations of decline: religious change in 20th-century Britain. *Journal for the Scientific Study of Religion*, 45(4), 567–584. https://doi.org/10.1111/j.1468-5906.2006.00328.x

Cronin, C. (2013). Interpreting research results of parish mystagogy. *Australasian Catholic Record*, 90(1), 71–80. https://search.informit.org/doi/epdf/10.3316/informit.246311803077022

Crook, A. (2010, March 17). Journalism media couples: an updated *Crikey* list. *Crikey*, https://www.crikey.com.au/2010/03/17/journalism-media-couples-an-updated-crikey-list/

Curran, C. (1997). The Catholic identity of Catholic institutions. *Theological Studies*, 58, 90-108. https://www.xavier.edu/jesuitresource/online-resources/documents/Curran.pdf

Dantis, T., Bowell, P., Reid, S., & Dudfield, L. (2019). *Final report for the Plenary Council Phase 1 – Listening and Dialogue*, https://plenarycouncil.catholic.org.au/wp-content/uploads/2020/03/Diocesan-Final-Report-Phase-1-Sydney.pdf

Darwin Diocesan Development Fund. (n.d.). *Special purpose report year ended 30 June 2020*, https://static1.squarespace.com/static/602f24d61f1de445374ae9fd/t/602f386b97cbab7fdd5cb77a/1613707375400/S3.+DDDF+Annual+Financial+Statement+FY20.pdf

Daughters of Charity of St Vincent De Paul, Rosalie Rendu. (2024). *Financial overview (2023)*, https://www.acnc.gov.au/charity/charities/19d0bada-39afe811-a961-000d3ad24182/profile

Day, L. (1964). Fertility differentials among Catholics in Australia. *The Milbank Memorial Fund Quarterly*, 42(2), 57–83. https://doi.org/10.2307/3348716

DDF Diocese of Sandhurst Development Fund. (n.d.). *Special purpose financial report for the year ended 30 June 2023*, https://www.sandhurst.catholic.org.au/diocese-of-sandhurst-publications/2036-ddf-annual-financial-report-30-june-2023/file

Diocesan Development Fund. (n.d.). *Special purpose annual report for the year ended 31 December 2023*, https://www.ddfrockhampton.com.au/wp-content/uploads/DDF-AUDITED-ANNUAL-FINANCIAL-STATEMENTS-2023-FINAL.pdf

Diocesan Provident Fund Diocese of Wagga Wagga. (n.d.). *Financial statements as at 30 June 2022*, https://wagga.catholic.org.au/wp-content/uploads/2022/09/2022-DPF_Financials-Signed.pdf

Diocese of Cairns Catholic Development Fund. (n.d.). *Special purpose financial statements for the year ended 31 December 2022*, https://cairns.catholic.org.au/files/media/original/313/522/cab/CDF-Financial-Statements-31.12.2022-Final-Signed.pdf

Diocese of Maitland-Newcastle Catholic Schools Office. (2023). *Financial report 2022*, https://www.acnc.gov.au/charity/charities/3223f2a8-38af-e811-a963-000d3ad244fd/documents/

Diocese of Parramatta Diocesan Development Fund. (n.d.). *Financial report for the financial year ended 30 June 2023*, https://parracatholic.org/wp-content/uploads/2023/09/DDF-Annual-Report-Financial-Year-2023.pdf

Diocese of Parramatta. (n.d.). Consecrated religious life. *Diocese of Parramatta*. https://parracatholic.org/contribute/discern-my-vocation/consecrated-religious/

Dixon, R. (1996). *The Catholics in Australia*. Bureau of Immigration, Multicultural and Population Research.

Dixon, R. (2024). Mass attenders' attitude to the sexual abuse crisis in the Catholic Church in Australia: Part 2: Detailed results from the most recent survey. *Pointers Bulletin of the Christian Research Association, 34*(2), 1–5.

Dixon, R., Bond, S., Engebretson, K., Rymarz, R., Cussen, B., & Wright, K. (2007). *Research project on Catholics who have stopped attending Mass: final report February 2007*. ACBC Pastoral Projects Office, https://ncpr.catholic.org.au/pdf/DCReport.pdf

Dixon, R., Kunciunas, A., & Reid, S. (2008). *Mass attendance in Australia*. ACBC Pastoral Projects Office, https://www.ncpr.catholic.org.au/pdf/SummaryReport_MassAttendanceInAustralia.pdf

Dixon, R., Reid, S., & Connolly, N. (2011). 'See I am doing a new thing': The 2009 survey of Catholic religious institutes in Australia. *Australasian Catholic Record, 88*(3), 271–283.

Dixon, R., Webber, R., & Reid, S. (2021). Contemporary approaches to religious vocations in Australia. *Australasian Catholic Record, 98*(3), 335–348.

Dixon, R., Webber, R., Reid, S., Rymarz, R., Martin, J., & Connolly, N. (2018). *Understanding religious vocation in Australia today: report of a study of vocations to religious life 2000-2015 for Catholic Vocations Ministry Australia*, https://ncpr.catholic.org.au/wp-content/uploads/2021/07/CVMA-Report-Final-report-Feb-2018-Rev.pdf

Donnelly, K. (2019). Danger: the threats to Australia's Catholic schools. *The Catholic Weekly*, https://catholicweekly.com.au/danger-the-threats-to-australias-catholic-schools/

Drewitt-Smith, A. (2023, June 22). Paedophile cult leader 'Little Pebble' William Kamm granted bail after alleged breach of court orders. *ABC News*, https://www.abc.net.au/news/2023-06-22/paedophile-cult-leader-faces-court-alleged-breach-of-bail/102509370

Duncan, G. (2024, July 2). The rise of South Carolina's Catholic population. *Catholic World Report*, https://www.catholicworldreport.com/2024/07/02/the-rise-of-south-carolinas-catholic-population/

Dunlea Centre. (2024). *Financial overview (2023)*, https://www.acnc.gov.au/charity/charities/ad0f75b9-38af-e811-a960-000d3ad24282/documents/

Editors. (1986, March 29). The Charles Curran case: From March 29, 1986. *America: the Jesuit Review*, https://www.americamagazine.org/issue/100/charles-curran-case

English, R. (2015). Use your freedom of choice: reasons for choosing homeschool in Australia. *Journal of Unschooling and Alternative Learning*, 9(17), 1-18.

EWTN Global Catholic Network. (2022, July 15). New poll from EWTN News and RealClear Opinion research finds likely Catholic voters disagree with transgender ideology, support increased border security. *PR Newswire*, https://www.prnewswire.com/news-releases/new-poll-from-ewtn-news-and-realclear-opinion-research-finds-likely-catholic-voters-disagree-with-transgender-ideology-support-increased-border-security-301587505.html

Farrow, M. (2024, November 5). 'Boots on the ground' – Catholic life for a consecrated virgin. *The Pillar*, https://www.pillarcatholic.com/p/boots-on-the-ground-catholic-life

Fewtrell, T. (2022, July 5). Canberra Catholics say Church's Plenary Council could be a last chance for reform. *The Riot Act*, https://the-riotact.com/canberra-catholics-say-churchs-plenary-council-could-be-a-last-chance-for-reform/572400

Figge, J. (2024, October 12). Homeschooling: 'Super weird,' or future of the Church? *The Pillar*, https://www.pillarcatholic.com/p/homeschooling-super-weird-or-future

Fisher, A. (2012). *Catholic bioethics for a new millennium*. Cambridge University Press, 275-301.

Fisher, A. (2024, June 9). Religious freedom in a secular world: Doomed or doable? *The Catholic Weekly*, 12-13. https://www.sydneycatholic.org/addresses-and-statements/2024/religious-freedom-in-a-secular-world-doomed-or-doable-31-may-2024/

Fisher, S. (2014). *The sinner's guide to Natural Family Planning*. Our Sunday Visitor.

Fisher, S. (2024, April 26). Restored order of sacraments and family catechesis: a combination that works. *The Catholic Weekly*, https://catholicweekly.com.au/restored-order-of-sacraments-and-family-catechesis-a-combination-that-works/

Gilchrist, M. (1986). New class, new church. *Quadrant*, 30(9), 44-47.

Gleeson, J., & O'Neill, M. (2018). Student-teachers' perspectives on the purposes and characteristics of faith-based schools: an Australian view. *British Journal of Religious Education*, 40(1), 55–69. https://doi.org/10.1080/01416200.2016.1256266

Grantham, J. (2018, May 16). Hildegarde of Bingen, part 2. *Catholic Outlook*, https://catholicoutlook.org/part-two-hildegard-bingen/

Gray, M., & Popčak, G. (2023). *Future Faithful Families Project: successfully raising Catholic children to be active Catholics as adults*. Center for Applied Research in the Apostolate (CARA). https://275132.fs1.hubspotusercontent-na1.net/hubfs/275132/_peytoninstitute/Research/HCFM-CARA%20Summary%20FFF%20Report.pdf

Gregory the Great, Pope St. (c.500s). *Pastoral rule*, https://www.documentacatholicaomnia.eu/01p/0590-0604,_SS_Gregorius_I_Magnus,_Regulae_Pastoralis_Liber_[Schaff],_EN.pdf

Haddad, R. (2023). George Cardinal Pell's contribution to tertiary chaplaincy reform: a personal recollection. *Journal of the Australian Catholic Historical Society*, 44, 154-.

Hadro, M. (2016, June 26). How not to be a 'beige Catholic', according to Bishop Barron. *Catholic News Agency*, https://www.catholicnewsagency.com/news/34095/how-to-not-be-a-beige-catholic-according-to-bishop-barron

Higgins, J. (2024, February 19). Hundreds take the next step on path to baptism and confirmation in Brisbane. *Catholic Leader*, https://catholicleader.com.au/news/qld/hundreds-take-the-next-step-on-path-to-baptism-and-confirmation-in-brisbane/

Higgins, J. (2024, October 14). Pope Francis appoints Bishop Tim Norton as the Bishop of Broome. *Catholic Leader*, https://catholicleader.com.au/news/australia/pope-francis-appoints-bishop-tim-norton-as-the-bishop-of-broome/

Hitchens, C. (2003, October 20). Mommie dearest: The pope beatifies Mother Teresa, a fanatic, a fundamentalist, and a fraud. *Slate*, https://slate.com/news-and-politics/2003/10/the-fanatic-fraudulent-mother-teresa.html

Hitchens, D. (2023, September 23). Inside the fastest growing – and shrinking – churches in the UK. *Spectator*, https://www.spectator.co.uk/article/inside-the-fastest-growing-and-shrinking-churches-in-the-uk/

Hitchings, A. (2019, May 2). For want of a lot of good men. *The Catholic Weekly*, https://www.catholicweekly.com.au/for-want-of-a-lot-of-good-men/

Hodge, B. (2024, April 4.) The faith of the next generation. *The Pillar*, https://www.pillarcatholic.com/p/the-faith-of-the-next-generation

Hughes, P. (2013). Organization of leadership in rural parishes: Some Australian Catholic case-studies. *Rural Theology*, 11(1), 3–14. https://doi.org/10.1179/1470499413Z.0000000003

Hyndman-Rizik, N. (2010). At my mother's table: migration, (re)production and return between Hadchit, North Lebanon and Sydney. PhD Diss., Australian National University. https://openresearch-repository.anu.edu.au/bitstream/1885/49372/5/02whole.pdf

Ignatius of Antioch (c.110). *Letter to the Magnesians* 2, https://www.newadvent.org/fathers/0105.htm

Implementation Advisory Group and the Governance Review Project Team. (2020). *The light from the Southern Cross: promoting co-responsible governance in the Catholic Church in Australia*, https://www.catholic.au/s/article/Church-Governance

Independent Education Union of Australia, NSW Branch (2024, June 4). Union rejects Catholic Archbishop of Sydney's threat to close schools. *MediaNet*, https://newshub.medianet.com.au/2024/06/union-rejects-catholic-archbishop-of-sydneys-threat-to-close-schools/51749/

International Theological Commission. (2014). *Sensus fidei in the life of the Church*, https://www.vatican.va/roman_curia/congregations/cfaith/cti_documents/rc_cti_20140610_sensus-fidei_en.html

Janis, I. (1971). Groupthink. *Psychology Today* (magazine), November, 84-89. https://agcommtheory.pbworks.com/f/GroupThink.pdf

John Jay College of Criminal Justice. (2004). *The nature and scope of sexual abuse of minors by Catholic priests and deacons in the United States 1950-2002*, https://www.usccb.org/sites/default/files/issues-and-action/child-and-youth-protection/upload/The-Nature-and-Scope-of-Sexual-Abuse-of-Minors-by-Catholic-Priests-and-Deacons-in-the-United-States-1950-2002.pdf

John Paul II, Pope St. (1996, March 25). *Vita consecrata*, https://www.vatican.va/content/john-paul-ii/en/apost_exhortations/documents/hf_jp-ii_exh_25031996_vita-consecrata.html

Keating, A. (2017, October 2). The perfect family is an idol. *Church Life Journal*, https://churchlifejournal.nd.edu/articles/the-perfect-family-is-an-idol/

Keating, J. (2016, September 13). Single by default. *Church Life Journal*, https://churchlifejournal.nd.edu/articles/single-by-default-by-jessica-keating/

Kessler, G. (2012, February 17). The claim that 98 percent of Catholic women use contraception: a media foul. *Washington Post*, https://www.washingtonpost.com/blogs/fact-checker/post/the-claim-that-98-percent-of-catholic-women-use-contraception-a-media-foul/2012/02/16/gIQAkPeqIR_blog.html

Klein, J. (n.d.). A former Evangelical discovers why we need the sacraments. *Catholic Digest*, https://www.catholicdigest.com/faith/sacraments/a-former-evangelical-discovers-why-we-need-the-sacraments/

Klesko, R. (2024, August 3). Deacons are emissaries of Jesus Christ. *National Catholic Register*, https://www.ncregister.com/blog/klesko-deacons-emissaries

La Rosa, M. (2024, May 4). 'To find your people' – How Catholics are building intentional communities. *The Pillar*, https://www.pillarcatholic.com/p/to-find-your-people-how-catholics

Lane, S. (2024, March 6). Tradwife ideology won't save you. *The American Mind*, https://americanmind.org/salvo/tradwife-ideology-wont-save-you/

de Lassus, D. (2020). *Risques et derives de la vie religieuse*. Cerf; available in English as *Abuses in the religious life and the path to healing*. Sophia Institute Press.

Lewis, C. (1952). *The Screwtape letters*. Geoffrey Bles.

Lockwood, G. (2011, February 21). *The Catholic right in SA Labor*. Australasian Society for the Study of Labor History, https://labourhistorycanberra.org/2015/04/the-catholic-right-in-sa-labor/

Longenecker, D. (2017, April 29). Restoring beauty in church buildings. *Crux*, https://cruxnow.com/church-in-the-usa/2017/04/restoring-beauty-church-buildings

Longenecker, D. (2019, October 29). Pachamama, witchcraft and women's ordination. *Dwightlongenecker.com*, https://dwightlongenecker.com/pachamama-witchcraft-and-womens-ordination/

Lucas, A. (2023, March 13). Boomers or bust? On Vatican II and generational arguments. *Catholic World Report*, https://www.catholicworldreport.com/2023/03/13/boomers-or-bust-on-vatican-ii-and-generational-arguments/

MacKillop Family Services. (2024). *2023 – 2024 Financial report – collaboration*, https://www.mackillop.org.au/uploads/About-MacKillop/Publications/Annual-reports/2024_MacKillop_Financial-Report.pdf

MacKinley, S. (2020, February 18). *'Listen to what the Spirit is saying': Monsignor Peter Jeffrey Oration*, https://sandhurst.catholic.org.au/news-events/1309-listen-to-what-the-spirit-is-saying-shepparton-feb-2020/file

Maiden, J. (2019). The emergence of Catholic charismatic renewal 'in a country': Australia and transnational Catholic Charismatic Renewal. *Studies in World Christianity*, 25(3), 274-296.

Mares, C. (2023, February 14). Nigeria's newest cardinal shares secret behind the highest Mass attendance in the world. *Catholic News Agency*, https://www.catholicnewsagency.com/news/253640/nigeria-s-newest-cardinal-shares-secret-behind-the-highest-mass-attendance-in-the-world

Marist 180 (Marist Youth Care Ltd). (2024). *Financial overview (2023)*, https://www.acnc.gov.au/charity/charities/096d6c8a-38af-e811-a962-000d3ad24a0d/profile

Martyr, P. (2023, August 18). How do Aussie Catholics rate their bishops' leadership? *The Catholic Weekly*, https://www.catholicweekly.com.au/philippa-martyr-how-do-aussie-catholics-rate-their-bishops-leadership/

Martyr, P. (2012, December 1). Reaping the whirlwind. *Quadrant*, https://quadrant.org.au/magazine/2012/12/reaping-the-whirlwind/

Martyr, P. (2018). Let's call the whole thing off? God, truth, and Buckminster Fuller. In D. Daintree (Ed.), *Creative subversion: The liberal arts and human educational fulfilment*. Connor Court.

Martyr, P. (2019, August 17). Fault lines for Catholic agencies. *The Catholic Weekly*, https://catholicweekly.com.au/philippa-martyr-fault-lines-for-catholic-agencies/

Martyr, P. (2019, July 18). A catechesis Australia needs. *The Catholic Weekly*, https://www.catholicweekly.com.au/phillipa-martyr-a-catechesis-australia-needs/

Martyr, P. (2019, November 21). Why get over it isn't enough for victims of clerical sexual abuse. *Church Life Journal*, https://churchlifejournal.nd.edu/articles/why-get-over-it-isnt-enough-for-victims-of-clerical-sexual-abuse/

Martyr, P. (2019, November 3). Righting the clergy imbalance. *The Catholic Weekly*, https://catholicweekly.com.au/philippa-martyr-righting-the-clergy-imbalance/

Martyr, P. (2020). Clothed with the sun: Christianity and the liberation of women. In D. Daintree (Ed.), *Heart to heart: thriving in a post-Christian world*. Dawson Colloquium.

Martyr, P. (2020, April 21). Women deacons misses the point. *The Catholic Weekly*, https://catholicweekly.com.au/women-deacons-misses-the-point/

Martyr, P. (2020, June 17). Precisely which Church? A response to the Plenary Discernment papers. *The Catholic Weekly*, https://catholicweekly.com.au/precisely-which-church-a-response-to-the-plenary-discernment-papers/

Martyr, P. (2020, March 5). Secret wildfire of Adoration. *The Catholic Weekly*, https://catholicweekly.com.au/philippa-martyr-secret-wildfire-of-adoration/

Martyr, P. (2020, May 7). The lay role in covering up abuse. *The Catholic Weekly*, https://www.catholicweekly.com.au/the-lay-role-in-covering-up-abuse/

Martyr, P. (2021, April 25). Small is beautiful for this particular age. *The Catholic Weekly*, https://catholicweekly.com.au/philippa-martyr-small-is-beautiful-for-this-particular-age/

Martyr, P. (2021, August 26). Liturgical fallout of the 70s. *The Catholic Weekly*, https://catholicweekly.com.au/dr-philippa-martyr-liturgical-fallout-of-the-70s/

Martyr, P. (2021, February 16). Ditch the cha-cha and try a little chant. *The Catholic Weekly*, https://catholicweekly.com.au/philippa-martyr-ditch-the-cha-cha-and-try-a-little-chant/

Martyr, P. (2021, February 3). Condensed milk liturgical music. *The Catholic Weekly*, https://catholicweekly.com.au/philippa-martyr-condensed-milk-liturgical-music/

Martyr, P. (2021, July 19). A conversation about bogus mysticism and the rule of fear. *Gaudium et Spes 22*, https://gaudiumetspes22.com/blog/a-conversation-about-bogus-mysticism-and-the-rule-of-fear

Martyr, P. (2021, March 5). Stranded under the Southern Cross: news from a shrinking Church. *Gaudium et Spes 22*, https://gaudiumetspes22.com/blog/stranded-under-the-southern-cross-news-from-a-shrinking-church

Martyr, P. (2021, October 6). Plenary voices: Philippa Martyr. *The Catholic Weekly*, https://catholicweekly.com.au/plenary-voices-philippa-martyr/

Martyr, P. (2021, September 28). Beige Catholicism emptied our churches. *The Catholic Weekly*, https://catholicweekly.com.au/dr-philippa-martyr-beige-catholicism-emptied-our-churches

Martyr, P. (2022). Factors affecting Australian Catholics' return to Mass after COVID19 church closures. *Journal of Religion and Health*, 61(5), 4245-4259. https://link.springer.com/article/10.1007/s10943-022-01618-1

Martyr, P. (2022, May 30). The bishops' Praetorian Guards. *The Catholic Weekly*, https://www.catholicweekly.com.au/philippa-martyr-the-bishops-praetorian-guards/

Martyr, P. (2022, September 8). Neither Fr Relaxo nor Fr Apocalypto. *The Catholic Weekly*, https://catholicweekly.com.au/dr-philippa-martyr-neither-fr-relaxo-nor-fr-apocalypto/

Martyr, P. (2023). Australian Catholics' lived experiences of COVID19 church closures. *Journal of Religion and Health*, 62, 2881-2898. https://doi.org/10.1007/s10943-023-01823-6

Martyr, P. (2023). We don't want bishops made in our own image, do we? *The Catholic Weekly*, https://www.catholicweekly.com.au/philippa-martyr-we-dont-want-bishops-made-in-our-own-image-do-we/

Martyr, P. (2023, December 7). When getting out is the only way to go on. *The Catholic Weekly*, https://catholicweekly.com.au/when-getting-out-is-the-only-way-to-go-on/

Martyr, P. (2023, January 12). Cardinal George Pell: Moments of true greatness. *The Catholic Weekly*, https://www.catholicweekly.com.au/cardinal-george-pell-moments-of-true-greatness/

Martyr, P. (2024, January 29). Reject romance, return to clothes-swaps. *The Catholic Weekly*, https://catholicweekly.com.au/philippa-martyr-reject-romance-return-to-clothes-swaps/

Martyr, P. (2024, July 18). How to be ignored during the synodal process. *The Catholic Weekly*, https://www.catholicweekly.com.au/instrumentum-laboris-synod-2024/

Martyr, P. (2024, June 14). Who's responsible for bringing back the church's lost sheep? *The Catholic Weekly*, https://catholicweekly.com.au/lay-evangelisation/

Martyr, P. (2024, May 11). Money and ministry: Are we serving the right master? *The Catholic Weekly*, https://catholicweekly.com.au/money-and-ministry-are-we-serving-the-right-master/

Martyr, P. (2024, May 20). The reasons why we don't need women deacons. *The Catholic Weekly*, https://catholicweekly.com.au/philippa-martyr-the-reasons-why-we-dont-need-women-deacons/

Martyr, P. (2024, May 23). Pope Francis made it clear the church can't ordain women as deacons. *The Catholic Weekly*, https://catholicweekly.com.au/pope-francis-made-it-clear-the-church-cant-ordain-women-as-deacons-heres-why-some-people-will-always-disagree/

Martyr, P. (2024, May 4). Should Catholics reconsider their financial habits? *The Catholic Weekly*, https://catholicweekly.com.au/should-catholics-reconsider-their-financial-habits/

Martyr, P. (2024, October 23). Make room in your heart for the poor and the weird. *The Catholic Weekly*, https://catholicweekly.com.au/catholic-church-australia-present-and-future/

Martyr, P. (2024, October 28). Don't forget to pray for the dead, *The Catholic Weekly*, https://catholicweekly.com.au/dont-forget-to-pray-for-those-in-purgatory/

Martyr, P., & Bullivant, S. (2023). *The Catholics in Australia Survey 1 – Mass attendance*, https://papers.ssrn.com/sol3/papers.cfm?abstract_id=4646161

Martyr, P., & Bullivant, S. (2024). *The Catholics in Australia Survey 3 – Believing*, https://papers.ssrn.com/sol3/papers.cfm?abstract_id=4723637

Martyr, P., & Bullivant, S. (2024). *The Catholics in Australia Survey 4 – Belonging*, https://papers.ssrn.com/sol3/papers.cfm?abstract_id=4767155

Martyr, P., & Bullivant, S. (2024). *The Catholics in Australia Survey 5 – Behaving*, https://papers.ssrn.com/sol3/papers.cfm?abstract_id=4850676

Martyr, P., & Bullivant, S. (2024). *The Catholics in Australia Survey 6 – Family life*, https://papers.ssrn.com/sol3/papers.cfm?abstract_id=4855996

Martyr, P., & Bullivant, S. (2024). *The Catholics in Australia Survey 7 – Family planning*, https://papers.ssrn.com/sol3/papers.cfm?abstract_id=4856022

Martyr, P., & Bullivant, S. (2024). *The Catholics in Australia Survey 8 – Irregulars and Nevers*, https://papers.ssrn.com/sol3/papers.cfm?abstract_id=4912660

Martyr, P., & Bullivant, S. (2024). *The Catholics in Australia Survey 9 – Traditional Latin Mass (TLM) attenders*, https://papers.ssrn.com/sol3/papers.cfm?abstract_id=4942220

Martyr, P., & Bullivant, S. (2024). *The Catholics in Australia Survey 10 – Parish life*, https://papers.ssrn.com/sol3/papers.cfm?abstract_id=4942224

Martyr, P., & Bullivant, S. (2024). *The Catholics in Australia Survey 11 – Catholic schooling*, https://papers.ssrn.com/sol3/papers.cfm?abstract_id=5016420

Marymead CatholicCare Canberra & Goulburn. (2024). *Financial overview (2023)*, https://www.acnc.gov.au/charity/charities/5a8843db-39af-e811-a960-000d3ad24282/profile

Mauro, J-P. (2023, January 13). Survey: Catholic contraception use diverges from Church teaching. *Aleteia*, https://aleteia.org/2023/01/13/survey-catholic-contraception-use-diverges-from-church-teaching/

McAlpine, S. (2017, November 7). Does your church have a spiritual Spacey? *Stephen McAlpine*, https://stephenmcalpine.com/does-your-church-have-a-spiritual-spacey/

McAlpine, S. (2019, October 14). Bully vol. 3. *Stephen McAlpine*, https://stephenmcalpine.com/bully-vol-3/

McAlpine, S. (2021, February 6). Clerical bullying and spiritual abuse: Are they the same thing? *Stephen McAlpine*, https://stephenmcalpine.com/clerical-bullying-and-spiritual-abuse-are-they-the-same-thing/

McCallum, J. (1987). Secularisation in Australia between 1966 and 1985: a research note. *Australian and New Zealand Journal of Sociology*, 23(3), 407–422. https://doi.org/10.1177/144078338702300306

McDermott, R., Fowler, J., & Christakis, N. (2013). Breaking up is hard to do, unless everyone else is doing it too: social network effects on divorce in a longitudinal sample. *Social Forces, 92*(2), 491–519. https://doi.org/10.1093/sf/sot096

McGillion, G., & O'Carroll, J. (2011). *Our fathers: what Australian Catholic priests really think about their lives and their Church*. John Garratt.

McKeown, J. (2024, May 15). Vatican halts some parish closures in St. Louis following appeals. *Catholic World Report*, https://www.catholicworldreport.com/2024/05/15/vatican-halts-some-parish-closures-in-st-louis-following-appeals/

McLean, F. (2018, May 3). Why we sent our children to local state schools. *The Gospel Coalition* (Australian edition), https://au.thegospelcoalition.org/article/sent-children-local-state-schools/

McMullen, G., & Laverty, M. (2020). Learnings from the development of new lay-led church entities in Australia. *Australasian Catholic Record, 97*(2), 131–143.

McNeill, H. (2021, January 21). Catholic Church makes record payout in child sex abuse case. *WA Today*, https://www.watoday.com.au/national/western-australia/catholic-church-makes-record-payout-in-child-sex-abuse-case-20210120-p56vng.html

Melbourne Archdiocese Catholic Schools. (2023). *Financial report 2023*, https://www.acnc.gov.au/charity/charities/35e4116b-1596-ed11-aad1-0022489733de/documents/

Melbourne Catholic. (2023, February 28). The journey to Easter: catechumens and candidates celebrate the Rite of Election. *Melbourne Catholic*, https://melbournecatholic.org/news/the-journey-to-easter-catechumens-and-candidates-celebrate-the-rite-of-election

Melbourne Catholic. (2024, November 8). Two new auxiliary bishops appointed for Melbourne. *Melbourne Catholic*, https://melbournecatholic.org/news/two-new-auxiliary-bishops-appointed-for-melbourne

Meloy, D. (2024, April 14). First-year seminarians will unplug from technology starting in fall at Detroit seminary. *Catholic World Report*, https://www.catholicworldreport.com/2024/04/14/first-year-seminarians-will-unplug-from-technology-starting-in-fall-at-detroit-seminary/

Milligan, L., Fallman, M., & Zillman, S. (2023, January 31). Federal government writes to regulators investigating Opus Dei-affiliated schools that former students say caused 'pain and suffering'. *ABC News*, https://www.abc.net.au/news/2023-01-31/government-investigation-considered-over-opus-dei-schools/101910228

Mol, H. (1970). Mixed marriages in Australia. *Journal of Marriage and Family, 32*(2), 293–300. https://doi.org/10.2307/350137

Mol, J. (1965). The decline in religious participation of migrants. *International Migration*, 3(3), 137–145. https://doi.org/10.1111/j.1468-2435.1965.tb00878.x

Monk, D. & Christian, P. (2024, February 20). Beacons of Light backlash: Closures have begun and Catholics aren't happy about it. *WCPO Cincinnati*, https://www.wcpo.com/news/local-news/i-team/beacons-of-light-backlash-closures-have-begun-and-catholics-arent-happy-about-it

MRA Consulting Group. (2021). *Measuring the impact of the charitable reuse and recycling sector: A comparative study using clothing donated to charitable enterprises*, https://www.charitablerecycling.org.au/wp-content/uploads/2021/06/Charitable-Recycling-Australia-Recycled-Clothing-Impact-Assessment-240521.pdf

Murphy, H. (2024, April 18). Australians are having fewer babies – experts say it could have more consequences than we realise. *ABC News*, https://www.abc.net.au/news/2024-04-18/australia-fertility-rate-could-predict-the-next-five-years/103692844

National Catholic Education Commission (NCEC). (2022). *Annual report 2022*, https://ncec.catholic.edu.au/wp-content/uploads/2023/08/2022-NCEC-Annual-Report.pdf

NCEC. (2020). *Annual report 2019*, https://ncec.catholic.edu.au/resource-centre/2019-annual-report/

NCEC. (2024). *Annual report 2023*, https://ncec.catholic.edu.au/wp-content/uploads/2023/04/NCEC-2023-Annual-Report_Final.pdf

National Centre for Pastoral Research (NCPR). (2024). *Australian Catholic Mass Attendance Report 2021*, https://ncpr.catholic.org.au/wp-content/uploads/2024/05/Mass-attendance-in-Australia-2021-FINAL.pdf

NCPR. (2021). *Australian Catholic Mass attendance report 2016*, https://ncpr.catholic.org.au/wp-content/uploads/2021/07/Mass-attendance-in-Australia-2016-Revised-July-2021.pdf

NCPR. (2023). *2021 Census parish social profile – Albury-Lavington*, https://ncpr.catholic.org.au/2021-Parish-Social-Profiles/Wagga%20Wagga/Albury-Lavington.pdf

NCPR. (2023). *2021 Census parish social profile – Buranda*, https://ncpr.catholic.org.au/2021-Parish-Social-Profiles/Brisbane/Buranda.pdf

NCPR. (2023). *2021 Census parish social profile – Casino*, https://ncpr.catholic.org.au/2021-Parish-Social-Profiles/Lismore/Casino.pdf

NCPR. (2023). *2021 Census parish social profile – Jabiru*, https://ncpr.catholic.org.au/2021-Parish-Social-Profiles/Darwin/Jabiru.pdf

NCPR. (2023). *2021 Census parish social profile – Kalgoorlie-Boulder*, https://ncpr.catholic.org.au/2021-Parish-Social-Profiles/Perth/Kalgoorlie-Boulder.pdf

NCPR. (2023). *2021 Census parish social profile – Toongabbie*, https://ncpr.catholic.org.au/2021-Parish-Social-Profiles/Parramatta/Toongabbie.pdf

NCPR. (2023). *2021 Census parish social profile – Willetton*, https://ncpr.catholic.org.au/2021-Parish-Social-Profiles/Perth/Willetton.pdf

NCPR. (2023). *2021 Census parish social profile – Wodonga*, https://ncpr.catholic.org.au/2021-Parish-Social-Profiles/Sandhurst/Wodonga.pdf

NCPR. (2023). *2021 Census Parish Social Profiles – Bankstown (Archdiocese of Sydney)*. https://ncpr.catholic.org.au/2021-Parish-Social-Profiles/Sydney/Bankstown.pdf

NCPR. (2023). *Social profile of the Catholic community in Australia, based on the 2021 Australian Census*, https://ncpr.catholic.org.au/wp-content/uploads/2023/04/2021-Social-Profile-of-the-Catholic-Community-in-Australia-R.pdf

NCPR. (2024). *A profile of Catholic clergy in Australia*, https://ncpr.catholic.org.au/a-profile-of-catholic-clergy-in-australia/

National Museum Australia. (2022). *Aid for non-government schools*, https://www.nma.gov.au/defining-moments/resources/aid-for-non-government-schools

Norman, K. (2022, March 10). Why sacraments are important for your faith. *Crosswalk*, https://www.crosswalk.com/faith/spiritual-life/why-sacraments-are-important-for-your-faith.html

O'Brien, J. (2024, August 22). Words of Deuteronomy fulfilled: Redemptoris Mater Seminary celebrates 30 years of the Lord letting us know the way forward. *The Record*, https://therecord.com.au/news/anniversaries/words-of-deuteronomy-fulfilled-redemptoris-mater-seminary-celebrates-30-years-of-the-lord-letting-us-know-the-way-forward

O'Connor, S. (2018, November 22). Confessions of a Catholic whistleblower. *First Things*, https://www.firstthings.com/web-exclusives/2018/11/confessions-of-a-catholic-whistleblower

O'Loughlin, M. (2016, September 28). Poll finds many US Catholics breaking with church over contraception, abortion and LGBT rights. *America: the Jesuit Review*, https://www.americamagazine.org/faith/2016/09/28/poll-finds-many-us-catholics-breaking-church-over-contraception-abortion-and-lgbt

O'Shea, G. (2017). A comparison of Catechesis of the Good Shepherd and Godly Play. *British Journal of Religious Education*, 40(3), 308-316. https://www.tandfonline.com/doi/full/10.1080/01416200.2017.1292209

O'Shea, G. (2017). Confronting dualism in religious education. *Journal of Religious Education*, 64, 197-206. https://link.springer.com/article/10.1007/s40839-017-0044-6

O'Sullivan, F. (2015, October 15). Where Europeans are most likely to be single vs married. *Bloomberg*, https://www.bloomberg.com/news/articles/2015-10-14/maps-of-where-europeans-are-more-likely-to-be-single-instead-of-married

Osborne, P. (2024, November 7). Bishops hear from Cardinal-designate Mykola Bychok. *ACBC Media Blog*, https://mediablog.catholic.org.au/bishops-hear-from-cardinal-designate-mykola-bychok/

Osborne, P. (2024, October 14). Bishop Timothy Norton SVD appointed to Diocese of Broome. *ACBC Media Blog*, https://mediablog.catholic.org.au/bishop-timothy-norton-svd-appointed-to-diocese-of-broome/

Pakaluk, C. (2024). *Hannah's children: the women quietly defying the birth dearth*. Regnery.

Paul VI, Pope St. (1967, June 18). *Sacrum diaconatus ordinem*, https://www.vatican.va/content/paul-vi/en/motu_proprio/documents/hf_p-vi_motu-proprio_19670618_sacrum-diaconatus.html

Paul VI, Pope St. (1968, July 25). *Humanae vitae*, https://www.vatican.va/content/paulvi/en/encyclicals/documents/hf_p-vi_enc_25071968_humanae-vitae.html

Payne, D. (2024, September 11). 'Harsh realities': Diocese of Buffalo announces final list of parish mergers, closures. *Catholic World Report*, https://www.catholicworldreport.com/2024/09/11/harsh-realities-diocese-of-buffalo-announces-final-list-of-parish-mergers-closures/

Pentin, E. (2021, May 3). Australian Catholics petition Vatican to remove their bishop over his stance on homosexuality. *National Catholic Register*, https://www.ncregister.com/news/australian-catholics-petition-vatican-to-remove-their-bishop-over-his-stance-on-homosexuality

Pew Research Center. (2016, March 22). The gender gap in religion around the world. *Pew Research Center*, https://www.pewresearch.org/religion/2016/03/22/the-gender-gap-in-religion-around-the-world/

Pew Research Center. (2017, May 10). *Religious belief and national belonging in central and eastern Europe*, http://assets.pewresearch.org/wp-content/uploads/sites/11/2017/05/15120244/CEUP-FULL-REPORT.pdf

Philips, W. (1987). Religion. In W. Vamplew (Ed.), *Australian historical statistics*, Academy of the Social Sciences in Australia, https://socialsciences.org.au/wp-content/uploads/2019/10/29-Historical-Statisitics-Chapter-25-final.pdf

Pinedo, P. (2024, May 29). Diocese of Buffalo to merge a third of its parishes. *Catholic World Report*, https://www.catholicworldreport.com/2024/05/29/diocese-of-buffalo-to-merge-a-third-of-its-parishes/

Piotrowski, D. (2020, May 7). What George Pell knew: Bombshell report reveals Cardinal failed to remove a notorious paedophile priest who 'repeatedly sexually abused children in the confession booth'. *Daily Mail*, https://www.dailymail.co.uk/news/article-8294783/Cardinal-George-Pell-Redacted-royal-commission-report-released.html

Plenary Council. (2020). *Thematic Discernment Paper 1: missionary and evangelising*, 6. https://plenarycouncil.catholic.org.au/wp-content/uploads/2020/05/PC2020-thematic-papers-1.pdf

Poncini, A. (2024). Formation fit for purpose: empowering religious educators working in Catholic schools. *Religions, 15*(6), 665-. https://doi.org/10.3390/rel15060665.

Porteous, J. (2022). Consecration of canonical hermits: hidden with Christ in God. *Archdiocese of Hobart*, https://hobart.catholic.org.au/2022/04/20/consecration-of-canonical-hermits-hidden-with-christ-in-god/

Prichard, J. (2008, July 10). Catholic community shuts after Archbishop's apology. *WA Today*, https://www.watoday.com.au/national/western-australia/catholic-community-shuts-after-archbishops-apology-20080710-3crr.html

Queensland Catholic Education Commission. (n.d.). *2023 annual report*, https://qcec.catholic.edu.au/wp-content/uploads/2024/05/QCEC-2023-Annual-Report-FINAL-web-version.pdf

Roberson, R. (2024). *The Eastern Christian Churches*. Catholic Near East Welfare Association, https://cnewa.org/eastern-christian-churches/the-catholic-eastern-churches/from-the-assyrian-church-of-the-east/the-syro-malabar-catholic-church/

Rodrigues, M. (2024, April 18). I come from a land down Umbers. *The Catholic Weekly*, https://www.catholicweekly.com.au/i-come-from-a-land-down-umbers/

Rodrigues, M. (2024, July 29). Seminary sees promising rise in future priests for regional Australia. *The Catholic Weekly*, https://www.catholicweekly.com.au/sydney-seminary-sees-regional-vocations-up/

Roman Catholic Church Trust Corporation of the Archdiocese of Hobart, trading as Catholic Development Fund Tasmania. (n.d.). *Financial report for the year ended 30 June 2022*, https://www.cdftas.com/wp-content/uploads/2022/11/Signed-2022-Financial-Statements.pdf

Roman Catholic Diocese of Bathurst Catholic Development Fund. (n.d.). *Financial statement for the year ended 30 June 2023*, https://cdn.prod.website-files.com/6181fbcf194a7c60ab81c6a8/650b9651063c7194288b1f72_Signed%2030%20June%202023%20CDF%20Financial%20Statements.pdf

Roman Catholic Diocese of Toowoomba Diocesan Development Fund. (n.d.). *Financial statements for the year ended 30 June 2023*, https://www.twb.catholic.org.au/site/wp-content/uploads/2023/10/20230630-Financial-Report-and-Audit-Report-Diocese-of-Toowoomba-Diocesan-Development-Fund.pdf

Rose, M. (2000). *The renovation manipulation: the Church counter-renovation handbook*. Aquinas.

Rose, M. (2001). *Ugly as sin*. Sophia Institute Press.

Rosengren, P. (2008, October 29). Alone, but not lonely: A new hermit for Perth. *The Record*, https://therecord.com.au/news/local/alone-but-not-lonely-a-new-hermit-for-perth/

Rossi, M., & Scappini, E. (2014). Church attendance, problems of measurement, and interpreting indicators: a study of religious practice in the United States, 1975–2010. *Journal for the Scientific Study of Religion, 53*(2), 249-267.

Rowland, T. (2024). *Unconformed to the age: essays in Catholic ecclesiology*. Emmaus.

Royal Commission on Aged Care Safety and Quality. (2019). *Interim report: neglect*, (3 vols), https://www.royalcommission.gov.au/aged-care/interim-report

Rymarz, R. (2019). Catholic parish-based youth ministers: a preliminary study. *Journal of Youth and Theology, 18*(1), 49–64.

Rymarz, R. (2019). Youth ministers: Another Catholic narrative? *Australasian Catholic Record, 96*(4), 445–457.

Rymarz, R. (2023). A narrative approach to discerning some key issues for Catholic education in a more synodal Church. *Religions, 14*, 1121. https://doi.org/10.3390/rel14091121

Rymarz, R., & Cleary, A. (2016). Some religious beliefs and behaviours of Australian Catholic school students. *Journal of Beliefs and Values, 37*(1), 68–77. https://doi.org/10.1080/13617672.2016.1141530

Rytel-Andrianik, P., & Zielenkiewicz, T. (2024, March 19). US Diocese of Columbus doubles number of seminarians in two years. *Vatican News*, https://www.vaticannews.va/en/church/news/2024-03/columbus-ohio-bishop-fernandes-doubles-vocations-two-years.html

Sadewo, G., Bullivant, S., & Cranney, S. (2021). McCarrick, the kingmaker? A social network analysis of episcopal promotion in the Roman Catholic Church. *Catholic Social Science Review, 26*, 247–261. https://www.pdcnet.org/cssr/content/cssr_2021_0026_0247_0261

Samie, Y., Maldini, I., & Vladimirova, K. (2024, November 21). Overwhelmed by ever more clothing donations, charities are exporting the problem. Local governments must step up. *The Conversation*, https://theconversation.com/

overwhelmed-by-ever-more-clothing-donations-charities-are-exporting-the-problem-local-governments-must-step-up-243709

Sandeman, J. (2024, April 28). Mythbusting: conservative denominations grow, progressive ones shrink. *The Other Cheek*, https://theothercheek.com.au/mythbusting-conservative-denominations-grow-progressive-ones-shrink/

Sato, K. (2023, December 7). Baby boomers are scapegoats for ills of the world, Charles Sturt University researcher says. *ABC News*, https://www.abc.net.au/news/2023-12-07/baby-boomers-scapegoats-clive-hamilton-history-csu/103179636

Seedling. (n.d.). How much should a charity spend on admin? And what else you should ask to make sure your donation isn't wasted. *Seedling*, https://seedlinggiving.com.au/blog-article/how-much-should-a-charity-spend-on-admin

Separation Guide. (2024). *How much does it cost to get a divorce or separate?* https://theseparationguide.com.au/how-much-does-it-cost-to-get-a-divorce-or-separate/

Shearer, C. (2017, June 28). Number of Australian Anglicans falls by 580,000 in five years: Census 2016. *Melbourne Anglican*, https://tma.melbourneanglican.org.au/2017/06/number-of-australian-anglicans-falls-by-580000-in-five-years-census-2016/

Silva, W. (2024, June 22). The Catholic Church in France will have 105 new priests in 2024. *Catholic World Report*, https://www.catholicworldreport.com/2024/06/22/the-catholic-church-in-france-will-have-105-new-priests-in-2024/

Sisters State Advisory Research Groups. (1977). *National statistical survey of religious personnel, Australia 1976.* Conferences of Major Superiors of Australia.

Skojec, S. (2021, July 26). It's time to pass the torch. *One Peter Five*, https://onepeterfive.com/its-time-to-pass-the-torch/

Slater, E., Burton, K., & McKillop, D. (2022). Reasons for home educating in Australia: who and why? *Educational Review (Birmingham)*, 74(2), 263–280. https://doi.org/10.1080/00131911.2020.1728232;

Smith, A., & Carroll, L. (2023, January 28). War of words erupts between Opus Dei schools and the ABC. *Sydney Morning Herald*, https://www.smh.com.au/national/nsw/war-of-words-erupts-between-opus-dei-schools-and-the-abc-20230127-p5cfvs.html

Smith, C., & Adamcyzk, A. (2020). *Handing down the faith: How parents pass their religion on to the next generation.* Oxford University Press.

Smith, R. (2007). Don't blame Vatican II: Modernism and modern Catholic church architecture. *Sacred Architecture*, 13, 12-18. https://www.catholicculture.org/culture/library/view.cfm?recnum=8000

St Agnes Care and Lifestyle. (2024). *Financial overview (2023)*, https://www.acnc.gov.au/charity/charities/cf3426dd-2daf-e811-a963-000d3ad24077/profile

St Cecilia's Abbey, Ryde. (n.d.). *The history of Gregorian chant*, https://stceciliasabbey.org.uk/wp-content/uploads/2022/07/CHANT-HISTORY-1.pdf

St Cuthbert's House, Hermitage of the Diocese of Nottingham. (n.d.). *How to be a hermit*, http://www.stcuthbertshouse.co.uk/howtobeahermit.html.

St Francis Social Services. (2024). *Financial overview (2023)*, https://www.acnc.gov.au/charity/charities/fb86ed2c-39af-e811-a95e-000d3ad24c60/profile

St Vincent de Paul Society. (2011). *Submission to Treasury review of not-for-profit governance arrangements*, https://treasury.gov.au/sites/default/files/2019-03/St-Vincent-de-Paul-1.pdf

St Vincent de Paul Society. (2024). *Frequently asked questions*, https://www.vinnies.org.au/about-us/frequently-asked-questions

Staff Writers. (2015, September 23). Redemptoris Mater: the seminary the little old ladies built. *The Catholic Weekly*, https://www.catholicweekly.com.au/redemptoris-mater-neocatechumenal-seminary-sydney/

Staff Writers. (2024, May 20). Conservative American 'chastity speaker' Jason Evert's visits to NSW schools cancelled after backlash. *ABC News*, https://www.abc.net.au/news/2024-05-20/schools-cancel-visit-by-us-chastity-speaker-jason-evert/103868358

Staudt, R. (2024, August 8). The power of silence and the problem of sound in adoration. *Catholic World Report*, https://www.catholicworldreport.com/2024/08/08/299691/

Stimpson, E. (2012). *The Catholic girl's survival guide for the single years*, Emmaus Road.

Taouk, Y., Ghosn, M., Steel, A., & Butcher, J. (2012). Maronite church and youth identity in Australia: at the crossroads. *Australasian Catholic Record*, 89(3), 299–310.

Taylor, A. (2016, September 1). Why Mother Teresa is still no saint to many of her critics. *Washington Post*, https://www.washingtonpost.com/news/worldviews/wp/2015/02/25/why-to-many-critics-mother-teresa-is-still-no-saint/

The Pillar (2024, August 15). NJ diocese and priests sue State Department over visa policy change. *The Pillar*, https://www.pillarcatholic.com/p/nj-diocese-and-priests-sue-state

The Pillar. (2021, January 22). What is a bishop's conference, anyway? *The Pillar*, https://www.pillarcatholic.com/p/what-is-a-bishops-conference-anyway

The Pillar. (2024). Glemkowski: Why the National Eucharistic Congress worked. *The Pillar*, https://www.pillarcatholic.com/p/glemkowski-why-the-national-eucharistic

The Pillar. (2025, September 5). Newlywed IOR employees fall foul of nepotism rule. *The Pillar*, https://www.pillarcatholic.com/p/newlywed-ior-employees-fall-foul

The Record. (2008, October 22). New religious vows in Perth. *The Record*, https://therecord.com.au/news/local/new-religious-vows-in-perth/

The Record. (2009, January 7). New community to throw open its doors. *The Record*, https://therecord.com.au/news/local/new-community-to-throw-open-its-doors/

Thomas, G. (2013). *The sacred search*. David C Cook.

Thompson, H. (2024, August 12). More WA families are opting to home-school their kids. Here's why. *WA Today*, https://www.watoday.com.au/national/western-australia/more-wa-families-are-opting-to-home-school-their-kids-here-s-why-20240725-p5jwkd.html

Tierney, K. (2024, May 19). Opinion: The dynamism and challenge of 'DIY Traditionalism'. *Catholic World Report*, https://www.catholicworldreport.com/2024/05/19/opinion-the-dynamism-and-challenge-of-diy-traditionalsm/

Tomlinson, H. (2024, June 26). Potential pitfalls of Catholic Parish Summit's evangelising spirit. *Catholic Herald*, https://catholicherald.co.uk/potential-pitfalls-of-the-catholic-parish-summits-evangelising-spirit/

Topliss, J., Gourlay, T., & Chua, R. (2024). In Altum – 'Put Out into the Deep': a formation program for missionary discipleship for students at the University of Notre Dame Australia. *Religions*, 15(2). https://doi.org/10.3390/rel15020147

Townsville Diocesan Development Fund. (n.d.). *Financial statements for the year ended 31 December 2023*, https://os-data.s3-ap-southeast-2.amazonaws.com/tsv-catholic-org-au/bundle31/signed_financial_report_31.12.23.pdf

Trustees of Mary Aikenhead Ministries. (2024). *Financial overview (2023)*, https://www.acnc.gov.au/charity/charities/503bf532-38af-e811-a962-000d3ad24a0d/profile

Trustees of the Roman Catholic Church for the Diocese of Lismore as Trustee for Diocesan Investment Fund. (n.d.). *Concise financial report for the year ended 31 March 2024*, https://dif.au/important/uploads/2024/07/DIF_Annual-ReportWeb2024.pdf

Vaidyanathan, B., Jacobi, C., Kelly, C., White, S., & Perla, S. (2022). *Well-being, trust, and policy in a time of crisis: highlights from the National Study of Catholic Priests,* https://catholicproject.catholic.edu/wp-content/uploads/2022/10/Catholic-Project-Final.pdf

Vermurlen, B., Cranney, S., & Regnerus, M. (2021, October 28). *Introducing the 2021 Survey of American Catholic priests: overview and selected findings,* https://ssrn.com/abstract=3951931

Victorian Catholic Education Authority. (2023). *Victorian Catholic Education Authority annual report 2023,* 32-33. https://vcea.catholic.edu.au/about-us/governance/#annual-reports

Warhurst, J. (2024, May 19). Painful times for church reformers. *Eureka Street,* https://www.eurekastreet.com.au/article/painful-times-for-church-reformers

Waters, I., & McGuckin, R. (2016). Eastern Catholic churches in Australia: canonical issues for Catholic clergy and pastoral workers. *Australasian Catholic Record, 93*(1), 81–89.

Weber, K. (2024, April 18). What happens when a diocese takes a synodal approach to parish restructuring? *America: the Jesuit Review,* https://www.americamagazine.org/faith/2024/04/18/catholic-diocese-parish-closings-mergers-247747

Weigel, G. (2024, March 17). The good news is that the bad news isn't all the news there is. *The Catholic Weekly,* https://catholicweekly.com.au/the-good-news-is-that-the-bad-news-isnt-all-the-news-there-is/

Wesselinoff, A. (2022, September 23). New campus approach goes for discipleship. *The Catholic Weekly,* https://catholicweekly.com.au/new-campus-approach-goes-for-discipleship/

White, S. (2020, March 26). False allegations are rare – and real. *Ethics and Public Policy Center,* https://eppc.org/publication/false-allegations-are-rare-and-real/

Williams, L., & Jurich, J. (1995). Predicting marital success after five years: assessing the predictive validity of FOCCUS. *Journal of Marital and Family Therapy, 21*(2), 141–153. https://doi.org/10.1111/j.1752-0606.1995.tb00149.x

Williby, B. (2019, July 29). Public schooling Catholic kids. *Blessed Is She,* https://blessedisshe.net/en-au/blogs/blog/public-schooling-catholic-kids

Willis, O. (2018, June 17). 'I don't yearn for someone to complete me': Why more women are staying single. *ABC News,* https://www.abc.net.au/news/health/2018-06-17/why-women-are-staying-single/9873956

Wilson, T. (n.d.). *Good works: the Catholic Church as an employer in Australia,* https://s3.ap-southeast-2.amazonaws.com/acbcwebsite/Articles/Documents/ACBC/nla.obj-1766235550-1.pdf

Wooden, C. (2016, June 18). Too many couples do not understand marriage is for life, Pope says. *National Catholic Reporter*, https://www.ncronline.org/too-many-couples-do-not-understand-marriage-life-pope-says

Zenit. (2006). On liturgical norms for the Neocatechumenal Way. *Zenit/EWTN*, https://www.ewtn.com/catholicism/library/on-liturgical-norms-for-the-neocatechumenal-way-4286

Zurlo, L. (2019). *Single for a greater purpose: a hidden joy in the Catholic Church*. Sophia Institute.

INDEX

Aboriginal and Torres Strait Islanders, 81, 92, 206

Acts of the Apostles, 198

adult faith formation, 57, 60, 119, 242, 247, 265
- Anima Network, 267
- Catechesis of the Good Shepherd (child and family formation), 266
- Centre for Evangelisation, Sydney, 177, 267
- FORMED program (US catechesis and evangelisation program), 281
- Parousia Media, 266
- St Paul Centre, 266
- Word on Fire, 281

aged care, Catholic, 81, 82, 169, 249, 279

Altenburger, Michael (US writer), 65

Andrews, Dan (Victorian premier), 133

Anglican communion, 3, 28, 34, 44, 113, 118, 222

Annuarium Statisticum Ecclesiae, 31, 46, 140

Argüello, Francisco (Kiko) (religious figure), 183

Australian Broadcasting Corporation (ABC), 182

Australian Bureau of Statistics (ABS), 29, 31, 69

Australian Catholic Bishops' Conference (ACBC), 23, 24, 25, 28, 56, 103, 130, 131, 139, 156, 228, 264
- *Statement of Conclusions (1998)*, 12

Australian Catholic Migrant and Refugee Office, 147

Balthasar, Hans Urs von (theologian), 18, 36, 134, 239

Benedict XVI, Pope, 16, 74

Benedict, St, 180

biases
- in-group bias, 133
- recall bias, 26
- social desirability bias, 27

bishops, 7, 8, 10, 12, 15, 16, 18, 27, 28, 37, 39, 41, 42, 43, 46, 74, 99, 104, 115, 118, 122, 128, 129, 130, 131, 132, 133, 134, 135, 136, 137, 140, 145, 146, 150, 151, 153, 155, 156, 163, 171, 175, 177, 179, 180, 183, 185, 195, 197, 200, 202, 209, 257, 258, 260, 265, 268, 269, 270, 271, 276, 277

Barron, Bishop Robert, 4, 33, 281

Bychok, Cardinal Mykola, 42

Costelloe, Archbishop Timothy, 39, 184

Fisher, Archbishop Anthony, 177, 221, 274

Hickey, Archbishop Barry, 184

Kolodziej, Bishop-elect George, 39

Long, Bishop Vincent, 134

Macbeth-Green, Bishop Columba, 176

Morrissey, Bishop Michael, 39

Nguyen, Bishop-elect Thinh, 150

Norton, Bishop Tim, 39

Pell, Cardinal George, 3, 133, 177, 181, 197, 217, 227

Porteous, Archbishop Julian, 176, 178

Ramirez, Bishop-elect Rene, 150

Robinson, Bishop Geoffrey, 131

bogus mysticism, 97, 122, 184

Bonacci, Mary Beth (US writer), 65

Boomers, 9, 11, 12, 14, 15, 16, 17, 30, 81, 112, 116, 131, 150, 174, 231, 243, 261, 271
Brown, Dan (novelist), 275
Bruyn, Joe de (former union leader), 219
Bullivant, Stephen (UK researcher), xii, 15, 26, 36, 83, 142, 200

Catechism of the Catholic Church, 56, 73, 115
Catherine of Siena, St, 179
Catholic Charities USA, 194
Catholic Church Life Survey (1996), 25
Catholic Football Club (CFC), 1, 2, 190
Catholic Institute of Sydney, 217
Catholic Theological College, 217
Catholic Vocations Ministry Australia, 167
Catholic weird, 36, 57, 142, 216, 244, 256
Catholics in Australia 2022 survey (CIA2022), 15, 16, 17, 26, 31, 34, 35, 58, 59, 60, 64, 68, 70, 77, 78, 80, 82, 92, 94, 105, 113, 132, 134, 146, 147, 181, 207, 211, 227, 240
Catholics in Britain survey 2019, 15
Census (Australia), 23, 29, 41, 42, 48, 70, 76, 92, 207, 214, 274
Central Office of Church Statistics, 31
Chapp, Larry (US writer), 4, 90, 242
charities, Catholic-origin, 14, 190, 193, 194, 204, 223, 225, 226, 229, 231, 262, 274
    funding, 225
    Mass attendance rates, 231
Chicago (US), 121
Cincinnati (US), 121

Cleary, Anthony (researcher), 206, 210, 217
Clements, Ben (UK researcher), 15, 36, 83
Code of Canon Law, 6, 73, 114, 153, 203, 239
converts, 11, 30, 33, 34, 35, 68, 105, 207, 245, 266
COVID19, 24, 59, 62, 81, 114, 133, 208, 255, 267
cults, 18
    Bethel Community, 18
    Kamm, William ('The Little Pebble', cult leader), 18, 184
Cupcake School of Lady Catholic Journalism, 64
Curran, Fr Charles E (US writer), 192, 194, 220

Dawson, Christopher (academic)
    Dawson Centre (Melbourne), 267
    Dawson Society (Perth), 267
deacons, 128, 129, 151, 152, 153, 155
    women, 2, 16, 152
Deuteronomy, Book of, 191
dioceses
    Adelaide, 48
    Armidale, 45
    Bathurst, 45
    Brisbane, 34, 45, 91, 96, 253
    Broken Bay, 209
    Broome, 39, 45, 260
    Buffalo (US), 202
    Bunbury, 39, 45, 151
    Cairns, 45
    Darwin, 45, 92, 170
    Geraldton, 39, 45
    Hobart, 39, 45, 176, 177, 180, 260

Lismore, 47, 92, 176
Melbourne, 34, 45, 96, 105, 150, 177, 197, 218, 253, 260
Parramatta, 92, 134
Perth, 34, 39, 45, 91, 92, 96, 104, 144, 151, 171, 180, 195, 253
Port Pirie, 45, 170
Rockhampton, 45
Sandhurst, 91
Southwark (UK), 144, 281
Sydney, viii, 34, 45, 47, 93, 96, 109, 111, 142, 143, 144, 177, 181, 182, 206, 217, 221, 253, 267
Toowoomba, 45
Townsville, 45
Wagga Wagga, 91
Wilcannia-Forbes, 45, 47, 176
Dixon, Robert (Bob), 23, 24, 25, 166

Eastern rites, 45, 49, 51, 91, 93, 113
  Chaldeans, 24, 37, 42, 43
  Maronites, 24, 41, 82, 93, 109, 171, 227, 267
  Melkites, 24, 37, 41, 151
  Syro-Malabars, 24, 37, 43, 147, 171, 251, 267
  Ukrainians, 24, 37, 42
Escriva, St Josemaria, 180
euthanasia, 82, 279
Evert, Jason (US speaker), 209, 276

families, Catholic, 5, 18, 30, 56, 57, 63, 66, 76, 77, 82, 84, 85, 93, 98, 104, 105, 106, 110, 117, 118, 119, 120, 141, 142, 149, 150, 154, 164, 174, 175, 203, 209, 225, 240, 242, 244, 245, 248, 249, 251, 252, 253, 257, 258, 259, 266, 270, 272, 277, 280
  birth control and family planning, 27, 63, 73, 77, 78, 79, 80, 207, 248
  cohabitation, 94, 112, 119
  divorce, 63, 64, 65, 66, 70, 72, 73, 75, 76, 109, 112
  family size, 77, 78, 150, 249
  fatherhood, 57, 144, *See also* parishes, Catholic:men's ministry
  home schooling, 59, 60, 61, 62, 211, 247, 253, 259, 276, 279
  single Catholics, 63, 65, 66, 67, 80, 248
  spousal abuse, 73, 74, 75
France, 150
Francis, Pope, 42, 74, 134, 200, 227, 259
Fuller, Buckminster (US futurist), 13

General Instruction of the Roman Missal (GIRM), 104
Germany, 134, 135, 146
Glemkowski, Tim (US conference organiser), 198
governance, 3, 13, 136, 171, 175, 197, 199, 202, 231, 261
  'Mission and Identity', 193, 200, 264
  'professional Catholics', 3, 6, 8, 9, 10, 14, 16, 131, 262
  'carapace' or Borg, 6
  Catholic industrial complex, 190, 220, 228, 230
  consultation, 8
  data collection and sharing, 30, 31, 33, 34, 67, 92, 147, 206, 220, 268
  diocesan bureaucracies, 7, 9, 134, 136, 195, 197, 261, 269
  lay clericalism, 197
  non-disclosure agreements, 199

social networks, 197, 200
diocesan marriage tribunals, 74, 201, 202
Diocesan Pastoral Councils, 10, 18
groupthink, 201
in persona episcopi, 39
'inclusion', 66
liturgy specialists, 104
parochial-diocesan Church, 5, 6, 37, 131, 155, 190, 192, 195, 204, 221, 230, 240, 268, 275, 276
spiritual abuse, 198
subsidiarity, 19, 265, 277, 279
subsidies, government, 2, 5, 6, 18, 190, 194, 203, 220, 222, 225, 229, 262, 263, 279
transparency, financial, 3, 131, 156, 195
trust, 7, 8, 18, 109, 132, 145, 146, 155, 156, 185, 227, 228, 229, 242, 253, 257, 258, 269, 271
whistleblowers, 201, 202
Groeschel, Fr Benedict (US priest-psychologist), 65

Hahn, Scott (US evangelist), 246
health care, Catholic-origin, 14, 171, 192, 193, 220, 262, 278
    Calvary Health Care Bethlehem Kooyong Precinct, 221
    Calvary Hospital (ACT), 222, 274
    funding, 223
    hospital chaplaincies, 222, 278
Hernández, Carmen (religious figure), 183
Humanae Vitae, 25, 27, 78, 242

Ignatius Press, 12, 281
India, 43, 147, 252

Ivereigh, Austen (UK writer), 227

John Paul II, Pope St, 12, 175, 184, 280
John XXIII Fellowship, 12

Keating, Jessica (US writer), 65
Knights of the Southern Cross, 202

laity, 17, 44, 75, 97, 99, 100, 103, 114, 128, 129, 135, 136, 148, 152, 154, 156, 164, 172, 174, 179, 185, 192, 197, 198, 223, 242, 269, 278
Laudato Si', 263
Leviticus, Book of, 191
Liturgy of the Hours, 144, 180

Mackillop, St Mary, 166
Marshall, Taylor (US media figure), 33
Martyr's Law, 36
Mass attendance, 1, 5, 23, 24, 25, 26, 29, 32, 34, 35, 36, 45, 48, 50, 62, 70, 79, 80, 81, 107, 113, 118, 192, 195, 200, 213, 218, 228, 241, 244, 260, 261
    'Irregulars', 32, 35, 36, 58, 68, 70
    National Count of Attendance, 24, 50
    'Nevers', 32, 35, 36, 58, 68, 70, 71
    'Weeklies', 32, 34, 35, 58, 59, 68, 70, 77, 78, 79, 82, 94
McAlpine, Stephen (Protestant pastor), 198
McCarrick, Theodore (former priest), 200
media, Catholic, 23, 191, 226
    AD2000 (magazine), 12
    America, 226
    Catholic Herald (UK), 226

Catholic World Report, 226
Crisis (magazine), 12
Crux, 226
Fidelity (Australia), 12
outside Australia, 226
The Catholic Weekly (Sydney), viii, 133, 227, 245
The Pillar, 226
migrants, Catholic, 30, 35, 45, 49, 50, 68, 69, 77, 92, 93, 100, 109, 110, 117, 147, 150, 166, 170, 245, 251

National Assessment Program-Literacy and Numeracy (NAPLAN), 214
National Centre for Pastoral Research (NCPR), 24, 28, 92, 146, 147, 180, 228
National Civic Council, 12
National Health Service (UK), 149
Nehemiah, Book of, 19
new movements
   Catholic Charismatic Renewal, 183
   Communion and Liberation, 178
   Disciples of Jesus Covenant Community, 178, 182
   Emmanuel Community, 182
   Neocatechumenal Way, 143, 178, 183
   Personal Prelature of the Holy Cross and Opus Dei, 44, 133, 178, 180, 181, 182, 183, 210, 279
Nigeria, 147
Norwich, Julian of, 180

O'Connor, Siobhan (whistleblower), 202
O'Shea, Gerard (educator), 266

Official Directory of the Catholic Church in Australia, 44, 46, 140, 143
opinion polls, 36
Ordinariates
   Military Ordinariate, 44, 151
   Personal Ordinariate of Our Lady of the Southern Cross, 44

Papua New Guinea, 166
parishes
   Albury-Lavington, 91
   Bankstown, 93
   Buranda (St Luke's), 91
   Casino, 92
   Jabiru, 92
   Kalgoorlie-Boulder, 91
   St Mary Mackillop, Western Border, 250
   Toongabbie, 92
   Willetton, 92
   Wodonga, 91
parishes, Catholic
   beige Catholicism, 4, 91
   boutique parishes, 97, 121, 122, 254
   children's liturgy, 94, 106, 107, 111
   church decoration and interiors, 14, 99
   church rage, 118, 123
   Extraordinary Ministers of Holy Communion, 94, 255
   feminised liturgy, 4, 273
   house groups, 250
   intentional communities, 93, 245, 253
   liturgical abuses, 97, 98, 115, 121, 254
   liturgical nomads, 11, 97, 115, 250
   liturgical silos, 99, 122, 254

'Lying Masses', 106, 107, 258
men's ministry, 47, 57, 65, 94, 120
music ministry, 14, 47, 91, 100, 101, 103, 111, 117, 118, 123
offertory collection, 196
parish closures, 121, 250
parish councils, 14, 118, 148, 251
sacramental preparation, 258
silence, 103
undeclared guerilla wars, 15, 90
weekday Masses, 111, 252
participants
    Alan, 7, 61, 104, 105
    Annie, 62
    Belinda, 62
    Ben, 105, 120, 272
    Charlotte, 61
    Colin, 8, 257
    Daisy, 61
    Dominican Sisters of St Cecilia, 71, 164, 168, 174, 177
    Eloise, 148
    Ethan, 16, 178, 210, 212, 220, 251, 256, 264
    Fr Geoffrey, 4, 11
    Fr Harrison, 10, 15, 33, 83, 138, 273
    Fr Jason, 6, 11, 145, 154, 272, 273
    Fr Joshua, 34
    Fr Michael, 10, 139, 212, 213, 250, 270
    Fr Robert, 1, 5, 33, 119, 132, 145, 257
    Fr Stephen, 97, 139, 145, 209, 215
    Fr Vincent, 50, 75, 101, 109, 132
    Gerard, 61
    Isla, 98, 104, 208, 211, 216
    John, 257
    Josh, 105, 240
    Katrina, 63, 66, 98, 112, 117, 120, 148, 154, 246, 247, 248, 252, 259, 263, 266
    Lauren, 106, 240
    Lawrence, 62
    Leah, 105, 110, 116, 118, 120, 212, 247, 251, 253, 254, 256
    Miriam, 59, 110, 120, 253, 258, 265
    Oliver, 71, 121
    Paul, 5, 71, 72, 130
    Petra, 57, 246, 271
    Rachel, 64
    Sr Yvette, 165, 175, 251
    Steve and Helen, 116, 266, 269, 276
    Tori, 4, 130, 243, 245, 270, 272, 274
    William, 8, 231, 240, 269
Paul VI, Pope St, 78, 151
Paul, St, 198
Peter, St, 91, 241
Peterson, Jordan (US psychologist), 33
Philippines, 147, 252
Plenary Council, 2, 3, 10, 12, 14, 35, 112, 117, 133, 261
political parties
    Australian Christians, 17
    Australian Labor Party (ALP), 17, 181
    Greens, 17, 274
    Liberal-National coalition, 17
    One Nation, 17
    Teal Independents, 17, 274
    United Australia Party, 17
Popiełuszko, Blessed Jerzy, 216
priests, 10, 15, 16, 17, 26, 27, 31, 37, 43, 44, 45, 46, 47, 51, 57, 59, 65, 74, 75, 77, 97, 98, 99, 103, 104, 114, 115, 121, 122, 123, 128, 129, 130, 132, 136, 137, 138, 139, 140, 141, 142, 143, 144,

145, 147, 148, 149, 150, 152, 153, 154, 155, 156, 176, 180, 183, 195, 196, 242, 248, 251, 256, 260, 261, 264, 268, 269, 271, 272, 273, 278, 279
Allain, Fr Dominic, 144
Berg, Fr Thomas, 144
clergy abuse, 8, 25, 26, 27, 135, 136, 138, 144, 145, 146, 156, 171, 190, 197, 202, 227, 242, 260
   Royal Commission into Institutional Responses to Child Sexual Abuse (2012-2017), 197
clericalism, 128, 197
diocesan, 43, 45, 46, 47, 48, 138, 139, 140, 146, 147, 155, 156, 170, 171
   relationship with local bishop, 146, 155, 156
Fr Apocalypto, 121, 122
Fr Charm, 202
Fr Directo, 110
Fr Fixit, 202
Fr Relaxo, 121
incardination, 140, 260
leaving the active ministry, 140
married, 2, 10, 16, 41, 42, 43, 147, 154, 249
older, 47, 138, 140, 146, 271
overseas, 147, 148, 149, 150, 252, 261
religious, 46, 138, 148, 162, 170, 171
Schmitz, Fr Mike, 246
Searson, Fr Peter, 197
seminary formation, 141, 143, 145, 156
   Redemptoris Mater seminaries, 144
   Seminary of the Good Shepherd, 144, 177
suicide, 152, 156
supporting each other, 154, 155
surveys
   National Study of Catholic Priests (2022), 146
   NCPR survey (2024), 146
   Our Fathers survey (2011), 146
   Survey of American Catholic Priests (2021), 146
wearing clerical dress, 143, 153
women, 2, 10, 28, 152, 249
younger, 11, 140, 142, 146, 271
Protestant churches, 3, 28, 61, 62, 63, 105, 198, 247
purgatory, 82, 83

Reagan, Ronald (US president), 199
religious and religious life, 10, 15, 17, 41, 42, 43, 44, 46, 49, 65, 66, 71, 138, 150, 152, 162, 163, 164, 165, 166, 167, 168, 169, 170, 171, 172, 174, 175, 176, 177, 179, 180, 184, 185, 191, 192, 194, 195, 203, 204, 213, 221, 223, 278, 279, 281
   abuses, 58, 168, 171, 174
   Antonine Maronite Order, 171
   associates, tertiaries and oblates, 179
   Benedictines, 176
   Carmelites, 176
   Catholic Religious Australia, 175
   charisms, 163, 169
   Christian Brothers, 58, 166
   Conferences of Major Superiors of Australia, 166
   consecrated virginity, 179
   Council of Major Superiors of Women Religious, 175
   departures from, 166, 167, 168

Dominicans of St Cecilia, 177, 281
formation, 164, 167, 175
Franciscans, 143
habits, 162, 165, 169, 170, 174, 177
hermits, 180
Josephites, 166, 179
Lebanese Maronite Order, 171
Maronite Lebanese Missionaries (Kreimists), 171
Ministerial Public Juridic Persons (MPJPs), 171, 177, 192, 195, 204, 223, 231, 278
Missionaries of God's Love, 178
Missionaries of the Gospel, 184
Noonan, Dom Pius, 176
Notre Dame Priory, 176
Salesians of Don Bosco, 184
Sisters of Life, 281
Sisters of Mercy of Alma, Michigan, 177, 281
Sisters of the Immaculata, 178
spiritualised anticlerical feminism, 174
surveys
 National statistical survey of religious personnel, Australia (1976), 166
Vincentians (Syro-Malabar), 171
Rite of Christian Initiation of Adults (RCIA), 33, 34, 47, 118, 218
Rose of Lima, St, 179
Rosengren, Peter (editor), viii
Rowland, Tracey (Australian theologian), 6, 130, 136, 144, 145
Rymarz, Richard (researcher), 109, 206, 210, 213, 217

sacraments
 Anointing of the Sick, 129
 Baptism, 31, 33, 56, 57, 90, 119, 121, 128, 151, 212, 239, 268
 Confirmation, 31, 107, 129, 212, 259
 Eucharist, 129, 213
  Adoration, 119, 120, 143, 150, 170, 178, 213, 255, 261, 270
  Holy Communion, 2, 31, 32, 72, 73, 76, 102, 119, 148, 149, 151, 152, 183, 213, 216, 254, 255, 256, 258, 266
 Marriage, 10, 27, 30, 31, 56, 63, 64, 65, 66, 67, 68, 71, 72, 74, 75, 76, 79, 84, 111, 119, 121, 128, 151, 154, 185, 201, 213, 219, 243, 247, 248
  'mixed' marriages, 27, 51, 58
  annulments, 31, 72, 73, 74, 201, 202
  marriage preparation, 75, 76, 248
  FOCCUS program (marriage preparation), 75
 Ordination, 31, 129, 140
 Reconciliation (Confession), 59, 60, 70, 113, 114, 117, 119, 121, 129, 207, 212, 256, 258, 259
  Third Rite of Reconciliation, 59
same sex attraction, 10, 16, 28, 65, 66, 74, 112, 117, 155, 156, 182, 211
Samoa, 166
Santamaria, Bob (Australian political figure), 181
Schaefer, Brian and Maureen (Australian publishers), 12
schools, Catholic-origin, 5, 7, 11, 12, 14, 15, 59, 60, 61, 62, 108, 110, 112, 117, 131, 142, 168, 171, 174, 177, 182, 190, 203, 204, 205, 209, 210, 219, 225, 228, 229, 240, 242, 256, 258, 262, 274, 275, 276, 277
 bullying, 61
 data collection and sharing, 213, 214

enrolments, 206, 207, 210
   Catholic, 206, 207
   non-Catholic, 206
   socio-economic status, 206
evangelisation effect, 207, 210, 215
faith formation, 212
funding, 203, 205, 211
governance, 204
Mass attendance rate, 206, 208
National Catholic Education Commission, 204, 205
non-systemic schools, 204
Opus Dei, 210
rejection of by Mass-going parents, 61, 211, 217
religious literacy testing, 214
School Masses, 215
systemic schools, 204
teachers, 208, 211, 229, 275
   Mass attendance, 212, 214
Secretariat of State, Vatican, 31
sensus fidei, 3, 35
South Carolina (US), 281
Spanish Civil War, 181
Synod on Synodality, 8, 10

TAFE students, 17, 218, 220
Teresa of Calcutta, St, 192
Tierney, Kendra (Catholic blogger), 246
Tierney, Kevin (US journalist), 256
Traditional Latin Mass (TLM), 34, 50, 77, 92, 93, 98, 112, 181, 256
traditionalism, 13, 33, 44, 77, 80, 98, 101, 122, 133, 146, 152, 165, 170, 176, 181, 240, 254, 258
United States, 42, 93, 150, 177, 200, 279, 281

universities, 59, 110, 142, 219, 228, 229
   Australian Catholic University, 219
   Campion College, 217, 218
   students
      Mass attendance rate, 218
   university chaplaincies, 92, 177, 217, 220
   University of Notre Dame Australia, 217, 218
   University of Sydney, 177
US Conference of Catholic Bishops (USCCB), 102

Vatican II, 4, 14, 99, 130, 133, 135, 165, 166, 177, 179, 242
   call to personal holiness, 13, 230, 239, 243
   Lumen Gentium, 90
   People of God, 90, 114, 193, 225, 266, 267
   Sacrosanctum Concilium, 99, 100, 101, 104
Vietnam, 147
Vita Consecrata, 175

Weigel, George (US writer), 227, 279
Wesselinoff, Adam (editor), viii, 227
women, 29, 63, 64, 76, 79, 94, 112, 113, 120, 133, 152, 156, 162, 164, 166, 167, 168, 171, 174, 176, 178, 179, 180, 181, 185, 191, 197, 211, 225, 246, 247, 249, 266, 267, 280, 281
World Youth Day, 109, 110, 177, 217, 280
youth, Catholic, 10, 14, 16, 47, 59, 60, 65, 94, 104, 106, 109, 110, 209, 210, 218, 241, 253, 257, 262
   Mass attendance rate, 218, 270

Zurlo, Luanne (US writer), 65

www.ingramcontent.com/pod-product-compliance
Lightning Source LLC
Chambersburg PA
CBHW060940230426
43665CB00015B/2008